TONY CROSLAND

Rarely have political and private life been
revealed with such vitality as in this extraordinary book. Tony Crosland was a complex,
passionate man, rude, kind, enigmatic. As
Labour's leading intellectual, he held five high
offices of State before his sudden death in
1977, only ten months after becoming Britain's
Foreign Secretary.

When the author met Crosland in 1956, the
same autumn that *The Future of Socialism* was
published, he was about to move into the most
active period of his political life. As the story
unfolds, their private life is increasingly invaded
by political battles; but there is still some time
for Crosland's quarrels about Kingsley Amis's
jazz records and *Match of the Day*.

Susan Crosland has written a story at several
levels – a political drama which can also be
read entirely in terms of a human drama and a
love story. The inter-weaving of intimacy and
candour, black comedy and tragedy are,
literally, spell-binding.

TONY CROSLAND

'It is hard to conceive of a more difficult task
than to write a good biography of one's dead
husband or wife ... but Susan Crosland has
met this task brilliantly. The book is both a
very moving story of love and affection and an
important political record. It is full of laughter
too – a fitting testament to his memory'
The Times

'This extended profile of the husband she
adored may serve as a memorial to them both.
It is beautifully written and, by the end,
intensely moving'
Daily Mail

'Mrs Crosland has written a very beautiful and
remarkable book'
Irish Times

'A remarkable insight into a man, a woman and
a marriage ... it will not just be friends who
read some of the passages in this book with
mist in their eyes. It is a labour of love, vividly
bringing to life a rare personality.
The Standard

TONY CROSLAND

'Susan Crosland has written a marvellous book, a masterpiece of its kind'
New Statesman

'Refreshing, touching and inspiriting ... an intimate portrait of a public man written by a woman who does not bother to try and hide the fact that she adored him'
New York Times Book Review

'None of the dramas of the political stage is omitted, but it is the sidelights, the candid comments, the human comedies, the sheer ebullience of the man that illumine these pages and make them brilliantly readable'
Plymouth Western Morning News

'A brilliant memoir-cum-biography ... a tender and unsentimental account of a relationship and a deeply affecting love story that is hard to read without shedding tears of laughter and of sadness'
New Society

TONY CROSLAND

'This is a remarkable, possibly unique book:
the biography of a politician written by
someone who loved him, was clearly loved by
him, and is more than a passable journalist'
Financial Times

'It's a witty, vivacious, telling and very
revealing portrait. Susan Crosland's loving,
perceptive but dashing book is an outstanding
and touching study of a man whose sudden
death in 1977 robbed both his friends and
British politics of a major character'
Bristol Evening News

'Susan Crosland's book is outstanding. She is
the best political profile writer in Britain and
here she has given not only a profile in depth
of her husband but of the whole Labour Party
during some of its most dramatic years'
Daily Mirror

'A deeply personal memoir and an unusual and
fascinating biography, very effective just
because it is so honest ... the end of the story
is one of the saddest and most moving I have
ever read'
Yorkshire Post

TONY CROSLAND

'This is one of the most gripping political biographies of recent years ... everyone will praise the honesty and courage of her portrait'
Spectator

'Mrs Crosland has succeeded in recreating the charm, the charisma and the sheer elan which surrounded Tony Crosland throughout his political career. That they loved each other deeply is apparent on every page of her book'
Guardian

'The story is told sensitively and affectionately but not sentimentally or uncritically, and what comes through above all is the sense of Tony Crosland's personality'
Hull Daily Mail

'No description can do it justice'
The Australian

Tony Crosland

Susan Crosland

CORONET BOOKS
Hodder and Stoughton

Copyright © 1982 by Susan Crosland

First published in Great Britain 1982
by Jonathan Cape Ltd

Coronet edition 1983

British Library C.I.P.

Crosland, Susan
    Tony Crosland
    1. Crosland, Anthony
    2. Statesmen—Great Britain—Biography
    I. Title
    941.085′092′4   DA591.C7

    ISBN 0–340–33785–0

Printed and bound in Great Britain for
Hodder and Stoughton Paperbacks, a
division of Hodder and Stoughton Ltd.,
Mill Road, Dunton Green, Sevenoaks,
Kent (Editorial Office: 47 Bedford
Square, London, WC1 3DP) by
Cox & Wyman Ltd, Reading

for

the people of Grimsby

and the Labour Party

Contents

Acknowledgments

In my pursuit of factual accuracy and different viewpoints, I have received enormous help. Some people, already working under great pressure, spent untold hours, untold days over the three plus years that it has taken me to research and write the book. Without their generosity, a very different biography would have emerged. I am particularly obliged to those who gave me time and material when their personal or political views were at odds with Tony's.

I did not set out to interview men and women who are currently leading politicians, as I felt it would be nearly impossible for them to be as candid as they might have wished. Many facts, however, could be checked and corroborated only with them. In every instance where I asked for help, they gave it. I do not thank them personally lest it seem that they have always approved of the way I have presented the material.

And while I want to thank the people whom I interviewed – numerous times in some cases, as they will recall only too well – I must make clear that they might not agree with the way I have interwoven my sources. I am very grateful to Lord Armstrong of Sanderstead, D. L. Atkins, Lord Balogh, Sir Ian Bancroft, Muriel Barker, Lilian Bontoft, Alec Bovill, Lord Brown, Raymond Carr, Thomas Caulcott, Roy Croft, Lady Donaldson of Kingsbridge, Sid Epton, Ewen Fergusson, T. N. Fox, Jack Franklin, Derek Gladwin, Fred Goshawk, Dr Amos Griffiths, Ivor Hanson, Peter Hardy, MP, Lord Kaldor, Lord Kennet, Professor Anthony King, Dr Henry Kissinger, Dick Leonard, Lord Lever, David Lipsey, I.M.D. Little, Lord McCarthy, David McDonald, Sir Donald MacDougall, Dr Keir MacKessack-Leitch, Sir Robert Marshall, John Rollit Mason, Sir Alan Neale, Professor Robert Neild, Sir Michael Palliser, Christopher Price, MP, Sir Idwal Pugh, Lord Roberthall, Irwin Ross, Edward Rowlands, MP, Andrew Semple, Lord Shackleton, Dennis Skinner, MP, Margaret Turner, Lord Vaizey, Sir Toby Weaver, Barbara Wilkinson, Philip Williams, Lord Young of Darlington. And I am grateful to Tony's sisters, Elsie Alexander and Evelyn Crosland, and his cousin, Michael Cavenagh. And to his step-daughters.

A number of people have accomplished prodigious feats of research, managing somehow to keep good humour each time I wrote or rang with yet another ghastly list of things to discover or check. I am indebted to, among others, the Secretary of the Parliamentary Labour Party, Bryan Davies, the Assistant Secretary, Phyllis Birt, and the Librarian and staff of the House of Commons Library. I greatly appreciate the patient strivings of Adrian Barker, Wilfred Beckerman, David Bryan, Tyrrell Burgess, Austin Mitchell, Michael Stewart.

Perhaps paramount thanks should go to seven martyred souls whose August holiday was hardly enhanced by having to slog through the first draft of the MS, and then, for their pains, being asked to comment once again on the second draft. I therefore award a special badge of fortitude to Terry Heiser, Anthony King, Irène and Dick Leonard, David Lipsey, Hilary Rubinstein, Michael Young. The fourth and final draft is immeasurably better because of their detailed comment earlier, though they cannot be held in any way responsible for the outcome.

How I would have got down the last furlong without immense encouragement from Cape, I cannot imagine – especially from Xandra Hardie and Tony Colwell and Graham C. Greene. And I'd like to thank Elizabeth Robinson, Brooke Snell and Jo South for all their help. As for my copy-editor, Jane Hill, we fell stretched out beside each other, in harness, when we completed the course.

I am grateful to the following for permission to quote from copyright material: the British Library of Political and Economic Science, for Hugh Dalton's unpublished diaries; Lord Vaizey, for Dalton's letters and diary extracts; Julia Gaitskell McNeal, for the correspondence between her father and Tony; Philip Williams, for letters; Auberon Waugh, for the postcard written to Jack Donaldson by Evelyn Waugh. James Callaghan, Frank Cox, Lord George-Brown, William Rodgers and A. J. P. Taylor have very kindly given me permission to quote from letters and other of their communications.

I am grateful to London Express News and Feature Services for permission to reproduce the cartoon by Jak on page 250.

In the text I have made clear where I have quoted from the following: *Inside The Treasury* by Joel Barnett (Andre Deutsch, 1982); *The Castle Diaries* by Barbara Castle (*Sunday Times*, 1980); *The Future of Socialism* by Anthony Crosland (Jonathan Cape, 1956, reissued 1980); *The Conservative Enemy* by Anthony Crosland (Jonathan Cape, 1962); *Socialism Now* by Anthony Crosland

(Jonathan Cape, 1974); *The Diaries of a Cabinet Minister*, Vols I-III, by Richard Crossman (Hamish Hamilton and Jonathan Cape, 1975-7); *Memoirs of a City Radical* by Nicholas Davenport (Weidenfeld and Nicolson, 1974); *The Politics of Education* by Maurice Kogan (Penguin, 1971); *The Labour Government 1964-70* by Harold Wilson (Weidenfeld and Michael Joseph, 1971).

Preface

I set out to write an unconventional biography in which things happen as they do in real life, and the reader is not frogmarched through the calendar. I wanted to describe how the characters behaved, talked, reacted to one another, leaving the reader to make any analysis.

In trying to get at 'truth' we are all aware that the same incident is perceived differently by each of us. To accommodate various viewpoints I decided to write a biography structured like a novel. Many of those I interviewed recalled events by dialogue: 'He said ... I said ...' In my diary people's reactions were often conveyed by what they said to one another. Instead of flattening out the personalities by paraphrase, I have incorporated the dialogue directly into the text so that the characters emerge in their own right. I have tried to bear in mind that some of us have a vested interest in an account, and factual accuracy has been checked down to the last detail when possible, the dialogue corroborated in substance.

A formidable amount of research was necessary because Tony's life covered so many areas. On the one hand the central points had to be extracted and got right; on the other hand I had to keep the story moving along. The task was made no easier by the fact that unless they have kept a diary or written a letter or whatever, many people cannot remember what they said or did five, let alone twenty, years ago. Politicians have notoriously bad memories, not so much because they want to adjust the past as because of the continuing surges of activity and emotion and the insecurity endemic to their profession: one moment they are on a pinnacle, the next moment on the ash heap, sometimes rising from the ashes, toppled again.

Civil servants, most of whom I'd scarcely met, proved astonishingly helpful. Perhaps because they are accustomed to taking minutes, or because their working lives are relatively ordered, their profession seems to enable them to reconstruct events as they were at the time rather than reshaped by hindsight. Civil servants from Ministers' Private Offices demonstrated a recall that was almost uncanny: the dialogue they quoted, its content often unknown to me previously, was word for word in Tony's cadence or that of someone else whose manner of speech was familiar to me.

Lord Armstrong (Sir William Armstrong at the time of my story) had kindly helped me in the past with the profiles I wrote under the name Susan Barnes, so I already knew that he was capable of describing events with exceptional dispassion, and that he had a marvellous ear for individuals' speech mannerisms. On page 125, for instance, the dialogue between the leading politicians is exactly as he reported it. Throughout the book the characters have been allowed the style of speech peculiar to them – for example, Lord Brown's account on page 191, Harold Lever's on pages 228–9. My sources are clearly flagged, and only occasionally in the Foreign Office chapters, for reasons which are self-evident, is the person speaking not named. As always with my interviews, I took copious notes at the time and later checked back with my sources.

By its nature my approach precluded footnotes. 'But how then do I know the story is true?' an Oxford professor asked me. 'How do you know it's true when there are footnotes?' I asked him, for footnotes have necessarily been filtered through at least two mental sieves. As it was essential to avoid constant interruption of the narrative, I took my sources directly into the story.

Tony had lived two-thirds of his life before our paths crossed. That period is covered in Part One. Its style and emphasis are different from the bulk of the book which deals with his life after we met in 1956, the same autumn that *The Future of Socialism* was published. The sources of the first section are interviews with people who knew him then, his commonplace book that survived the war, letters, and his own recollections of those years (though he dwelt very little on the past).

Interwoven in the main section are a host of interviews, two more of his commonplace books, once in a while material published by others and acknowledged within the text, and the diaries that I kept during those years.

My diaries have presented the usual moral problem. Except for the last pages, Tony read them – partly for relaxation, partly to check my accuracy as a reporter. He made a very few amendments in the margins. So the diaries have his authority. The judgment of selection is inevitably my own. In the end I have used the diaries largely to put his point of view or mine. When others were holding private conversation in our home or theirs, I have quoted it only with their permission or else because it had come into public currency, i.e. other versions of the conversation had already been retailed. When did I write my diaries? The circumstances varied. If one is in the midst of some happy or terrible turmoil, one is not likely – not this one, at any rate – to rush to her desk and scribble it down. When possible I made an *aide-mémoire* and then wrote the account the next morning – a chore but no great feat for someone whose profession requires a trained memory. Very infrequently I described an event as it was taking place in order not to jump out of my skin. When Ellen-Craig was being held in the police station and I was far too anxious to read or think of anything else, I took notes on Tony's side of the telephone conversations as a means of keeping some kind of perspective.

In his commonplace books I sometimes found a view that he had also put to me and others, such as the observation about politicians that begins on page 243. Rather than using the Hattersleys' or my perception of that conversation, it seemed sensible licence to take Tony's exact written words and put them in his mouth.

The material for the last two chapters comes from a separate diary. A month or so after he died, my memory of final events began to blur in places. With a considerable effort, I got in touch with the participants, wrote down what they thought had happened, found my own memory cleared. The knowledge thus secure, I put away the diary and reread it four-and-a-half years later. A few days after that I got up early in the morning and wrote the penultimate chapter, got up early the next morning and wrote the last chapter. Generally I rewrite a number of times, but in those two cases I left the chapters as I had first written them.

In order to keep the cast of characters from growing beyond a size comprehensible to the reader, I have had to omit friends who influenced Tony and were closer to him than many I have mentioned. I am sorry.

It took me ten years to sort out the basic initials and jargon peculiar to Westminster and Whitehall, and I have used them only when inescapable. There is a crash course at the back of the book.

Adderbury   S.C.
April 1982

PART ONE

A Short Happy Childhood

Tony Crosland was brought up in the intense, austere, narrow Christianity of the Plymouth Brethren, whose pleasure lay in the Word of God and endless discussion of it. More extreme than most non-conformist faiths, in common with them it had its own divisions. Tony's parents belonged to the Exclusive Brethren.

His father was a high-ranking civil servant. Joseph Beardsell Crosland came from Lancashire, went to Manchester Grammar School, won a scholarship to Trinity College, Oxford. Soon afterwards he was in Whitehall, where he applied an exceptional force of intellect to a successful career at the War Office. Tony had the impression that his father's father was perhaps a branch manager of a bank: when old enough to be curious about his ancestry, he was irritated that his mother displayed resolute ignorance of her husband's people. 'We are not a "*family*" family,' Jessie Crosland stubbornly declared in explanation of so little knowledge of her husband's kith and kin.

About her own family she was well-informed. She was a Raven. One of nine siblings, she grew up in the Royal Naval College at Greenwich where her father presided as civil governor. F. E. Raven was an unusual Victorian: he thought daughters as well as sons should be educated in case they didn't want to marry. Jessie got an MA at Bedford College and became a lecturer at Westfield College; her books on French medieval literature remain standard university textbooks. Alice was a barrister. Mary taught English. Edith taught Maths.

At the same time that F. E. Raven stood high in the civil service – hard to better in 'Establishment' attitudes – he was a leader in a sect whose dissent from the established Church was drastic. The Brethren were not founded: around 1820 they sprang up spontaneously in different places – proof of the Spirit's leading. Idealistic puritans reacting against the Church of England's laxity, they comprised a mixed bag – Haldanes and Ravens and Gosses as well as agricultural workers and fishermen. Class distinctions were supposedly disregarded, though the leaders were educated men who had succeeded in reconciling intellect with fundamentalist faith. They were known by their initials, all men being equal – at any rate in the sight of God. When F.E.R.'s wife bought silk for a tea-gown from the Greenwich draper – also a member of the Brethren – he addressed her as 'Sister'. Unlike her husband, Mrs Raven experienced conflicting feelings about this aspect of their religion.

The Exclusive Brethren had a creed, but it was difficult for an outsider to gather what it was. They didn't have rules: there were pressures, things one didn't do – these shibboleths. They didn't do that; they did do this. They didn't go to opera; they did go to concerts. They had some way of making the two consistent when they weren't. Ritual was shunned. Pleasure for its own sake was eschewed. Love for another human being must not overwhelm: total surrender to the physical and natural beauties of life could shut out the Spirit. When a beloved died, grief was curtailed: one should rejoice that the creature wrenched away was now with Jesus.

J. B. Crosland and Jessie Raven met through the Brethren. Their firstborn was named Richard. Two years later came Elsie. When Richard was four he got some incurable disease – probably leukaemia. His mother sat at his bedside and watched him die. It scarred her for life. A year after his death, several Brethren went to J.B.C. to complain that his wife was grieving too much. Despite her deep faith in the heaven virtually guaranteed Exclusive Brethren, she wasn't comforted. She was desperate to have another son. After three or four miscarriages, she was sent away from London by her doctor. Though the First World War was entering its final throes, Mr Crosland was given some leave from the War Office and joined his wife in Sussex. Again she conceived, and the doctor insisted she remain at St Leonards-on-Sea until the child was born – on 29 August 1918. He was christened Charles Anthony Raven Crosland. A few years later came Evelyn.

It was a loving family, the parents far less severe, forbidding than those of Edmund Gosse, described with terrible poignancy in *Father and Son*. But for Tony, the sect that constricted his family was as Gosse described it: 'Here was perfect purity, perfect intrepidity, perfect abnegation; yet here was also narrowness, isolation, an absence of perspective, let it be boldly admitted, an absence of humanity. And there was a curious mixture of humbleness and arrogance; entire resignation to the will of God and not less entire disdain of the judgment and opinion of man.'

J. B. Crosland disliked many things about the sect, but he parried the irritations: loyalty was involved. Well over six feet tall, impeccably dressed and groomed, he was a kind man. Despite his intellectual power, he was equally considerate to everyone. At the post-war conference in Egypt in 1921, the whole of the future of the Middle East was decided under the leadership of Churchill – then Colonial Secretary. J. B. Crosland always sat beside him. 'He can juggle the figures and make them come right,' Churchill said. To Mrs Crosland, who with her husband joined the Churchills' table at meals, he observed: 'Your husband is the truest Christian gentleman I've ever known.'

J. B. Crosland was not saintly in the chilly detached way. At Christmas charades when the word was 'job', he would sit with a rug over his head, using a lozenge tin to scrape himself. (All well-brought-up children knew about the boils that afflicted poor Job.) Though smoking wasn't permitted in the house, drink was, in moderation. Whatever the contradictions between the man and his religion, J. B. Crosland's sheer strength of character had a lasting influence on many people outside as well as inside his family.

Tony was his parents' pride and joy. Then when he was four he got tuberculosis. He was sent to Switzerland for a year, his mother spending the winter near his sanatorium and learning to ski. He was a chattery little boy, and when he returned from Switzerland, wholly fit again, he chattered in French.

The family lived in a typical Golders Green house: semi-detached, larger than it looked, three storeys but going back a long way to a big garden. It was of no avail that he said to journalists in later years: 'I was *not* born and bred in Highgate. I was raised in Golders Green.' His father had purchased an extra strip of land with the house so there could be a tennis court. His mother was noted for her deadly underarm serve. Nannies succeeded one another. Two, sometimes three women servants lived on the top floor. The cook, who was a dwarf, was called Little Lucy. Family holidays were spent in a rented house on the Isle of Wight, or at Aviemore or another of the prettier spots of Britain. In short, the way the professional middle classes lived before the Second World War.

One day when Tony was six or seven, his father suddenly couldn't play tennis on Saturdays, take walks on any day: he had a slight stroke, caused by a clot in his leg. The War Office used to pick him up and bring him home in a government car because he had to keep the leg up. As with 90 per cent of such strokes, recovery was complete.

J. B. Crosland and a Raven brother-in-law both turned down knighthoods, not because they disapproved of a KCB as such, but because it would have set them apart from their Brethren. Though Mrs Crosland took pleasure in demolishing pomposity and humbug, she suffered from petty jealousies. Frank Tribe, who lived along the road, accepted his knighthood. Mrs Crosland never lost a chance to say something sarcastic about Lady Tribe, always managing to convey 'Lady' in inverted commas.

She was extremely jealous for her family – wanting them to be seen to excel at anything they undertook – which was tiresome for them, though it taught Tony the folly of jealousy. 'Jealousy has been the downfall of my life,' she confessed.

When he was eleven, he started junior school at Highgate, a minor public school not far from the house in Golders Green. On the first night in their dormitory, he and Alan Neale became friends. Tony chattered about Italian drivers, motor-racing then his great interest. In those days there were hundreds of car-makers; he knew about all of them. Both were weekly boarders, going home at the weekend. The first time Neale went to Tony's house, his eleven-year-old host produced cigarettes in his little room. Naturally his mother smelt them out. 'She blamed me,' Neale said. 'In fact, I was timid. Tony owned up. He was strictly honest. He'd never let you down. But his parents preferred to think it was *my* influence rather than their own dear son's.'

Neale's people were shopkeepers. It's difficult to discuss snobbery in England and get it right. One might say that it wouldn't have occurred to Tony's parents that they were taking a morally superior position, but they couldn't quite believe there were others as useful as dons and civil servants. Certain areas were outside their knowledge.

Tony was eleven when the Croslands moved to Sheldon Avenue, an attractive tree-lined road in Highgate, not far from Kenwood, everything bigger and more comfortable than in Golders Green. It was usual in those days to say grace before meals. Most middle-class families went to church. The principal outward difference was that the Croslands were the only family in the street who twice every Sunday trooped out to the meeting. Between meetings, usually fifteen Exclusive Brethren were invited to tea at Sheldon Avenue, the doors thrown open between drawing-room and dining-room. Tony helped hand round the bread-and-butter plates.

The main things that families enjoy were enjoyed by the Crosland family. True, there was no radio in the house, no newspapers on Sunday. One didn't go to opera or ballet or the theatre. One didn't eat ice cream on Sunday. But if these restrictions are imposed by the religion of parents you love, you accept them when you are still a child.

By the time Tony was thirteen he chattered less. There was deep happiness in the family, and there was deep tension: the two were concurrent. Elsie, seven years older than her brother, watched his two sides develop. He could be withdrawn, absorbed in his own growing up; he could be high-spirited and amusing, especially after eight o'clock on Sunday evening when he was allowed to come downstairs in his dressing-gown. 'After the evening meeting we had a late dinner, which was exciting,' Elsie said. 'Mother always said that even *her* father had permitted everyone to read a secular book after 8 p.m. on Sunday. So Tony's coming down in his dressing-gown and it being after eight were larks.'

At school the withdrawn side didn't show. 'Few boys can have been less constrained by self-consciousness,' Alan Neale observed. 'The fascination of forbidden fruit led him into a good deal of minor trouble. He was a natural leader of others, and if he felt like enjoying himself in mischief, he'd lead others down that path. He saw this as not serious – as a game where nobody got hurt. He led others astray simply by charming the legs off them. I think a considerable element in his being so wayward was to see what would happen. He was reckless.' He didn't particularly mind being caught. The housemasters were usually bachelors, and some were the type that work themselves up about what they see as moral degradation. 'They never succeeded in deterring him for long: he had a natural courage and resilience,' said Neale.

A housemaster, not noted for sensitivity, beat him excessively and wrote to Mr Crosland about his errant son. By now Elsie was an undergraduate at Oxford; when her father came to see her, he talked largely about Tony: 'I think he's settling down now, although his mouth is still a little soft.' Tony was not yet fourteen.

At home he still did what was expected of him. Twice on Sunday he trooped down the street with his family, though now he sat in the back of the hall with other older boys who didn't want to take part in the meeting. That upset his mother, though she was pleased that he never seemed to mind accompanying his family to the meeting as his friends walked by to play tennis. He did mind. The early childhood identification with the Brethren, the intense imitation of his father at prayer had always been combined with total absence of emotional belief and faith. The 'unreality of prayer' was what struck him. It was a strain for this sensitive boy who knew he was not going the way of his parents, and who was so loved by his parents, and who loved them.

He joined the Left Book Club. As he grew more and more politically-minded, he felt the sheer illogicality of his family's position. J. B. Crosland had clearly formed political views – he was a Liberal – and he discussed politics with his family. Yet he didn't vote: that was another thing the Brethren didn't do. 'What's the point in discussing politics if you then don't vote?' Tony asked Elsie. Many of the Brethren were conscientious objectors in the First World War, some – unlike Quakers – refusing even to drive ambulances. Yet J. B. Crosland was No. 2 at the War Office.

The grip of his religion on this humane man had to be remarkable for him to require his son not to join the Officers' Training Corps at Highgate. For the Brethren, membership of the Corps was condoning the taking of human life. The Corps in itself was a fairly boring activity – boys in military uniforms meeting once a week for a little basic training and parades. But for Tony it offered a way to dissociate from the Brethren's pacifism, which he did not share. When his father enjoined him to take the pacifist role, he minded far more than a boy brought up without these acute and arbitrary moral pressures.

When he rejected the Exclusive Brethren's obsession with the next world, he didn't go to the other extreme of atheism: he was a religious agnostic. He was occupied with what was happening in this world: he felt the grossness of the inequality; he thought that some of the unfairness could be righted here and now. When he was sixteen he joined the Labour Party. His emotions and intelligence poured into the Labour Party. He could identify with the Labour Party.

In 1935 when J. B. Crosland was sixty, he automatically retired from the civil service. The last family holiday was in the Highlands. A week or two later, he and Elsie were strolling out to the car when he had the stroke that killed him. 'Don't bother Mother. I shall be all right,' he said and died outside the house. Mrs Crosland did the best she could to hold the family together, but the focal point was gone.

Tony had just had his seventeenth birthday. He ceased being a weekly boarder because his mother wanted him at home. He kept his word to his father, didn't join the Corps, but was without the pacifist's moral armour. It left him vulnerable. There are three ways to deal with the imputation of cowardice, shirking and suchlike. One is to give the true reason. The second is to dredge up a false reason to weasel out of the imputation. The third is to refuse to give any reason, because you'd rather have the false inference believed than have it thought that you were trying to weasel out of something – which was Tony's way. *One takes the consequences of one's actions:* presumably this overriding value of internal self-respect was instilled by his father.

At Highgate he was the champion mile runner. He was the most graceful long-distance runner his younger sister had ever seen: he had stamina and the capacity to pace himself. He was a prefect. He excelled in debate in the Sixth Form Society. But Alan Neale noticed he had become less outgoing. 'You knew', he said, 'that Tony had his private world of thought, and you didn't know what it was.' Some masters took sharp exception to a Sixth Form essay, 'Bread for the Masses, Cake for the Few'.

Friends still came home for tennis. Afterwards there were bowls of raspberries from the garden. Mrs Crosland always welcomed her children's friends, though when Tony brought them back for tennis on a Sunday, she was furious and turned them out. He still spent time at the family piano. But mostly when he was home he closed himself in his room and read his monthly volumes from the Left Book Club and listened to his radio. His mother was very angry when she found he'd smuggled the radio into the house, but she had to give way. When he wanted to think things out, he played ball alone against the house wall that faced the tennis court, for an hour or more at a time, throwing the tennis ball up against the wall, catching it, throwing it up again. He now took his holidays alone.

He failed his first exam for a scholarship to Trinity College, Oxford, had to sit for it a second time. When he left Highgate, his mother felt less than exaltation on Speech Day: another boy bore off a slightly taller pile of those gold-tooled leather-bound books. No matter that Alex Comfort's ambition to be a surgeon was jeopardised when he blew up much of his left hand in an accident with a home chemistry set. The sight of his prize books outnumbering those of her beloved son remained graven on her soul, and she never hesitated to slander the entire Comfort family. 'Everyone believed that his parents helped him with his homework,' she said with waspish nostalgia whenever another novel or book of poetry or medical biology by Alex Comfort was acclaimed. (Tony read his so-called rival's work with detached interest. The commonplace book he started during the war included comments on novels that interested him. One such précis began: 'Unpleasant as he may have been at school, Alex Comfort can certainly write. *The Power House*, for all its obvious faults, is a very big achievement indeed for a young man of 25. The faults are irritating but should be curable.')

Despite the prize-day setback to her vanity, Mrs Crosland gave her son a secondhand MG. He named it the Red Menace and drove it forthwith to Germany, determined to see the castles in the Black Forest before the inevitable act of aggression closed frontiers. Among the castles he encountered his first romance, with an American girl, though this proved rather less enduring than the passion he developed for architecture. He enjoyed solitude.

But solitude is very different from separateness – the keystone of the Exclusive Brethren. He had been inculcated with the sense of being apart from other people. 'It gave one a very odd feeling,' he said when, twenty years later, all at once he was able to talk about it.

2

Different Worlds

Trinity was an unlikely college for Tony: he went there because his father had. Most of the undergraduates were Conservative bloods – philistines and proud of it, 'typical of the English ruling classes before the war' was the way Richard Hillary put it, 'cliquey, extremely limited in our horizon, quite conscious of the fact and in no way dissatisfied with it.'

Tony and his left-wing friends in Trinity formed a small clique of their own, a number of them Marxists – fellow travellers or communists. Most were scholars, some – like Philip Williams – from grammar schools. Philip was a mine of information about Labour Party lore. Tony hadn't previously met anyone like him.

In 1937 the British Labour Party had ceased to be neutralist. It remained anti-communist. The Spanish Civil War was raging. All left-wingers supported the Loyalist Republicans against Franco. Communists fought side by side with Republicans and grew increasingly influential, which confused matters ideologically: one could be revolutionary, anti-fascist and patriotic at the same time. Idealistic English trade unionists along with poets and intellectuals – ten years older than Tony – went to Spain to fight the fascists, often becoming communists along the way.

At Oxford the Spanish War brought Labour and communist undergraduates together. Though accounts of the Moscow trials and purges filtered through, the Left didn't believe these as yet unsubstantiated stories. The Communist Party seemed to be the defender of democracy against fascism. Denis Healey and Iris Murdoch were card-carrying CP members; a great many gifted and able people were in the CP then. Tony went to the brink but was hauled back by Philip Williams. (After the war he reproached Philip for denying him experience of what the CP was like from the inside.) Transport House took no great interest in the Oxford Labour Club, which resembled the sex life of the amoeba – dividing itself incessantly.

The final collapse of Republican Spain came in 1939. Hitler had just seized Czechoslovakia, and in September he sent his army into Poland. Britain fulfilled her treaty obligations to Poland and declared war on Germany – but, with the signing of the treaty between Russia and Germany, the CP turned 180 degrees and opposed the war.

A few months after declaring her neutrality, Russia invaded Finland. That gave the English Left a further shock. Was communist totalitarianism as evil as fascist totalitarianism? The Oxford Labour Club put it to the vote. The fellow-travelling majority kept to the pro-communist, somehow pacifist line. The minority, led by Tony Crosland, got off that train and caught one going the other way, though with no vitriolic personal break. Early in 1940 they formed their own Democratic Socialist Club, loyal to national Labour Policy – anti-communist, anti-pacifist. Tony was its first chairman, Roy Jenkins treasurer. They became good friends. Roy, an undergraduate at Balliol, was two years the younger. Tony found it pleasant to have Roy around, treating him rather as a senior partner treats the junior ones, patronising him.

Meanwhile Tony and two other friends had moved into lodgings at 2 St John Street, run by the most snobbish lady in Oxford – high praise in a severely contested league. No doubt she was relieved that Philip Williams drank virtually nothing, Tony and Alan Neale no more than their fair share, unlikely to topple over the bannister on to her nicely polished floor as undergraduates elsewhere sometimes did. There was a young girl who worked for this lady. Tony thought she was having a rough time and found excuses to give her small amounts of money.

During the months of the 'phoney war', the two Left factions at Oxford went on arguing, Denis Healey still on the communist side, Tony Crosland leading the Labour side, each using Marxist arguments. Suddenly they had to stop arguing: France collapsed. They went off together to war. Britain, by the summer of 1940, was fighting Hitler entirely alone.

Undergraduates were exempted from military service until they had taken their degrees. Tony had started as a classics scholar, a four-year course at Oxford. He had one year to go. Walking down Piccadilly late in June 1940, he noticed two soldiers with a black flash emblazoned on the back of their tunics. Five black ribbons – which a century earlier would have bound the soldier's hair in a queue – each 2 inches wide ($9\frac{1}{2}$ inches long for officers, $7\frac{1}{2}$ inches for other ranks), spread out like a fan from the collar of the tunic.

Tony maintained his sole reason for joining the Royal Welch Fusiliers, which he did a few days later, was to wear their emblem, the flash.

He didn't talk about his five and a half years in the army. But a nightmare recurred for the rest of his life, always the same: he was trying to run but couldn't move one of his legs; he was armed, but somehow couldn't use his weapon; however hard he strained as the enemy advanced, he was unable to move. Just before death overtook him, he used to wake. He never brooded on whether our worst nightmare may foreshadow our destiny.

During the army years, he started a commonplace book. One war notebook went to the bottom of the Mediterranean, one survives – every strand of his personality appearing like signposts to the rest of his life. The signposts also appear in an astonishing correspondence with Philip Williams – letters which Tony said they should both keep ('we owe a duty to our biographers'). Army life not being designed for sustained thinking, he and Philip used the letters to keep their minds from deteriorating under the tedium of regimentation. Some ran to 25,000 words, argument growing heated as these two young men analysed international politics and mapped out problems they foresaw for democratic socialism. Many of the themes reappeared in *The Future of Socialism* – the resilience of capitalist economy, the ability of a gradualist but determined reforming government to change the balance of power in society. 'I am revising Marxism & will emerge as the modern Bernstein,' Tony wrote – at twenty-two.

In these dense missives neither man refers much to his individual experiences, so that to extract those fragments from Tony's letters gives a false impression of egocentricity. (He did like things to go his own way, however.) The two friends were going down different paths. Throughout Philip's years in the artillery, he avoided identifying with the army. Tony moved from a privileged and exclusive background into total involvement.

Previously having spoken up for the interests of the less fortunate from a comfortable distance, he was now at close quarters.

(AUGUST 1940, Cheshire) 'Dear Willie ... Army life is getting more bearable gradually. At first I was too miserable for words, and often literally on the verge of tears – the worst thing being the utter loneliness engendered by the impression of Cockneys en masse, loud-voiced, coarse, perpetually swearing, etc. I thought I should lead an existence of utter solitude. But gradually I have discovered that taken singly they are amazingly pleasant and really generous, though very stupid. I am treated very definitely as an intellectual from a different world, which helps matters, and altogether I get along with them far better than I ever thought I could. I am gradually ferreting out the relative intelligentsia of the place and spend the weekends with them. Everybody hates Army life, and frankly morale is non-existent.'

During the first exercise in handling the Bren, there was an incident. The Bren was a gun that stood on the ground. A private fired it, cleared the stoppage, fired again, leapt to his feet and shouted: 'No. 1 gun clear, Corporal!' Private Crosland leapt to his feet and shouted: 'No. 1 gun clear, Comrade!' He was confined to barracks for seven days.

(SEPTEMBER 1940, Cheshire) 'Dear Willie ... Actually I had heard from Roy that you had received the summons, so that the address was not a surprise. Please let me express my quite genuine sympathy and my sincere hopes that you will not find it too bad ... I'm very glad you've found at least one educated friend there. Quite honestly, if I hadn't found such a person here (a very intelligent man from Brecon who works in a bank), life would have been pretty near unbearable; you can't conceive the difference it makes if you have someone with whom to discuss the day's work, Army life, etc. from a more or less common standpoint – it prevents that awful feeling of loneliness and spiritual isolation which nearly killed me during the first few days here ... My greatest achievement to date in this place has been to give a political lecture to my platoon during a training period. We were supposed to be on anti-gas, but our N.C.O. was called away, and I took the squad instead, but turned 'anti-gas' into a political talk on why the war was not a mere capitalist war and financiers' romp. It was a great success, and I am becoming a sort of political commissar around here! ... If by any chance you are feeling slightly depressed, remember that the human body and mind will adapt themselves to anything.'

(SEPTEMBER 1940, Cheshire) 'Dear Willie ... On the whole you seem to have been definitely lucky – you can't conceive what you escape by being under a roof. A month ago I should have envied your happier lot; at the moment, with the prospect of a fairly early release from my woes, I am inclined to be glad of having had the worse experience.' When interviewed by the board who decided which soldiers should be trained as officers, Tony was asked why he had not been in his school's OTC. He replied that his reasons were pacifist ones, giving no hint of why he had minded so much.

At the officers' training camp in North Wales, Cadet Crosland found the release limited.

(DECEMBER 1940, Barmouth) 'Dear Willie ... It is true that the work offers slightly more scope for the use of one's intelligence, but this is more than countered by the appalling atmosphere of earnest-mindedness that pervades the place. The officers are young and "keen", very reminiscent of second-rate classical lecturers, & much in need of a course in elocution & public speaking; the cadets for the most part are horribly alert & serious about it all, & one badly misses that spirit of cynicism and revolt that was so evident in the ranks.

'I need hardly say that I do not fit very happily into this Sunday School atmosphere, & I am officially disapproved of. It is felt that my attitude is too casual, & I made a thoroughly bad start by omitting to remove my pipe from my mouth during a mock bayonet charge. The trouble is (& I'm sure you would find the same) that I refuse to degrade myself intellectually to the point of assuming an avid interest in the ridiculously piddling & unrealistic matters that absorb our time.'

Wrexham, North Wales, was the regimental depot – home base – of the Royal Welch Fusiliers. The second lieutenants were amateur soldiers. All officers who ranked above them were professionals. The young subalterns, waiting to be posted, were spared the grinding regimentation inflicted on other ranks. Even so, the Royal Welch laid great stress on conformity.

Like most subalterns, Lt John Mason was straight from school, keen to do the right thing. He shared a room with David Graves, Robert Graves's son by his first wife. Tony and David, Mason observed, were different from the others: they were thinking things out for themselves. David arrived at Wrexham with a great black mark against him. 'I have to be very careful what battalion they select for me. My father has offended virtually every regular officer in the regiment,' he said to Mason. 'And Tony has to be equally careful where they post him.'

'What's Tony done?' asked Mason.

'Well, you know that Tony is left-wing.'

'Oh.'

Professional officers in the line regiments were from the upper-

middle classes, all officers assumed to be Conservative. A socialist
from their background meant class betrayal. In any case, party
politics were not to be discussed during the war. Most left-wingers
kept quiet in the army.

David was impressed by Tony: 'Tony says . . . Tony thinks . . .'
Tony was in hospital for some minor ailment. 'All the nurses rave
about him.' David was more poetic than intellectual, hadn't Tony's
formal good looks; David's uniform was always untidy, his hair too
long even when it had just been cut. He and Tony became closely
attached. When David went on leave to his grandmother's home in
North Wales or Robert Graves's home in Devon, Tony was usually
with him.

At Wrexham, subalterns sought out girls at the Saturday-night
dances, though they couldn't take a girl back to their quarters –
that would mean a court-martial. Like most subalterns Tony and
David, disciplined by school and army, had limited sexual experience: relations with girls were mostly flirtations.

When the blitz on London intensified and Westfield College was
evacuated to Oxford, Mrs Crosland closed up the Highgate home
and moved with Evelyn into a little terrace house in North Oxford.
Tony divided his leaves between the Graves households and his
own family. Away from the army, his clothing was an individual
assemblage. He was wearing a camel's hair coat and buttonhole
when he swept into his old digs at 2 St John Street to find two girls
in occupation.

'Who said you could occupy my rooms?'

The discovery that one girl belonged to a high Establishment
family seemed to add to his irritation. The other girl, Barbara
Horsfield, her own family Conservative enough, was doted upon by
a bevy of young men. She was rude back, whereupon she and Tony
began a long friendship.

She had not encountered anything like him. He knew more
about architecture than anyone she had met and clearly loved
examining the special features of Oxfordshire's houses and
churches. On the other hand, he insisted he didn't know how to eat
asparagus or make polite conversation. Clambering over rocks,
teetering on the edge of a sixty-foot drop, he said: 'You must
tell me how one behaves with girls. How do girls' minds work?'
Skimming along in the Red Menace he asked: 'What do you
like?'

'Hunting,' Barbara said.

He drove straight into a ditch, and while they sat entangled in a hedge, he lectured her on people who were absolutely hopeless.

Back at Wrexham he began a two-month course to become a Signals Officer. 'Reading and sending Morse is extraordinarily amusing, I must say,' he told David after the first week. Shortly, however, he wrote to Philip: 'All that an Infantry S.O. needs to know could be learned in a month, instead of the two we actually have. We take a lamp or buzzer into a field outside the camp, & spend most of the day reading or sleeping, with an occasional pause for signalling ... To make things quite perfect, I am now sleeping with an officer under close arrest for trying to commit suicide while drunk. Although a little nervous at first of a savage attempt on my life (or even honour!) during the still hours of the night, I have gradually got to know him very well, and we get on admirably together ... I have got to know a very worthy man here, one Ted Jones, Sec. of the No. Wales Miners' Federation, and on the Executive of the MFGB. He is an excellent corrective to the Left intellectual line.'

No officer failed a Signals Course exam. One test was to plan a simple tactical exercise. To relieve his boredom, Lt Crosland produced a complex international operation involving the Russian Reds. The infuriated examiners tore it up. Amateur officers were bad enough, intellectual ones beyond the bloody pale. He became a Signals Officer only because the Commanding Officer had been rather amused by the incident.

At Wrexham the professional officers had their own magnificent mess, filled with treasures, the regimental colours draped over the main table. The port went round and round. The subalterns lived in an annex, had one glass of port – but paid the same mess rate as the senior officers. They had little money.

Tony said: 'Leave it to me.'

He went to a mess meeting of senior officers and wiped the floor with them. They were very put out indeed and he was promptly posted.

(AUGUST 1941, Worthing) 'Dear Willie ... an appalling rocket from the C.O. for going on leave a day early: he reported me to the Brigadier, and the result is no weekend leave for poor To-To until after his next 7 days. On the other hand, a nice compliment from the Div. Commander himself on a report which contained a brilliant and scathing analysis of this Battalion's operational role.'

Tony and David and John Mason were posted to different

battalions and were to have separate wars. There was no reason why Tony and Mason should meet again in civilian life, and they didn't. Mason saw him for the last time outside Brigade Headquarters at Piddlehinton Camp in Dorset: up came Tony on a motor cycle, wearing a skiing hat. The Brigadier appeared, looked coldly at the two subalterns, his eyes on Tony's hat. 'Good afternoon, Crosland.' Mason was astonished: a Brigadier, commanding three battalions, did not notice junior officers in wartime. The following day orders were issued: '*Officers will wear official headgear on all exercises.*'

There was every reason why Tony and David should meet when the war was over. They had embarked on a lifelong friendship.

While the professional soldiers deplored his socialism, Tony became increasingly at odds with Left intellectuals. To Philip he described himself early in 1941 as 'bang in the middle of the steady process of intellectual flux that started when my faith in the CP and 100% Marxism was shattered, & continued when my brief period of faith in the Left Intellectuals and 85% Marxism was shattered. Where I shall end Heaven knows – I am still moving.'

He was against those who sniped at the Labour Party in *Tribune* and the *New Statesman*; he found Fabians 'self-righteous and anti-patriotic'; he also got fed up with Philip's nit-picking. 'You look on me as a hopelessly complacent Transport House stooge, unwilling to allow any criticism of Party leaders,' he wrote to Philip, 'while I regard you as a permanently nagging Left intellectual, carried away by catch-phrases and determined (à la N.S.) to read the worst into everything and ignore "the case in favour".' Lt Crosland was already the Party man.

By the spring of 1942, browned off with journalists' attacks on 'British blunders', he was considering volunteering either for India or for an Airborne Division: 'If one has got to waste one's best years in the Army, one might as well have some valid experience to show for it.' David's battalion of the Royal Welch had just left England, shipped by convoy, destination unknown.

↤ 3 ↦

Some Valid Experience

In Whitehall the War Office was forming the 1st Airborne Division. They had one Parachute Brigade. They wanted a second. Because the casualty rate for paratroops was so high, soldiers had to volunteer. Parachutes were not as reliable as one would have liked. When they opened, their burden was liable to be shot before he reached the ground. If he reached the ground behind enemy lines, civilians might enthusiastically impale him on pitchforks while he was still disentangling himself from his harness. Members of the Parachute Brigade were trained to the same standard as commandos. They had an understanding with the German SS: behind enemy lines, they didn't take prisoners – there was nowhere to put them.

To form the Brigade quickly, the War Office chose one battalion each from the Royal Welch, Royal Scots and Royal Irish, and asked for volunteers. The soldiers were free to join another battalion, but well over half the Royal Welch volunteered (though not all were accepted); they proved the army right: group loyalty was stronger than the instinct for personal survival.

(JULY 1942, Piddlehinton) 'Dear Willie ... A sudden and unexpected change in my fortunes and those of my Battalion. At the end of next week I proceed to the hills of Derbyshire, undergo an intensive 3 weeks' P.T. course, and then do my first jump, and immediately afterwards (after a short interval, possibly, for running to my quarters and changing my fear-soiled trousers) my second. After the 7th jump I am granted the triple privilege of a parachute badge on my right sleeve, 2/- a day extra danger pay, and a liability to be shot for cowardice if I ever afterwards refuse to jump. How I came to volunteer for this I am still not quite sure. This time a year ago I should have regarded any such prospect with the utmost distaste and repugnance. But a second year of Army life has done more to me than add grey hairs to my bowed head. It has changed the ratio of my interests: politics have gone down to just that extent that military affairs have gone up. This combination of growing interest in, and self-identification with, the Army was psychologically the determining factor, tho' mixed with many others – vanity, bravado, browned-off-ness with the infantry, a feeling of the utter absurdity of spending 3 yrs. of one's life in khaki without even getting an interesting psychological experience for one's pains, etc. etc. etc. So there it is. So far I have no regrets, as I am still enjoying the pleasant experience of having something new and interesting to look forward to.'

(undated, no place) 'Dear Willie ... The actual act of jumping is far worse than I expected, and not faintly comparable with anything I have experienced before. Sitting, tense and keyed up, waiting to drop through a hole in the fuselage into empty space, then the awful 3 seconds plunging helpless through the air before the chute opens – it has taught me at least the true content of phrases which before meant little to me, such as "abject terror" and "cold sweat"!'

(SEPTEMBER 1942) 'Dear Willie ... We are under canvas "somewhere in England". I am extremely depressed at the moment, partly because I have just heard I have to do another jump on Monday, but even more at the general prospect of several weeks in tents, working extremely hard, being thoroughly regimental, & having nothing better to look forward to in the evenings than a dim, large, & freezing tent, which makes me think for some reason of what the Holy Tabernacle must have been like in Old Testament days: the main difference is that even the most ferocious Jehovah in his most wrathful moods would have seemed a very ray of cheerful sunshine compared with our new CO. But enough of these woes: Jack Tanner bids us to action, and I must try to be inspired by his earnest and high-minded desire for my premature decease.'

Jack Tanner, in his London office as General Secretary of the Engineers' union, was calling for a Second Front. As most of Tony's letter was about the recent TUC conference and Labour's influence in the coalition government under Churchill, any lessening of his interest in the Labour Party was presumably fleeting.

'I see you write a lot of letters,' Lt Crosland said.
'Yes. I'm writing to my wife,' Lt Atkins said.
'I don't think I should write that many letters.'
'I shouldn't write that many letters to *your* wife.'
From then on the two men clicked. Dougie Atkins, like Tony, was twenty-four. Having volunteered for the Parachute Brigade, Dougie hastened to marry his childhood sweetheart. He wrote to her each day. He was a socialist – from Barry, South Glamorgan-

shire, where his father was a successful butcher and a radical local councillor. When the Brigade was allowed under a roof he and Tony shared a room. What Dougie liked best was his companion's cheerfulness in trying circumstances. When the packed load of paratroops was waiting to jump, miserable and tense, Tony would say something flippant that broke through the nervous strain, made them laugh.

The new CO was absolute king. He'd been a Cambridge blue, so everyone had to go running before breakfast. He had the fanatic's concern for correct dress: all officers had to carry swagger-sticks. At meals he held court at one end of the table, officers waiting on his every word. One day he was holding forth on the glories of General Montgomery. From the lowly end of the table, Lt Crosland leant forward: 'Montgomery would not go down well with *your* regulations on dress, would he, Sir.' (Montgomery went in for battledress peculiar to his current whim.) Silence fell. There was no reply.

They moved to Salisbury Plain where they continued life of a sort under canvas when not engaged in something called the Parachute March (when, as part of their twenty-five-mile march, they walked and ran alternately for ten miles, packs on backs) or in leaping into an outdoor pool for their swim in the middle of winter (packs still secured firmly to backs).

Whenever Tony was home on leave, he saw Barbara. Her family also lived in Oxfordshire. Around the beginning of 1943, she introduced him to her younger sister, Pat, back from school in Canada with an attractive North American accent. She was about eighteen. Though Barbara's own relationship with Tony was platonic, rather to her chagrin he and Pat fell for one another.

It was his first experience of falling overwhelmingly in love. Previously, physical frolics were in one compartment, the serious side of his nature in another. With Pat, the compartments could open into one another. The song from the film *Casablanca* was a great tear-jerker at that stage of the war. Tony would always associate 'As Time Goes By' with his and Pat's last evening before the 2nd Parachute Brigade was shipped to North Africa.

People who haven't been in a war don't realise how much time soldiers spend waiting for action in unremitting monotony. In North Africa the tedium was broken only by discomfort. Most of the Brigade had never seen a desert before. A three-day exercise was devised to see how long they could go without water in tropical heat. Thirty-five years later Dougie Atkins could still remember the animal desire for water. 'Actually, the CO misjudged the desert heat and they had to send a tanker of water out to us. Even then we were only allowed to re-fill our flasks once. At the end of the three days when we got back to camp, there stands the CO with his swagger-stick, waiting to take the salute.' Tony's platoon was carrying anti-tank weapons, great cumbersome tubular things like drain-pipes. He should simply have ordered his men: 'Eyes right!' Instead he ordered: 'Present arms!' There was an absolute shambles as the soldiers swung these great tubes round. The CO was furious. Lt Crosland was hauled over the coals. He didn't care.

Dougie discussed it with some of the others. They all felt if Tony set his mind on being a success, he would be, whatever he chose to do. They were in a much sought-after regiment. He stood head and shoulders above the rest. But they couldn't imagine him ever wanting to be a general in the army, which above all expects you to conform.

On 9 July 1943 the airborne invasion of Sicily began. The 2nd Brigade was on the runway, fuselages of Dakotas crammed with men bulging in their parachute equipment, keyed up for what lay ahead. Then they were told that the 1st Brigade's drop had been so successful that their own was cancelled.

About this time a letter reached Tony in North Africa telling him of David's death in Burma. The Japanese were established in strongly protected positions, and David had gone ahead of his company to hurl grenades into two enemy posts. He returned for more grenades, then went forward again and flung them into a third enemy post. He was last seen as he was falling into the Japanese trench. Posthumously he was recommended for the Victoria Cross but didn't get it because an officer hadn't witnessed the action.

Two months after the first assault on Sicily, Italy surrendered. The Germans moved south to withstand the Allies' seaborne invasion. Paratroops make skilled foot soldiers in unknown terrain. British High Command decided to use the 2nd Parachute Brigade in the seaborne invasion; Tony's Battalion was split between two ships, Dougie Atkins on the first ship, the *Abdiel*, Tony on the second. They were to meet at Taranto, the Italian navy's main base.

When the Allied fleet entered Taranto harbour, they didn't know how many Germans awaited them. Dougie was on the *Abdiel*'s deck with the troops intended to disembark first, completely equipped – pistol, grenades in pockets, binoculars. As it was night and no one knew when they would land, he lay down on the deck and went to sleep.

There was a tremendous explosion. The *Abdiel* swung completely over on to one side, then back on to the other side. The Captain said: 'Don't panic. Every man for himself!' – like an Errol Flynn film. Dougie swam along the funnel, all the soldiers who'd been on deck accidentally kicking each other as they tried to swim. The *Abdiel* went down in two minutes. The suction dragged the swimmers down after the ship. Some got to the surface again before they drowned.

The Battalion's second ship reached Taranto. 'Is Dougie all right?' was the first thing Tony asked. Dougie was one who'd reached the surface in time and stayed there. The Commanding Officer and a quarter of the Battalion had been below deck; two days later their bodies started floating into shore. The senior officer, known as Roderick, took over. He appointed Tony to replace the injured Adjutant. Tony's first job was to get his comrades' bodies out of the water. Then the Battalion's supply ship hit a mine, everyone's personal possessions going down, along with the crew.

In a large, flat, lined Italian accountancy book, Tony began afresh, depicting countries he moved about in, peasant communities caught between opposing armies and reduced to rubble, reactions of diverse nationalities and individuals thrown together in arbitrary alliance or enmity, the pure bliss of rest leave and eating off a plate. Vivid, sometimes lyrical, in pictorial descriptions, he wrote of his own response to horror in a stilted manner, like someone distancing himself – no mention of the first job at Taranto until a fortnight after the episode.

(4 OCTOBER 1943) 'We are on the move again, back to Acquaviva. I am half glad and half sorry. I still have the novice's curiosity about battle: but much of my schoolboy enthusiasm for fighting has been damped by the unpleasant aftermath of the Abdiel sinking. I shall not soon forget the sight and stench of those washed up bodies, horribly and grotesquely swollen, limbs distorted, flesh decomposing: and the grim business of loading them on the lorries, travelling in the back of the lorry with that macabre load, and burying them in a huge communal pit, trying hard not to be sick.'

(8 DECEMBER) 'They were right about the shelling – the worst time is the 2–3 seconds between first hearing the whistle and the actual bomb-burst while you wonder how near it's coming. It's an

inhuman impersonal sort of warfare, the menace of death that suddenly comes out of the blue, and leaves you helpless to hit back. This morning a truck had a direct hit on the cab, and the driver, my old friend Johnson, had his head blown right off – a horrible sight, lolling over the driving wheel, with only a gory mess where his head should have been.'

(10 DECEMBER) 'This first experience of being under fire has been invaluable training, but I don't think we have shone particularly. Admittedly the Bn. is in a very sticky position, holding an almost isolated position in a very pronounced salient: we have enemy on two sides of us, and can therefore not concentrate our attentions in one particular direction. There is no doubt that we have let the Germans gain complete patrol (and therefore moral) superiority: last night they walked right into our positions and carried off a N. Z A/Tk [Anti-Tank] Sgt. alive – a very daring piece of work. Matters are made worse by the fact that they have our positions 100% pin-pointed & registered, whereas we must almost guess theirs: and this fact completely nullifies our immense artillery superiority. Roderick is inordinately cautious and refuses to be in any way offensive. He pays no attention to any suggestions from either Fleming or myself, & there is a certain amount of friction in Bn HQ.

'X has been evacuated with shell-shock. This is an excellent testing-ground – and it isn't the fine physical specimens or the battle drill kings who come out best.'

Friction in Battalion HQ increased. With the CO away in England, the Major called Roderick was again in command. Adjutants were usually chosen on social grounds: Capt. Crosland, as he now was, had presence, courage, intelligence (valued in that order by some). But he had an unfortunate habit: when he came to think that his superior officer had no sense of strategy, he would explain how to manage things better.

(11 DECEMBER) 'Tonight we are relieved by the Scots, thank God, and to celebrate the fact we have our worst day so far. As we drive out of the area, our hearts lighten and the oppressive feeling is lifted from the pit of my stomach. We all feel it, and by the time we stop to brew up some miles away from the firing line we feel like singing aloud, the rather excited relief that you feel after a parachute jump. I feel rather ashamed of myself, but no one could avoid that sudden cessation of strain and lightening of the tension. It is grand.'

(12 DECEMBER) 'Something of a shock for me today. Roderick

tells me he is removing me from post of Adjutant and making me I.O. [Intelligence Officer] with no immediate loss of rank but a possibility of going down later on. Reason given: he wants a good I.O., and he doesn't think I'm sufficiently regimental to be an Adjutant. This is fantastic. The opportunities for being either regimental or non-regimental in the line are not exactly considerable, and this is obviously not the real reason. The real reason is two-fold: (a) we are temperamentally complete opposites. (b) I make no attempt to hide my disagreement with him, and in general appear too casual and lackadaisical – in other words, not enough bullshit and hypocrisy. As I don't consider this an adequate reason for reversion, I ask for an interview with the Brigadier. I tell him frankly why I think Roderick has made the change, and ask for a transfer to another Bn. He says wait until Col. Barlow comes back, and meanwhile he will guarantee that there shall be no change in rank. I agree unwillingly.'

Three days later the new Intelligence Officer was given his first patrol, its purpose to discover where German troops were deployed along the route twisting up to the citadel – the once towering medieval monastery on top of Monte Cassino. German Headquarters were inside this rubble, commanding the heights. General Alexander's divisions were below, trying to scale them. The weather was appalling.

When used as foot soldiers the Parachute Brigade had relatively light casualties: they were too highly trained to waste in front-line slaughter. They were used when specialised troops were needed who could travel fast and light and thus were eminently suitable for reconnaissance patrol. Nothing was worse than local patrol: when you came back safely, you hated going out again; it was foreign to every instinct. Dougie Atkins sometimes thought that the more intelligent you were, the more difficult it was: you had more ability to imagine what might happen.

(17 DECEMBER) 'Was told at $\frac{1}{2}$-hour's notice that I was going on 36-hour reccc patrol to discover whether there was any sign of Guardiagrele being evacuated. I had with me an interpreter, an I [Intelligence] Sergeant, 2 Signallers with an 18 Set, and 3 men for protection. We started at 1400 hours, went as far as we dared in daylight, and then lay up in a house where the I Sergeant had been before. By this time I realised I couldn't answer the question without passing through strong enemy positions. I asked the C.O. over the wireless if he wanted me to do this: and after a long delay the reply came back "Yes – if you can without being caught." This

didn't help me at all, as the chances of doing so without being caught were remote.

'After questioning a civilian, who said the houses along the road were occupied by Germans in fair strength, I decided there could be no question of taking a large body. So I left everybody behind except the interpreter (an excellent Italian-born Sergeant from the 4th Battalion), and at 0300 hours he and I set out in the half-moon. The going was unbelievably bad: we had to cross a succession of gulleys and ravines so steep that the only way of getting down was on your bottom, and up on all fours. I fell down continually and slipped and slithered all over the place. Also, it was my first patrol: and every bush and cabbage patch was a German to me: but you can't do anything except go in and hope it isn't. Only once did we actually see a German patrol of three: we were walking on the edge of a precipice, and we went to ground right on the brink, wondering whether if they approached we should open up on them, or slide out of sight down this very disagreeable ravine. My heart was in my mouth: but fortunately they passed by.

'By 0600, when I had meant to be up to the lateral road which the Germans array, I was still some way away, with no hope of crossing it in daylight. We found a slit trench which gave very fair cover but which had a completely covered approach to it from the rear: so that anybody could have crept right up to us from behind, and dropped a grenade into the trench before we even knew he was there: every leaf rustling sounded uncannily like a stealthily-moving man.

'I thought I had better have a shit before daylight finally locked me up in my little trench. I had got my trousers down, and a steady flow was proceeding, when an accursed M.G. suddenly opened up with tracer in our direction. I pulled up my trousers and ran like hell for my trench, clutching at my pants as I ran: my Sergeant, seeing my pants gleaming white in the moonlight and me clutching haplessly at my legs, exclaimed: "You're wounded, Sir!"

'It was a queer feeling, sitting in that trench, knowing that we couldn't move from it until dusk 10 hours later, and wondering what daylight would show. Actually, we were some 400-500 yards away from the houses which we believed German-occupied. It was not one of the pleasantest days I have spent: bitterly cold – too cold to sleep; the trench so small that we suffered agonies from cramp; the continuous nervous tension of whether we had been spotted and whether a patrol would scotch us from behind. Never have I so longed for the blessed safety of darkness. At last dusk fell: at 17.15 we set out for the road. Across one bloody ravine, then up the steep slope to the road, making a terrific noise. Fifty yards from the road we were heard, and a rifleman fired several shots at us. It was perfectly clear that our chances of crossing the road were nil: and as I thought I had answered the question given me I deemed it wise to withdraw. But the journey back was a nightmare. It was pitch-black: one just slithered down and clambered up; it was a physical effort to move one mud-clogged boot in front of the other; each time we rested we had to fight against the almost unconquerable impulse to sleep – the most agonising physical effort I know: and in addition we were thirsty as hell.

'I reported to the Brigadier at once, and found him very pleased with our efforts, and very anxious about whether he would ever see us again.

'Apart from the extreme unpleasantness of the whole thing, and the nervous tension of half-expecting to see a body of Germans at every step, my abiding impression of the affair is the extreme kindness of the Italian peasants. They take a great risk in receiving us. If the Germans heard of it they would unhesitatingly shoot them. Three days ago they shot a whole family who had given away a Jerry patrol to one of ours. The Italians here are much more friendly than those round Santeramo who never knew what German occupation meant.'

(20 DECEMBER) 'An unexpected pleasure. The Brigadier took me to see General Freyburg [Commander of the 2nd New Zealand Division] and report on the country south of Guardiagrele. Freyburg is impressive: a cheerful rotund personality of medium height with a round open face and a pair of very alert eyes: a man who asks unexpected and penetrating questions with a most disarming politeness. I told him the route in from the South was out of the question: but I think he disbelieved me. General Dempsey was also there, tall, nervous, red-faced with surprised popping eyes; he looked as though the situation had got beyond him – which is hardly surprising.'

(14 JANUARY 1944) 'This is a devil of a place. The most terrifying thing of all was when the village was dive-bombed ... We were much aided by a German patrol of four which walked straight into an ambush: we killed two and captured two, which raised our morale not a little. Opposite us is 26 Pz [Panzer] Div. Their recce patrol walked straight into our trap, and we have killed three more who exposed themselves very carelessly. We have pushed forward

a good deal, and I think Colonel Barlow, now back from England, is a good soldier with bags of initiative.'

(31 JANUARY) 'Edwards, of my I Section, has been killed by a mortar bomb: poor Edwards, with his violin and his studious spectacles, always itching to get at a piano: he was the most un-military person I ever met. It really is a beastly business . . . One's attitude to the Germans out here is strangely paradoxical. When you meet them in the flesh, as individual P/Ws [Prisoners of War], they cease to be hated foes, and become human beings, for whom one feels sympathy. But thinking of them impersonally, say after you have just been the wrong end of some nasty shelling, one feels the most bitter hatred for them, and gloats at the news that they are wounded or killed . . . The reputation our Bde. has won for itself on this front is staggering. We have been very lucky in bringing in proportionately more P/Ws than any other formation, and as a result we are looked upon as the crack Brigade in the Allied armies. We are even having officers and men from the 8th Indian attached to us to study our patrolling methods.'

(7 MARCH) 'The Brigadier arrived back to-day after a week of conference with Alexander, Leese & others. So perhaps we shall soon know what the future holds in store for us. We were to have come up for 3 weeks: instead we have been fighting as infantry for well over 3 months. Personally I have no desire to go back & train for a parachute operation – I should be quite happy if I never had to jump again.'

Dougie Atkins thought it was during these months that Tony was recommended for an MC and was turned down. He was offhand about it to Dougie. Thirty years later, he and David McDonald, a young Ulsterman in his Private Office at the Environment Department, were talking about how, at different times in one's life, things matter differently. Tony said that at a later stage in his own life an MC would have mattered only to his vanity, but then he had deeply resented some man in the War Office turning down a commendation without knowing anything about it. At the time it seemed the most terrible thing that had ever happened to him.

(10 MARCH) 'I append opposite, as a matter of interest, a brief account of last night's battle. One of the reasons for our rather heavy casualties was that general over-confidence makes us quite careless about swanning around in full view – and the CO is the worst offender. The most pathetic story of the battle was the fate of our solitary P/W. He was bandaged up at Co. HQ in House 1,

a bandage also put over his eyes. He was only 19: wounded, very dazed and frightened, & quite ready to talk. Then in the confusion at the end, he got separated from his guards, and was wandering about, lost and helpless, the bandage still over his eyes. He bumped into a wall, groped his way on again, & quite unknowing started to wander towards German houses. 9 Pl. were themselves somewhat beset by enemy at this stage: they had no time to go after him, so put 2 bullets through his head. 11 Pl. were first-class – cheerful, blinding & swearing, making attempt after attempt to recover the bodies from under House 2. And the morning after, we heard that 70,000 miners are on strike over the £5 minimum wage: these lads are not very sympathetic.'

(24 MARCH) 'After being told yesterday that there would positively be no move before March 30th, one could be fairly certain that we should in fact move at once. And sure enough, at 0130 hours this morning I was woken out of a beautiful sleep by the Adjt. and warned to be ready by 0630 hours to move off with the Recce Party. I very nearly wept tears of mingled rage and grief: partly because I had been looking forward immensely to 7 days' rest; partly because I loathe the mental and physical effort of getting up and packing up in the middle watches of the night; and partly from a strong fear that we were due for the Cassino front. I have seldom felt so wretched as when I crawled out of bed at 4.30.

'However, the morning turned out brilliantly fine, and one's spirits gradually rose. Our last view of the Maiella was terrific – the early sun just tinging the snow-clad slopes with pink: one of the most lovely sights I have ever seen in my life. And one would have a few days of seeing new places.'

(31 MARCH) ' I think it's true that the private soldier is Britain's best ambassador – when he's sober. The officers and senior N.C.O.s tend (though with many exceptions) to be rather overbearing towards the locals: but the Fusiliers soon get on famously with them. They have all picked up the odd word of Italian: and they crack jokes with them, and soon get invited into their homes. I think it is the product of a genuine tolerance, a certain fundamental kindness, a lack of brutality and cruelty, a cheerful take-what-you-find attitude; and one notes an admirable scrupulousness about paying for goods received.'

(22 APRIL) 'This mountain warfare is at least a change. Like the Germans, we live on reverse slopes by day, in dug-outs and sangars, and occupy crests and forward slopes by night. Diffugere nives:

redeuntiam gramina campis arboribus que comae. Horace must
have written that at exactly this time of year. Primroses everywhere,
and wild pansies: cuckoos and nightingales.'

(26 APRIL) 'After 3 days of picking primroses, one is almost
inclined to forget how beastly war is. Last night a party was out
sweeping a minefield: something went wrong, and two of the mines
went off; Jerry Pearson had one leg blown clean off (the other was
amputated this morning at the M.D.S.), a L/Cpl. was killed, a
Sapper lost an eye, and two more were wounded. The idea of Jerry
Pearson with no legs makes me feel physically sick.'

(28 APRIL) '. . . What amazing fantasies the ordinary working man
can believe in: Talking to two this afternoon – one believed our
main war aim should be to seize French N. Africa as a British
colony; the other that the withdrawal of the Allied Armies from the
Rhine was the direct cause of Hitler's rise to power.'

(2 MAY) 'Fred Ashby has just come back from Santeramo with
a most interesting account of the May Day demonstration they had
there: the first free May Day for 22 years. The crowd was terrific:
excitable (some with vino, most with genuine emotion); all sorts of
hymns were sung – from "God Save the King" to "The Red
Flag".'

Fred Ashby used to say to Dougie Atkins: 'If I can only get
through, I'll settle for losing a leg.' On patrol he stepped on a mine
and his terms were met.

As General Alexander's army drove north in Italy, deeper into
German positions, it was essential to locate enemy troops and
anticipate their movements. Fifteen months after reaching Taranto
harbour, Tony left Italy for a five-week course in air photograph
interpretation – suddenly a peaceful, civilised life in Egypt after a
prolonged period under stress.

(22 JUNE, Port Said) 'Unhappily our Transit Camp is nothing
more than a piece of desert with a lot of tents on it. However,
things looked a little brighter when we met up with two rather
lovely French sisters at the swimming club. But they are very
deceptive, combining a good deal of make-up and the most daring,
revealing bathing slips, with an almost prudish respectability. They
had to be back at home by 9 o'clock, except on special occasions
when Papa gave his permission for a late night: and they were, in
general, far less flirtatious than two corresponding English girls
would have been. I'm afraid I got rather bored after the first two
days.

'God save me from the British bourgeoisie (especially represented by the officer class) when it tries to be serious! What a mass of imbecile myths and illusions it lives in. (1) Dislike for the Yanks: they can't fight, they're poking all the girls at home, etc. (2) Almost equal contempt for all Wops, Frogs, Wogs, Gyppies, etc., etc.: only the old Hun and the old Rusky have won their respect at all – and even so they want to shoot all Germans after the war, and wonder idly if we shall fight Russia when Germany is beaten. (3) Dislike of Labour, who caused the war by forcing disarmament on an unwilling country. (4) Mistrust of all politicians, who are notoriously crooked and in any case have sold their consciences to the Party Whips. (5) A belief that the Party system has killed democracy in G.B. (6) Belief that all civilian workers are living in luxury on £20 a week, are cowards, shirkers, etc., etc., etc. My little circle here suggests that 60% swallow all the myths emotionally and passionately, and that 30% do in general, but are slightly more open to persuasion.

'The most that can be said for this attitude is that it breeds a national self-confidence which, though irritating and dangerous in peacetime, is no small asset in war. But no wonder foreigners sometimes hate us! Confession: when I read the N.S. and Tribune, I react so violently that I am in grave danger of adopting some of the prejudices myself!

'My feelings have been mixed during the enforced stay at Port Said. One half of me hated the idea of sitting miles away while exciting things were happening in Italy: the other half loved the opportunity for reading. Like Tartarin, my personality is dual: one wants a V.C., the other a quiet cultured life.'

His course completed, he returned to his battalion, high up in the Italian mountains. The summer of 1944 was advancing; General Alexander was pushing hard before the winter set in. Capt. Crosland rang through to Lt Atkins. 'I've got some marvellous news, Dougie. I'll tell you when I see you.'

Dougie thought: 'Good. We're being taken out of the front line.' Later that day, shells breaking round them, both pretending not to notice, Tony told his marvellous news: he'd been invited to become Labour candidate for Henley. Dougie concealed his disappointment.

A week or two afterwards, Tony and part of the Royal Welch battalion resumed the original purpose of the 2nd Parachute Brigade. They were to be dropped where they could prevent German reinforcements from counter-attacking the Allied Division that invaded the South of France from the sea.

(13 AUGUST 1944) 'The last supper in camp. Everybody tried to be normal and talk about something else: but conversation always comes back to the op ... Most people are in quite high spirits, composed part of nervousness, part of expectancy.' The entry breaks off when Tony went to France, is resumed back in the camp outside Rome.

(30 AUGUST) 'D-1 was fortunately too crowded to leave one much time for depressing reflections. Finally by 8 p.m. we were all ready at the airfield, and settled down to a few hours' sleep. This was when I started worrying: would I trip over a static line: would the stick be so long that I should drop in the hills: would my pin fit all right: what sort of a landing would I have, and so on. Most of the men were feeling similarly excited, and no one got much sleep. At midnight we had our last meal, an early breakfast: at that time, by some freak of temperament, I was feeling very cheerful, and was the life and soul of the party.

'Finally, at 0130 hours we filed into our planes, and began the awful business of trying to get on our chutes inside the fuselage. Just before we took off it was accomplished, and we settled down in our plane – not comfortable, for our grotesque and swollen shapes made that an impossibility, but at least static. The take-off must have been a wonderful sight for a spectator – plane after plane in a never-ending stream wheeling onto the runway and speeding down to a perfect take-off. We had a smooth 3 hour flight, passing over Corsica. I dozed as far as I could, and was by this time fairly resigned to my fate. 30 minutes to go, we hooked up, feeling hollow and dry. Fifteen minutes to go, and over the coast: the first surprise – no flak, what a relief. Five minutes to go, we stood up and No. 1 stood to the door. Red light, then green, fortunately no time to think and wonder now. An uneven stick: my batman just in front of me tripped over a static line and dived out headfirst and I went out in shit order. A very strong slip-stream which swung me about madly, and then a comforting jerk as my chute opened.

'After the noise and bustle of the plane, the stillness was very eerie, made more so by the cloud which completely hid the earth below us. But I had no time to enjoy the stillness, as almost immediately I found myself oscillating violently towards another chute, and then found to my horror my legs collided with his rigging lines and got momentarily caught up in them. I managed to kick myself free, but it gave me a moment of absolute panic, a fleeting nightmare of the two of us hurtling down together. A moment later the earth opened up into sight. Spasmodic firing from various directions: but this worried me much less than the terrific speed I was descending at. I knew I was in for an awful landing, and by God I was: flat on my face, extremely hard! My nose received a very bloody bash from my steel helmet, and I strained a ligament in my left knee. I was stunned temporarily, and it took me some moments to struggle out of my harness. At that time there was dead silence, and I had no idea where I was. I called to Knox, and found him only a few yards away. We were moving off, when a single shot was fired nearby. But there was nothing we could do about it, so we moved on. Then we joined up with five more signallers, and pushed on for what I thought to be the right direction. There were still more odd shots being fired, and we had one bad moment when a long burst from a Tommy gun kicked up the earth 2 yards in front of us. We were joined by more and more people, and made slow progress onwards, until we knocked up a Frenchman from a house: after getting the shock of his life when we told him who we were, he directed us to Le Mitan, which we reached just as full daylight broke, at 6 a.m., exactly an hour after landing. We found more of Brigade H.Q., including the Brigadier looking slightly tired and strained, but physically O.K.'

After the initial casualties when paratroops were shot before they could get out of their harness, most of the Royal Welch reached their rendezvous, then separated for the 'mopping up' part of the operation. This lasted only three days – the Germans split into small parties and demoralised by the confusion. Next day, the seaborne Allied armoured cars linked up with the Royal Welch. On day eight paratroop patrols approached Cannes. When confident that only a handful of Germans remained in the town, Tony and a few other paratroops borrowed jeeps and entered Cannes, to be greeted with wild acclaim. Drinking champagne they sat on the bonnets of their jeeps – 'in a loutish way no doubt' – cheering the American Sherman tanks that poured in and officially captured the town.

A fortnight after leaving the Rome airfield in fear and trembling, Tony and the larger part of his battalion returned to it. A fortnight after that, he was on rest leave high up a mountain in an unscarred village far from the havoc below.

(SEPTEMBER 1944) 'Until I went to Ravello I did not, I think, appreciate the real essence, the peculiar flavour, of all that is best in Italy. I have just spent three days there in a state of such

complete surrender to the physical and natural beauties of life as I
can never remember achieving before.'

During that three-day leave he turned twenty-six years old. Back
at Brigade Headquarters outside Rome, several letters awaited him.
After a couple of weeks, he answered one of them.

(17 SEPTEMBER) 'Dear Willie ... I got your letter on the same
day that I had two others: one from my "beloved" at home,
announcing her engagement to a Canadian pilot: and the other
from Henley [his would-be constituency], informing me politely
that they got tired of waiting for a reply, and have chosen our old
friend Stewart Cook. Like you I haven't the youthful spirit left for
a 24-page effort.'

Some soldiers, dashing in their uniforms, appeared before constituency selection committees and became candidates for the
general election to be held when one day the war would end. A
dozen different constituencies invited Tony to stand for selection.
Sometimes the letters reached him after the committees had actually met, Labour secretaries not always conscious of the virtues
of airmail. He had no home leave.

During the earlier months of patrol duty in the mountains, he'd
made an uncharacteristic entry in his commonplace book – a dream
he'd had the previous night about Pat. The dream was described
at the bottom of a page, making it easy to excise: he simply cut it off.
Cutting off his emotions was more difficult.

→ 4 ←

The Most Nauseating Act

The Exclusive Brethren shunned opera. Tony fell in love with it during his six weeks in Rome. He ended up his 'Rome opera season' with two Puccini before the next 'disagreeable' security operation.

(29 DECEMBER 1944) 'Fresh woods and pastures new. I am now with 6 Armoured Division as P.I. [Photographic Interpretation]: back again to the sights and sounds that one got to know so well last winter. The snow has come already, and it is perishing cold; but at least I did get my Christmas dinner this year. And another improvement is that Divisional HQ is well out of range of hostile missiles, and it is only when visiting a Brigade or Battalion that one really comes into the battle zone.'

Private Sid Epton was a foot soldier in the Royal Welch Fusiliers. Wounded at Monte Cassino, he was translated into a driver for the 6th Armoured Division – and became Tony's closest companion for the first half of 1945. Two officers and two batmen-drivers formed a little unit slightly behind the front line, none of them minding that. Positions were photographed from the air and brought straight to Captain Crosland and Captain Aveline, who examined them for every enemy gun or transport position in the area where the next day's advance was to be; then one of the two batmen took the deciphered photographs to the Divisional Commander.

In a battalion, officers and other ranks were socially miles apart. Other ranks got drunk and fraternised with women collaborators; in his six years in the army, Private Epton never knew an officer to engage in either activity. In Aveline's jeep, as in most, the driver never spoke unless spoken to. In the other jeep, comradeship developed: 'He called me Eppie. I called him Tony, but whenever anyone else was there, he was "Sir".'

Mostly under canvas, they'd pitch the tent in pouring rain and just get cleaned up when the order would come to move. 'Tony was happy-go-lucky, but when we could get into a closed building and he had a bed, he was the happiest guy in the world. I would get his bed ready, boil up his water for shaving. After a period of this, you like someone or hate him. We got on fabulously. Whenever we moved back to Divisional headquarters, he played football. He was never shy with soldiers he hadn't met before: he'd play football with them and then try to convert them to socialism. When we were in the jeep, he would talk about socialism.'

In April, General Alexander's army broke into the Po Valley and made a three-Divisional drive to cut off the German army south of the river. The pace was hectic, as Sid Epton put it. At the beginning of May, Alexander's forces linked up with their Yugoslav allies at the River Isonzo. Tito always claimed the river as the Yugoslav frontier. So far so good. But advancing down the western side of the river were the first of some half-million people looking to the British for sanctuary: Chetniks, Croats, Slovenes were trying to escape Tito; Cossacks, Ukrainians, White Russians were trying to escape Stalin. The Chetniks were in the vanguard. British battalion COs were faced with political negotiations for which they had neither warning nor instruction.

(4 MAY) 'They were hopelessly handicapped by total ignorance of what high-level agreement had in fact been made with Tito and also of the whole Yugo-slav set-up. (One of them remarked to me that he had always thought Cetnik [sic] was some patent medicine.) On our side of the Isonzo, an army of no less than 12,000 Cetniks was moving slowly west. "The tents are struck, and the caravan of humanity is on the move" with a vengeance. It was a sight so medieval, so unreal, so Hollywood almost, that one could hardly credit one's eyes. Of the men, many were giant bearded figures, others wore their hair long, so that it fell over their shoulders Elizabethan-fashion and one couldn't tell from behind whether they were men or girls. Amongst them were old men of 60 and young boys of 15 ... drawn wagons piled with baggage, and riding on them the sick and the older women. Behind the wagons marched more women, looking very strong and wiry. Their uniforms appear mostly German, save for those who wear the brown uniform of the old Serb regular army. I had come to look on them as Fascists: whereas these people, or at least all the rank and file, were peasant and worker types, kindly and cheerful, and anything but a collection of mercenary thugs.

'In an effort to get the thing straight, I went with our interrogator to the little Italian town of Gorizia where the Cetnik force had set up its HQ. They freely, and in fact proudly, admitted that since 1942 they had been only fighting Tito. When one pointed out to these people that we were bound to treat them as enemy, they couldn't see it at all: they are genuinely pro-British themselves, and seem to think we shall help them against Tito.

'Well, what are we to do with this army? Clearly we have no alternative to treating them as P/W, or at least internees. Tomorrow they will be concentrated South of Udine and disarmed. Their sick and wounded are being looked after by us, and eventually the whole lot will be evacuated South in our Transport. After that, who knows? At least the British Army on the spot, despite having no warning, has shown its usual gift for improvisation – and more important, for humanity of action.'

Before the day was out, a Tito battalion had marched up to the town of Cormons with orders to take it over.

(5 MAY) 'The British Bn. Commander on the spot wirelessed frantically for orders, & was told to keep the Tito forces out until the Cetniks were clear, & then let them in the town: which he did, thus avoiding a massacre.'

Two days later Tony's division was aware of the presence in the mountains of no fewer than 35,000 Cossacks, complete with wives and families, expecting to be received by the British as refugees. Meanwhile the Italian workers conscripted as German labour were returning.

(7 MAY) 'A sad never-ending procession, huge packs or cases on their backs, bent double beneath the weight. What they did for food, God knows, but if one gave them a cigarette they were so grateful it made one ashamed. They were amazingly cheerful, dogged, enduring, and could manage a smile though their hands were so tired they could hardly hold a cigarette from the trembling. Well, the slaves are free at last, thank God: but their release is costing them something near the limit of physical suffering.'

On 8 May Churchill's voice came on the radio: he said that Germany had surrendered.

Sid Epton recalled the day dispassionately.

' "Get the jeep, Eppie. We're going to cross the border into Austria," Tony said. We passed droves of men and women who'd been hiding in the mountains, making their way back to Italy. Droves of them. I passed no comment: it was just another phase of war. But I remember Tony saying: "Terrible. Terrible." '

(9 MAY) 'Once over the frontier, we were presented with the astonishing spectacle of the German Army still free and in occupation. They had been ordered to stay put, and concentration had not yet begun: so they were lounging about the cafés, standing in

the roadside, often armed, watching us curiously, in fact behaving quite normally. Austrian flags have appeared everywhere, thus giving the impression that we have liberated a friend rather than occupied a foe. Sitting on top of an A.C.V., I got a good deal of satisfaction from watching their rather awed reaction (especially the soldiers) to our unending stream of tanks and trucks passing through. No doubt this pleasure would be even greater in Germany proper, but it won't do the Austrians any harm to have a good look at this display of force.'

(11 MAY) 'Never did I dream in my wildest nightmares that such complete and utter chaos could exist in so small an area. In our own Div. area, quite apart from the civil population, there must be nearly 200,000 people on the move . . . Whoever is responsible for this complete lack of foresight and planning should be shot. The result is that soldiers are having to deal with all sorts of political and diplomatic questions: and on the whole are coping with a great degree of discretion and commonsense. 1. The civilian population . . . 2. The disarming and concentration of the 3 German Corps who were here at the time of our entry . . . 3. Large and varied Quisling forces . . .

'The fantastic thing is that we still have no news of any Tito-Alex. agreement on a demarcation line.'

A fortnight after the British Army had shown 'its usual gift for humanity of action', orders came direct from British High Command: to hand over the people they had just disarmed.

(18 MAY) 'The problem of the anti-Tito Croats and Slovenes is almost causing a civil war within the British Army. We have on our hands at the moment some 50,000 of them. When we accepted their surrender, they certainly assumed that they would not be returned by us to Yugo-slavia. It was then decided as a matter of higher policy that they were to be handed back to Tito.

'The armed lot South of the Drava were dealt with thus: our troops all withdrew North of the river, and behind them took out the centre section of the bridge; after we had gone, firing broke out, a number of Croats swam back across the river, and more tried to repair the broken bridge: so we put up wire and other obstacles to stop them getting back to safety.

'The unarmed lot were shepherded into trains and told they were going to Italy: they crowded on in the best of spirits, and were driven off under a British guard to the entrance of a tunnel at the frontier: there the guard left them, and the train drove off into the tunnel. Among officers here, there is great revolt and resentment against the deception and dishonesty involved.'

'The most nauseating and cold-blooded act of war I have ever taken part in,' he wrote to Philip. 'Like you I am too mentally weak & spiritually weatherbeaten for anything more.'

(29 MAY) 'I witness today the handing over to the Soviet Army of large numbers of Russian nationals who had been fighting in the ranks of the Wehrmacht. There are thousands and thousands of these men all told, mainly Cossacks, Ukrainians and White Russians. What prompted them to join the Germans I do not know: mainly, probably, the prospect of food and release from German prison camps. When we first came in to Austria, they all made strenuous and ultimately successful efforts to surrender to us rather than to the Russians or Tito. But now the Russians have demanded them back, and this was apparently agreed at Yalta: we hand them over disarmed to the Russians.

'The secret of their fate somehow leaked out a few days ago; some have already committed suicide, others tried to escape and were shot. This morning a deputation arrived, asking if they could be shot on the spot instead of being handed over. Eventually, however, the great majority are got away somehow or other.

'The scene of this particular hand-over was the bridge at Judenberg which is the frontier between our zone and the Russians. The road down to the bridge was lined for half a mile with armed British soldiers, and the armoured cars sat at vantage points in the town, to guard against any last-minute breakaway. Across the bridge was the Russian committee of welcome.

'At length the convoy rolled up under heavy guard. One knew that these Cossacks had committed some of the worst atrocities of the war: one knew they thoroughly deserved a traitor's fate: yet as they craned their heads out of the trucks to try and see what lay in front of them, one forgot all that, and felt nothing but pity. All one saw was a lot of simple uncomprehending men being shepherded off under guard to a black and hopeless future: in the case of the officers, going to certain death.

'However, it all went off with only a single hitch – one man leapt out of his truck and hurled himself over the parapet. One by one the trucks crossed the bridge: the prisoners off-loaded, and were marched off by the Russians. The bridge itself was like a paper-chase: when they knew beyond a doubt that it was true, they frantically tore up and threw away all letters and photographs which might have incriminated fresh victims.

'For a few moments, as I looked at the youngsters particularly, I could hardly stand the whole scene, and nearly broke down.'

In Britain the Labour Party won a landslide victory. 'Not being able to get back to the election has been, I must confess, exasperating,' he wrote to Philip, listing the twelve constituencies which over the past year had invited him to their selection committees. 'If one European country doesn't very quickly prove that you can be both Socialist and democratic at the same time, I shall drown myself.'

In the Pacific the Second World War continued. In Austria Captain Crosland prepared to join the South-East Asia Campaign, where highly trained Intelligence officers were needed. His luggage was on a plane when the army, true to form, stopped IOs leaving Italy. A few days later the Americans dropped atomic bombs on Hiroshima and Nagasaki. Five days after that the Japanese surrendered.

Tony was now twenty-seven and expected to be demobilised in a year. But the British Government decided to release three thousand Arts students to resume their studies. To Philip, he wrote:

(9 SEPTEMBER 1945) 'I have never previously even considered the thought of going back, growing hair on my chest, to use an attractive figure of speech, being my main post-war objective. A quite different situation now arises, since it would merely mean exchanging one's last and probably barren year of Army life for a slightly less barren year at Oxford; and this I am prepared to do if pressed, even with Trinity thrown in.'

Then the Government changed its mind again. He was, however, to have a home leave as soon as troop ships could sail from Italy.

(4 NOVEMBER 1945) 'Dear Willie . . . I am still waiting on account of these storms. I have been seeing a certain amount of Denis Healey recently, and he has given me a lot of gossip about old Labour Club stalwarts; but they are such ghostly and half-remembered figures, and the gossip so largely concerned with their tedious and squalid matrimonial failures, that it is honestly not worth retailing. I think, however, that I did him an injustice in my last letter. It appears he has swung away from the C.P., and is very much in a state of flux. In fact one can hardly describe him at the moment as holding any coherent attitude.

'I still have it in mind to contact the release authorities when I actually get home, and if there were any chance of getting out before I was due to come back to Italy I might take it. But I have not set my heart on it – I am weary to the point of indifference with the whole business.'

Twelve or thirteen years later, he was induced by someone he loved, who knew nothing about the war, to tell her what he minded most. He spoke of David's death in Burma. He spoke of the early episode in Taranto harbour: he hadn't known that bodies change so much after two days in the sea that he would be unable to recognise comrades. He spoke of the episode at the end: the train of cheerful, unsuspecting men going into the tunnel, the trucks with those who knew crossing the bridge. He didn't go into detail. He really didn't want to talk about it.

5

The Break Out

Oxford undergraduates in 1946 presented the bizarre spectacle of fresh-faced boys straight from school sitting at lectures alongside glamorous veterans of the war, the younger species awed. Tony had switched from Classics to Philosophy, Politics and Economics. He was highly motivated, wanting to learn all he possibly could in the time he had set himself. It was not a moment for abandonment to pleasure. The Red Menace, lent to the Labour Party during the election, had been retrieved and resprayed. Possession of a car during this period of national austerity was a treasured luxury. 'You take it, Dougie. I'm so busy with exams I won't have time to use it.'

Dougie Atkins, waiting to be demobbed, was on home leave with his wife. They returned the Red Menace to Highgate: Mrs Crosland had moved back to the family home in Sheldon Avenue. Evelyn was still living with her mother. After all those years of knitting socks and sweaters for her absent brother, she and he rapidly slipped back into the unsettled relationship they customarily enjoyed. The Atkinses found them engaged in one of their bouts, Tony saying to his mother: 'Would you inform your daughter of such and such?' Evelyn, in the same room, hopped up and down with rage.

When he was decanted into the civilian world, he again considered a political career; he became President of the Oxford Union and again – after the five-and-a-half-year gap – Chairman of the Democratic Socialist Club, both positions requiring hard work when he was already working flat out. He completed his papers, took his finals, got his first. It was December 1946. He was twenty-eight years old. He was free.

At once he turned his thoughts to growing hair on his chest: he had a lot of catching up to do. He delayed long enough to arrange subsistence: a general election being unlikely for another three years, some basic form of earning had to be found. Tony lacked that nostalgia for his old college that some men carry to their graves. His decision to stay on at Trinity as an economics lecturer was a practical one.

That settled, he broke out. Encouragement was offered by Raymond Carr, a Fellow of All Souls College in substance but not in spirit. Raymond felt constricted by All Souls's Establishment conventions. His books would include a history of fox-hunting as well as tomes on Spanish history. Tall, thin, bespectacled, he affected a premature stoop. His gait was of that shambling character that suggests mild drunkenness in the soberest of men. Neither he nor Tony would have dreamt of drinking at lunchtime; playtime began at 7.15 p.m. Then drink flowed, the less intellectual aspects of women top of the agenda.

In the Crosland lexicon, 'tiddly' was broadly applied, embracing every state induced by alcohol, from lightheadedness to extreme intoxication. 'A bit tiddly' could mean one was far advanced, sometimes deplorably, into the latter state. He had a strong head and rarely got drunk inadvertently: it was for fun.

On Friday nights they ran a poker school that met in Tony's rooms at Trinity. Once in a way these assemblages got out of hand. Raymond had a trick: after finishing his drink, he chewed up the glass. One of the more sophisticated undergraduates, Jill Rowe-Dutton (who would later marry Peter Parker), was taken to Tony's rooms. Perhaps because she was preparing to be a GP, she was deeply shocked to see Raymond eating his glass, and left. In other respects, Raymond was more prudent than Tony who, faced with rules imposed in what he saw as an arbitrary manner, knocked them aside like a bull on the rampage. He then erected temporary rules for himself and made casual judgments on others accordingly. Sometimes the rules were slightly dotty – how much one should sleep, drink, smoke. Others might think a young don should set an example: Tony felt passionately that you ought to be free to do things that affect only yourself – or to the extent that others don't mind if they have the same freedom.

He worked hard during the day: that was the compartment where Philip Williams met him, Raymond sometimes wandering in. Philip, now an Oxford lecturer in politics, steadfastly refused to accommodate Tony, only sherry opened. In the playtime compartment, Tony consorted with Raymond. Anyone meeting them in the evening had every reason to think them slightly drunk, one of them – Tony – very brash.

Raymond's bad heart barred him from war service, and during those years he'd been a master at Wellington, where he founded a political club. He asked Tony to give a talk to the club about socialism. They drove down to that orthodox school in the Red

Menace, Tony wearing his paratroop beret. The students were frightfully impressed by this socialist – handsome, suave, incredibly patronising in a polite way, with a 'good war' background. In the evening, Tony and Raymond called at the house where Raymond had been a master. The entrance hall displayed the usual notice-board: 'Boys must be up at 7.30' and other mandates on how boys must comport themselves. Tony reached into his pocket for his cigarette-lighter and set the board on fire. Committing arson upon the notice-board of a major public school was poorly regarded.

But he always took his intellectual life seriously. In 1947 when his post-war tutor, Robert Hall, went off to become Economic Adviser to the Labour Government, Tony replaced him as Trinity's Fellow and Lecturer in Economics – teaching, writing, converting undergraduates to socialism.

'What the hell is that?' asked Raymond, peering at a notebook lying open on one of Tony's bookshelves.

'My notes on the novels and biographies I'm reading. When I read about Nelson's death, it reduces me to tears.' Raymond found this a very rum remark, stunned that an intellectual should be sentimental about Nelson of all people. He felt it was connected in a strange way with Tony's refusal to believe that anyone in Britain would steal his car: 'Never lock my car.' He and Raymond had a terrible quarrel about this subject. When Raymond by chance left his keys in his car and it was stolen, it was a great triumph over Tony.

While Oxford authorities were fairly relaxed about drink, a girl found in a don's room could jeopardise his job. Aid was required from time to time. When illness put Angus Ogilvy badly behind in his final year, Tony, who was very kind to undergraduates, got him through his exams. Angus, in turn, took the rap for some of his tutor's infringements of Trinity's regulations. A scout – as some college servants were aptly known – encountered a girl emerging early in the morning from the bathroom on Crosland's staircase. Tony knocked on Angus's door· 'Frightfully sorry to ask you to do this again, Angus.'

Raymond inclined to flatter the girl he was pursuing. Tony's method of getting into contact was to challenge, needle, tease. Some girls found his manner of confrontation irresistible. Others didn't respond, shrank into their shells, wondered what it was all about, thought: 'rude, brutal man'. He wanted a comeback. If they didn't have it, he dismissed them. His approach to pleasure was lighthearted rather than ruthless. If he didn't get his own way, he was not greatly stricken. Always honest about his intentions, he was equally candid when his interest ceased.

When Raymond was infatuated, all his nervous energies were directed to a single goal. Tony admonished him for letting his emotions run amok. Raymond, groaning aloud, amorous anguish coupled with annoyance at the other man's capacity to switch off, admonished Tony for compartmentalising his life. They quarrelled about a number of things, but then Tony quite enjoyed intellectual rows.

One girl held his interest. Her name was Hilary Sarson. She was seventeen when they first met, her father a respectable Conservative living comfortably in Berkshire. Some member of the family had made a successful business out of vinegar. Tony was not the person Mr Sarson would have selected for his daughter to fall in love with. And Tony fell in love with Hilary. She was pretty, playful, good-natured, sexy. Chemically they matched. He was promiscuous, but sooner or later he returned to Hilary. One day, she was determined, she would be his wife.

Running through his life was his enormous pleasure in the company of off-beat intellectuals. Often they weren't British. With a number of them he formed an enduring friendship. One was Robert Hall, whom he greatly admired – a robust, worldly Australian. At weekends the Government's Chief Economic Adviser joined his distinguished academic wife and their daughters in the family's home in Oxford. To be near the Treasury during the week, he kept a London flat. There was a mysterious air of successive unseen females in the flat. Robert Hall sensed that Tony was quite taken by the way his former tutor managed the different compartments.

A second economist to become a lifelong friend was Ian Little. They first met in 1948 at an All Souls dinner when Tony was Raymond's guest. Ian was a handsome, wry Old Etonian. When smoking, he maximised the nicotine: he drew in on his cigarette, removed it from his lips, opened his mouth so that one saw the noxious cloud being held there just before he inhaled so deeply that one never saw the cloud again, only the faintest wisp of smoke eventually emerging from Ian's nostrils. He'd been in the RAF throughout the war, was awarded the AFC for his work as a test pilot – an occupation that few envied – and fell in love with a member of a Ministry of Aircraft Production Experimental Team; her name was Dobs. They married when the war ended. Tony worked on the draft of Ian's first book – *A Critique of Welfare Economics* – whose publication established I. M. D. Little as one of the most brilliant economists of his generation. Subsequently, Ian advised on all the economic sections in the drafts of Tony's books. Sometimes the Littles and Tony went on holiday together. If Dobs was tied down with children, Ian and Tony set off alone. On their tour of Romanesque architecture in southern France, they went a full day without speaking – so Tony claimed – because Ian had said the five domes of Saint Frond, Périgueux, weren't really Romanesque and were vulgar besides.

A third lifelong friendship which began in this period was with Michael Young – an unconventional sociologist at a time when Oxbridge regarded the subject as not quite respectable. From 1945 to 1951, Michael was head of the research department of the Labour Party, and Tony was one of the people he found to supply ideas for the 1950 election manifesto. (Michael left Transport House in order to learn first-hand what people actually want – as distinct from what planners think they want. In Bethnal Green he set up the Institute of Community Studies; he founded the Consumers' Association and the magazine *Which?* and made it viable; he originated the Open University.) A social and intellectual maverick, he was Tony's sociology mentor. Each liked creative tension, enjoyed the abrasiveness that was part of their relationship.

The friendship begun in a paratroop training camp was also to continue throughout Tony's life. When Dougie Atkins was at last demobbed, he became a schoolteacher in South Glamorganshire. He and Tony went together to a regimental reunion dinner; even the least morbid of men felt this strange desire to see again, if only once, people who had shared the experience. A professional officer, puzzled that Atkins and Crosland remained friends, crudely asked: 'What have you two got in common?'

'We both have such nice eyes,' Tony replied.

He was always irritated by consumers voicing complaint to one another rather than doing something about it. When he and Dougie went to a film, if Tony didn't like it he complained to the manager. Dougie tried this once when he was on his own; the manager thought he was mad.

So far as Dougie could discern, others didn't resent Tony's grumblings. Not everyone felt as Dougie did. Tony was appreciative by nature, but he had his own way of showing it. He showed his friends he liked them by insulting them. Raymond, who had always been attracted to what he saw as the libertarianism of the upper classes, now married one of their members. He and Sara invited Tony for a weekend. Always an exigent houseguest, he complained that the hot water ran out during his bath. 'Extraordinary that women cannot cook eggs. My mother could never boil an egg,' he grumbled over breakfast. Raymond was amused. A young wife in her first home was not. Tony's and Raymond's paths began to diverge.

He'd joined the Fabian Society just before joining the Royal Welch Fusiliers but was unable to identify with the former. He was deeply impressed by the exemplary work of its founders, Beatrice and Sidney Webb, their dedication to the Labour Party. But after pages in his commonplace book about their achievements, he goes on to say:

What is one, then, to make of this extraordinary pair? Their devotion & conscientious single-mindedness clearly made them v. *admirable* characters. Yet their considerable indifference to all forms of art or culture, their lack of temptation towards any of the emotional or physical pleasures of life, the consequent priggish puritanism – all this is v. unattractive & *would*, if universally influential, make the Socialist State into the dull functional nightmare which many fear. Unlike most other critics, I personally do not feel any antipathy to the blue-book part of their lives: I like blue-books, & like research – but it all becomes v. unattractive when it is *unrelieved* by any recreation or alternative interest. This complete temperamental inability ever to be off-duty comes out also in their purely utilitarian attitude to social life – in the characteristic but damning phrase 'a useful little dinner'.

No, I shouldn't have liked the Webbs. I should have admired them, been fascinated by them: enjoyed talking shop with them: recognised that they had achieved a happiness & peace of mind (tho' B.W. only after gt. struggles) that was far beyond my powers & comprehension: recognised indeed that they were saintly where I was sinful. But with what a feeling of relief & release I should have walked out of their house!

Hugh Dalton was the antithesis of the Webbs. He was Chancellor of the Exchequer when he and Tony met and another close friendship began. The son of a canon at Windsor Castle, Dalton had been a day boy at Eton; at Cambridge he became a socialist and with his beloved Rupert Brooke founded the Cambridge Fabian Society.

He allowed the Labour Party's puritanism to restrain his boisterousness as little as possible.

Latter-day psychiatrists have speculated about the sexually inverted aspect of the Hugh Dalton–Rupert Brooke friendship. As the poet was in his twenties when he died in the First World War, his emotional development must remain a mystery. The politician lived to be an old man. The marked homosexual element in Dalton was repressed throughout his life. He might put his hand on a protégé's arm – that sort of thing. What he minded terribly was his protégés having girlfriends.

The Chancellor spent many weekends at the Berkshire home of another economist, Nicholas Davenport, and in August 1947 celebrated his sixtieth birthday there. Davenport described it in his memoirs: 'Hugh had asked me specially to invite his young friend who was the economics Fellow of Trinity College. "I want to see how he behaves when he is drunk," he said. Tony came in his bright red sports car, wearing the red beret of the Parachute Regiment. We had an entertaining evening of drink and talk and Tony drove back to Oxford as steadily as he had come. He could obviously hold his drink. As he drove away I could see in Hugh's eyes the rekindling of his romantic love for gallant and handsome young men. After another weekend occasion, when Tony had left abruptly to catch a train with a girl to London, leaving Hugh and me alone to dine, Hugh actually refused to eat or speak. He paced about the room as if he had been jilted as a lover.' Elsewhere in his memoirs, Davenport mentioned the fact that 'Tony was greatly embarrassed by this attention.'

Once or twice Tony dragged Raymond Carr into driving Big Hugh through Oxfordshire. Dalton had a way of suddenly turning round and booming: 'What's happening in Poland?' Raymond hadn't the faintest idea what was happening in Poland. He sympathised with the story of Churchill during the wartime coalition government hearing really colossal bellowing in an ante-room at No. 10. 'It's Dalton speaking to Glasgow,' a Private Secretary explained. 'Why doesn't he use the telephone?' said Churchill.

Hugh Dalton was not a sensitive husband, and when his only child died at the age of four his marriage collapsed in on itself, though Ruth Dalton continued, very courageously, to provide a home for him. This highly intelligent and cultivated woman was made to appear pinched and chilly in contrast to Dalton's physique and force of personality. He was well over six feet tall with an enormous head and fleshy face, his eyes of that pale-blue pigment that perpetually sparkles. Because of his seniority and his height, he was known as Big Hugh.

Gaitskell was Little Hugh. In 1947 when he and Tony met, Gaitskell had one of the less coveted jobs in the Labour Government: he was Minister of Fuel and Power – 'the most overworked man in Britain,' Herbert Morrison said a year later. Little Hugh was of medium height with wavy brown hair. He too had blue eyes, but their expression was different from Dalton's. Gaitskell was more sensitive altogether. When he was serious, he was intense. When he was lighthearted, his smile was puckish.

A few weeks after the Davenports' birthday party for Dalton, the Chancellor was on his way into the Chamber of the House of Commons to deliver an autumn Budget speech. He passed a political reporter and mentioned some of the Budget's contents. There was just time for the reporter to phone through to his paper and catch the edition that was on the streets before the Chancellor had finished delivering his speech. In theory this Budget leak might have permitted last-minute profiteering on the stock exchange. In fact it didn't, but Dalton felt he had to offer his resignation to the Prime Minister. Attlee accepted it and made Sir Stafford Cripps the Chancellor.

In his new role of elder statesman, Big Hugh took time and immense pride in spotting young talent and helping advance it in the Labour Party. Some men want adulation in their disciples. Others despise it. Dalton belonged to the second category and liked those who stood up to his hectoring. George Brown, Jim Callaghan, Barbara Castle, Denis Healey, Tony – all were encouraged by Dalton. The protégé he loved best was Tony.

6

Insufficient 'Gravitas'

In those days a senior Cabinet Minister was more influential in local Labour Parties than in years to come. Tony hadn't to hawk himself around in order to get a foot in the door: Hugh Dalton had prepared the ground in South Gloucestershire where a new constituency was created, and in the autumn of 1949 Tony went down to the selection conference. He had, of course, to sell himself to the committee – and did so.

The general election was called early in 1950. For part of the three-week campaign, Dougie Atkins came up from South Glamorganshire to help. He and Jack Donaldson, an active member of the local Party, accompanied Tony on the invasion of the Duke of Beaufort's domain – Badminton. At that time British Rail actually stopped its Bristol–London express at Badminton in the morning in case any of the Duke's household wanted to go up to London, stopped again at Badminton on the way back in the evening. No Labour candidate had dared set foot in Badminton. 1950 seemed a good year to start. The Duke's weekend guests and his farmworkers, along with the local gentry, took their places in the hall – the Duke sitting in the back row, the better to survey his flock and perhaps get out easily. The gentry asked their questions.

'If you are elected, Mr Crosland, do you intend taking a house in Gloucestershire?'

'Yes. I'm taking a little cottage in Badminton.' Handclaps and laughter from the farmworkers.

'Why is it, Mr Crosland, that when my daughter had her gas cooker repaired, it was necessary to send three fitters to do the job?'

He hadn't the least idea. 'I can only suggest, Madam, that if your daughter's beauty resembles yours in any way, two were gazing at her in admiration while the other one was working.' More laughter from the farmworkers. No converts were made, but morale rose among those made uneasy at having His Grace observing their political activity.

Attlee's Government was returned, just, and Tony became MP for South Gloucestershire with a 6,000 majority, at first commuting to the House of Commons from his rooms at Trinity. Academic obligations completed – he recommended Ian Little to succeed him as Trinity's Fellow in Economics, and Ian did – Tony found a flat of his own in South Kensington. The run-up to a big speech was always disagreeable, and he took comfort years later in reading that both Churchill and Macmillan invariably felt sick before speaking. 'Can't possibly get through it,' he said as his maiden speech in the House approached.

There is a convention that in a maiden speech one doesn't attack the other side. 'There is no convention preventing attacks on one's own side,' he said, going on to assault the Labour Government's fiscal policy for being too soft. As with most good speakers, once he had launched himself on the ordeal, some nervous mechanism threw its own switch, and the speech took on a momentum of its own. He was not a great orator. His style was the light touch and the heavy argument. Dalton was gratified. 'A very striking personal success and a few good points!' he scrawled on a card.

At this time he and Tony dined together every couple of months. Little Hugh and Tony met for a meal at similar intervals, their friendship growing. In the autumn of 1950, Gaitskell succeeded the critically ill Sir Stafford Cripps as Chancellor of the Exchequer. At forty-two he was the youngest Chancellor since 1903. As yet he had little following among the rank and file, and he incurred the wrath of Nye Bevan who wanted the job and felt he had a claim to it. Cripps himself had recommended Gaitskell to Attlee.

In South Gloucestershire, Tony's constituents sometimes heard that his private life was fairly riotous. They didn't seem to mind: they saw him apply himself to their problems. In the neighbouring constituency at Bristol, he helped Anthony Wedgwood Benn in his quest for the seat. He had taught Tony Benn at Oxford. The local agent, Frank Cox, had an instinctive grasp of the coexistence of Tony Crosland's work and play compartments.

4/11/50

Dear Crosland,
         In answer to your shocking letter of the 1st inst. I would like to inform you that I have done precisely B.A. in the South Glos. Const in the past month. My whole energies have been concentrated on getting Tony Benn into the House. (This Benn incidentally is obviously a much better type than you, so he had absolute priority.) The rest of the criticism in the letter comes very well from a geezer who has contributed nothing to anything for the past

three weeks, except gad about Europe, with Strasbourg as an excuse. And I am willing to bet a round of drinks that you were one of the 'unfortunates' who, owing to conditions were 'marooned' in Paris for the week-end. My boy, when I read of this, my heart bled for you. I could imagine you sitting in some second class Parisian boarding house, eating your heart out because you could not get back to dear old flood ridden England for at least another day, and steadfastly refusing to visit any part of Gay Paris, as a penance.

To work. You will find enclosed . . .

Yours Frank

At the Bristol by-election Tony Benn won the seat, whereupon he made a public announcement that he must lose the stigma of being an intellectual. 'You'd better acquire the stigma before worrying about losing it,' his former teacher said.

When visiting his constituency, the Member for South Gloucestershire would usually stay the night with the Donaldsons. Jack was then a farmer. Son of a clergyman, Old Etonian, onetime saxophonist in Fred Elizalde's Cambridge band, Jack was attracted by the libertarian strand of the Labour Party. As a young man he'd engrossed himself in prison reform. He worked hard in the constituency Party. Frankie, rather a reluctant convert to socialism, became, as reluctant converts do, hotly defensive about her new creed. Ready to bait her was her arch-Conservative friend and neighbour, Evelyn Waugh, who dispatched the occasional postcard to the Donaldsons:

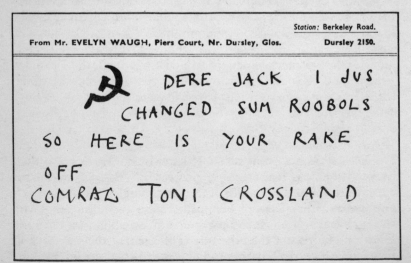

Station: Berkeley Road.
From Mr. EVELYN WAUGH, Piers Court, Nr. Dursley, Glos.   Dursley 2150.

DERE JACK I JUS CHANGED SUM ROOBOLS SO HERE IS YOUR RAKE OFF COMRAD TONI CROSSLAND

The Donaldsons were very tolerant of their MP. Over lunch when one of them asked what he would like to be if he was not a politician, Tony replied: 'A racing driver.' Rose Donaldson, aged fourteen, slipped away from the table and returned with her photograph album. She silently displayed a picture captioned 'Crosland Comes to Stay': one of the Donaldsons' fence posts was lying broken on the ground beside Tony's car. Until then no one had indicated the Donaldsons' annoyance about their broken fence post.

Frankie was already a biographer, though her best-selling work lay ahead. She worried about Tony. 'Most of us have a little man on our shoulder who can say to us: "Now watch out",' she said to Jack. 'Tony doesn't have one of these little men. He is so reckless, so uncalculating that he'll never get anywhere.'

Twenty-five years later, when Jack Donaldson gave an address at Westminster Abbey for the late Foreign Secretary, he described Tony's visits:

My whole family looked forward to these visits for weeks beforehand. The flatness after he had gone was relieved by the knowledge that he would come again. This was not merely because his presence was very stimulating but because he was so much fun. He was never an easy guest. He was always determined to put off meals until he felt sufficiently relaxed to enjoy them, and he used to deploy his considerable armoury in delaying tactics until sometimes we had lunch an hour or more late. He closed all conversations which did not interest him, and he never refrained from complaining of any lapse in the standards of comfort of the house. My wife kept up a running battle with him, but almost invariably gave in, gracefully.

She was less tolerant of a distinguished young actress who sometimes accompanied Tony on his visits and was inseparable from a small dog that liked to relieve itself, unfortunately, on the Donaldsons' drawing-room carpet.

And there were other occasions when neither Donaldson was allowed the option of giving in, gracefully or otherwise, to their houseguest. Tom Driberg, a Bevanite MP, was speaking in the constituency and Tony asked if they both could spend the night. On Sunday, while Driberg went round for a pre-lunch drink with Evelyn Waugh who'd been at school with him, Tony said to Jack: 'How on earth am I to endure driving Tom all the way back to London? All he really wants to talk about is his squalid sex life.'

'Well, you can't leave him here,' said Jack.

Halfway through lunch, Tony leant down the table to Driberg. 'Tom, I must be setting off for London, but there's a train that goes at 4.15. I'm sure you'd rather not rush through your lunch, and Jack can take you to catch the train.' Driberg said that would be very nice. Tony waved and was off.

Big Hugh kept an erratic diary, some entries made late at night after too much to drink. He sent two pages from it to Tony, who read them in deepening gloom:

(5/11/50) Tonight Tony is dining in King's with Kaldor. I don't think he's ever dined there before, where the ghosts of all my undergraduate friends walk. *They* are all dead; nearly all of them died in the First World War. I have no personal links with King's now. Kaldor is an immigrant from Central Europe and L.S.E. Also a good Economist & Socialist. But not real King's.

Am thinking of Tony, with all his youth and beauty and gaiety and charm and energy and social success and good brains – and a better Economist & a better Socialist than Kaldor, & with his feet on the road of political success now, if he survives to middle age – I weep. I am more fond and more proud of that young man than I can put in words. I think of him – I've said this earlier – as something between a beloved only son and a gay and adorable younger brother.

May he live to reap all the harvest of happiness and achievement which his gifts deserve!

My weekend has been brightened by that brilliant paper of his!

The word 'gay' had not yet been adopted by a minority group. Even so.

Urged on by Michael Young, Tony was smitten with sociology and psychiatry. 'Not one of us wouldn't benefit from five years' psychoanalysis,' he was prone to say at this time, brushing aside his own preference for reflection in his bath when his psyche showed signs of needing examination. Never imagining anyone could get self-analysis 100 per cent right, he was capable of a marked degree of objectivity. He judged himself by higher standards than he judged anyone else. The capacity to laugh at himself not only made him entertaining: it ultimately prevented him from being neurotic. He could recognise what he was doing.

A few weeks after receiving Dalton's diary entry, he decided to stave off any more by bringing psychiatry to the fore. He did so in

Strasbourg, where the Council of Europe was meeting. Things began simply enough with Dalton looking forward to an evening in Strasbourg brightened by dinner with Tony. During it the younger man raised one of Freud's theories – until then almost certainly unfamiliar to Dalton. The next day Big Hugh dispatched an enormous letter to Tony's hotel. At the top of the letter was scrawled: 'Written after a wakeful night.'

Strasbourg.
Saturday afternoon.
25/11/50

Dear Tony,
    ... I shan't expect, or try, to see much of you when we are back in England. I have come to the conclusion that I have been fussing you too much since you came into Parliament and that this has bored you and made a setback, on your side, in our friendship, which was, and is, very precious to me.

    ... I sense that you have found the life of an M.P. disappointing, boring and narrowing. You say that, apart from those you knew before, John Freeman (whom I too like very much) is the only politician you've discovered, with whom you wish to have a close friendship and that, had you stayed at Oxford, you would have made many more new discoveries by this time. And you would have had a much more comfortable and intellectually satisfactory life.

    ... I arranged for you to come out here . . . because I thought you'd do it well, and because I thought it would widen – if you'll forgive the word! – your practical political experience. And you *have* done well, both in the G.A. Ctee and in your speech in the Assembly, & generally in your political contacts here ...

And I know you've got some pleasure out of food and drink and night life here. And you know that I am wholly in favour of all that, and that one reason for my affection for you is that you are such an artist, and so quick on the ball, on all that side of life's playing field!

You are splendidly gifted – physically, mentally and socially – and you have been going through a period of great and varied successes, even in politics which you find so second rate and dreary.

I have told you last summer how I feel towards you – that I believe tremendously in you and your future, and admire immensely your wonderful diversity of gifts, and am *very* fond of you (but with no disturbing carnal thoughts about you), and get great stimulus from your company and from what you say and write, and would do anything any time, if you asked me, to help you.

I said to Jim [Callaghan] this morning that we can't fail to lose the next election, but we must try to lose it by as little as possible, so as to make the rebound quicker and easier and minimise casualties among our good young men. If you and he, and others who matter, hold your seats, you'll have a fine time in opposition and then, if we come back, you'll be in office – Jim in the Cab and you in a good junior office, or perhaps even in a No. 1 job outside the Cab to begin with. (You'll find politics more fun then!)

... I've fussed and focussed you too much lately. I shall do it no more. I shall leave you alone. Any initiatives must come from your side now, and I don't expect many, because your life, apart from politics, will be fuller and fuller. And I don't expect an answer to this letter. And I shall never write or say all this to you again. But my feelings towards you will never change.

So good luck always!

Hugh

A month after the dinner at Strasbourg, Tony and Dalton met for a drink, and Freud's spectre was evoked more cheerfully. The next day's missive from Big Hugh reverted to his usual robust style: 'As between you and me, all is now clear and understood and adjusted. No need of Freud; only to be, and go on being, totally frank.'

Tony greatly enjoyed Dalton's company, took account of his political advice, appreciated his help. Big Hugh's personal counselling was less welcome. Another missive arrived:

(25/1/51) Take three more years before starting – or even purporting to start – on monogamic monotony. I now think you may go right to the top. So you want somebody extra good, that will outlast first bloom, and shine and please in every likely later setting. Sic item ad astra ... And you needn't feel remorse much – or long. For you'll have given them all great fun while it lasted.

Probably, you, being what you are, will have to say No to some others before you make someone, who'll really fill all the bill, say Yes.

Enjoy yourself in Paris, and report to me officially when you come back, and let me see your powerful Political Quarterly article.

Three years had passed since Tony first met Hilary Sarson. Others sought her hand in marriage. She wanted to marry Tony. He was clear that they weren't cut out to be partners in marriage. In any case, he didn't want to be fenced in. Behaving less than well in one's personal life was one's own affair. Having it endorsed in the hearty manner of Dalton's letter made one uncomfortable all round.

Then another meeting of the Council of Europe produced another unwelcome epistle, this one from a different quarter. Nicholas Kaldor, the Hungarian-born economist, became a delegate to the Council largely because Dalton was impressed: Kaldor was one of the authors of the UN Report on *National and International Measures for Full Employment* which created a tremendous stir, especially in British Labour circles. Tony's and Kaldor's joint contribution to the Council's 1951 Report on *Full Employment Objectives* was substantial. Also substantial was their appreciation of the social life of Strasbourg. It was the latter that led the eminent historian A. J. P. Taylor to put pen to paper. By then married to Tony's sister, Evelyn, Alan Taylor was a close friend of an *enfant terrible* among Tory MPs, Bob Boothby.

27.v.51

Dear Tony,
        I asked Bob what he had been saying about you; and he said – that you drank too much every evening at Strasbourg and lay in bed every morning recovering. I couldn't possibly protest; I've heard the same from so many others. You'll forgive me, I hope, for writing to you about this – I've no concern but your future. You're extremely able; have a high reputation as an economist; and speak exceedingly well. You ought to be a junior minister by now, & would have been if it wasn't for drinking too much. I know on the very best authority that Attlee has said as much: he won't give you an appointment, because he has seen you drunk too often in the smoking room.

This is really deadly serious for you and your future. I know you'll say it is exaggerated; it doesn't matter if it is – it's what people think & say. It's the worst thing that can happen to an intellectual – I've seen it with one of my colleagues, and it's ruin. You can go to rot when you've had a career, but not when your career is beginning; and I do urge you most humbly to face this danger.

In my opinion, the wise – as well as the heroic – course would be to lay off drink altogether; tiresome though that is. If you think it too difficult or too dramatic, you should make the resolution – beer and never anything else. But do please reflect that your whole life is at stake.

I think you'd also be wise to use your great abilities to get a regular job in journalism in some economic activity. But that's another question.

Don't answer this letter & don't refer to it. Forget it was ever written; but don't forget what's in it.

Yours ever
Alan

Evelyn, who took an irreverent view of the Boothby-Taylor save-Tony-from-drink campaign, was pleased to see her husband shaken by the letter he received telling him it was none of his business. Alan's next letter to his brother-in-law confined itself to suggestions of hotels he might enjoy on his August holiday in France.

John Freeman, another Dalton protégé, talked to Big Hugh about Tony. Shouldn't he have stayed at Oxford a bit longer as a socialist don, influencing the young? Who would do that job now? Also, Tony's speeches in the House sometimes lacked 'gravitas'. He ought to be doing something part-time in business, said John Freeman.

Tony was asked to be a part-time financial adviser to the John Lewis Partnership, one of the most enlightened and innovative business firms. He needed the money. None the less, he felt the job might be inconsistent with his politics. After he turned it down, it was offered to Roy Jenkins who sensibly accepted.

Dalton began to fuss. *He* knew that the languid attitude concealed intellectual austerity: Tony's first book, *Britain's Economic Problem*, on which he was then working, wasn't written in bed. Dalton was famous for his 'prods' which impelled a protégé to make a worthwhile speech he might otherwise have neglected. Fussing was something else – it drove Tony mad.

He had begun a new commonplace book after the war, and on his holiday alone in France in 1951, his entries included a précis of Graham Greene's *The End of the Affair*. The précis began: 'I have to admit that much of it moved me almost beyond endurance, because it came just at the moment when I had finally ended my affair with Hilary: so much of it was unbearably poignant & well-understood – walking across the Common in the hope of a chance meeting, & the self-deceit that this wouldn't be breaking the vow: waiting by the telephone waiting for it to ring, & then when it does the let-down because it's only a wrong number: & the fingers itching to dial in turn. But all the same it isn't a successful novel . . .'

Meanwhile Attlee's second Labour Government was having a very different experience from his first one: the majority was so small that little controversial legislation could be got through the Commons. Trouble over the Budget was expected: it had to favour a big rearmament programme on top of Labour's social policies.

One of nature's owls, Tony started his day as late as possible, continuing it long after most had retired for a night's respite. His spare room was used by Dobs and Ian Little when they were in London. On Budget Day 1951 Dalton's diary began: 'I ring up Tony's flat at 8.30. Ian answers the phone ... Then I ask to speak to Tony – still asleep as usual after late nights. I tell him there is a very bad political situation. Nye, Harold Wilson, Strachey are resigning, now perhaps John Freeman ... We face an early election & heavy defeat. Will he come & discuss in my office? He comes at 11:30. He says he is very pro-Nye, but he is against him on this.'

Gaitskell's Budget speech later in the day turned out more palatable than the PLP expected. It was the Tories who attacked it fiercely for not making significant cuts in the social services. Nevertheless, ten days later Nye, Wilson, Freeman resigned. Tony was the most aggressive defender of the Budget.

Dalton wasn't jealous of his protégés' men friends, and he was generous in acknowledging Hugh Gaitskell's strengths. (19 AUGUST 1951) 'Lunch with Jim Callaghan & Tony at Josef's; all very cheerful. Jim thinks we may win the election; Tony doesn't ... Tony praised my loyalty to HG & his to me in a world where most spoke ill of one another.'

In October 1951 the Conservatives won a narrow victory. In Opposition Attlee stayed on as Labour's Leader. Gaitskell was the Party's main spokesman on finance, Herbert Morrison on foreign affairs; Dalton, as a senior ex-Minister, spoke on both. Tony kept his South Gloucestershire seat, his majority very slightly down.

Once more he applied his interest in psychiatry to Dalton, who wrote in his diary: (26 JUNE 1952) 'Tony came to lunch at my flat today ... He'd been lecturing in W. Germany under FO auspices ... He said I had a neurosis about German Rearmament, & my hatred for H. Morrison was a matter for psycho-analysis.'

A few weeks later Big Hugh's diary records drastic alteration in two colleagues' lives. (7 JULY 1952) 'Today I read of Zita Crossman's death, & Tony Crosland tells me on the telephone that he and Hilary Sarson are going to get married. This is, as John Freeman, walking up & down the terrace, says to me "a very moving day."'

Dalton closed the entry with the observation that Tony had been
a playboy long enough. Sadly, the about-to-be-bridegroom held a
different view.

Tony had resumed his affair with Hilary not only because the
chemical attraction remained compelling; when they were alone,
their temperaments went together. He found her sympathetic in
every way except intellectually. When at last he agreed to marry, he
returned alone to his flat and wept. She had successfully appealed
to his better nature. He knew the marriage wouldn't work. He
blamed himself for having let it happen.

After the announcement of their engagement, she went to Nor-
thumberland to stay with friends and start buying furniture from
auction sales. She wrote to Tony about these purchases for their
coming marriage. She wrote to him about how much she missed
him and wished he would come to visit her. Her letters were those
of someone terribly in love, intending to make him a good wife.

Hilary was twenty-two, Tony thirty-four, when they married
late in the autumn of 1952. The honeymoon was as inauspicious as
it could be. Perhaps unconsciously planned to keep at bay the word
'wedlock', it was a motor tour of southern Spain with Nicky Kaldor
and his wife, Clarisse.

'You're going on your honeymoon with the Kaldors?' said Ian in
disbelief.

'Buying furniture. Haven't money to spare. The Kaldors are
taking their car to Andalusia. Seemed a good idea to travel with
them.' Ian's astonishment had nothing to do with the choice of
companions: it was the general concept. Also, Nicky's driving
unsettled everyone else's nerves. He gripped the steering wheel like
Toad of Toad Hall, but – unlike Toad – Nicky talked as his
motorcar plunged along, as often as not his eyes fixed on the face
of the person beside him. Meanwhile his passengers stared ahead,
mesmerised, wondering how they would avoid the next oncoming
lorry.

At the beginning things went pretty well: they were conveyed
by ship as far as the Mediterranean. As well as the honeymooners
and the Kaldors, there was another chap from Trinity and his wife,
plus Ian Little's brother, an eccentric doctor who lived in Tangiers.
They all formed a party in Gibraltar, which wasn't too bad. It was
when the tour of southern Spain began that trouble started.

Nicky taxed himself ever afterwards. 'It was disaster. If I'd taken
the back seat and given Tony and Hilary the front seat, it might
have made all the difference. But he never said he wanted to drive.

Clarisse is an angel and couldn't care two hoots whether she sat in the front seat or the back seat. But she felt bride and bridegroom should not be divided. Every time Hilary opened her mouth, I made caustic remarks. I couldn't help it. Tony, in the back seat, tense, must have been thinking: "I'll kill him. I'll take the wheel and drive the car into the ditch." He was irritated with me for being irritated with Hilary.'

They toured round Andalusia – through Seville, Cordoba, Granada, Xerez where all the Tio Pepe is made. Finally Tony said, 'I think Hilary and I will fly to Paris.' Clarisse and Nicky drove on alone.

Nicky felt his friendship with Tony never fully recovered. 'A terrible, terrible mistake,' he sighed whenever he reflected on the unlucky honeymoon.

Not long after it, *Britain's Economic Problem* by C. A. R. Crosland was published. (The use of initials was an Oxbridge habit. 'But why *still* dead initials and not live first name?' Dalton wrote after hearing C. A. R. Crosland on the radio. 'How can you expect all that Light Programme audience of girls in love with your voice and lads who like your style, really to become your fans without knowing your name?' C.A.R. persisted for another six or seven years.) The book met with Dalton's approval. (7 JUNE 1953) 'No doubt, since you already thought well of yourself (on most counts), you will not regard it as a shattering new revelation of your gifts (as an economist and writer), if I say that no other member of either House of Parliament could have written so good a book on this subject at this time. On the other hand, you have been swotting at this subject for years, and have often lectured on it, both drunk and sober. I now pass to details . . .'

By now the nationalised industries were very controversial, their prices going up, especially coal. Tony was unusual: he was campaigning for still higher prices. 'We criminally underpriced coal,' he said of the Attlee Government. (If a policy was adopted by his Party in government, he thenceforth referred to it as 'our' policy, however much he deplored it.) Private industries should have been charged whatever they would pay, he argued, so that the coal industry would become self-supporting and able to re-invest instead of having to keep asking the government for more money. It was the subject of a lecture he gave at a Fabian School. Margaret Cole, *directrice* of Webb socialism, was in the chair. Tony prefaced the lecture with an attack on the Webbs. Dick Leonard, a young Fabian who hoped to get into the Commons, had never heard a

Crosland lecture, found it refreshing that someone said what he thought, regardless of whether anyone else liked it.

Although Tony served on the Fabian Society's Executive Committee for fifteen years, at one time its Chairman, his attitude to Fabians remained ambivalent. They mattered because they influenced Labour Party policy, if only indirectly. On the other hand, their obeisance to the strictures of their founders annoyed him. He saw no virtue in sitting on a bed of nails when there was a comfortable armchair in the same room.

Fabian summer schools met frequently in the pastoral surroundings of Buscot Park, home of the Labour peer – and Bevanite – Lord Faringdon. In the evenings refreshment was taken amidst the choice furnishings that Lord Faringdon had collected. Having delivered a lecture earlier in the day, C. A. R. Crosland fortified himself for the rigours of an evening with all these Fabians. Somewhat later, making his departure as soon as courtesy permitted, he lingered in the lofty entrance hall for a conversation about price controls, resting an elbow against a stupendous vase standing sedately on its pedestal. The vase was one of a pair. As he leant upon it, to his horror it toppled slowly sideways, colliding at last with the marble floor where with a fearsome crash it shattered into a thousand pieces.

The following day he rang Gavin Faringdon. 'I'm really frightfully sorry about last night. Of course I must replace the vase.'

'It is irreplaceable,' said Lord Faringdon. For some years afterwards, Tony was not invited to Buscot.

7

The Future of Socialism

The top-floor flat of 19 The Boltons was bought after Tony and Hilary married. She had hoped that his moving away from his previous bachelor flat would translate him into a monogamist. This was not the case. Feeling he'd been forced into the marriage, he then behaved badly. Some of his friends found Hilary's seeming lack of intelligence irritating, but Robert Hall thought Tony could have encouraged her, developed her personality and intelligence. He didn't. He would never have flaunted before Hilary the fact of his liaisons, but she wasn't a fool.

About a year after their marriage she gave up and left The Boltons, taking with her the furniture she'd acquired with such happy hopes, taking away any air of domesticity. She was very considerate about the divorce, which in the 1950s was bound to be sordid unless the grounds were desertion; after the required three years' formal separation, the divorce was obtained on those grounds. From the moment Hilary moved out of the flat in 1953, Tony effectively was a bachelor again. He was free.

The puritan's self-discipline predominated in his life: he preferred to work at home, and until he finished the task he set himself, playtime could not begin. When he was writing, it was almost impossible to lure him into social company of any kind. He could concentrate intellectually for fourteen, fifteen hours a day, pacing himself with breaks to make a pot of tea, walking to some café for a meal. But once it was time for play, there he was – over a longish period – drinking, smoking, womanising in the most undisciplined way some could remember. Like many, he regarded cocktail parties as a venue for making new sexual contact. (When that function of these gatherings at last ceased to interest him, his attendance also ceased, cocktail parties being hopeless for conversation or general comfort.) He was not a professional womaniser collecting scalps: Nor was he prurient. The lascivious joke trundled out by male after-dinner speakers made Tony bleak. 'It really astounds me that if you put together a collection of middle-class Englishmen, they seem to be obliged to indulge in schoolboy humour,' he said. One reason for his not belonging to a men's club was that he actually liked women.

Physically he was uninhibited in sexual relationships, imaginative, considerate. Yet, as with his non-sexual friendships, he was shy of articulating his emotions, instead employing a verbal code rapidly cracked – intended to be cracked – by anyone involved with him. Like some others raised on puritan mores, when he gave free rein to the hedonistic side of his nature, his enjoyment of the senses was heightened – perhaps felt more intensely than by people raised in a casually libertarian atmosphere. He saw a relationship as designed for the pleasure of both parties, and that pleasure was maximised with care. When he – or she – ended an affair, he didn't simply disappear without a word: he made it a proper ending, so to speak. Quite a few one-time girlfriends, as well as Hilary, continued to get in touch with him – to talk again if nothing else, out of curiosity, because of crises in their own lives.

He was in no hurry to fall deeply in love. If he ever did, the last thing he intended was a liaison with a married woman. He didn't go in for adultery.

On entering the flat at 19 The Boltons one felt that the atmosphere was charged. The furnishings themselves were donnish. Books lined a long wall, and manuscripts were systematically organised in piles on the seat of the sofa, on its arms, along the floor directly in front of it. Depending on the stage of writing he'd reached, further piles might be carefully set along the back of the sofa – fortunately of deep, squat design. 'Wedding present from Ian and Dobs,' he said, as if this were relevant to the fact that most of the time no one could actually sit on it. Two capacious armchairs, somewhat battered, stood one each side of the fireplace with its gas-fire. If a party was imminent, a considerable operation was required to move the papers, maintaining them in their proper piles, into the back of the flat where they were temporarily lined up on the floor. He was what the English call 'an armchair man'. All his writing was done in longhand from the comfort of three successive armchairs, the first two having collapsed after many years of service. His preference for working at home was one cause of misunderstanding with parliamentary colleagues.

He found constituency work absorbing. Regional meetings, going down the pits, these interested him, and he interested the people there: they didn't mind his accent because they liked his manner. The problem was the House of Commons: here he suffered agonies of boredom. He disliked the low level of argument, the exchange of Party platitudes. Nor did he care for the bickering and back-stabbing that then – even more than usual – characterised the Parliamentary Labour Party.

Of the three colleagues who had overlapped at Oxford, Denis Healey was the most diligent in his attendance at the House: he was never accused of having a dilettante attitude to Parliament. Roy Jenkins was less diligent, but he did produce a Private Member's Bill, and he was on a Select Committee on Malta. He had a bit of a reputation as a dilettante – writing biographies and so on – but he was always in evidence as a parliamentarian, unlike Tony Crosland.

Tony was more ambivalent in his ambition than most politicians because he had an alternative means of self-fulfilment – writing political philosophy which would shape democratic socialism. He hated the life of a backbencher and refused to volunteer for committee work, imagining it would be tedious. He yearned to work at home and did so. His most critical and criticised period in the House of Commons was when he was writing *The Future of Socialism*. With his flat only fifteen minutes' drive from the House, he could stroll into the chamber long enough to listen to the few speeches that interested him, occasionally deliver an incisive speech of his own, stroll out again and go home. He was a figure in the House, but not one who endeared himself to many colleagues. When he came back for evening divisions he would sometimes be accompanied by one or other young woman who was clearly not interested in politics. Dick Crossman, himself unruly, said:

'Tony, you really shouldn't get so drunk when you're going to come into the House.'

'How else is one to endure being here?'

Most MPs saw only his attitude and thought him a dilettante. The Shadow Chancellor, Hugh Gaitskell, worried about it. During a Budget debate, another Labour MP, Harold Lever, criticised an economic argument advanced by the Member for South Gloucestershire. Opening on a teasing note, Lever said his Honourable Friend was a typical example of an academic: if the grandfather clock happened to strike midnight on a sunny afternoon, he would put out the cat, put on his pyjamas and go to bed. Tony found this image entertaining and was still laughing about it afterwards, but when Harold Lever ran into Hugh Gaitskell, the Shadow Chancellor was irate.

'That was heinous what you did to Tony.'

'Good heavens, I was pulling his leg.'

Hugh remained furious. He was more concerned for Tony's parliamentary reputation than Tony was himself. During the last two months of 1954, he was in the United States on a grant. The trip was invaluable in developing his knowledge of sociology, its influence obvious in the book to be published two years later. He missed the whole of the new term of Parliament.

But his ambivalence about a political career didn't mean he wanted it ended when it had scarcely begun: he had the non-academic's desire to translate ideas into action. As the 1955 general election approached, the heavyweights at Westminster judged that South Gloucestershire, its boundaries lately redrawn in favour of the Conservatives, would inevitably change Parties. The local Labour Party believed the seat could be held by a personal vote for their Member, a view he dismissed as sentimentality. He decided to stand instead for Southampton Test, a new constituency that Hugh Dalton & Co. believed he had a good chance of winning for Labour, despite the foregone conclusion that a Conservative Government would be swept back to office.

He was selected for Southampton Test only three weeks before nomination date, six weeks in all before the election in May. The agent was shown a picture of him and went to meet him at the station when he arrived for the campaign. Recalling newspaper photographs of Tony and Hilary outside the Register Office, the agent had moved out of his own bedroom with its double bed to put up this great chap and his wife. When the candidate got off the train he was alone.

'Will Mrs Crosland be coming?' the agent asked.

'There will be no Mrs Crosland during this campaign,' replied the candidate. It was the first and last time that she was mentioned. The agent and his wife moved back into the double bed.

When the election results came in, the Conservative majority at Southampton Test was nearly 4,000 larger than at South Gloucestershire where it was a near thing. Tony felt he'd made a bad mistake in not taking local advice, saw it as a salutary lesson that those 'in the know' at Westminster may have antennae less sensitive than people on the spot.

'Best thing that could have happened,' he said years later when some cast-down young man or woman lamented the loss of a seat in Parliament. 'If one hadn't been away from that place, one could never have written *The Future of Socialism*.' In bolstering the spirits of whoever had come for solace, he stretched the facts a bit, as he was working on the book before losing his seat. Certainly, however, this spell outside the House – whatever it may have cost him in political terms – spared him another stint on the back-benches.

After the 1955 defeat, Attlee stood down and Gaitskell was elected Leader of the Labour Party. He was forty-nine. He had not campaigned earlier to succeed Attlee, feeling it was not yet his turn: he would willingly have served under another acceptable Leader. The Party chose him over Bevan and Morrison. Well aware that politics involve compromise, Gaitskell had already sought an accommodation with the more moderate of the Bevanite Left. Some of Bevan's supporters were quick to respond; he himself did so more slowly; a few of his friends were never reconciled to Gaitskell's leadership.

Like Dalton, Gaitskell encouraged younger men. He didn't want sycophants around him: he wanted politicians who were congenial and candid. He was deeply attracted to Tony Crosland's combination of intellectual astringency and unabashed insistence on the right to private enjoyment. The two men were eventually to quarrel about this matter of private pleasure, though the roles of critic and criticised turned out differently from what one would have guessed in the early years of their friendship.

The Future of Socialism was published in October 1956. That put paid to the view that Tony Crosland was squandering his gifts. The book appeared at a time when there was an ideological vacuum within the Labour Party which had just suffered a second consecutive defeat at the polls. Its author saw values and ideals as central to politics. He separated these from the means of achieving them. Means change as society changes, he argued, and the revisionist needs continually to examine the range of means available.

Using sociological analyses, he cleared away what he saw as irrelevant to present needs, and made the first systematic attempt since Bernstein's famous work published in 1898 to answer the question: what is socialism now about? The result was a cohesive theory of socialism that provided the ideological base that non-Marxists within the Party had previously lacked.

He began by analysing the changes that had occurred since the pre-war programmes were constructed. In the light of these changes, he re-interpreted the meaning of socialism. He then set out practical policies to which this re-interpretation seemed to point.

The Marxist theory of the inevitable collapse of capitalism had

been invalidated by cumulative democratic pressures. The economy was growing at a rapid pace, and there seemed every prospect
of its continuing to do so. (He was over-optimistic about economic
growth, as he readily admitted a few years later.) There was now a
quite different configuration of economic power from what faced
pre-war socialists. Primary poverty was substantially reduced.
Radical social welfare programmes were established – not least a
comprehensive National Health Service. Key industries had been
nationalised. Full employment had strengthened trade unions'
bargaining positions. The traditional power of the capitalist had
been broken, and ownership of industry was increasingly irrelevant: what mattered was who managed it and how; that was what
labour relations and industrial democracy were all about. Industry
was now in the hands of professional managers, and a significant
change had taken place in the social attitudes and behaviour of the
business class. Britain was no longer a 'capitalist' society as that
term had been generally understood.

The fundamentalists were fighting battles already won. The
devotion to Clause IV – common ownership – was misplaced:
nationalisation was a *means*, not an end; it was to be used to achieve
the socialist's ideals, not pursued for its own sake. The Attlee
Government's planning failures stemmed not from a lack of economic power – it was a failure of will: 'If socialists want bolder
planning, they must simply choose bolder Ministers'.

While Britain was no longer a 'capitalist' country, it was still far
from the ideals of democratic socialism. Socialists could not be
content if the Labour Party became 'the Party for defending 1945-
51 and a little more'. He set out detailed means for renewed,
vigorous pursuit of the welfare and equality ideals. To further
social welfare, a Labour Government must commit itself to increase
social expenditure; the broad priorities were the familiar ones of
the old, the sick, and those with large families; to these he added
what in 1956 were looked on as 'special cases', such as neglected
children and people with serious psychological disorders.

The commitment to equality was 'self-evident'. 'The socialist
seeks a distribution of rewards, status, and privileges egalitarian
enough to minimise social resentment, to secure justice between
individuals, and to equalise opportunities; and he seeks to weaken
the existing deep-seated class stratification, with its concomitant
feelings of envy and inferiority, and its barriers to uninhibited
mingling between the classes.'

Besides taxation changes, two main reforms were required to

break down barriers in our society. One was in education: the comprehensive principle must be propagated; entry into the public schools must be democratised. Education, not nationalisation, was to be the main engine in the creation of a more just society.

The second reform lay in the field of industrial policy. Some alienation of the work force was inevitable in large-scale industry, whoever owned it. But as well as industrial democracy at board level, there must be more effective consultation and worker influence at the point of production.

In laying out his blueprint for far more than equality of opportunity – he argued for the virtual destruction of the existing social hierarchy – he provided a closely argued moral justification. Ability was a chance factor, not something earned; it should be rewarded only while it was useful to society, not for its own sake. 'No one deserves either so generous a reward or so severe a penalty for a quality implanted from the outside and for which he can claim only a limited responsibility.' It was inequality that had to be justified, not equality.

He was a pluralist. He wanted state ownership, private ownership, the co-operative principle to coexist. His entire philosophy was designed to widen free choice, not narrow it. In the blood of the socialist, he asserted, 'there should always run a trace of the anarchist and the libertarian, and not too much of the prig and the prude.' The pursuit of equality must always be weighed against too great a loss of personal liberty. He did not propose a grey egalitarianism that would free the individual from gross injustice only to lock him in bureaucracy.

He thought that a wholesale effort to suppress the motive of personal gain could have undesirable side effects as well as being unrealistic. Furthermore, if the Party pledged itself to absolute economic equality, it might jeopardise Labour's chances at the polls, and unless it was elected to govern, none of its aspirations could be achieved. He argued that greater equality in a democratic society could best be secured by economic growth – using the dividend of growth to improve the relative standard of the poor. The Left should turn to the question of restrictions already imposed by society on the individual's private life and liberty: divorce laws, restrictions on equal rights for women, 'prehistoric' abortion laws, obsolete penalties for deviation from what is regarded as the sexual norm, illiterate censorship of books and plays, licensing laws. 'The enemy in all this will often be in unexpected guise; it is not only dark Satanic things and people that now bar the road to the new Jerusalem, but also, if not mainly, hygienic, respectable, virtuous things and people, lacking only in grace and gaiety.'

He rejected the Webbs' ideal of continuous sacrifice of private pleasure to public duty:

We realise that we must guard against romantic or Utopian notions: that hard work and research are virtues: that we must do nothing foolish or impulsive: and that Fabian pamphlets must be diligently studied. We know these things too well. Posthumously, the Webbs have won their battle, and converted a generation to their standards. Now the time has come for a reaction: for a greater emphasis on private life, on freedom and dissent, on culture, beauty, leisure, and even frivolity. Total abstinence and a good filing-system are not now the right sign-posts to the socialist's Utopia: or at least, if they are, some of us will fall by the wayside.

He acknowledged his belief that 'a definite limit exists to the degree of equality which is desirable ... But where en route, before we reach some drab extreme, we shall wish to stop, I have no idea. Our society will look quite different when we have carried through the changes mentioned earlier; and the whole argument will then need to be re-stated, and thought out afresh, by a younger generation than mine.'

Several of the book's major themes were by no means original, but *The Future of Socialism* was the first attempt to mould them into a comprehensive programme. The impact was immediate and explosive.

Fundamentalists (largely but not wholly on the Left of the Party) were enraged. Crosland had judged nationalisation to be a relatively unimportant means of achieving economic planning and social justice. He had displayed insufficient outrage at the inadequacies of the welfare state. He should have incorporated into the contemporary meaning of socialism the full co-operative ideal: surely the state could do something to combat the primitive urge for personal gain. Among his critics he achieved what Bernard Crick described as an 'almost diabolical status'. *Tribune* granted him 'intellectual agility, the lucidity of his writing, and the scope of his learning', but on the whole feelings were well summed up by a future editor of the *New Left Review* who later wrote in *Socialist Commentary* that the book was 'thoughtful, well-argued, stimulating – and wrong'.

To make matters more intolerable for them, their reaction had been anticipated in the book. Its author wrote of a 'subtle reason why revisionism has, historically, always been resented. This is because many working-class militants, and still more some middle-class people who have espoused the workers' cause, feel their whole status and psychological security to depend on preserving a traditional, proletarian philosophy of class-struggle.'

None the less, many democratic socialists enthusiastically seized upon the book. It added an ideological new dimension to revisionist writing. It provided an account of present needs for which they'd been groping. But perhaps the book's ultimate importance was its assessment of how to pursue socialism in current circumstances without abandoning the ethical idealism that underpinned so much socialist thought in the past.

The Labour Party found Tony Crosland hard to place. He held the old Left in contempt. He therefore appeared to align himself with the Right. Yet his credentials as a democratic socialist could not be doubted. His tough-mindedness made him impatient with the Right's caution, its tendency to woolly-mindedness. In later years as many on the Right became readier to compromise with existing social structures, his impatience bordered on hostility. He said he was an egalitarian and meant it. Those who knew him best thought his position on Labour's spectrum between the 1950s and 1977 was centre-right, centre, centre-left. His view was that he moved from the far left of his pre-war years to the centre of the Party and stayed there.

At the same time as Labour MPs responded to the influence of *The Future of Socialism*, they judged its author by his public demeanour. His image as a dilettante was to linger overlong, as myths do. He was not going to make the slightest effort to alter that opinion of him: to do so would be squalid.

PART TWO

⊶ 8 ⊷

Another Happy Childhood

Tony was born just before the First World War ended. At the same time that his father was at the War Office in London, my father was a young major in the American Expeditionary Forces in France. When he returned to civilian life, he resumed journalism in New York and then moved south to work for the *Baltimore Sun*. That's when he met my mother. After their marriage Baltimore became his home, though they went north every summer to the shores of Lake Champlain where he was born and bred.

My father's New England upbringing had a strong Puritan ethic and esteemed work for its own sake. Even so, some of his people permitted themselves pleasure in the creature comforts. Beginning with the first of them, a governor of Plymouth Colony, they produced a succession of New England governors as they moved across Massachusetts and Vermont to the shores of the vast lake which sweeps down from the Canadian border, dividing New England from up-state New York. Testimony to prosperity stands in the fine houses they built along the way. But by my grandfather's time the Watsons had developed a positive gift for losing money. Tony later claimed to be the only British politician with an American wife who was not an heiress.

As the youngest child of a youngest child of a youngest child it was perhaps not all that odd that I was raised on Victorian mores entangled with women's emancipation. When she was a young reporter on the *Baltimore Sun* my mother flew in a tiny aeroplane – uncommon transport in those days – scattering leaflets over the city, exhorting women to vote. At the same time she was the prototype 'Southern lady', pretty, gay, admired and sought; she accepted the sexual mores on which she'd been raised. She married relatively late and had miscarriages, so she was nearly forty when her children were born.

Although my mother ran the household, everything seemed to revolve around my father. Mark Watson made his name internationally as a war correspondent for the *Baltimore Sun* during the Second World War. Ultimately he was doyen of American defence ⌐

correspondents, his column read as a matter of course in the White House. His prizes included the Pulitzer and the Presidential Medal of Freedom, though when my father and Jean Monnet and the twenty-nine other recipients actually received the latter award, President Kennedy lay two weeks dead. Each time my father walked through the front door at home the whole atmosphere was charged. He was warm. He was entertaining. He was exciting. The contrast between the light eyes and the nearly black hair fascinated me.

In Baltimore my sister and I were brought up in an environment not fully recovered from the trauma of the Civil War and the 'reconstruction' of the South that followed. During that excessively poignant war, Maryland, though south of the Mason-Dixon line, did not secede from the Union. President Lincoln's cannon commanded Baltimore's harbour and business centre; Baltimore merchants had an economic interest at odds with that of the landed class which presided in southern Maryland and most of Dixieland. Maryland families were therefore peculiarly tormented. Those who chose to fight on the Southern side had to swim the Potomac to reach Virginia. If they were captured by the Union forces they were shot as traitors.

My mother's people had grown the tobacco leaf in southern Maryland since the early-seventeenth century. After the twenty years of reconstruction were done, my grandparents uprooted themselves from what little remained of their way of life and moved to Baltimore with their six small children, lived with relations while my grandfather, bred for leisure, looked for work. He quietly died. Those of my mother's people who coped with their alteration placed strong emphasis on blood and 'interests of the mind' – sensible priorities when your wealth is gone. Those who became prosperous again still emphasised the fact that 'old' Baltimoreans were highly cultivated people. 'Is it a *suitable* marriage?' was the accepted way of inquiring if one's betrothed came from a colonial – preferably Maryland – family. As for personal publicity, that was shunned. When I first came to London and observed upper-class families who make an industry of self-publicity I was astounded.

Three of my grandmother's six children were alive when I was born. Genteel poverty had enabled my mother alone to graduate from the state high school. The eldest son, John Owens, went out to work when he was fourteen, became a journalist on the *Baltimore Sun* where he and H. L. Mencken fell in love with the same young woman. She married my uncle who became the *Sun*'s most distinguished Editor-in-Chief, winning a couple of Pulitzer Prizes. The day after America dropped the atom bomb on Hiroshima, my uncle sat all afternoon on our veranda, smoking a cigar, stricken by the moral implications of what had been done.

My grandmother's second son was fourteen when he ran away from home and enlisted in the army, later becoming a Brigadier-General. Like all the Owenses, he had charm and humour, and with time and effort did pretty well in keeping his temper under control.

'Why did he leave home when he was so young?' I asked, unable to conceive of such a venture into the unknown. My mother, whom I loved dearly, adopted her vague voice: he'd been hunting and shot a deer; on his way home he was set upon by older boys who tried to divest him of it.

'He got angry, naturally,' said my mother. 'After all, it was his deer. He hit one of the boys.'

'Did he *hurt* the boy?' I asked, enthralled as only well-brought-up children can be.

'Well, dear, I guess he hurt him pretty badly.' Reared in the late-Victorian manner, my mother was a staunch believer in the euphemism. Not until I was grown up did I inadvertently discover that my uncle had killed him.

Another of my mother's brothers reached manhood but was shot through the temple when he was a young officer in the Philippines during the First World War. My grandmother taught me that he was my guardian angel. It was a stray bullet from a rifle range, my mother said each time I asked about my guardian angel. Only much later did I learn – again inadvertently – that he received a letter from his fiancée breaking off their engagement and went AWOL, his fellow officers finally tracing him to a 'disorderly house'. He asked them to give him until morning before they took him back for court-martial, went off to some room by himself. In the morning when they knocked at the door, they heard the shot, so presumably he hadn't wanted to pull the trigger. Some Baltimoreans were strengthened by the post-bellum emphasis on not letting the family down; others found it an insupportable strain. Whatever was happening in their lives, their manners were the most beautiful I have ever encountered.

Two months of each year in my sister's and my childhood were passed in family solitude on the Vermont shore of Lake Champlain, away from Baltimore's heat, suspended in time on a derelict enchanted farm belonging to my father's people. My great-uncle lived in the rundown colonial house. My mother and sister and I lived in the rundown Victorian house with its cupola, designed as an elegant summer house, occupied throughout the year by my father's unmarried brother. The only transport was a rowing boat named Emmy. No other soul lived for miles around. My father himself joined us for his three-week holiday. Only my mother, I think, was conscious of the place being other than ravishingly beautiful.

Hours on end I occupied myself in the high-ceilinged music room, whose only concession to its original purpose was a gramophone – called the Victrola – with a tuba-like speaker and a crank. *Song of the Volga Boatmen*, Sousa's *Military Marches*, *Triumphal March from Aida* were favoured in pre-pubescent years, my fantasies briefly interrupted while I rewound the Victrola. The fantasies were not of a bellicose nature: Joan of Arc was adapted freely, my sword symbolic, as I rode my white horse into rural villages, bringing peace, mutual aid, prosperity to all.

Of the once flourishing livestock on the farm, two fat brown horses remained to draw the wagon bearing what hay my uncle still harvested. Atop this chariot, grasping my pitchfork, flanked by two knights borrowed from the Vermont State Reformatory to help with the summer crop, I dreamed my dreams of glory until one day when I was, I suppose, twelve years old. Evidently I fainted and fell from my chariot, regaining consciousness in my parents' enormous double bed where, in my father's absence, I was to spend the next seven days, coming round and then fainting again from horror. The old-fashioned telephone, for some reason installed in the dining-room, was cranked to summon the doctor from the distant town of Vergennes (pop. 1,700), my mother fearing this young girl was suffering from a heart attack as well as the onset of menstruation. My sister imagined someone else had forewarned me of this occurrence. No one had.

In our Baltimore home, while surrounded with the pleasures of my parents' generosity and their continuous hospitality (called 'open house' in the South), whenever the opposite sex was concerned my sister's and my upbringing was exceptionally strict. Like most people we knew, we went to a single-sex private day school. When we went out on dates we had to be home before anyone else. Other girls were allowed to go with boys for an overnight sail on Chesapeake Bay, but this was forbidden us unless there was a chaperone, which there never was, that no doubt being the main point of the sail. My mother inculcated in me the belief that I should kiss no one unless I intended marrying him. As I was still in my fourteenth year when I fell passionately in love with a youth a couple of years my senior, a dilemma presented itself. This I sought to resolve by not discussing further with my mother the question of kissing. By the time I was fifteen I was most eager to marry my *beau*, as such were known in Baltimore. My mother dealt with the dilemma by forbidding me to see my *beau* for a year. It says something for her common sense that when the youth and I joyfully met for our reunion at the end of this painful year I found I had 'got over it'.

As a girl I did most of what was expected of me, excelling at studies, captaining various team sports, more often than not being president of my class, and so on. And much was expected of me by my mother because I had 'everything', being nice to look at, intelligent, popular, not to mention possessing this boon of belonging to an old Maryland family.

Until I set off for Vassar when I was seventeen, I'd never lived apart from my family. On the railway platform I burst into tears. Then an odd thing occurred. As soon as I was away from my much-loved home, I immediately stopped doing all the things that had been expected of me. Nothing could induce me to participate in Vassar's student government. My room-mates forged my name on those slips that testify to attendance at chapel. All blandishments to play games were resisted, a racking cough brought into play when compulsory sport was mentioned. An unpermitted number of weekends were spent in New York or Boston or the Ivy League men's universities by the simple device of informing no one in authority that I intended departing Vassar's campus, writing an illegible name in the sullen porter's book when I made my return. If rather 'wild', I wasn't 'fast'. Germaine Greer might put this down to two thousand years' brainwashing culminating in my mother's admonishments. Whatever the cause, I am what a psychiatrist friend, Eustace Chesser, called 'monoerotic' – unable to be physically attracted to two people at the same time.

Instilled by my childhood was the psychology of being the youngest among first cousins whose birthdays spanned twenty years: I was protected and dared simultaneously. Because their mother died when they were small, two cousins spent much of their life in our house, we in theirs. 'If anything happens to me,' was my mother's ritual remark as she went out, 'just telephone the other house.' The glamorous sister and farouche, dark-haired brother were objects of my adoration from earliest days. I liked to pretend that Johnny Owens was my brother and I wept bitterly when it was decreed that I was getting too old to play in his bedroom. I can't have been more than eight years old when this ban was imposed.

As a war correspondent, my father was rarely home from North Africa, Italy, France. Only occasionally did my sister and I see our mother break down. 'You are too young to understand what it is like for me without him,' she said. My older cousins had joined up after Pearl Harbor, most of them as officers serving in the Pacific. Johnny was a long time in the Pacific islands as an enlisted man – what the English call other ranks – in the Marines. I especially liked the song 'When Johnny comes marching home again, hurrah, hurrah'.

He returned very late after the war.

Time passed. As I grew up the semi-sibling adoration grew complicated, taboo and mutual attraction mixed. Running concurrently were the usual teenage infatuations, but better than anything else was driving fast with Johnny, sitting astride his shoulders when he dived into a water-filled quarry, target-shooting with the revolver he had. I knew he played Russian roulette with it sometimes. 'Show me how,' I said. 'Don't be silly,' he replied. We laughed in almost everything we did together, acted as if no melancholy was there; it wasn't caused solely by the years in the islands: he was always an outsider. Every desire for involvement seemed to lead him to a dead-end.

Largely to oblige his father who had wanted as a young man to study law but been unable to afford it, Johnny started at the Maryland School of Law. Why not try anything? He was already in a dead-end, emotion blocked by taboo. There was nothing to lose. Few professions could have been worse chosen for someone struggling against despair.

Johnny drove me to the station. My next term at Vassar began. A student meeting was in progress while I lay on my bed, listening to my room-mate's record of the Love Music from *Tristan and Isolde*, when someone knocked on the door to say there was a long-distance call for me. The telephone boxes stood along one side of the main hall. What I remember most clearly when the caller told me that Johnny had shot himself was how the group of students, sitting at their meeting on the other side of the hall, were at once located at some other distance from where they'd been a moment before.

The period ushered in by the telephone call included the sort of thing one would expect. In Baltimore the family took turns giving each other support. But when away from home, at Vassar more or less, I was determinedly irresponsible, driving my friends' cars – they sometimes hapless passengers – with a recklessness disagreeable to recall, leaping into an allegedly lethal whirlpool (its reputation, I correctly guessed, exaggerated), playing with guns obsessively, involving myself with the most unsuitable man whose path crossed mine. These things I kept from my mother, though a few glimmerings must have made their way south. 'I sometimes worry, dear, that you are a little highly strung,' she said.

When I was twenty I graduated from Vassar, returned to live at home, began teaching at the Baltimore Museum of Art, met and fell in love with Patrick Skene Catling. Anglo-Irish, he was tall, handsome, auburn-haired. His sense of humour was sardonic. At that time he was a reporter on the *Baltimore Sun*. Despite being born and bred in London, Patrick was declared suitable. We had a church wedding, which required special permission from the bishop as Patrick had been divorced. His first wife was neatly discounted because he'd been only nineteen when he married her, there were no children, and furthermore – my mother pointed out – she was a New York model.

Throughout my childhood three Negro women served as mainstays. Mamie, whom I loved most, cooked and waited at table; her sister-in-law, Carrie, was our laundress; Queenie was seamstress – the latter two waiting on table when we had company. All three warned my sister and me of the cataclysm of marriage that lay ahead. 'You don't know nothin' 'bout marriage,' said Mamie. 'You think it gwine be like your parents' marriage. Ain't no other two people live together like Mister–Miz Watson. You in for a big surprise.'

In 1956 Patrick was assigned to head the *Baltimore Sun*'s London bureau for two years. That spring, along with our two infant daughters, I joined him in London. Mamie was right. Our marriage was very rocky indeed. Despite some terrific discouragements, neither of us wanted a divorce, and I didn't dream of a life outside my marriage.

We lived in a rented flat in Knightsbridge on an expense account that allowed me independence unknown since our marriage. We could afford a 'daily' who came in the mornings, and, crucially, a 'mother's help' who lived in – which meant I could go where I liked when I liked.

The first thing I did with my new freedom was to go regularly to the Reading Room of the British Museum. I was younger than most when I was at Vassar, and though I took my degree at America's most renowned women's college in three years instead of the usual four, no one could call it a good degree. Belatedly I discovered the urge for further education. The second thing I did was to start going to parties again. These abounded in London, every size and shape. The British were in a kind of exaltation that post-war austerity had run its course.

At the beginning of November 1956 the Conservative Government poised British troops for the invasion of Egypt. Patrick flew to the Middle East to report events as they unfolded there. I attended a small cocktail party given by a friend from Vassar. In her drawing-room, the Suez fiasco was one topic of heated conversation. Another was *The Future of Socialism*, about which everyone else present seemed to hold a strong view, I alone oblivious to its recent publication and its author's name until our hostess introduced us.

9

An Interlude

'Let's sit down,' Tony Crosland said, settling in our hostess's unoccupied sofa. 'Cannot understand why people want to stand round while holding a conversation. I expect you'd like to discuss your psychoanalyst.'

'I've never been analysed, as it happens.'

'Nonsense. Every female American has been psychoanalysed. Generally twice.'

Over dinner I said to him: 'What exactly is *The Future of Socialism*? Is it one of those pamphlets?'

That gave him great pleasure.

Unusually tall, broadshouldered, to me he looked raffish and was compelling at the same time. I'd never seen irises so pale; I was fascinated by their contrast with the nearly black hair.

19 The Boltons was an oasis. I could scarcely credit it. I still can scarcely credit what happened to my life.

Patrick returned a month later, and I invited round for a drink at our Knightsbridge flat the Labour Party intellectual I'd met in his absence. The two men liked each other. For the remaining fourteen months of the London assignment, conviviality was active at 19 The Boltons, or in the Catling flat, or with those of Tony's friends who now became Patrick's and my friends. The oasis of happiness was camouflaged.

The author of *The Future of Socialism* gave me a copy, marking chapters I should skim, others for me to skip altogether: previously I'd read nothing about political philosophy or sociology, let alone economics, and he was too good a teacher to overburden a novice.

My Vassar friend had introduced me to him as 'Sunie' – the name I was called in Baltimore and elsewhere by Americans who knew me. At the front of my copy of *The Future of Socialism* he wrote: 'To Sunie Catling – who *thinks* she disproves p. 250, ll. 7–16; though the author still agrees with Margaret Mead.' On page 250 he'd contrasted the pigeon-holes of English society with the ladder which Mead used to classify American society, where the 'upper' classes, he quoted from her study, are merely those 'whose

only possible social movement is downwards ... They have no
distinguishing manners and no distinguishing morals and no distinguishing occupation or lack of it ... If a member of the upper
class of Baltimore should turn up in shabby clothes in Billings,
Montana, he would find it very difficult to document his position
... Former residents of Baltimore might be able to identify him if
they had known him personally, but not by his bearing and accent,
as would be the case in England.' Without having ever brooded
upon the matter, I was astonished by this information; I'd never
even heard of Billings, Montana.

He opened my eyes to all manner of concepts, attitudes I'd never
analysed, aspects of human nature, pleasure, needs I hadn't realised
before. A whole new education began.

Paradoxically, because I had my private oasis, the Catling marriage stabilised, looked as if it would survive.

One afternoon in 1957 Tony said: 'I'm putting my promiscuity
aside until you leave England.'

'Why? You've taken trouble enough to make me understand that
it doesn't diminish what we have.'

'Which it doesn't. But I want to make the most of this.'

His habit of total separation between work and play remained
unchanged. He was writing polemics for periodicals. He was giving
the Co-ops the rapt attention that he applied to everything that
caught his interest. The Co-operative Movement's Annual Congress had voted to set up an Independent Commission to discover
how to revitalise their methods of production and marketing. They
had markedly failed to adapt to the new world of large-scale retailing introduced by Marks and Spencer. Gaitskell, chairman of the
Commission, appointed Tony to take charge and write the Report.
Throughout 1957 he examined Co-ops up and down the country,
determined to get to the bottom of the problem, involving himself
with it.

Though infrequent, a party at 19 The Boltons was always event-
ful, composed of perhaps fifteen people who tended to be economists, actresses, writers, painters. Hugh Gaitskell was usually the
only politician invited. At that time Tony was interested in American jazz. A fair bit of noise was generated. While various occupants
of the flats on lower floors were placated in advance by being
invited to look in, the host was strangely indifferent to the sensi-
bilities of the family that occupied the whole of the large adjoining
house. A game, much favoured during this period at 19 The

Boltons, caused stress at 20 The Boltons. 'Pat-ball' consisted of two contestants, each with a tennis racket, hitting a rubber ball against a wall of the landing just inside the flat's front door. Bets were placed by onlookers. Guests at Tony's party were stricken with a sense of inconsiderateness whenever a ferocious pounding on the wall commenced from the other side, the handle of a broom or similar-shaped object being wielded to hammer out an entirely justified complaint. The rest of us looked guiltily at one another and desisted from pat-ball. Our host seized one of the tennis rackets and with its handle pounded back on the communicating wall.

'Tony, you really shouldn't do that. We *are* making rather a lot of noise for whoever lives next door.'

'That may be. But as the person who lives next door wears a beard, is a rich Catholic and a peer, and has eight children, one sees no reason for him to complain.' Pat-ball was resumed.

One party was smaller and ended sooner than most. At a *Spectator* gathering earlier in the evening, Tony and a so-called Angry Young Man met for the first time and rather took to one another; Kingsley Amis, a Labour supporter, was a lecturer at the University College of Swansea, writing his best-selling novels when he could find the time. It was arranged that after a meal he and his wife and another married couple, ex-pupils, turn up at 19 The Boltons with Kingsley's favourite jazz records, carried in a special black case. Tony had a meal with Patrick and me, after which some ten people converged on the flat. Patrick was an expert on American jazz, probably the most expert of those present.

From the start, tensions declared themselves. One of the guests went into the room adjoining the drawing-room, taking with him the wife of another guest, closing the connecting glass door. While engaging in no flagrant act of impropriety, they made plain their feelings for one another. As their respective mates were on our side of the glass door, Tony regarded the situation as squalid, intolerable. He sauntered next door and broke up the tête-à-tête, thus adding two more angry people to the already angry mates.

Patrick and Kingsley had a violent altercation about whether Coleman Hawkins or Lester Young was the superior tenor saxophonist. Patrick's aquiline face was drained of all colour, and he drew in his nostrils – always an ominous sign – before suggesting that, if Kingsley persisted in his ignorant dogmatism, he would certainly strike him. Tony had to dissuade him.

Kingsley took it upon himself to rearrange his own records on the turntable of Tony's gramophone. Tony was rather particular about this gramophone. 'Wedding present from Hugh Dalton. Cost him a lot of money. One would rather you let one deal with the gramophone.'

'Look, Crosland, they're my records.'

'It's one's gramophone.'

Following this dialogue, four guests filed down the short flight of stairs to the entrance hall, Kingsley leading the way, the rear drawn up by one of the ex-pupils carrying the black case with Kingsley's jazz records, all of them clear that this intellectual socialist was not only aggravating: he was childish as well.

Normal life for the Catlings was about to resume: the *Baltimore Sun* assignment in London reached its end. A traditional luxury of these expenses-paid foreign assignments was the return trip by sea, first class. The ship sailed from Cannes. The night before we flew to Cannes, there was a party at 19 The Boltons to bid us goodbye. Hugh Gaitskell's eyes filled with tears as we revolved to the lilt of 'Teacher's Pet'. He did not speak of his awareness of the full farewell taking place.

The following morning, when Patrick and the children and I set off for Cannes, two of us were distinctly unfit. A few hours later Tony woke not only to feel unfit: he realised something further needed to be said. We would not communicate again when I returned to my homeland. No regular commercial flight being available, he chartered a small plane, arranged with his bank manager to guarantee the cheque, left word with Hugh's secretary that he would have to miss their lunch appointment, sent a telegram to Cannes, got himself and a woman friend of ours to Croydon Airport, and the two of them arrived in Cannes before the tender set out for the ship waiting in the harbour.

This time the farewell was final.

Looking back on the pain that followed – lying in a deckchair as the January sun shone palely on the southern Atlantic route, trying physically to absorb the pain, painting our entire flat in Baltimore, trying physically to absorb the pain, at the same time marvelling at what had made the pain inevitable – it was a rehearsal.

After several months in Baltimore, Patrick found he preferred life in London and arranged to work in Fleet Street as a reporter for the *Guardian*. We sold our Baltimore flat and along with four early American hickory chairs, some silver that was a wedding present from my aunts and uncles, a Persian rug that was a wedding present from Patrick's parents, a secondhand Buick convertible bought with a bequest left by my godfather, we boarded a ship bound for England. In November 1958, ten months after leaving London for ever, we returned to make it our home.

⇥ 10 ⇤

A Self-appointed Chief of Staff

When the Independent Co-operative Commission Report was presented to the 1958 Co-op Congress, Gaitskell and Crosland were angry and depressed when the traditionalists defeated the central recommendations of the Report. With dogged resolution the Co-operative Movement refused to advance into the second half of the twentieth century.

In a thoroughly bad temper, Tony allowed Gaitskell to persuade him that he would be more influential in Parliament and that as his work for the Co-op stood him in good stead with its more progressive elements he should go for a seat suddenly vacated at Tottenham where the Co-op had influence. He officially joined the Co-operative Party three weeks before appearing as their nominee before the selection committee. Ian Mikardo wrote in *Tribune* that it was scandalous. Tony – for once – agreed with him. He was not selected and was not sorry. He and Gaitskell continued their argument about Tony's ambivalence to being an MP.

The two men admired, loved, maddened one another. The bonds between them were far stronger than mutual censure. They shared what might be called an egalitarian attitude to people, their manner unaffected by someone's position – though Tony carried to extremes his treatment of others with concentrated attention or unconcealed dismissiveness according to mood or his assessment of their personalities. Both men threw themselves into their work. Both had a large capacity for enjoyment. Both viewed power as a vehicle for putting principles into practice, not as an end in itself. Both believed in political teamwork. The main and continuing contention between them was Tony's concern that Hugh was insufficiently radical for a left-wing leader.

In 1959, with a general election approaching, the MP for Grimsby, Kenneth Younger, decided very reluctantly not to stand again and went to see his Leader to tell him. Gaitskell devoted exactly one sentence to expressing regret before asking Younger whether he thought the seat could be won by Tony Crosland. Until the Second World War Grimsby dockers and railwaymen, traditionally Labour, were heavily outnumbered at the polling booth: fishermen were Tory by nature. Wartime service produced awareness of a broader world. Newly discovered methods for freezing fish brought more industry to Grimsby. When Labour swept the country in the post-war general election, Grimsby elected its first Labour MP. Younger was the high-minded son of a brewery baron, part-heir to a fortune, Winchester–Oxford educated, a major in Intelligence during the war.

Most Grimsby working people lead hard lives. Until recent technological advances in trawling, the number of young widows was horrifying. But in fifteen years a deckie-learner could be a skipper: he was self-assured and admired self-assurance in others. Cut off on the northernmost tip of old Lincolnshire, Grimbarians as a breed are exceptionally independent-minded. They don't suck up. They admire the man who knows what he's doing. Even if a skipper is a bastard, he wins their respect: 'He knows his job.'

Grimbarians didn't mind that Younger was cultivated, worldly, different from Grimsby's former Conservative MPs, mostly self-made chaps who'd clawed their way up. They appreciated that he could have been a leading Tory: he chose to be Labour.

At the Conservative Club in the fine broad street lined with brick mansions – testimony to rewards reaped by enterprising late-Victorian businessmen – the Labour MP was slandered, naturally enough. A few actually believed that Younger left London in a Rolls-Royce, drove as far as Louth, changed his clothes, then stepped on the train for the last few miles to Grimsby where he descended in plebeian guise.

While irritating, the absurd myth did no real damage to his reputation as an excellent constituency MP. In the Attlee Government he was a junior minister, certain to be in the next Labour Cabinet. By 1959 Labour had been in Opposition for eight long years, cruelly frustrating for a talented man. Others might think that Labour under Gaitskell's leadership would win the 1959 election. Younger was not so sure. He was invited to become Director-General of Chatham House and, after anguished soul-searching, he decided to accept – which meant leaving politics. He was deeply hurt by Gaitskell's off-hand response to this news.

The leading Fabians in Grimsby were the Franklins and the Barkers. Bill Rodgers used to meet them at Fabian summer schools. When Muriel and Jeremy Barker learned of Younger's decision to stand down they asked Bill if they could nominate him for the seat. He accepted their offer.

Lill Bontoft rounded up the local Co-ops to nominate Tony Crosland. Blonde, pretty, Lill was a dynamo. Her friend Bill Brumby worked on the trade union vote. Councillor Ivor Hanson was thirsty: the nomination meeting in his own ward was dragging on, perilously near closing time. He knew Lily Bontoft wanted this bloke called Crosland. 'Mr Chairman, I think Mr Crosland is the best person,' he said. A quarter of an hour later he was in the pub enjoying his beer.

Bill Rodgers arrived five days before the selection committee met and stayed with the Barkers, Jeremy acting as his campaign manager. On selection day Tony Crosland appeared in Grimsby for the first time. His supporters asked Alderman Franklin in his business role to provide lunch at the Franklins' café. Bill barely had time to finish his lunch; he left behind a humorous note saying he'd been turfed out by Tony's people. Upstairs was a room where Crosland supporters could come and meet him. As proprietor of the café, Alderman Franklin had to lay on their tea; he decided Tony was the better man, even if rather high-handed.

There were five candidates in all, including an important local figure, Matt Quinn. Crosland won by a healthy majority. That August, instead of the gentler pleasures of a continental holiday, he spent a fortnight in a Grimsby trawler as it pitched and heaved upon the bleak North Sea. It reminded him of the army – a rugged physical life, camaraderie, no one showing the slightest interest in Westminster politics.

The day before the general election in October 1959, Joanna Kilmartin drove her yellow convertible from her Queen Anne house in Chelsea to a seedy little hotel in Earls Court. Joanna, a journalist, and Terry, her husband and the *Observer*'s literary editor, were friends of Tony before I knew him. The seedy little hotel in Earls Court was my latest abode, where the children and the mother's help and I were holed up in an attic room along with a sewing machine – borrowed from the Kilmartins – with which the mother's help was making curtains. We had sole use of the bathroom along the corridor, owing to the fact that the builders hadn't completed the floor, and we were the only residents prepared to step across the spaces between the joists. Patrick, trying to write a book in his spare time from *Punch* – for which he had changed his *Guardian* job – rightly guessed the Earls Court set-up to be unconducive to literary creativity. I've forgotten where he was living. We were waiting for a solicitor called John Silkin to negotiate a 110 per cent mortgage/loan for a leasehold house in Hobury Street, World's

End – that indeterminate area where Chelsea dissolves into Fulham. Silkin aspired to enter Parliament one day. Meanwhile Tony recommended him for this task.

Joanna and I set off in her yellow convertible on the four-hour drive to Grimsby. Neither of us had been there before, but it wasn't hard to find the lorry, all trimmed up with Labour Party placards, from which the candidate was speaking. Lill Bontoft took one look at us. 'My God, Tony, whoever are they?'

He'd mentioned that he had some friends coming from London, and there we were – 'so obviously Chelsea set, long chiffon scarves flying', was how Lill saw us, fairly accurately. She was not going to have it.

'When you get off that lorry,' she said to the candidate, 'for goodness' sake, walk the other way. I know Grimsby better than you do. You're not in yet. You can do what you want after the count.'

'Welcome to Grimsby,' he said, jumping down from the lorry to introduce us to some of the Party workers. Lill glared.

The following afternoon the eve-of-poll cavalcade commenced, Lill's van leading, the candidate riding immediately behind in a Party worker's car adorned with red and yellow ribbons and a red and yellow pennant stitched with the letters CROSLAND. (Embroidered by a constituent in South Gloucestershire, when the pennant wore out in Grimsby, Lill made another.) In the yellow convertible Joanna and I trailed in the rear.

Halfway through the cavalcade, the candidate's car broke down. He strode down the street canvassing every third house, while his campaign committee discussed the overwhelming fact that the cavalcade had ground to a halt.

'Why don't you have Tony ride with us?' said Joanna helpfully. 'My car's open and it's even the right colour.'

Lill accepted the car on the condition that we vacate it and a Party worker take over the wheel. We were permitted to get in another car though its driver was sternly admonished: 'Whatever you do, keep far back.'

It is a privilege to be allowed into the count inside the Town Hall as the contents of the ballot boxes are separated and deposited in clumps in wooden troughs stretching down tables lined end to end. As Grimsby had only two candidates, there were only two troughs, and the wads of votes growing in each were unnervingly even in number. Joanna and I were among the unprivileged crowded in the square outside, shivering in the wind blowing off the North Sea, waiting for the result. Word spread that a recount was taking place. People with car radios said that Conservatives throughout the country were being returned with vastly increased majorities. One lot in the square cheered. The other lot told them to belt up. Both lots stamped their freezing feet.

Inside Grimsby Town Hall, the Labour candidate strolled around, apparently unruffled, talking to his supporters. Lill Bontoft had a perceptive eye; she kept it on his complexion. 'I watched that lad change from red to white to green to grey. I never went to a count again.'

Outside we all looked up when the balcony doors above us opened. The Town Clerk announced that Anthony Crosland had won by 101 votes.

'If you'd let my London friends stay in the car, we might have won by 201 votes,' he said to Lill.

'Wouldn't have got in at all,' she replied.

When television showed Gaitskell conceding defeat, his dignity didn't conceal his pain. In defeat he gave the wider public its first perception of this highly emotional man whom Bevanites had labelled 'a desiccated calculating machine'.

During the election – fought by the Conservatives in a campaign summed up by Harold Macmillan's phrase 'You've never had it so good' – Gaitskell made a bad blunder by committing his future government not to raise income tax. He thereby averted the scare campaign he had feared – that Labour's programme would entail a massive tax increase – but was denounced instead for fiscal irresponsibility and turning the election into an auction. None the less he expected to win.

The countrywide defeat of the Labour Party shattered its morale. Two evenings after the election, Hugh gave an already arranged farewell dinner party at Frognal Gardens for Big Hugh. Dalton had stood down from his safe seat to make way for a younger man. The guests were friends of both Hughs – Tony, Douglas Jay, Roy Jenkins, Gordon Walker – Labour intellectuals lumped together by the press as the 'Hampstead Set'. They were neither sober nor drunk. They were punch drunk. Tony left the party early for an engagement at The Boltons with one of his actress friends.

The following morning, Sunday, he was back at Frognal Gardens – in his work compartment. Already Gaitskell was set on 'reshaping' the Party, his first aim being to alter Clause IV of the Party's constitution. Clause IV is printed in small letters on the back of everyone's Labour Party membership card – beneath the large space that most members notice because it's where their annual subscription is recorded. If one examines Clause IV, there is no doubt that in the middle of it is the phrase 'common ownership of the means of production, distribution and exchange'. No election had been fought on this piece of doctrine. Many members were unaware of its existence. But Gaitskell saw its alteration as a symbol of the need to modernise the Party. He put his view to the Hampstead Set.

The Hampstead Set at no time influenced Gaitskell's values: these were fixed by him. Their own values were diverse: for Tony, equality and personal freedom were the essentials; Roy Jenkins made personal freedom and the Common Market his priorities; and so on. What they attempted, together or individually, was to influence the Leader's strategy and tactics. Although Roy and Douglas Jay were against all nationalisation, they didn't actually suggest altering Clause IV; it was Gaitskell who got this bee in his bonnet.

Tony disowned the full literal meaning of Clause IV. But he strongly opposed tampering at this moment with a bit of doctrine that no one – so far – much noticed. 'Why draw everyone's attention to this shibboleth? You will start a battle in the Party that will cause far more trouble than the thing is worth,' he said to Gaitskell and the others.

Tony lost the argument.

'I shall be very surprised if Hugh hasn't overestimated the number of MPs who are prepared to throw nationalisation so gaily overboard in the full public eye,' Dick Crossman commented to his diary only ten days after the defeat at the polls. The following week he recorded: 'The net effect of this morning's meeting was to show that the Jenkins–Jay line has no chance whatsoever of being accepted.'

Disaster struck. Douglas Jay wrote an article suggesting that the Party needed to shed its working-class image, and – since nationalisation was so unpopular – might drop the idea of renationalising steel. The Left wing of the Party imagined that this member of the Hampstead Set must be flying a kite for the Leader who, they supposed, was plotting some far-reaching abandonment of socialism. In fact, Gaitskell was irate with Jay; he did not wish to prevent public ownership. He intended only to expand the Party's doctrinal statement of aims to include its other agreed purposes, and he believed he could do so in a way that would command general assent.

By the time he reached Blackpool for the Party's post-election conference in November, both the Left wing and the trade union working-class Centre were convinced they were under attack. Left-wing constituency militants, led by Michael Foot, began what they saw as a defensive battle. Before 1959 was out, the Labour Party had embarked on two years of internecine warfare.

Whenever the Clause IV shambles was referred to afterwards, Tony said: 'We made a frightful mistake.'

'Why do you always say "we" when you argued against it at the outset?' another of Gaitskell's supporters once asked.

'We went into it together.' (Many years later, Tony was drawn in a television interview to admit that he had advised against the abortive attempt on Clause IV. Almost his first words after the programme were: 'I feel rather a heel.')

He didn't go in for saying 'I told you so'. When Clause IV blew up in Gaitskell's face, Tony became his most ferocious defender. With the Left wing and trade union Centre unexpectedly unified it was crucial for the leadership to win back the Centre – the working-class vote on which Gaitskell depended. To that end Tony bombarded the Left with speeches and articles, deriding them as conservatives in their orthodoxy.

By January 1960, the *New Statesman*, then edited by John Freeman, approached near obsession on the subject of Crosland, giving pleasure not only to the Left but to right-wing economists who equally resented his attacks on them for being reactionary. One such economist – his latest book reviewed by C. A. R. Crosland – was still dispatching letters about writs he was preparing to issue. With more than a little satisfaction he addressed yet another letter to 19 The Boltons, quoting from the *New Statesman*: 'When he gets on to politics or economics he sometimes reveals an assertive arrogance which confirms his colleagues' worst impression of intellectuals.' That was an excellent description, he said, of Tony's 'disgusting behaviour' to him the year before.

This aggrieved man was to receive further satisfaction some weeks later when the *New Statesman* published an anonymous profile of Tony, laced with innuendo, describing him as Mr Gaitskell's cup-bearing Ganymede. Hugh Dalton wrote to Tony:

(20 MARCH 1960) I have been very angry, for two days and nights, with the Statesman. You arouse, in some vile groups, a pent-up hatred, spitefulness and jealousy which is almost unbelievable. In that office they must all have frightfully evil states of mind. I

suppose they all sit around in a ring and contribute to all the malice and personal nastiness and sheer error of a piece like last Friday's . . .

I don't think it would do any good if either I or you wrote to the Bloody Paper. They'd only use their right of comment and reply to worm their way even deeper into the shit. Labour politics is fuller now of personal stinks and stinkers than ever before.

'I don't think the profile is *that* terrible,' I said, when its subject showed me Dalton's letter. 'It's quite interesting. I love that Vicky cartoon of you. Looks just like you.'

'Good. Too bad it's not you that's lunching with my poor old mother.'

'Surely she doesn't read the *New Statesman*.'

'She will have by now. Some candid friend will see to that. They always do.'

Tony's mother suffered from a pathological hatred of the press. 1960 was the first of many trying years. 'CROSLAND LEAPS TO BACK GAITSKELL.' 'CRITIC CROSLAND TO BE RAPPED.' 'MR CROSLAND ON THE OFFENSIVE.' 'CROSLAND HITS AT THE LABOUR LEADERSHIP.' 'MR CROSLAND SLAMS THE LOT IN NEW LABOUR ROW.'

'These press people,' said his mother, 'they really ought to be put down. They've put Tony's name in the paper again.' Whatever they said about him wasn't right.

In February Gaitskell delivered a major speech, largely written by Tony, in which he tried to undo the damage started by Douglas Jay's article. He was *not*, he repeated, against extending public ownership. His objection to Clause IV was that it was too narrow in omitting many basic aims, too broad in hinting at nationalising everything.

In March a kind of truce was reached, the trade unions having now begun to move back to Gaitskell as they realised a conspiracy was afoot to overthrow him. That month a constitutional amendment was approved by the NEC – with Clause IV now redrafted: '. . . Common ownership takes varying forms . . . Recognising that both public and private enterprise have a place in the economy . . .'

Long before the amendment could be ratified by conference, it received a fatal blow. Left-wing unilateralists seized the opportunity to exploit the resentment of trade unionists and the older generation, still simmering from the attack on Clause IV. The battle was reopened and joined to a second passionately emotive issue: unilateral disarmament. Trade union leaders didn't want to fight on two fronts: in order to support Gaitskell over defence they abandoned the attempt to persuade their members to accept an amended Clause IV. The issue of defence weapons has always symbolised a basic divide in the Labour Party: is the Party intended as a protest movement or as a prospective government? The question was faced by Tony in a brutally frank Fabian pamphlet he wrote at this time – *Can Labour Win?*

In this same spring of 1960, the leadership in disarray, he appointed himself Gaitskell's chief of staff.

Gaitskell kept a very few files of correspondence from individuals, only one of whom became a leading politician. The letters in the Crosland file were not written to please:

(SPRING 1960) Basic question: how to avoid the tactical errors which we all agree that we made from Oct. to March. These were fundamentally due to: (a) bad intelligence: i.e. through lack of consultation we were wrong about how different people & groups would react. (b) bad analysis: i.e. we spent much too little time thinking & planning every move ahead ...

You, facing what will be a 2-year fight to modernise the Party, face a number of handicaps ... First, you lack the resources to create a full-time staff ... Secondly, while a committee system exists (N.E.C. & Shadow Cab.), it's no damned good for the task in hand.

Can we then do anything to make our leadership-system more professional, less amateur & haphazard?

I would make the following suggestions.

Chapter and verse followed. Hugh's marginalia suggest that he took this advice in good part. The next planning letter, written a few weeks later on 4 May, maddened him. It began: 'Recent events demonstrate that your leadership still lacks a proper system of intelligence and Forward Planning.' Tony then gave three examples of errors caused, he said, by Hugh's unawareness of PLP feeling changing on the H-bomb:

As a consequence of this faulty intelligence, no forward planning occurred; and two snap decisions had to be made by Brown and Wilson (both of them, in my view, correct decisions) while you were absent in New York, Paris and Haifa.

The question of going abroad so much at critical moments must be one between you and your conscience.

This personal jab led to irate marginalia by Hugh. Tony's letter went on:

But whatever the outcome of that inner struggle, the wider question remains. It may be summed up in this way. In the 7 months since the election, we have suffered a major defeat over Clause 4; we are now fighting an unplanned defensive battle over the H-bomb; we have achieved not one single one of the positive reforms which the moderates wanted (a change in the composition of the N.E.C. and/or an explicit change in the balance of power between N.E.C. and Parliamentary Party, a new set-up at Transport House, a systematic study of survey material, etc. etc.); your own position is weaker, and you yourself more criticised, than at any time since you assumed the leadership; and the morale of the Right-wing of the Party is appallingly low ...

I therefore make the following recommendations ...

Hugh's writing, never the easiest to read, became nearly indecipherable as he scribbled furiously on the margins, sometimes driven to elementary protest: 'Rot!' 'Really!!'

Meanwhile the Catlings moved into Hobury Street and hung the curtains the mother's help had made in the Earls Court attic. My father wanted to pay for his grandchildren's education, and Sheila was at a private school a short bus-ride away. Ellen-Craig was four years old by now. Patrick didn't like the idea of his wife going out to work. On the other hand, though his salary at *Punch* had gone up, so had his caprice in its disposal. When he agreed that a second earner was essential, he said: 'Always apply at the top,' telling me how to spell John Junor's surname. Junor was editor of the *Sunday Express* and we'd met, Patrick was certain, at a recent *Spectator* party. I wrote to Mr Junor, referring to our meeting, and asked if I could come to see him to discuss writing for his paper. He wrote back to say he'd not been to a *Spectator* party in years, but if I rang his secretary, she would arrange an appointment.

At the appointed hour, I did my best to implant the strong impression that I was a free-lance writer much in demand by American magazines and on that account uncertain that I could meet the *Sunday Express*'s requirement that its staff write for it alone. Whether John Junor believed me I do not know, but a week or two later his features editor rang to ask me to write an article about holidays. Patrick helped me. The result was published the following Sunday, and I was then offered a contract whose terms of pay I managed to push up by 80 per cent on the grounds of my reluctance to give up my earnings from American journals. In 1960 I began my first job as a journalist.

As my husband's surname, my father's surname, my mother's surname were familiar bylines, I didn't want to ride on their coat-tails. I called myself Susan Barnes, using what Americans call their middle name – often a surname that events have curtailed.

If family or friends were visiting London, the Catlings usually asked Tony to come round to Hobury Street and put himself out. Once clear what was required, he never let us down. Also, he particularly liked Americans. I found him a helpful guest. This view was not widely shared. Others found that unless his interest was caught he withheld himself or, far worse, made a conscious effort at sociability, thereby reducing a conversation until then cheerful to strained discomfort.

Eddie Shackleton, a Labour life peer, described to me the costs and benefits of having Tony as a guest: 'You knew he would bring a special intellectual quality. The trouble was you had no idea whether he'd be extremely reserved, or charming, or behave frightfully badly. I liked having pretty girls at my parties. Unlike some men, Tony felt no need to imprint his personality upon every woman in the room. He somehow managed to establish a situation where they, not he, sought to please. But if he was attracted to one of them, in no time at all he and she would depart and that was the last to be seen of them.

'At a party after the 1959 defeat, he went round the room and asked every single person present how they'd voted. When my young cousin said she'd voted Conservative, he was so rude to her that I later found her weeping. I suppose she may also have minded the fact that he went off with some other girl. A few weeks after that my wife found another young relation with tears falling down *her* face, *The Future of Socialism* on her lap. She was so besotted with Tony that she was trying to read his books. She'd never read political theory before.'

In the spring of 1960, after long, sad indecision, neither of us willing to accept that the marriage had failed, Patrick moved out of Hobury Street. My job made it possible – just – to afford a trial separation. The next day I dyed my hair pink, not then a common-place hue. Quite prepared to let various males provide opera and theatre tickets and meals rather more sumptuous than those that the children and the mother's help and I ate at Hobury Street, in other respects I was notably unreceptive. When pressed as to whether there was someone in my life, I replied: 'What an impertinent question.'

->- 11 -<-

Comrades in Arms

It was still spring 1960. At a pub near Westminster, Tony and Bill Rodgers met for a drink. Bill, just completing a six-year stint as General Secretary of the Fabians, was one of those stirred by *The Future of Socialism*. He had shared Tony's attraction to some Bevanite policy, though Bill didn't care much for the Bevanites' personalities. On the issue of unilateral disarmament Nye himself was opposing the Left. He said: 'We cannot go naked into the conference chamber.' In 1960 Nye was dying from cancer. Most of his followers disregarded their hero's advice. They'd routed Gaitskell over Clause IV and were out to finish him off, 'Ban the Bomb' their rallying cry.

Was it not possible, Bill asked, to get some sort of continuous liaison among Centre and Right activists in the Party, from members of the PLP to candidates and key workers in the constituencies? Why should it be only the extreme Left that fired its members at all levels with a sense of purpose? Thus began the Campaign for Democratic Socialism.

Of the original thirteen members of CDS, four were MPs, the rest journalists, local councillors, and little-known parliamentary candidates; all were highly articulate. The manifesto was discussed in several long sessions, Tony and Philip Williams doing the drafting. The growing pressure to topple Gaitskell made CDS more of a defence of his leadership than its sponsors had at first intended, for if Gaitskell fell, the Party was bound to swing sharply to the Left. He did not fall, and CDS played a major role in bringing the Centre of the Party back together with the leadership. It took the greater part of eighteen months.

Bill Rodgers had heard a fair bit about Tony's dilettante reputation in the House. He was now introduced into the work compartment, which he described (early in 1964) in his notes on CDS:

Throughout the period of preparation before the launching of the Campaign, Tony Crosland's role was crucial. Not only did he give the intellectual lead reflected in the Manifesto: he also showed a single-mindedness of purpose and discipline which most of us had previously believed he had not possessed. It was he who kept us at it when we met, mainly at his flat, refusing, for example, to let us have a drink until we had done three hours' solid work. He had the authority to keep us together and although he in no way dominated the group, he gave it a lead without which much less would have been done.

The campaign kept sympathetic members in touch with one another in the unions and constituency parties, helping with propaganda material, political advice, draft resolutions. Above all it reassured Gaitskell's grassroot supporters that they were not isolated; it stopped them dropping out of political activity.

Tony greatly enjoyed CDS. He liked teamwork. His organisational role, as he saw it, was to get things off the ground. Once CDS was going, he left the detailed running of it to others and concentrated on two different functions: forward planner ('apart from the fact that you usually reject my plans!' he wrote to Gaitskell) and ideological aggressor ploughing as wide a field as his articles and speeches could reach.

He took only a week's break that summer and was grim when he wrote: 'A middle-aged conservatism, parochial and complacent, has settled over the country.' In the essays published as a book called *The Conservative Enemy*, it was the Left and Right of his own Party that he was addressing under that title.

On 1 September 1960 he wrote a short letter to Gaitskell:

My long letters have no effect, so this is a very short one!!

The events of the last year have proved two things. (1) We were wrong (*all* of us) to go for *doctrine*; we should have gone for *power*. (2) In the present bloody-minded state of the Party, you alone + Hampstead group + occasional T.U. leaders are not strong enough to force through major changes.

The conclusion must be that (1) next year we must go for power, & (2) you need systematic alliances.

I therefore think that after Conference you should invite Brown, Wilson & Callaghan for a talk, & say roughly this: Let's forget our disagreements over Cl. 4 – that's all water under the bridge. But we're all intelligent enough to realise that major changes are needed if the Party is ever to win another election. Are you prepared to join me in a collective systematic effort to get: (1) ... (2) ... (3)

... (4) ... (5) ... The aims of course are old; what is new is the view that we shan't *achieve* any of them without (disagreeable tho' it may be) an open alliance with the next 3 leading men in the Party (or such of them as are willing to play).

In Gaitskell's five-page, single-spaced reply setting out in detail how he saw the next twelve months, he said of that particular suggestion:

(4 SEPTEMBER 1960) The three people cannot really be regarded as just rational human beings, each principally interested in winning the next Election. They are all able and talented, but they are *not* like that! A discussion with them at present on the lines you suggest would be inhibited by an unwillingness to speak frankly in front of each other or even to me. There is no need for me to explain why – you must surely understand this since you know them well and the circumstances of the moment. It would not even be safe for me to speak frankly to them – one could not rule out the risk that one or other might use this against us in the present struggle. The attitude of at least one of them in this is by no means clear and may well be hostile ...

So much for that tactical approach. Tony switched to another. On 3 October, just as the 1960 conference at Scarborough began, an American magazine, the *New Leader*, published a long article in which he argued that a narrow victory for Gaitskell's leadership might be worse than an initial defeat. 'The Left-wing constituency militants would then simply redouble their efforts. The party would face exactly the same damaging crisis next year and the year after. Moreover, it would be quite apparent to the country that the victory rested solely on manipulation of one of the big unions' block votes.' If, however, Gaitskell lost, stood for re-election as leader as an avowed supporter of NATO and opponent of neutralism, he 'would no doubt be challenged by some rival (perhaps Harold Wilson) fighting on the conference platform. We should then have, for the first time in the party's history, a direct confrontation of the Parliamentary group and the conference. From the resulting crisis and confusion there might, eventually, emerge a much-altered, radical Labour party attuned to the reality of the 1960s.' Sparks flew. (Three weeks later the *Daily Express* reported yet another rowdy meeting of MPs, during which Tony denounced Left-wingers for hawking his piece in the *New Leader* 'around the House of Commons tea room ... like a dirty postcard'.)

At conference Gaitskell was narrowly defeated by the Left on the issue of unilateral nuclear disarmament. He decided not to resign but to fight to reverse the decision – 'fight and fight and fight again to save the Party we love'. Fifteen days later Wilson challenged Gaitskell for the leadership.

The next letter in Gaitskell's Crosland file was written the following day, 21 October 1960:

These are my immediate reactions to the Wilson decision: (1) *Object*. In the next 10 days, we have one single over-riding object: to make sure that his vote is as low as possible, and yours as high as possible. Our possibilities over the next 12 months will depend entirely on this; & to achieve this we must resort to any degree of chicanery, lying, etc. etc.

Most of this was characteristic hyperbole, but Tony was prepared to use methods for a collective purpose which he was temperamentally unable to employ when his own personal advantage was at stake. '(2) *Tactics* ...' the letter went on.

Gaitskell defeated Wilson's challenge, 166 to 81 votes. The following week Tony produced the systematic planning paper he'd been asked for: the objectives the leadership must pursue before conference a year later and the objectives after that conference. First came the task of reversing the Scarborough decision in favour of unilateral disarmament. The leadership's defence policies had been much too detailed, he wrote:

(7 NOVEMBER 1960) The Tories never went into this degree of written detail ... The detail may at any time be rendered obsolete by new weapons or new strategic thinking; therefore we have to bring out frequent new policies, each causing endless argument and wasting an immense amount of valuable time. Again, the greater the detail, the stronger the pressure for compromise formulae and papering over the cracks ... And all these disadvantages are *unnecessary*, since we don't need a detailed policy while in Opposition ...

Isn't it possible for us to make more positive running on questions such as multilateral disarmament and the switch to a less nuclear strategy? Some of our difficulties would surely come out in the wash if we weren't always *defending* weapons, but were also consistently banging away for multilateral disarmament and for the necessary changes in our strategy ...

How to strengthen Gaitskell's personal position in the PLP and elsewhere? The letter went on:

Every party must have its extremist wing ... But our Left is clearly too numerous; it constantly pulls us towards the Left when the electorate is moving Right, it forces us into constant, damaging paper compromises, and generally it makes the Party virtually ungovernable ...

To see what should be done, let us (very crudely) analyse the Wilson vote into its component parts. (a) 10-15 genuine pacifists, who of course must be allowed to stay in the party. (b) 5 personal malcontents such as Shinwell and Ness Edwards. Too trivial to worry about. (c) 20 hard-boiled extreme Left ... This is the crucial group which must be expelled ... (d) 30 *New Statesmen* or ex-I.L.P. ... Many of these are intolerable and neurotic people who will always oppose us, but who nevertheless belong in the party and (if we could get rid of group c) would constitute a perfectly normal Left wing ... (e) 10-15 people, Left of Centre, who voted Wilson on his 'unity and compromise' appeal, and because they think you lead the party from too far to the Right. (f) probably 20-25 people who voted *for* you, but reluctantly – for the reasons just mentioned ...

There's a limit to the amount of disaffection which any party can stand and still be successful in the country; to rely always on the T.U. hatchets is absolutely fatal electorally in the long run ...

I therefore think it vital, before next year's election to the leadership, to seduce some of group (d), to win over group (e) completely, and of course to consolidate group (f). THE CRUCIAL TASK FOR THE NEXT YEAR IS TO ISOLATE THE EXTREME LEFT AND WIN BACK OR CONSOLIDATE THE LEFT–CENTRE.

He lists Wilson supporters with whom Gaitskell should make contact: 'if you can't do this, hateful as it is, you have no right to be a political leader!' One he named was Tony Benn:

Benn (who incidentally voted for you against Bevan in 1955) is a more controversial case; but I can personally see nothing against consulting him on the whole question of public relations, propaganda and reform of the machine, on which he holds quite enlightened views . . . Of course he's a hopeless neurotic; but he could be won back – and this whole field of reform is a crucial one . . .

Lastly, an obvious enough point . . . Every selection for a Labour seat must now be treated *as a major operation*. We have often let seats go by default in the past; we must never do so again.

A distinct note in the Crosland file was the over-rating of the far Right of the Labour Party. 'Of course the morale of the Right is important too. But the militant Right is much smaller than one often thinks.'

At about this same time in November, I wrote a long letter to my parents about my separation from Patrick. Aware how distressed they would be for the children and him and me, for six months I'd written to them each week without mentioning that Patrick was no longer at Hobury Street. While waiting for a reply, I began having stabbing pains in my stomach. Anxiety often expressed itself in my stomach. I imagined the increasingly spectacular spasms must be psychosomatic.

On his way to King's Cross station on a Friday morning, Tony stopped by Hobury Street to lend me his car while he was in Grimsby for the weekend. The second-hand Buick transported across the Atlantic along with the Catlings had been sold within months of our resettlement in London. The No. 11 bus was my usual transport to the *Sunday Express*. While discussing when I would return his car, I was seized by such pain that to ease it I had to squat on my own front steps.

'Why on earth don't you go to a doctor? Haven't the slightest sympathy for someone who complains and then refuses to do anything about it.'

My GP was away when I called in at the morning surgery. The locum said he didn't think it was psychosomatic: 'It may be a twisted colon. If it persists, come back.'

Determined to finish my article before leaving the *Sunday Express* – my editor excused me from Saturday attendance if I finished my work on Friday – I extracted from colleagues the supplies of Alka-Seltzer saved for their moments of gastric discomfort. By the end of the afternoon the pain was more than bad. Driving back through the rain to Hobury Street, I was caught in a traffic jam and before I got out of it my appendix evidently burst.

The children and the mother's help were informed which hospital I'd been taken to. Morphine, then shock, made me such a docile patient on my trolley in Casualty that it was eight hours before the registrar realised an operation was overdue, acute peri-tonitis far advanced. Was there someone, he asked, apart from my young children, who could be contacted? I said I hadn't any other family in this country, but perhaps he could ring Mr and Mrs Gaitskell. I told him their telephone number.

When Hugh walked into the ward on the Saturday morning, I was aware of his unhappiness. Almost certainly the healthy person worries unduly that the desperately ill are tormented by mental anguish about the welfare of their young children and so on. In my experience, one's energies are so concentrated on dealing with the physical pain that surprisingly little concern is left over for anything else.

When it was possible to leave hospital, Tony and Hugh drove me home. Mary Gottardo, the mother's help, set up a little table in my bedroom for them to have the lunch she'd prepared. It was during my long confinement in this bedroom that I read Edmund Gosse's *Father and Son*: someone had told me it was about Gosse's upbringing in the Plymouth Brethren, and I'd asked a friend to get it for me. Tony never discussed his own upbringing among the Brethren.

The doorbell rang. The English and Italian voices cordially exchanged courtesies. How was Mary? How was Mr Crosland? How was Mrs Catling getting on? He came up to my first-floor bedroom. Any exchange of courtesies between us was cut short when he saw the book on my bedside table.

'Why don't you mind your own bloody business?'

I watched him deciding whether to turn on his heel and go down the stairs again. After hesitation, he went over to the table where Mary had set up a drinks tray and poured himself a whisky. 'If you must probe into my upbringing, I suppose I might as well tell you about it.'

He talked for more than an hour in a quiet flow of recollections, acknowledging their significance, calmly stubbing out one cigarette and lighting another. When he finished, he said: 'I feel better.' He sounded surprised. Thenceforth he referred to his Exclusive Brethren childhood with casual forbearance, sometimes almost fondly, as a trying but intrinsic part of his past with which he now felt at ease. He seemed always to have been at ease with the non-puritan side of his nature – the hedonistic side.

Most of 1961 was devoted to the campaign to reassert Gaitskell's authority over the Party. A recurrent theme in the Crosland file was most unwelcome to the Leader: Tony thought that in having to concentrate on the fight against the Left, Gaitskell had allowed his speeches to sound conservative. In the planning paper of 7 November 1960 he wrote to Gaitskell:

We must face the fact that the impression has got around – and, alas, I myself largely share it – that the middle class leadership of the party (yourself, Gordon Walker, Soskice, etc.) is leading from an extreme and rather rigid Right-wing position, and has no emotional desire to change any major aspect of the society in which we are living. The element of radicalism and discontent, which even the most moderate Left-wing party must possess, seems lacking; even Kennedy sounds more radical than we do.

He suggested Gaitskell get some help for his speeches from the head of the research department at Transport House, Peter Shore, who had backed Wilson in the recent leadership election. 'As a pleasant irony, you could get Peter Shore to prepare large chunks of them – he would do it very well.'

Gaitskell put ticks or queries or comments down the margins of the planning papers and sent photocopies back to Tony. Alongside the latest rebuke of the leadership Hugh wrote in reply: 'It's you who are looked on as *Right* wing not I!' This whole matter had become a sore subject, not just for its criticism of Gaitskell's style of politics; it also related to a private argument that stood between him and his self-appointed chief of staff.

In middle age, as Leader of the Opposition, Gaitskell's political power attracted a glamorous London world he'd not previously encountered. He'd always enjoyed dancing. Now he began in his private life to enjoy occasional dancing with fashionable Tories, absolutely clear that their values could not erode his. Tony didn't for an instant imagine Gaitskell being entrapped – à la Ramsay MacDonald – in the aristocratic embrace, but he feared Hugh's left-wing convictions might be subtly softened in an indirect way by these pastimes. Hugh, naturally enough, resented the reproofs. I sided with him – not that my view made the slightest difference.

'What about your own Duke's Daughters Period?' I said to Tony. The expression was his own, designating a short phase in his earlier years when he consorted with several of the nobility's more wayward offspring. Having dipped into their world, seen what it was about, he became impervious to its attractions. He felt not guilty but a trifle sheepish about this period.

'Lamentable. I was, however, twenty years younger than Hugh is now. And I was not Leader of the Labour Party.'

'Well, what is he meant to do in the tiny bit of time he has to relax? Would you prefer him to go to the Stork Club for his dancing? Or perhaps go to bed with some little actress?' In those days the Stork Club, located in a narrow lane just off Piccadilly, flourished by virtue of a discriminating seediness; the diversity of the clientele allowed privacy impossible to find in smarter night-clubs. It was much favoured by intellectuals when inebriated.

'If you must make these debating points, I'll explain why there actually is a basic difference. Going to bed with some little actress, as you so prettily say, is hardly likely to affect one's political standpoint. If you choose to associate, as Hugh does, with intelligent people whose political values are the opposite to your own, an insidious erosion of your political values can occur. I mightn't think that if I hadn't seen what's happened to Roy.'

Somewhat irritably Tony and Hugh agreed to disagree, on the understanding that Tony did not have to hear from Hugh about his very infrequent socialising with these Tories. When some people from Oxford told Gaitskell that All Souls was offering Crosland a fellowship to write a book about British government, Hugh said: 'Splendid idea. He'd be admirable at that. You must get him.' He thought they'd said Crossman. He then realised they meant Crosland. 'Good God. You can't have him. I need him.'

In the autumn of 1961 Gaitskell won his conference battle to reverse the unilateral disarmament policy. His authority was restored. The Left-Centre of the PLP was won back, the extreme Left entirely isolated. A handful of MPs had the Whip temporarily withdrawn, but there was no need for expulsions. Increasingly friend and foe accepted that he would be Britain's next prime minister; a year later, no one had any doubts.

✦12✦

An Ending

Late one evening in 1961, more than a year since Patrick and I had
separated, he called at Hobury Street unexpectedly. From adolescence he'd been a fan of Peggy Lee. She was completing a series of
jazz concerts in Europe, after which she and Patrick were going to
her home in Los Angeles. They would like to marry. Mexico, as
well as conveniently placed on the other side of California's border,
issued divorce certificates like autumn leaves. Was this OK with
me?

No one was clear whether a Mexican divorce was recognised in
England. Constantine FitzGibbon, a writer versed in matrimonial
difficulties, offered his advice: 'Let me give you the name of the
solicitor who handled my last divorce, Susan. A man of the
world, knows the ins and outs of international law. You'll like him.'

I did. At last this worldly man satisfied himself that as Patrick,
like me, was now an American citizen, the Mexican divorce was
acceptable; he wrote the pleasant news to Patrick's solicitor in Los
Angeles. Weeks passed. Months passed. It transpired that Patrick
and Peggy Lee, still the best of friends, were no longer keen on
marriage. For the first time I had a faint sense of limbo. My
solicitor suggested I take a turn, this time in a British court of law.
He would arrange for a petition to be filed.

Weeks passed. Months passed. I called upon my solicitor. His
New York partner had tried all his excellent contacts in Los Angeles. Unfortunately, none could discover where Peggy Lee, let
alone Patrick, was currently to be found.

'She's in New York,' I said.

'How do you know that? Have you heard from Mr Catling?'

'No. I read it in yesterday's *Daily Express*. It was in the William
Hickey column. It said she's singing at the Waldorf Astoria for
another week.'

While my solicitor's secretary searched out a copy of the previous
day's *Daily Express*, I suppressed a niggling doubt about this New
York partner.

'That's what it says. Extraordinary. Perhaps Mr Catling is also in New York. Do you know where he might be staying if he is there?'

'In the circumstances, I suppose he might be staying at the Waldorf Astoria.'

'Yes. People can become unco-operative, Mrs Catling, when they are suddenly served with a writ. I'd like to manage this another way. Has Mr Catling a club in New York?'

'What kind of club?'

'A club. A dining club. A men's club.'

'Oh. I've heard him speak of staying at something called a player's club. I don't suppose it's the kind of club you mean.'

'Excellent. My New York partner belongs to The Players. The old-boy network succeeds where all else fails. When two men belong to the same club, it's an easy matter for them to be in conversation at the bar. My New York partner will find some way to introduce this subject, put it to Mr Catling that the decent thing would be for him now to make a divorce uncomplicated. My partner won't actually say that the rest of the club will take it amiss if Mr Catling behaves badly, but it will be implicit.'

'Patrick's not all that susceptible to this old-boy thing. That's one of the reasons I like him.'

'My dear girl, you do not understand about Englishmen and their clubs. When you and I next meet, the problem will be resolved.'

We met a fortnight later. My solicitor looked uncomfortable. 'I'd better tell you straight away, Mrs Catling. My New York partner failed. He called in at The Players the same evening of the day I rang him. He asked the hall porter if Mr Catling happened to be present. The hall porter said Mr Catling had been asked never again to be present at The Players. There was a dispute in the bar the previous night, and I'm sorry to tell you that an unfortunate incident followed. It's frightfully bad luck. My partner only missed Mr Catling by twenty-four hours.'

Early in 1962 Big Hugh died. He'd had a severe stroke nearly three years before. Tony took trouble in visiting him and Ruth, bullying others to do so as well. After Dalton's death, Tony's friendship with Ruth continued.

1962 highlighted fresh divisions in the Labour Party. Until then the Common Market had evoked comparatively little interest among the comrades. Roy Jenkins, it was true, was always a passionate advocate of entering the Market. So now were Bill

Rodgers and others of Gaitskell's supporters. As an internationalist, Tony was emotionally in favour of entry, though sceptical of some of the arguments advanced by the enthusiasts. Rather suddenly the subject became a burning issue in the Party, and though it didn't polarise Left and Right, the Left wing was predominantly against entry.

A few days before the autumn conference, Tony wrote to Hugh: 'This is not of course a letter on the politics of Europe as to which every argument that could be used in recent days has been flogged to death.' Several pages followed, pros and cons set out. The letter concluded: 'None of this means that I think the present terms are adequate – only that a lot of study in the last ten days makes me think the odds are on the final terms being reasonable. NO REPLY!! Yrs. Tony (Crosland, not Greenwood).' Tony Greenwood was a leading left-wing anti-Marketeer. This was the last letter Hugh put in the Crosland file.

Three days later, in his conference speech, Gaitskell not only rejected entry into the Common Market on present terms, but rejected it in such emotive language – recalling British heroism at Gallipoli – that he ended by rallying the anti-Market forces. The pro-European Gaitskellites managed to produce a few ironic hand-claps when their Leader finished speaking, but it was with conspicuous lack of enthusiasm that they got to their feet to show loyalty. Bill Rodgers was even more conspicuous: outraged by the timing of Gaitskell's anti-Europe torpedo, he sat defiantly on his chair.

Two days later Tony departed for his long deferred visit to the United States on a grant, so he was not present when Gaitskell met with his aggrieved CDS supporters a week after conference. Hugh told them he thought the Common Market had nothing to do with the basic principles for which CDS stood. He had never felt strongly either way about Europe and in this he realised he differed from most of those present who felt a warmth towards Europe. He regarded the whole matter as a bore and a nuisance and it always had been. The discussion then ranged closely over manifold aspects of the Market problem. As the evening wore on, he showed increasing signs of weariness. A number of those present thought this reflected his regret that he'd been forced to take this stand on an issue about which he cared little.

December 1962 ushered in one of the coldest winters Britons could remember. Fire-engines fastened generators to mains pipes in an effort to unfreeze householders' water supply. In the middle of December Hugh went into hospital, then went home for

Christmas. Dora called in at Hobury Street with presents for Sheila
and Ellen-Craig; I was touched that she could think of these
children when anxious about her husband – though at that point
no one yet realised what was happening.

Tony went to see Hugh at Frognal Gardens, stayed two hours.
They argued about the Common Market. There was a lot to talk
about, Hugh recorded, and he – Hugh – was at fault, for trying to
bridge their differences over Europe. He found Tony's attitude
unconvincing and unsatisfactory precisely because Tony was very
anti-Federalist and didn't expect any political integration in foreign
policy and defence; Tony was not really very strongly pro on
economic grounds and yet counted himself in favour of Britain's
entry. A lot of it seemed to Hugh to be rationalising – not the first
time Tony arrived at an attitude emotionally and then rationalised
it. The conversation was 'properly amicable', but slightly irritating
for both men. Tony told me the same.

Roy went to see Hugh a day or two later. It was a short visit.
Hugh wrote that he found Roy's attitude on Europe more intelli-
gible than Tony's, though he disagreed with it more. He and Roy
talked on the basis of understanding the differences between them
rather than trying to bridge them. Hugh always found it easier to
avoid argument with Roy – less irritant and more desire to please
on both sides, he wrote.

I went to Frognal Gardens the day after that. Hugh was sitting
up against pillows in his and Dora's big bed; the slate-coloured
knitted shawl around his shoulders made his eyes look especially
blue. Where his neck showed in the folds of the shawl, it had that
falling away look. He returned to hospital at the beginning of
January. Ten days later his friends and the British public learned
that his condition was critical.

Sheila had received a radio for Christmas. Every news item gave
the latest report from the hospital. I flicked off the radio; I had to
do an interview with Kingsley Amis for the *Sunday Express*. We
hadn't met since the evening, six years earlier, when he and his wife
and his two ex-pupils from Swansea had tramped down the stairs
from 19 The Boltons following the disagreement about his gramophone records. Weeks earlier I'd arranged that we meet over lunch
at a Cypriot restaurant in the King's Road, where Hugh and Tony
– occasionally Hugh and I – used to have a quiet meal. The
restaurant was nearing the end of its existence, and as usual no one
else was present except the ancient patriarchal Cypriot who ran the
place. He wore a black suit so faded that one wondered when it

would disintegrate, but it was always carefully pressed, the frayed white shirt freshly laundered. He brought a tiny wireless over to my table, and we listened to the beginning of the one o'clock news. Mr Gaitskell had not responded to the kidney machine. His condition was deteriorating. The old man put a hand on my arm, then got out his handkerchief and wiped his eyes. Kingsley sauntered in. I made for the ladies' room, passing my guest without speaking. When I returned to the table, Kingsley said: 'You shouldn't be upset. I'm not that difficult to interview.'

After the children were in bed that night, Tony came round for supper. Mary Gottardo, the mother's help, asked to borrow Sheila's radio. We were glad of an excuse not to flick it on and off obsessively.

There was a knock on the drawing-room door and simultaneously Mary pushed it open. 'I've just heard it on the radio. Mr Gaitskell is dead.'

Later that night Tony paid tribute on television. It was unscripted, and one sentence, unnoticed by most in the emotional impact, dealt with the old argument between them: 'Whether he was a sufficiently radical leader for a left-wing party is another question.' Then he went on, 'But he was a leader. You had complete confidence in him. You trusted him. You knew absolutely where you were with him, and of how many other politicians in Britain at the moment could you say the same? Most of the others are dwarfs and pygmies beside him ... My last thought of this man is of his huge vitality, because he was immensely vital, he was as strong as an ox, he was as gay as a child, and it simply seems to me wrong that now he should be dead.'

The winter did not let up. The congregation of friends dispersed from Hampstead Parish Church into bone-chilling frost. Tony never talked much when he was driving. We were both silent.

'Do you suppose that man actually believes the things he said?' His voice was so sudden that I jumped.

'What man?'

'The vicar.'

We both looked silently through the windscreen. After a while he said, 'I wonder what Dora and Julie and Cressida felt when he put those unctuous questions?'

I glanced sideways at him. 'Which questions?'

As he said nothing further, concentrating on the road to keep from crying, I thought he was going to leave it at that, when all at once he repeated, stonily, the vicar's rhetorical questions: 'Death where is thy sting? Grave where is thy victory?'

The memorial service at Westminster Abbey was held while the winter kept its grip. Bill Rodgers always associated that service with the sight of Tony afterwards, wearing a long overcoat, striding rapidly down Victoria Street, by himself.

A couple of weeks later, I was with Tony on one of his visits to Dora. By then Cressida had returned to Oxford. Dora was in the drawing-room, its familiar sense of comfort gone. All the colours seemed drained. Tony sat in a chair near Dora, Julie on the arm of her mother's chair. Empathy enclosed all three. They talked about Dora's plans. Watching them from a little distance, outside their collective gallantry, I found compassion for these two women overwhelming. Upstairs I was restoring my face when Julie came in.

'Is there anything I can do, Susan?'

'It's ludicrous. Why should I go to pieces when you and Dora manage to be so dignified? I don't see how you bear it.'

'There's no alternative.'

⇥ 13 ⇤

Re-embarking

As is the custom, before Hugh Gaitskell's body was cold others were moving into position to determine who would succeed him. Most of the Gaitskellites, reeling, took a few days to pull themselves together. Early the next week several met at 19 The Boltons. The only thing on which they all agreed was that they would oppose Harold Wilson. Nobody considered him a dangerous left-wing leader; they were hostile because they considered him an opportunist, preoccupied with tactics, conservative. Even had they assessed his character less harshly, they could not have voted for him: he had challenged Hugh.

As Deputy Leader, George Brown was a major contender. He was visiting Herbert Morrison the night Hugh died. 'It's come too soon,' George said. 'I'm not ready for it.'

'Don't worry,' Morrison said. 'The Labour Party will never elect its leader from the working class.'

The difficulty with George was not his background: it was his volatility coupled with drink. Too many depressing instances of his eruptive nature had been witnessed. At first the Gaitskellites favoured Callaghan as their candidate and believed he could defeat Wilson in a straight fight. But with the Deputy Leader also standing, they doubted whether Callaghan could get through the first ballot.

Tony went to see George alone in his room at the House, told him that he would not finally make up his mind until the morning but expected to support Callaghan. He told George the reason. The following day George wrote to him:

Friday [25 JANUARY 1963]

Dear Tony,

    I was so glad you came & talked with me last night. I do hope I wasn't too vehement!

As you know, I, like you, care passionately about the *issues* involved in all this. I am deeply worried & anxious about the future. And it's very lonely with everybody telling me to 'keep quiet'!

Please keep in touch – good luck with your decision.
May God be kind to our movement at this moment.

Yours
George

The Gaitskellites went on meeting. Tony then called on Callaghan
and told him their collective view was that he'd be knocked off in
the first ballot. George Thomson urged Jim to stand whatever the
outcome, and that seemed to clinch Jim's decision. From then on
Callaghan's faction was led by Tony.

The Brownites argued that a three-way race would permit Wilson to establish a lead which, given voters' psychology, he was
bound to increase on the second ballot and win. (Most MPs did
not accept that the election system was devised expressly for the
purpose of allowing them to show their personal preference on the
first ballot, and then, their man knocked off, vote for their second
preference.) Callaghan's supporters argued that Brown couldn't
win in any circumstances: his temperament was too alarming.

Bill Rodgers, newly elected to Parliament, was a leading Brown-
ite. Tony liked Bill. He disliked the strong-arm methods, what he
called 'the gang mentality', when Bill, pressing his case, habitually
said: '*We* think . . .'

'*I* think . . .' Tony would reply to Bill, each of them smiling
faintly, angry.

The results of the first ballot were: Wilson 115, Brown 88,
Callaghan 41. In the second round Tony supported George; it was
emotionally impossible for him to vote for Harold Wilson, who
won the second ballot, 144 to 103 votes.

A few days later Philip Williams wrote a long letter to Tony
about how CDS should come to terms with the new Leader:

(27 FEBRUARY 1963) I think there may have been some misunderstanding last night about what Bernard Donoughue and I were
saying about our relations with Harold. Neither he nor I – nor I
imagine anyone – have ever conceived that relations with Harold
could exist as they did with Hugh (or might have with George
Brown if he had won). Obviously mistrust goes far too deep for
that. But we do think it not just necessary, but urgent, to decide
among ourselves what our attitude should be and then open communications – and soon.

Philip discussed the effect of Wilson's having already appointed a
senior Gaitskellite – Patrick Gordon Walker – as Shadow Foreign

Secretary. From the beginning Wilson, like any canny Leader, used his powers of patronage to win over individuals and at the same time disrupt the group to which they belonged by sowing personal dissension through his picking and choosing. Urging Tony to help heal a breach which might damage the Party, Philip's letter concluded:

Of course it will be a distasteful operation . . . I'd be very sorry, but not too surprised if you or some others dropped out of politics now; but if you stay in you have to take the world as it is and not as we'd like it to be (as we have so often said to the Left). This is not only my view but that of every CDS non-MP I've spoken to . . . Bernard Donoughue . . . and (I'm told) David Marquand . . .

Tony's reply was curt, declining to parley with Wilson.

Jim Callaghan and Tony became friends when both were protégés of Dalton. After Merlyn Rees won the South Leeds seat vacated on Gaitskell's death, Tony suggested that Callaghan ask Rees to be his PPS – Parliamentary Private Secretary. Jim wrote back: '. . . so I have talked to Merlin [sic] Rees & he seems to be thrilled to bits at the idea . . . So we are both pleased. What good advice you do give me!' This was not always Jim's view. Nevertheless, despite their dissensions, his friendship with Tony was pretty continuous, though it hadn't the complete openness that marked Tony's relationship with Gaitskell whatever their quarrels.

That autumn when the Labour Party held elections for its Parliamentary Committee – the Shadow Cabinet – Tony decided to stand for the first time. Bill Rodgers asked him not to, saying that Tony would get only four or five votes, which wouldn't do him any good and would otherwise go to Roy Jenkins. Tony ignored the advice, polling 72 votes to Roy's 64 – neither getting into the top twelve who then made up the Shadow Cabinet. Bill's unheeded advice was the first intimation that at least one of the disciples of *The Future of Socialism* saw his mentor's personal entry into practical politics as a threat to Roy. The concept came as a surprise.

1964 began. In February Tony and I were married at Chelsea Register Office. After Patrick had asked me for a divorce, Tony made his interesting proposal to which I responded with surprise and pleasure at his having thought of such a thing (consciously I hadn't considered the possibility); tears of regret (I didn't want to give up the oasis at 19 The Boltons); apprehension (marriage wouldn't work: he'd feel fenced in).

Some months later I came round to his view. Instantly he grew uneasy. The matter was left in abeyance until the day when I might actually be in a position to remarry. In time this came about – without publicity, owing to the fact that my worldly solicitor had satisfied himself that Peggy Lee really was christened Norma Egstrom and could be cited in the divorce courts under that homespun name.

'Perhaps the best thing,' Tony said, 'would be for you and the children to live at Sandwich and I come there at weekends. Most MPs' families live outside London.'

I loved Sandwich, but the coast of Kent lies a considerable distance from the London life which I also enjoyed. The No. 11 bus to Fleet Street paused one road away from Hobury Street. The No. 31 bus to the children's school actually had its terminus around the corner from Hobury Street. I brooded upon Tony's latest proposal.

'The thing has become hopelessly complicated. I have cleared my mind. We must stop seeing each other,' I said.

Miserable, disjointed, I tried to concentrate on children and journalism. When the telephone rang and it was some male who didn't remotely interest me, momentarily I hated the caller for being the wrong person. Five days passed. The telephone rang. It was Tony's voice: 'I'm coming round to Hobury Street in twenty minutes' time. You'd better be there. I don't like these unilateral decisions.'

Dora Gaitskell and Ruth Dalton were the witnesses at the Register Office. Tony extracted the ring from its velvet box and, without looking behind him, chucked the box towards a bench at the back of the room where Sheila and Ellen-Craig sat side by side in their best coats, the hems let down the previous day. My mother flew from Baltimore for the wedding. 'Otherwise, dear, someone might say we didn't think the marriage was suitable.'

The honeymoon covered the same terrain as Tony's first honeymoon – Gibraltar, Seville, Cordoba, Granada, Xerez – this time round successful. Our last stop was a little fishing port, where on the final day Tony wanted once more to walk through the hills overlooking the sea.

'Wouldn't you like to come too?' he said, making the mistake we all sometimes do when we issue an invitation in the belief that the other party will turn it down.

'That would be nice,' I replied.

After some hundreds of yards, I grew conscious of a looming silence and glanced up to observe what Sheila called 'Tony beetling the brow, pressing the lips'. Grasping that my company was unwanted – it implied that he could never again be solitary – I turned smartly on my heel and returned to our sunny balcony, where I was reclining comfortably when he returned later in the morning. ('Since that last day at Nerja, it has required all my persuasion to induce you to take a walk with me again,' he observed for the next thirteen years.)

He moved body and other essentials into Hobury Street, retaining his own flat in The Boltons while I looked for a larger house. We'd assumed there would be a certain asymmetry in the marriage – that he would once in a way benefit from an 'adventure', without any disadvantage for anyone else. He was forty-five and hadn't tried to convince either of us that his promiscuity had altogether run its course. Escape hatches were constructed in advance. Until we found a house with a study and two bathrooms, we would live at Hobury Street, but on Sunday nights he would return to 19 The Boltons. 'Nowhere else to keep one's books. Must get things sorted out before Monday.'

He was too considerate of my feelings to contemplate an adventure with anyone I knew. (My Scottish psychiatrist friend, Eustace Chesser, sometimes despaired of human intelligence. 'Wives will put up with a husband who is a menace to family life. He can be a drunk, a brute. He can be unreliable, which is more destructive to a relationship than anything else. But if the best of husbands has a meaningless flirtation and his wife hears of it, she rushes to the divorce courts. Nothing whatsoever has suffered except her vanity, yet she insists on wrecking her life, wrecking her husband's life, wrecking her children's lives. The stupidity of the thing never ceases to astound me.') The precedent was already established that the children and I should return to Baltimore for the annual summer holiday. My vanity could hardly suffer if an adventure occurred thousands of miles away when Tony took his own August holiday in southern Europe.

'What about London?' I said.

'That's my problem, not yours.'

The existence of escape clauses in the understanding meant he didn't feel confined. It's hard to say which of us was more surprised when it turned out that the hatches weren't used.

The first night he went back to The Boltons proved the last. It was the middle of winter and the flat was freezing cold, the hot water turned off, a bottle of Vermouth standing bleakly in an otherwise empty drinks cupboard, not a trace of Nescafé to be found in the kitchen. 'No one looking at you would guess how cunning you are,' he said when he returned to Hobury Street in the morning before going on to the House of Commons. 'In principle you accede to poor old Toto retaining a fragment of his freedom. Then you make absolutely certain that his life will be so disagreeable when he returns to his bachelor flat that he never wants to go there again. It's not right.'

While waiting for the Tory Prime Minister, Sir Alec Douglas-Home, to choose an election date, the Opposition prepared itself. Harold Wilson intended setting up a second economic planning department to be at least as powerful as the Treasury. The Shadow Chancellor, Callaghan, would go to the Treasury, George Brown – runner-up for the leadership – would head the new department. Douglas-Home and his Chancellor, Reginald Maudling, gave permission for high-ranking civil servants to discuss the machinery of such a department in case Labour won.

Everyone knew that Wilson's face was set against devaluing the pound and that his personal economic adviser, Thomas Balogh, was also against it. Tony's overriding concern in the pre-election months was that the Shadow Chancellor be made to see that if Labour policies were not to be crippled, it was essential to promote economic growth, and this depended on devaluing sterling as soon as Labour came into office. It must be done at once to forestall international bankers creating a sterling crisis that could be very damaging to confidence in the Government.

Most economists sympathetic to Labour shared this view. One was Nicky Kaldor who was already earmarked to work for the Chancellor on taxation if Labour won. Another was Robert Neild; both Callaghan and Brown wanted him as a personal economic adviser.

In addition, there was Sir Donald MacDougall. In his professional life he deliberately avoided Party affiliation. In 1964, on leave from Nuffield College, Oxford, he was Economic Director of Neddy – the National Economic Development Council. Wilson asked him to join the new department – coming into the civil service proper virtually at the top – if Labour won. MacDougall agreed to do so. He was pro-devaluation.

He, Kaldor, Neild came to Hobury Street to talk with Tony

throughout 1964. The four men separately put the case to Callaghan numerous times. MacDougall put the case to Brown.

During these same months, Callaghan had cheerfully agreed to seminars on economic policy. Tony had asked Ian Little – then a Fellow of Nuffield College where Jim was a Visiting Fellow – if Ian could arrange a set of special seminars. In London, Robert Neild arranged further seminars for the Shadow Chancellor. Callaghan listened to the argument for devaluation but was deadpan.

⤜ 14 ⤛

Bang, It Was Done

Late on a Thursday night in October 1964, as the contents of the ballot boxes were being separated in Grimsby Town Hall, the Labour candidate strolled casually round, talking with his Party workers. To his second bride he said quietly: 'Don't give the bloody Tories the pleasure of knowing you're nervous.' I tried to simulate his nonchalance.

The Town Clerk sternly admonished Labour supporters to make less noise: they could see how the count was going. This time their candidate won by something over 4,000 votes. I felt sorry for the Tory candidate, a decent local fish-merchant, whose supporters were silent, their remaining hope being that the rest of the country might return a Conservative Government for the fourth consecutive time.

Everyone woke on Friday, 16 October to discover the overall outcome unknown. I shoved clothes into a suitcase. We called on Lill Bontoft, who never now went to a count. (She and I had accepted one another and become friends.) Then Tony and I set off on the four-hour drive to London. The Sunbeam was a nice car, but it lacked a radio. At Lincoln we stopped at the inn overlooking the cathedral, for once ignoring ecclesiastical architecture as we ate our sandwich lunch in an upstairs room which contained a television set. Just after 2.30 p.m. the result came in that gave Labour an overall majority.

While we'd been driving from Grimsby to Lincoln, Whitehall was suspended in a limbo of its own. During the three weeks that politicians were electioneering, civil servants in every department prepared two briefs – identical in facts about the state of the nation, differing in conclusions. Civil servants can read election manifestos as well as anyone else: alternative advice must be ready. One brief was red, the other blue.

The red brief was the larger: it had to include plans for Harold Wilson's second economic department to vie with the Treasury, 'creative tension' being the idea. The new empire would be called the Department of Economic Affairs – DEA. Sir William Armstrong was not the only civil servant to wonder if Wilson might have conceived the DEA to divide and rule his two strongest colleagues. Armstrong, then Permanent Secretary at the Treasury, had seen enough comings and goings to encourage this thought.

At 9.30 that Friday morning, Tom Caulcott turned up smartly in the Chancellor's Private Office where, as No. 2 Private Secretary, he shared a desk with Ian Bancroft, the Principal Private Secretary, the two men sitting on opposite sides of this enormous piece of furniture. Caulcott never forgot the scenes that followed:

'By the way, Tom,' Bancroft said, 'if Labour wins the election and if George Brown is Secretary of State at DEA and if he'll have you, we propose that you go there as Principal Private Secretary.' Tom Caulcott was flabbergasted.

At 2.47 p.m., when Labour's majority was announced, it was as if at that moment a wall was set up across the desk. Treasury papers came to Bancroft and not to Caulcott.

'Right,' said Caulcott to himself. He quietly commandeered a copy of the enormous red brief intended for Callaghan. He still had a set of keys to the Chancellor's boxes. He kept them. He had to act in a buccaneering role, he said to himself. He knew that offices further down the same building had been kept empty just in case Labour won and the new DEA was set up. What state they were in he didn't know. He found teams of men in overalls frantically decorating offices deficient in the fundamentals. He got on to the Ministry of Works: 'You will by tomorrow have finished the decoration, and the Post Office will have installed some telephones.'

He returned to the Chancellor's Private Office to clear out his possessions from the desk shared with Bancroft until less than two hours ago. 'This is going to strain our relationship,' Caulcott said. Bancroft then let him take one secretary – a Diary Secretary.

Caulcott had never met George Brown in his life. He now knew that Sir Eric Roll was to be Permanent Secretary at DEA. But where on earth was Roll? Two days before he was living in Washington, D.C. as Britain's representative on the International Monetary Fund.

By Friday evening everyone knew Harold Wilson had been to the Palace. Caulcott was still sitting in the Chancellor's Private Office, no one talking to him. By 6.30 he'd discovered the telephone number of the Browns' flat near Marble Arch. George's secretary answered.

'Is Sir Eric Roll there?'

He came to the phone.

'Look, Eric, I don't know whether there is a DEA, but if there is, I have a set of papers that the Secretary of State ought to read tonight.'

After a pause, the mellifluous Brown voice came on the line, unmistakable in its capacity to range over an octave in one sentence, favouring the higher end of the scale when under stress. 'Who are you?' demanded this voice.

'I'm Tom Caulcott. I've been proposed to run your Private Office. I have some work you ought to get on with.'

'You'd better come up.'

Jim Callaghan didn't rush to return from his Wales constituency. He had his Party workers to thank. Cardiff is a long way from London. Ordinarily the brief prepared for the Chancellor is intended for him alone. It doesn't even go to the Prime Minister unless the Chancellor requests it. How should Jim have known that the Chancellor's brief was being handed round George Brown's flat?

By Friday evening the flat was like the cabin in the Marx Brothers film. Tom Caulcott was giving out envelopes marked SECRET to those in the crush who had been cleared for security. Two economists, Robert Neild and Thomas Balogh, were in the crush; both expected to be made temporary civil servants. Caulcott took Neild into the bathroom to give him his envelope: Tommy Balogh hadn't yet been cleared by security and mustn't have his feelings hurt (though Caulcott relented later in the evening and let Tommy have a SECRET envelope too).

At the Treasury, waiting for Callaghan, Sir William Armstrong received a telephone call from Sir Eric Roll at George Brown's flat. Sir Eric had rung to say they had a copy of the Chancellor's brief. Already well on the way to becoming the most powerful civil servant Whitehall has known, Armstrong could still be startled. He was. The Chancellor, he pointed out, had not yet clapped eyes on his brief. A few minutes later No. 10 rang Armstrong and asked for the Chancellor's brief. 'It's hard to say no to the Prime Minister,' Armstrong said, 'so we coughed it up.'

In the United States, two months elapse between the election of a President and his taking office: he has time to calm down, reflect a bit. Even in France a fortnight is allowed between charging round the hustings and deciding on one's Cabinet. The British system results in men taking decisions with all the adrenalin still rocketing through them, before they've had a night's sleep, let alone two days in which to unwind.

When Callaghan at last got back from Cardiff that Friday night, his Permanent Secretary was waiting at No. 11 to give the Chancellor his brief, now read by a good many others. Armstrong was against devaluation; the brief argued against devaluation. Armstrong also had a message that the PM wanted a meeting later that night. 'No one was to be present but the three of them – Harold, George, Jim. We were led to believe that the futures of the economists – Tony Crosland and Robert Neild – were to be discussed,' Armstrong told me when he reconstructed these events. He remained in No. 11 with Callaghan who was waiting to be called next door. In came George Brown with his Permanent Secretary, Sir Eric Roll, and his other senior official, Sir Donald MacDougall.

George Brown said: 'I don't know when the boss will call us in. We might as well settle what we're going to say about devaluation.'

Armstrong said: 'We thought you were meeting to discuss the appointment of economists.'

George said: 'That's just a cover.'

George Brown was against devaluation because he said the trade unions would not like it, Armstrong said, continuing his account: 'Donald argued that without devaluation, Labour's growth plans would be wrecked. He could see that the one moment to devalue was the first day in the coming week. He was told to shut up. Jim said little.

'Then George and Jim were summoned into No. 10. It was a long discussion, and after a time a message was sent out saying we needn't wait. That's when they did it. The devaluation decision was over in a flash – on Friday night. There was no great debate. Bang, it was done.'

When the meeting between the three Ministers broke up that night, Sir Eric Roll was informed of the decision. He rang MacDougall at home to tell him. MacDougall was dismayed.

On Saturday morning the Prime Minister and his two colleagues were accompanied by their Permanent Secretaries at the formal meeting held in the Cabinet Room. Armstrong described it. The Prime Minister began: 'We three have decided that the exchange rate should stay where it is.'

'We went on from there,' Armstrong said. 'Although the Treasury brief had argued against devaluation, I don't think any of us influenced Harold. I think he was determined to avoid having "The

Labour Party is the Party of Devaluation" hung around his neck. He was determined to kill the myth that Labour squandered money, didn't have the confidence of bankers. He was going to put that myth right.'

Later on Saturday more ministerial appointments were settled and the division of economists dealt with. Crosland would go to George Brown as No. 2 at DEA, Robert Neild would go to Callaghan as a temporary civil servant. 'It was a trade-off of a kind,' Armstrong said. 'At the Treasury we wondered whether it was Harold bent on divide-and-rule. Tony had championed Jim in the leadership election. If two people are friendly, you'd better separate them. It also could have been that George wanted all the re-enforcement he could get. If Tony was with Jim, George would have had Crosland and the Treasury faced against him.'

Meanwhile at Hobury Street on Saturday, Tony decided he'd stay in earshot of the telephone. He thought there was a fair chance of being No. 2 to the Chancellor, and he knew there'd been talk that George Brown wanted him. He also knew that others questioned whether he would be offered any office in a Wilson Government: during the leadership contest he was an extremely outspoken critic of Wilson.

'I wonder how many people are sitting round just like this, waiting for a telephone call,' he said as I set out for the newsagent at the corner where King's Road bends.

World's End contained a mix of the working classes who'd lived there for generations and the middle classes who took over houses as the old leaseholds expired (the poignant alteration of a neighbourhood known as gentrification). A middle-class, middle-aged, corpulent man with large moustache and deep-hued complexion, probably a bit deranged at the best of times, had lost all control and was bawling at the newsagent.

'Mark my words, they'll be begging us to come back in a few weeks' time. Socialist cowards! Yellow-bellied *cowards!* They'll be crawling on their knees, the way they did before. They'll be crying for us to come back. You'll see.'

The newsagent winked at me. I went home with the newspapers.

When the telephone rang I answered. George Brown's voice said: 'It's the Pope. May I speak with your husband?'

To Tony he said: 'Economic Secretary. Minister of State. Department of Economic Affairs. Can you and Susan come round tonight?'

That afternoon Nicky Kaldor and Robert Neild came to Hobury Street. The three men were in passionate agreement: whoever got at Callaghan or Brown first would say that the crucial thing was to devalue the pound immediately. They knew that if that was done, the onus would be placed where it belonged – on the previous Government. What they didn't know was that the decision had already been taken.

That evening, on our way to the Browns' flat, Tony said: 'It's essential I have a word alone with George. Harold's bound to feel the psychological need to announce policy on Day One next week. It's imperative to persuade George and Jim to hold the argument before deciding about devaluation.'

The flat was near Marble Arch; we'd not been there before. George swung open the door. In his wine-red velvet smoking jacket, exuding self-confidence, expansive in the role of beneficent host, he was pouring out drinks when Tony mentioned that after George rang him earlier, he – Tony – had spoken on the telephone with Jim Callaghan about the broad division of functions between the two economic departments. George's mouth turned into an 'O', his eyes popping until he found his voice, which emerged in a shriek.

'*Treason!*'

The long harangue began. I think he was genuinely shocked. Tony pointed out that he understood the Treasury and DEA were to co-operate, that he couldn't possibly accept the job without mentioning it to Jim.

'*Treason!* Back-stabber! I'll have to re-think the whole thing. How could any man *do* such a thing?'

Tony's face was like a weather-map. The outlook was bad, rapidly worsening, when Roy Jenkins and Bill Rodgers turned up with their wives. Both men had been close associates of Brown since the attempt to win the leadership for him after Gaitskell's death. Sophie Brown ambled in and out, apparently oblivious to her husband's volume of sound. His denunciation of the traitor went on unabated.

Silvia Rodgers, a woman of spirit, said: 'George, do you think this is the way a man should talk to his friends?'

George calmed down. Somewhat unfortunately, Tony was so nettled by now that each time the First Secretary of State began to talk rationally about what DEA should do first, the proposed Minister of State said:

'I must excuse myself long enough to telephone Jim and tell him that. Where did you say you keep your telephone?'

The First Secretary of State literally shot up in the air again.

As this routine appeared to be going on for ever, my curiosity and amusement dwindled. To my fury, tears of outrage began to fill my eyes. I concentrated on fitting a cigarette into the eleven-inch holder I used in those days, fixed my eyes on the ceiling, waiting for the wretched tears to go back from where they'd come.

'If this is what one has to put up with, to hell with George and the job and the lot,' I said to Jennifer Jenkins who was sitting beside me on the sofa. I kept my eyes fixed on the ceiling and didn't get up and leave, sorely tempting as it was to a novice.

On our way home I learned of the far more serious, violent altercation that had occurred privately between the two men. George told Tony the decision had already been taken not to devalue the pound and the subject was never, *never* to be raised again. Tony was horrified and angry. By the time we reached Hobury Street, he was acutely depressed as well, saying he'd make up his mind about the job in the morning.

As in other Labour households, that Sunday at Hobury Street was not a day of rest. The telephone refused to stop ringing. People came and went. Nicky Kaldor got through on the telephone, his voice melancholy. He'd just been stitched up in hospital following a motor accident. His car had overturned. His mind had been on devaluation instead of the fact that he was about to drive across a one-way thoroughfare. He'd been to see Callaghan the night before and learned the same thing that Tony had learned from Brown. Nicky had told Callaghan that such a decision shouldn't be taken after virtually no sleep. 'Tony and Robert Neild and I are in agreement that the whole Labour Party policy is jeopardised if we don't devalue now,' Nicky said to Callaghan.

'If you want to work for me, you must not argue against things that have already been decided,' Callaghan said to Kaldor.

So Nicky agreed to work for the Chancellor as a temporary civil servant – on taxation policy only. On Sunday Callaghan rang Robert Neild, who also agreed to go to the Treasury, though appalled that the three men at the top had taken the crucial decision in the excitability of three children at a birthday party.

⇢ 15 ⇠

A Department Is Born

Throughout Whitehall on the Monday morning, civil servants ceremoniously welcomed their new masters, none of whom had had experience of government for the past thirteen years. Most had not governed at all. Only the Department of Economic Affairs failed to make the transition smoothly, not having existed before.

Shortly before noon Tony left Hobury Street in the Sunbeam to call at No. 10 where the Prime Minister officially appointed him Economic Secretary to the Treasury, this being the only way he could be paid a salary until Parliament reconvened and passed an Act enabling him to take his intended title of Minister of State at DEA.

Meanwhile in the offices at Storey's Gate, things weren't too good. True, there was some improvement over Saturday when George Brown had arrived there expecting to find a full Department in existence, the day printed for ever on Tom Caulcott's mind: 'Here was George, who legitimately believed his was the No. 2 job in the Government, finding he had Eric Roll, Donald Mac-Dougall and me. And one Diary Secretary.' Except for the First Secretary of State, who had a chair, everyone sat on the floor like buddhas. By Monday Caulcott, who'd hardly slept for three days, had got together a Private Office. He himself had tramped over to the Treasury, seized a typewriter from the Chancellor's Private Office, carried it away in his arms. But there still wasn't any DEA writing paper. The chaos was terrible, George erupting the whole time. Caulcott's nerves were strained. He felt a presence, wheeled to find a tall figure standing in the doorway, surveying the turmoil.

'Who are you?' demanded Caulcott.

'My name's Crosland.'

The Future of Socialism and *The Conservative Enemy* stood in the bookshelves in the Caulcott home. 'I'd seen many photographs of Tony Crosland,' Caulcott said. 'By then I knew he was coming to DEA – "Tony is coming" – and had an office organised for him with a Private Secretary. But such was the pressure that when he walked in I didn't recognise him at first.'

That night at Hobury Street the day's highlights were retailed for my entertainment, but largely Tony was preoccupied: he refused to accept that devaluation should be raised 'never, *never* again'. Balogh told me it was during that first week that the Prime Minister received from Tony a paper setting out why he strongly disagreed with the economic course that Wilson was pursuing. 'It was a very courageous thing to do,' Balogh remarked. 'People don't argue with prime ministers.'

By the beginning of the second week DEA had a reasonable stock of desks, chairs, typewriters, even writing paper, though the stress in the Secretary of State's Private Office did not appreciably diminish. After the empty boxes from the new writing paper had been lying round for two days, the Principal Private Secretary could stand it no longer.

'I'm going to throw them all out the window,' Tom Caulcott announced to the rest of Private Office who were preparing to go home, yearning for an evening's respite. He flung open the window on to St James's Park.

'You mustn't do that, Tom.'

'I've stumbled over those boxes for the eighteenth time. I can stand it no longer.'

He threw them out of the window one by one. With a sweeping overarm throw, he pitched them towards the railings of St James's Park.

From the Treasury's end of the same building, a close eye was kept on the new rival economic department, not least because the Chancellor was taking quite a time to gain confidence. 'Jim was still catching up on his reading, so to speak,' said his Permanent Secretary. 'George made the running to start with.' It seemed to Armstrong that George had feel but couldn't build an organisation: 'Everything was a deal on its own: you go from deal to deal. That was George. He had the trade unionist's outlook; he had insights; he had negotiating skills. He was good at demolishing silly arguments. But he didn't seem interested in long-term philosophy. What mattered was that he *had* the National Plan, not what was in it.'

He hurled himself into assembling a powerful team. It had team-spirit and loyalty. It learned to cope with the Secretary of State. But it was under-used. One economist, brought in from outside, sat in a room for months doing nothing. George had forgotten he was there.

'The great role that Tony played in the early days', said Caulcott, 'was to establish some order in which advice could at least be presented to George so that he would know the facts when taking a policy decision. Tony got some rational discussion going on the major issues of economic policy: devaluation – on which he refused to keep quiet – the import surcharge, economic councils, the autumn budget of that year.'

Tony had the politician's irritation with academic abstraction, but he wanted clarity. He would go through the argument intellectually, then decide whether its philosophic values fitted his own or whether they were ones he could adapt. 'Right. I see the shape of the thing. A ... B ... C ... D ... E ... I can't go all the way, however, for political reasons.'

Although he believed George Brown's temperament could be disastrous in a prime minister, he greatly respected many of George's qualities. 'The man has genius,' he said. George would get hold of an idea and charge off with passion, eloquence, animal vitality of a quite remarkable kind. If he sometimes charged in the wrong direction, he did it with distinction. In those days he was a formidable figure, Tony tireless in his support.

Proud of his working–class background, George knew he had a brilliant mind. However, he resented the lack of a university education. One was never sure which of his emotions would predominate. His volatility made him unreliable in ways that were tiresome. Occasionally when he was to address leading Conservative industrialists after a lunch, his staff feared the worst. 'And then George got to his feet and dealt with each point superbly. He didn't put a foot wrong, had them completely under his control. It is an immense pleasure to watch him in his element like that,' Tony said.

George said: 'You couldn't have found two people more different in manner than Tony and me. He could irritate every part of me – drape his hand on the mantelpiece, look at me in that patronising way – but he couldn't make me dislike him. You knew where you were with Tony. He was the one bloke who would fight me to my face – in the Department, in private. Others would give way because I was overbearing: then in my absence they'd run me down. Tony, having lost the argument, was totally loyal to me. I could make allowances for him; he could make allowances for me. At the end of the bloody day, whatever the rows, I knew he'd be there.'

The Secretary of State handled Prices, Incomes, Neddies, Little Neddies. As Minister of State, Tony took general responsibility for the rest of the field rather than having one or two specific jobs – prodding and shoving in all directions on the broad economic front.

At the beginning of the third week of Government, the Prime Minister was extremely worried by growing hostility to Britain's new import surcharge. He dispatched DEA's Minister of State to Strasbourg, a decision taken so suddenly that a small plane had to be chartered to get Tony to the Council of Europe before they voted. He made a 'hard-hitting' speech which won reluctant support for the Labour Government's unpopular measure, after which he returned to London in time to make the 9.30 winding-up speech in the House of Commons, explaining what he'd done and why. He knew the subject backwards and assumed that was why the speech – made at the hour when the House is its most tumultuous – had been successful. Some months later he was to discover painfully that it was not always so easy.

I paid my second visit to the Browns' flat, this time their official residence in Carlton Gardens. By their nature few ministerial flats are home-like, the impersonality of this residence reinforced by the route required to reach it. After being decanted from the lift located at the other end of the building, one walked through an echoing corridor scattered with workmen's tools, stretching between half-completed offices. As well as DEA itself, an official home had to be created from scratch for the No. 2 member of Her Majesty's Government.

George was at his most charming, alluding to our last highly disagreeable meeting and removing any lingering embarrassment. 'Susan! Are you going to weep tonight?' he merrily demanded when we arrived. Before leaving the cavernous drawing-room to go to his study with Tony, he turned back to say: 'Now don't weep while I'm gone.' I realised I liked him.

I also liked Sophie's directness. She didn't suffer from piety nor did she mince her words. She made me laugh. Back at Hobury Street I asked Tony about the Browns.

'I gather things get slightly fraught because they get depressed at the same time. You and I are luckier: we take turns,' he said.

About this time we went to see our own new house. It was built around 1840. 'Will it be like the New Forest?' Sheila asked. 'After we've lived there twenty years, will we still call it the new house?' For a long time we did.

I began searching for the new house after our marriage in February. Not until the eve of the wedding did I clear out my desk at the

Sunday Express, having only three weeks earlier screwed myself up to tell John Junor of my intention. An editor ready to savage, he showed me paternalist consideration during the four years I worked for him. When I began as a features writer, Fleet Street expected interviewers to display at least as much of their own personality as that of their subject. Female journalists were virtually confined to the Women's Page. John Junor allowed me to break out of both moulds. I didn't look forward to telling him I was leaving.

'I know why. Tony Crosland doesn't want his wife to write for the *Sunday Express*.'

'It's not that exactly,' I said vaguely – with little hope of misleading that canny Scot, but wanting to stave off a vendetta. 'It's just that I'd like to be at home while this marriage gets under way.' Junor simply grinned. 'And I have to find a new house,' I added, abandoning further explanation.

The geography of our home was a crucial factor in our marriage. At forty-five Tony was taking on two partly-grown children. He and I needed privacy. Each child – and the mother's help – needed privacy. Yet there had to be some means for a sense of parental supervision when, in a not too distant future, boyfriends were certain to step into the picture; the ground floor had to be such that these youths could be entertained downstairs; Tony and I weren't cast for the 1960s permissive parents scene. And there had to be a hub of family life. To achieve all this, the actual shape of the house was fundamental.

On a Grimsby weekend he stepped off the train to be handed a message that it was urgent to ring me in London. He always stayed at the County Hotel, which despite its name stands in the centre of Grimsby Town in a short street called Brighowgate, separated from the railway station by little except the lines. The only telephone is in a callbox in the entrance hall.

The telephone rang in Hobury Street.

'Something has happened to one of the children,' Tony said.

'No no. They're at school. Everyone's fine.'

'Wish you wouldn't send messages like that. You scared me.'

'I know. I'm sorry. The thing is, I've found the new house.'

'Good. I'll hear about it when I get back tomorrow night.'

'But the thing is, it has to be decided today.'

'Don't be ridiculous.'

'I'm not being. It came on the market this morning. I've looked at hundreds of houses, and I *know* this one is good value and will be sold before the day is out. It's on three floors, and there are three rooms on each floor, so we could have a family floor and a you-and-me floor and a floor for the children and Edeltraud.' Edeltraud was the current mother's help. 'And there's a second bathroom for them. And the garden faces the right way. It's on the western slope of Notting Hill. The sunsets must be terrific.'

'How much does it cost?' Receiving no answer, he began to mutter. 'Detest callboxes. Are you still there, Susan? How much does it cost?'

'Well, it's a freehold, which you've always said is a good investment.'

'How much does it cost?'

'Over £30,000.'

'*What?!*'

'I know. But there's a self-contained flat that goes with the house. We could get a bigger mortgage than we planned, and the flat could help pay the mortgage.' Silence at the other end of the line. 'Actually it costs £35,000.'

'Out of the question. You know we agreed £25,000 was the *absolute* outside limit.'

'I mean the house and the flat *together* cost that. Well, £35,500 to be exact. That includes carpets and the flat's furniture.'

'You're quite sure you've finished telling me how much this house costs?'

'Yes.'

'We can't afford it.'

'I know. But maybe we'll get more money than we've counted on when we sell your flat and Hobury Street.'

'We've been over this before. You borrowed every penny that Hobury Street cost. When that's paid back, there won't be much left.'

'But this house is the right shape. One of the bedrooms on what would be our floor would make a marvellous study.'

'Not sure one wants one's study beside our bedroom. You'd have to start looking for a job next week. You have two children to raise. You do owe some responsibility to me. Are you certain you also want to manage what has to be a fairly large flat if it's going to help pay for the world's most expensive house?'

'I don't mind if it's the only way to have this house.'

'You know I hate long conversations in this bloody callbox. If you can get Ben Hooberman to make an agreement that is not absolutely binding but will keep the house until I get back, I suppose you'll have to go ahead. This marriage won't last if we have to take another major decision in this preposterous manner.'

'I'll ring Ben now. Thank you very very very very much.'
'I must go.' He rang off.

With the election and delays in raising a £25,000 mortgage, six months passed before we owned the new house in Lansdowne Road. On a Saturday in November we went to see it. The builder had nearly completed bookshelves to line the walls of the study beside our bedroom. After a grumpy start, Tony began warming to the remaining decisions, though it seemed a sensible insurance policy for me to nip round to the off-licence for some whisky while he went out 'to inspect my garden'.

At Hobury Street that evening, paterfamilias was in his element. 'Just going into the dining-room to chastise the children for wasting good reading time looking at television,' he said. We'd rented our first set the week before. Intrigued by *Gideon's Way*, he sat down with the children to watch.

The telephone rang. Nora Beloff wanted to speak with him before writing her article for the *Observer*.

'Ask her what she wants,' he said, concentrating on the screen. She wanted to discuss the general economic situation. 'Ask her if she'd be so kind as to ring back at the end of *Gideon's Way*.'

She did so, five minutes too late: Sheila had distributed invitations to Clea's birthday party, and the four of us were engaged in writing acceptances. Clea was the Siamese cat that Tony had given the children shortly before we married.

'Sheila, ask Miss Beloff if she could hang on for two minutes. Perhaps you'd better explain that I can't talk now because I'm writing a letter to my cat.'

At weekends economists brought into Government came privately to Hobury Street: Robert Neild and Nicky Kaldor from Callaghan's office, Tommy Balogh from No. 10. They were distrusted – with very good reason – by the regular civil service. Balogh had previously advised Wilson against devaluation. Three weeks after the election Tommy switched: 'I thought it shouldn't be done until we had an incomes policy. Harold didn't want to say the economy was overheated – which it was – for fear of the confidence crash. So we pretended it wasn't overheated. I thought an adviser could influence timing: I realised too late that he can only influence the next seven days; beyond that it's too complicated. Once you've said the economy is not overheated, then that's that. Finished. Things change in a new way. The marvellous opportunity has been rubbed out.'

In November a moment came when it seemed possible that 'The Unmentionable' could be made to happen. At DEA Sir Donald MacDougall received a message from Sir William Armstrong at the Treasury. The two men met. 'Look. We've lost 25 million today,' Armstrong said – a lot of money in 1964. Callaghan was wobbling, he said.

MacDougall went straight to his own Secretary of State and together they arrived at No. 11 where the Chancellor and his Permanent Secretary awaited them. After dinner at home Mac-Dougall was rung by the First Secretary of State and told to come round at once. MacDougall did so.

Brown said to him that Callaghan was threatening to devalue the pound after the Government had just announced they weren't going to. MacDougall pointed out that Cripps had done the same thing. That made George even more against devaluation: Cripps – that ascetic vegetarian teetotaller – was the opposite of everything George was. In any case someone had told him that if the pound was devalued, the real wages of the working classes would go down.

I think it was probably the next day that a minuscule side-effect of this flurry was Tony's and my late arrival for a reception at Buckingham Palace in George Brown's honour. I drove to DEA to collect Tony.

The Secretary of State emerged and set off in his official car.

A Private Secretary came out. 'The Minister wonders whether you'd be more comfortable waiting upstairs.' I was reading the *Evening Standard* by the car light and said I was content.

After a time Tony emerged. 'I'm sorry you've had to wait, but there's a crisis on. It's The Unmentionable.'

A relaxed courtier was waiting inside the front door of Buckingham Palace. As he took us up to the drawing-room where 'George's party' was in progress, he said it didn't matter in the slightest that the Queen and Prince Philip had already gone in. Until then I hadn't known that when the hostess is Queen one is expected to arrive before her – though I daresay Tony was informed of this by his Private Office.

In a day or two it was again made clear that the three men at the head of government would not be moved by any argument for devaluation.

Within three months of coming into office, George Brown had established a national reputation – a force to be reckoned with.

Inside DEA, the force took a form nearly intolerable to Private Office. Part of the difficulty was George's unorthodox humour: he didn't expect all his shrieking to be taken seriously. Part was his distrust of civil servants. His Principal Private Secretary – until he was sacked/resigned for the seventh and last time – was himself a Labour supporter. Tom Caulcott felt there was misunderstanding on both sides:

'The Civil Service didn't appreciate how much thirteen years in Opposition had made the Labour Party dubious of the official machine. In fact, there was good will for the incoming Labour Government, and Jim Callaghan's great strength, after a slow start, was to learn to use it. George never did. He seemed to be trapped by the trade unionist's traditional approach. They are used to playing by the rules of procedure to gain influence over someone else. You're brothers in one sense, but you don't trust one another. I think George was distrustful of nearly everyone.'

Tony would simply say as we exchanged gossip when he got home: 'Afraid George's Private Office is not having an easy time. Tom Caulcott's just resigned again.'

At their Departments, Ministers communicate through their Private Offices. Caulcott rang No. 10 about something or other. George didn't believe his Principal Private Secretary's report of what was said. 'Make the phone call again where I can *hear* you. Make it from my room.'

Caulcott arranged for the call to be switched through to George's desk and went in to hold his repeat conversation with the Private Secretary at No. 10. The Secretary of State paced his vast room. His Principal Private Secretary sat down at the desk and began the telephone conversation afresh. The Secretary of State swung round in his pacing and saw the spot where Caulcott sat.

'Get out of my chair! *Get out of my chair!*'

The Principal Private Secretary conducted the rest of the conversation standing up – as he should have done in the first place. Maybe he had set out to be provocative.

'I suppose,' Caulcott said when he thought about it later, 'subconsciously I may have said to myself: "He's called me a liar. I'm going to sit in his chair."'

Rows between them went on for months. 'Leave my sight! *Go away.* I never want to see you again.' The next morning the Secretary of State would say: 'I didn't mean it.'

The Permanent Secretary proposed someone to replace Caulcott. The candidate went to see the First Secretary of State. Success as a Minister's Private Secretary is an important mark in a civil servant's progress. The intended replacement rang up Caulcott: 'I don't care what it does to my career. I'm not coming.'

The Secretary of State told Caulcott he'd better stay.

Another crisis presented itself. This time the Secretary of State called in other officials to watch him berate his Principal Private Secretary. They stood there, amazed, embarrassed.

Caulcott said: 'If you're going to do this, I'm going to leave.' That time he did.

Yet there was a great admiration for George Brown among civil servants. He'd brought in stupendous energy, and they thought they'd be making decisive economic policy. Planning Councils were set up throughout the country. The Industrial Reorganisation Bill was pushed through – both Industry and DEA claimed its parentage. The Prices and Incomes Board was created.

When eventually George Brown left his first Department to become Foreign Secretary, officials at DEA made touching speeches. They admired his enormous vitality and drive. Without him DEA would fade away.

Towards the end of January 1965, I got back to Lansdowne Road late one Friday afternoon, having interviewed Enoch Powell for the *Sun*, the new paper lately risen from the ashes of the *Daily Herald*, Hugh Cudlipp optimistically aiming for a profit-making middlebrow left-wing journal. The effort of moving into the new house in Lansdowne Road had been no less ghastly than most such moves. We fondly hoped this weekend would be easier than the last.

The previous one was dominated by books. The workmen hadn't yet collected their half-used tins of paint which stood in the ground-floor hall. The tin containing ink-blue paint – looked very nice on the kitchen boiler – must have had its lid loose. The hall was one of many places where Tony's books from The Boltons had been stacked. He and the children carried armload after armload to the drawing-room shelves before anyone looked down and observed ink-blue footprints trailing back and forth across the russet Wilton carpet, the only new carpet that was ever to adorn the house in the nearly thirteen years we lived there. We gazed upon these footprints in silent horror. No one spoke as all four set to with rags and scrubbing brushes and turpentine, Sheila scrubbing the most urgently as it was plain that the footprints matched her size. After half an hour of this employment, Tony announced that he thought he had done his share and would retire to his study where several thousand other books were waiting attention.

This weekend, however, would be more serene, I said to myself as I took off my coat late that Friday afternoon. Propped on the chest in the entrance hall was a note in Ellen-Craig's giant handwriting: MAMA PLEASE RING GEORGE BROWN. I rang. The familiar mellifluous voice came on the line:

'May I be the first to call you Madam Secretary of State?'

At this early stage of my political development, I had no idea that all heads of departments are designated Secretary of State. Why was George hailing me as his partner? He clarified the position. Tony had just been made Secretary of State for Education and Science. Would I join them for a celebration drink at DEA?

Tony had the Sunbeam that day, so I took a taxi, stepping out where Tom Caulcott had hurled the empty boxes, proceeding upstairs in my black-velvet trouser suit and high-heeled sandals, click-clacking into George Brown's office where the drinks were. His eyes grew rounder. He shrieked.

'No more of that! No more of that! You must realise that you are now the wife of a Cabinet Minister. No more trousers. No more open sandals. Look down and let me see your eyelids.'

I looked down.

'No more eyeshadow!'

He reached for the telephone to Private Office. 'Have we a skirt for the Secretary of State's wife?'

To me he shouted: 'Do you realise you may be photographed when you're leaving DEA tonight?'

By now I'd got used to George. So far as I know, women were never the object of his abuse. It seemed to me that his underlying attitude to them was one of respect: it was his presentation that was unorthodox. Later that night when the photographers arrived at Lansdowne Road, I was still in my velvet trouser suit and high-heeled sandals.

The next day, as our quiet weekend commenced, a brace of television men tramped upstairs to the study, followed in due course by reporters and photographers. Tony was wearing a pullover and his usual weekend trousers, a relic of the war, for some reason dyed bottle green, considerably the worse for twenty years' wear.

'Don't think this would be very good for the image,' he said, disappearing into our bedroom to change, one imagined, into more presentable trousers, reappearing in the study a minute or two later

in shirt, tie and jacket for the cameras, the lower half of him still
clothed in the moth-eaten army fatigues. Evidently he got fed up
with the image as midday approached: two of the Sunday newspaper photographs showed the Secretary of State for Education
re-clad in his pullover, a small whisky glass in one hand, a cheroot
in the other.

During the first few weeks at Curzon Street – where the Department of Education and Science was then housed – he found
his mind reverting to DEA and economic policy. Because he engrossed himself so completely in a subject that interested him, he
found it difficult to switch overnight. He wrote to George Brown
about DEA policy. 'The things which I still feel need chasing up
are as follows: (1) ... (2) ... (3) ... (4) ... (5) ... (6) ... (7) ... Life
is very dull without you.'

When I told Ruth Dalton that Tony was somewhat unhappy
about leaving DEA, she said he would find being a Cabinet Minister was enjoyable in a way he couldn't imagine in advance: 'The
authority, the briefings, being looked after, the car – they all
produce a different psychology from that of a No. 2, however
interested the No. 2 is in his Department.' In a month's time he
agreed that Ruth Dalton was right about the psychology. What she
didn't mention was the other side of the coin, knowing we would
discover it soon enough.

-›-16-‹-

Curzon Street

The move to Education resulted from a frightful blow to Patrick Gordon Walker, first of the Gaitskellites taken up by Wilson. On becoming Leader he made Gordon Walker his Shadow Foreign Secretary. While Labour MPs celebrated victory in the 1964 general election, Gordon Walker lost his seat at Smethwick; its white working people felt their jobs and homes threatened by immigrants; the Tory candidate ran a 'squalid' anti-immigration campaign and won. The Prime Minister, in an unusual but not unique arrangement, appointed Gordon Walker Foreign Secretary on the assumption he'd soon be back in the Commons. Pressure was put on the MP for Leyton to vacate his safe seat and go – most reluctantly – to the Lords, the local Party urged to select Gordon Walker as their candidate for the by-election called in January 1965. That Gordon Walker would win was taken for granted.

When the British electorate feels it is being used, its capacity for bloody-mindedness is signal. Also, the weather was bad. Huge numbers of Labour voters declined to attend Leyton's polling stations. After a recount, Gordon Walker – who lost by 205 votes – had to resign as Foreign Secretary. He was replaced by Michael Stewart, until then Secretary of State for Education. He in turn was replaced by Tony, who at forty-six became the youngest member of the Cabinet.

'The school system in Britain remains the most divisive, unjust, and wasteful of all aspects of social equality,' he wrote in *The Future of Socialism*. The system had been primarily geared to educating the middle classes. Working-class children, with rare exception, were faced with overcrowding, a shortage of teachers, deteriorating buildings and were segregated into separate schools. Nature assures that an élite is always rising and asserting itself in a democracy, but the state should do its utmost, he said, to make it possible for those without money or position or a literate family background to have equal access to the opportunity that a decent education bestows.

Not only was it morally wrong for the state to determine which eleven-year-olds could go to the grammar, which were deemed suited for the secondary mod; it was wasteful of resources. More unjust and most wasteful were those public schools – Eton, Winchester – that provided the finest academic education to youths who would mostly disappear into the City or other parasitic occupations. The new system he envisaged was to be built around the comprehensive school.

On that Saturday, after the television crew had lugged their equipment back through our front door, he set off in the Sunbeam for an already arranged visit. 'I suppose there is something one wants to do less than drive to Banstead,' he said, but it would have been inhuman to cancel the lunch. Great age had not mellowed his mother, her needling still tiresome for her children (though she directed none of it at me who had come into her life so late that she was happy to overlook my failings). Her jealousy for her son had not abated since the Speech Day at Highgate School when Alex Comfort bore off more of the gold-tooled leatherbound books than Tony. On this Saturday, however, she was like a schoolgirl in her delight.

When he returned to Lansdowne Road and we went up to the study, his first words were: 'I shall allow my wife to pour me a small whisky, if she would be so kind.' While she did so, he opened the first of the documents to arrive. Among them was a letter of archaic formality addressed to Anthony Crosland, Esq. (for the last time), MP, about procedure to be observed at the Council to be held by the Queen at Sandringham the next day. 'Country clothes will be worn,' it concluded. Attached was a piece of paper headed: *Careful Attention To These Instructions Is Requested.* Five paragraphs followed on which knee to bend on successive footstools while advancing to kiss the Queen's hand and become a member of Her Majesty's Most Honourable Privy Council. He summoned the children. Neither wanted to kiss the other's hand. He couldn't possibly remember the instructions without two rehearsals, he said, so they could each take a turn.

'Thank you very much,' he said. 'I should get through the thing quite nicely now.'

In choosing to affirm, rather than take the Oath, he was one of a small minority. Whatever their private views on the substance of the Oath, most Cabinet Ministers find it simplest to conform in the ritual. Oaths and affirmations are duly recorded in the *Daily Telegraph*'s Court Circular. 'Are we to understand', comes the inevitable question from a Tory during an election campaign, 'that you are against Christian practice in our country?'

(An earlier Education Minister, Sir Edward Boyle, though he was a believing High Anglican at the time he kissed hands, refused to take the Oath. One of the few Tories for whom Tony had any time, Boyle explained to me why he had gratuitously offended the Christians in his constituency: 'The idea that a promise is made more binding by holding a Bible in your hand is something I've always found offensive. I think one's word alone should be sufficient.')

On Sunday Tony took a train to Sandringham and back.

Monday morning the official car made its first appearance in Lansdowne Road. It was a stately Austin Princess, no longer young, those comfortable conveyances not yet compelled to give way to compact efficiency. It bore him away to Curzon Street. When Grimsby constituents asked me: 'What's it like to be a Cabinet Minister's wife?' and I answered that I now had sole use of the Sunbeam during weekdays, they and I suspected there must be something still to come.

Like others, Tony was influenced by Arthur Henderson's dictum: 'The first forty-eight hours decide whether a Minister is going to run his office or whether his office is going to run him.' Some Ministers make theatrical gestures intended to impress the Department with their strong personality: the furniture is turned round at once, the curtains replaced, sometimes the entire Private Office reshuffled. Tony didn't think this sort of thing much impressed civil servants: 'One imagines they give a smile of tolerant amusement.'

What he imposed at the outset was that he was not willing to accept their submissions automatically, that he would argue and reject when necessary, that he would take initiatives on his own. He couldn't hope to learn about the entire Department, so he concentrated on chunks. If officials in some section of the enormous machine had to wait for a decision, that was too bad.

The three problems he saw as most pressing were: secondary-school reorganisation, teacher supply and, after the Robbins Report, higher education. A decision on the first problem had been taken by the Labour Government before he went to Curzon Street: not to legislate. This was partly because the Government had such a small majority, partly because of a general feeling that most local authorities would reorganise if asked and given the chance to do so. Michael Stewart had a circular in draft when he was moved to the

Foreign Office. Tony took the draft out, polished it, and began negotiations with the multitude of local-authority, teacher and other pressure groups that surround Education.

At a later date he contemplated legislation on comprehensives, particularly when so many local authorities went Conservative. But in January 1965 he wasn't sorry that the Cabinet had already decided not to legislate: it was fundamental to his view of democracy that reform would 'stick' better *if* it could be achieved voluntarily. (When Mrs Thatcher took over Education in 1970, even she could not stem the move to comprehensives.)

He had to decide whether to 'require' or 'request' education authorities to go comprehensive. One of his characteristics was realism about himself and his position. His Minister of State, Reg Prentice, wanted to go for the tougher word – 'require'.

'It's an empty toughness,' Tony said. The Department couldn't cope with the pace already set. He didn't want the new system threatened by botching it – throwing together buildings that lacked the physical requirements for a sixth form; or amalgamating a grammar school and a secondary modern school so quickly that instead of creating a genuinely new school, the grammar school ethos prevailed. He issued Circular 10/65, laying down his 'request'. It was notable for its realism and flexibility as he came down firmly on the egalitarian side of the major argument in post-war educational policy.

'He was the first person to stop talking about comprehensive reorganisation and take a decisive step towards it,' a senior official, Toby Weaver, said. Brought up in the home of Sir Stafford Cripps, Weaver's quarrel with the existing educational system was that it arrogantly equated academic 'excellence' with human 'excellence'. Much – by no means all – of his advice was valued by Tony, 'though he didn't want positive advice from us,' Weaver said. 'He did not want to be led. He wanted good lieutenants. He was immensely generous in praising good work: when most Ministers would have left it to their Private Office, he would send you a personal note. On the other hand, if officials produced shoddy arguments, he wrote them off very quickly. While he was always courteous, he managed to convey when people should be kept out of his way.'

His civil servants didn't know it, but Tony never enjoyed the initial weeks in any job; he felt he wasn't yet on top of it. 'If I had more ministers and more time,' he said as he came up the stairs to our floor carrying three red boxes, 'it might be fun. But not now.'

He'd got away from the Commons after the 10.00 division, and before starting on the boxes he wanted to hear my day's gossip, tell me his.

'What's been happening?' meant my gossip came first while he began to unwind over a drink in his study. Anything good, bad, sad in the children's day. How my interview had gone. Family news. What else had I done, thought, felt? Once, long before, I'd expressed surprise at his insatiable curiosity about what I did. 'Never understood the male attitude that your day isn't at least as interesting as mine,' he said. If morbidity or depression invaded me, he showed me the way to dispel it. When either of us had a moral collision – I with the children or someone in my journalistic work, he with a colleague or anyone encountered in his day – we wanted to know how the other felt about it. He wanted to tell me about a new concept, or St James's Park at lunchtime, or some individual's behaviour that had amused or annoyed him. He might ask me to have a look at a passage in a speech if, after redrafting it, he still wasn't happy. Whatever made up our gossip, generally it was interlaced with the farce that asserts itself in every situation.

This time of day that we had entirely to ourselves was important. If he was going to be terribly late but I knew when he'd be back, I set the alarm, got some sleep, was awake when he came up the stairs. When he had to work after gossip, I made him a pot of tea before I went back to our bed.

The study had the atmosphere of his sitting-room at The Boltons – the same Victorian chandelier, the same floor-length gold-velvet curtains now sewn together to draw across the wall made almost entirely of glass, the same sense that the room was charged even when he hadn't yet walked through the front door. Most horizontal surfaces were covered with methodically-organised papers, files, books. Books lined two walls, a drinks tray on one shelf. On the remaining wall hung two large austere black and white portraits by Auerbach either side of a nearly lifesize drawing that Tony had commissioned – me, standing, wearing high-heeled sandals only. The walls were white until nicotine turned them brown, the carpet black – the thickest carpet in the house, given us by a friend after she had it taken up from her own husband's study because he said it made him think of death. The furniture was Victorian except for the chairs each side of the gas-fire. When we married, I gave Tony the Eames classic black-leather chair – designed to lie back in rather than sit upon – with its ottoman. He gave me Eames's white-leather rocking-chair. Mine faced the glass wall leading on to the balcony with its terrific view. His chair faced the pictures.

That night my gossip was partly about Susan Barnes's day in Hatfield for an interview with Barbara Cartland, who in the course of a three-hour *tour de force* made passing reference to 'not the grammar schools or the secondary modern schools. Co-operative? What *is* the name of those beastly schools?' 'Comprehensive,' I replied.

I said to Tony: 'I know you haven't come home to discuss educational policy with me, but could you be very kind and in three sentences tell me exactly what *is* a comprehensive?'

He told me in three sentences.

'Do you mean all this fuss is about nothing more nor less than high schools that have existed for a thousand years in America?'

'That is near enough correct. I cannot decide whether it is an irritation or a relief that you are the only mother in Britain who is both uninformed and without a passionate view about her children's education.'

I did, however, hold the view that as my children were content in the schools they were attending when Tony and I married, I didn't want them automatically shuffled about because of his ideals. Why shouldn't they go to a private day school as I had done, if my father wished to provide this? Tony grew increasingly out of sorts with people who preach comprehensives and always find very moving reasons why their own children do not attend one, but I didn't preach and the children weren't his. Compromise was reached: when Ellen-Craig started secondary school, she would go to a comprehensive. He then bided his time: he always preferred persuasion to coercion.

At family meals he and Sheila discussed aspects of democratic socialism. At first she was taken aback by the moral concept that children shouldn't inherit huge sums of money earned by others. She thought of her piggy bank, how nice it would be if someone filled it nightly. But Tony was a good teacher. He explained his reasons for urging privileged children to attend comprehensive schools:

'Of course St Paul's gives you a better academic education, but my own view is that if a girl brought up in a home with books has academic potential in her, she'll develop it whether or not she goes to an intensively academic school. I daresay the headmistress of St Paul's holds a different view. Much of the argument hangs on how you define education. Some would argue that a comprehensive school offers the privileged girl better preparation for the real world, though admittedly that's not the purpose of comprehensives.'

When Sheila asked us if she could go to Holland Park Comprehensive, I called on the headmistress of St Paul's, who told me we were using Sheila as a political pawn, but that it probably didn't matter too much as she was 'rather wet'.

'In what sense?' I inquired.

'She never wants to play sports.'

Not only that, when asked to write an essay about Guy Fawkes Day, Sheila had described how she imagined Fawkes felt as he awaited incineration. Her English teacher wrote on the essay: 'Excellent writing. But what a pity that so young a girl has such morbid thoughts.'

'What was your day like?' I asked Tony.

'Interminable. Barbara never stopped talking in Cabinet. The Vice-Chancellors this evening went on and on and on as if their precious universities weren't already rich and successful. I can understand about macro-economics. I can understand about sex. What I *cannot* understand is the desire of human beings to hear their own voices. Also, if one is to be truthful, I'm not frightfully interested in the universities.'

With the pot of tea on the ottoman, he resumed work, including preparation for another meeting with the Vice-Chancellors. I went back to bed and my novel. When he joined me he announced: 'Tomorrow I shall tell the Vice-Chancellors they can stuff themselves. "Enough of this niggling and nagging," I shall say. "I have other things on my mind than your petty preoccupations. Away with you!"

'On the other hand, I may say nothing of the sort. I shall just have had lunch with your friend Lord Pakenham. All verve may have been drained from me by Christianity and a meal at the House of Lords.' He persisted in referring to Lord Longford by his previous title, Lord Pakenham.

A few nights later it was Jennie Lee's advent at Curzon Street, as Minister for the Arts, which featured in the day's gossip. 'She is raising a great fuss about the fact she hasn't her own lavatory. She says she can't share one with the other junior ministers because they're male. I expect I'll end up in doing the decent thing and giving her mine while her own is being built at the taxpayers' expense. It's a bad business. Furthermore she thinks that everything in the entire Department should be subservient to the arts.

To tell the truth, I'm not frightfully interested in the arts at this moment.'

He was driven mad by the obtuseness of those who claimed grammar schools did not affect comprehensives despite the undeniable fact that the former creamed off the more gifted children. Following a dinner with four of the teachers' associations – 'Joint 4' – his tread was ominous as he mounted the stairs. He stopped at our bedroom door.

'Good evening. You'd better come in the study.'

I put my novel aside and got smartly out of our bed, wondering what had caused this latest vexation.

'If it's the last thing I do, I'm going to destroy every fucking grammar school in England,' he said. 'And Wales. And Northern Ireland.'

'Why not Scotland?' I asked out of pure curiosity.

'Because their schools come under the Secretary of State for Scotland.' He began to laugh at his inability to destroy their grammar schools.

Three years earlier he'd written in *The Conservative Enemy* that a Labour Government must give high priority to the reform of the public schools. The objective must be to assimilate them into the state system. The public schools should give most of their places to children who do not pay. A token number of free places was quite unacceptable. 'We must either have a radical reform or none at all.' A Labour Government should proceed if possible by agreement. To impose a scheme which wholly changed the character of the schools would cause all the teachers to leave. If the public schools refused to accept voluntary reform, then the Government must legislate. 'The object of legislation would be *not* to prohibit all private fee-paying, which would be an intolerable restriction of personal liberty, but, by regulating the *conditions* under which education is bought and sold, to secure a more equitable distribution of educational resources between different classes of the nation.'

There was no way for him to reform the public schools in 1965: no one knew how it should be done – how to select free places; no detailed scheme had been worked out in Opposition. To find a practicable scheme, he set up the Public Schools Commission, 'to advise on the best way of integrating the public schools with the state system of education'. Then he turned his mind back to the reforms that could be made now.

In casual conversation his hyperbole was shaped by a perversity that drove some people up the wall. He fastened on whatever long-existing social problem had just been discovered by the fashionable intelligentsia and he mocked them for over-simplifying the cure, regardless of whether he agreed with the aim of their current crusade. When stuck behind a car whose driver kept turning to face the front-seat passenger as they conversed, Tony invariably said in the 1960s (according to the appearance of the driver): 'Women never could drive.' 'Black men never could drive.' For good measure: 'Men with beards never could drive.' If I was in a good mood, I took it in part. If I was in a bad mood, it exasperated – and there was no point in making a rejoinder, as he'd only said it to try me.

'I'm not frightfully interested in the public schools,' he told a conceited, youngish journalist brought along by friends for an after-dinner drink one weekend.

'How can you say that after all you've written?' the journalist replied. 'I'd like to send my kids to a comprehensive school, but as long as the public schools exist, my wife feels we'd be letting our kids down if we sent them anywhere else. If you would abolish public schools, we'd have no hesitation in sending our kids to a comprehensive.'

'You really mustn't assume one's function is to ease the conscience of the middle classes. Why can't you and your wife take your own decisions?'

A deep flush of indignation was advancing up the young man's face. With patent weariness his host set out the arguments:

'One had thought one's writing was fairly clear. *A.* Arguments against abolishing fee-paying schools. (1) A democracy cannot forbid people to found schools and charge for going to them. (2) In any case, outright abolition unenforceable: parents and teachers would devise a way to get round the law. (3) Further waste of resources: many teachers at, say, Eton and Winchester, would emigrate.

'*B.* Since they exist, how does one utilise public schools? (1) Make their resources available to a wider public, perhaps 25 per cent of places available to fee-paying children, 75 per cent distributed in a manner to be advised upon by the Commission that I am setting up for that purpose. The Commission will take a couple of years to complete its findings, but that's OK as there's no money currently available at Education to reform the public schools. (2) The state sector must be strengthened so that it can match all but the very best fee-paying schools. Hence teacher supply is one of my priorities.'

Suddenly altogether bored by having to give this exposition, he drew it to a close. 'Once the state system is strong enough to compete, if parents want to send their children to some inferior fee-paying school for purely snobbish reasons, that's their affair. Why should they be denied the freedom to spend their money buttressing their egos if that's what they want?'

All visible flesh of the journalist was carmine with grievance; he made a stiff departure.

'Feel I've not made myself very popular with that young man. He does try one's patience. You were saying . . .?'

There were others with whom Tony did not make himself popular, among them a number of young MPs who entered Parliament in 1964. Bill McCarthy, eminently qualified to pronounce on the Labour Party, summed up the situation as he saw it. McCarthy won a trade union scholarship to Ruskin College, Oxford, and ever since has commuted between academia and politics. Barbara Castle brought him in as an adviser on industrial relations when she was running the Department of Employment and Productivity. Since then successive Governments have appointed him as an arbitrator in industrial strife. McCarthy likes metaphor in setting out his argument.

'Two streams flow through British socialism,' he said, 'those who are seeking a pope, those who are reacting to the very idea of a pope. I'm the second. If you belong to the stream that wants a pope, you don't mind that he has to be propped up. Popes can be petty, overbearing, overstrung. *You* know your pope goes stark raving bonkers from time to time. *You* know. But the world doesn't. There's a kind of attraction in this kind of character who needs *you*.'

Those who came into the Commons excited by *The Future of Socialism* looked about for its author. They'd been impressed. He identified the issues, then pointed the way. As the world changed, he recharted the course to reach the goal. They'd heard about his leadership in CDS, knew he threw himself wholeheartedly into a cause. The ball was at his feet – to use another metaphor – and they expected him to pick it up. When it came to himself, he didn't pick up the ball. They wanted to rally round, but he didn't present himself to be rallied round. They'd expected to be welcomed with open arms; they never got any open arms from Tony. They were greatly disappointed. Some felt it sharply.

On a Sunday in February we celebrated our first wedding anniversary. In the drawing-room we played records from The Boltons days, Tony and the children taking turns miming 'Singin' in the Rain' under a large black umbrella left behind by some educationalist. After Sheila and Ellen-Craig were in bed, we were listening to more records when I looked up to see tears streaming down his face.

'It's nothing to do with you,' he said lest I feel unduly flattered. 'I was thinking about Hugh. I miss him so. He's the only person who could have been here with us listening to these records tonight.'

It was two years since Gaitskell's death. There was no one older left with whom Tony could enjoy Hugh's complete candour.

→→ 17 →→

Mr Goshawk

Cabinet is a totally different forum from the Commons, debate genuine, no public to entertain, no need for childish exchange of Party slogans. Prime ministers vary in the way they conduct Cabinet. Wilson called first on those Ministers whose views were relevant, then the others, after which he 'interpreted' the consensus opinion. When differences were irreconcilable, he would ask the view of each Minister in turn, totting up the pros and cons as he went round the table.

Addressing one another by title helped depersonalise the issues, though Ministers, being human, still managed to display some facets of their personalities. Barbara Castle made speeches, pounding the table. Denis Healey, when in the ascendant, could not resist one-upmanship. The 'weak Ministers', as regrettably nearly half were known (Crossman called them the 'tiddlers'), would go along with the Prime Minister: they felt very uneasy, but at the end of the day, on balance, they supported the Prime Minister's view, they said.

When Tony first entered the Cabinet he was uncertain how it worked and initially said very little: 'I cannot offer comment because I haven't given the matter serious thought.' Jim Callaghan said to him after the first few weeks that while he might regard himself as 'knowing nothing about it', he was considerably more informed than most of his colleagues: 'You're too modest, Tony.' A couple of days later Callaghan pushed a note across the Cabinet table for the S of S Education: 'Splendid. You see how right you were to start joining in. In one bound you become an Opinion-former (and in this Cabinet that's a bloody marvel!). Jim.'

From then on, it was Callaghan's own Department, the Treasury, whose opinions Tony was primarily challenging. Why was a socialist Government not committing itself to the highest possible public expenditure? Why was it carrying out Treasury policy based on estimates for the previous Government's Tory objectives? Why did it not discuss the one economic measure that would allow the

British economy to expand? He didn't actually use the word 'devaluation' in Cabinet, but no one was in the slightest doubt that he was advocating The Unmentionable.

Without devaluation, the British balance of payments was under continuous pressure, hung like a cloud over Curzon Street and every other domestic spending department, gave the Treasury even more power than in the 1950s to restrict the public spending on which Labour's programme depended. By April, Dick Crossman observed to his diary, Tony was much more confident and was 'emerging in Cabinet as a man with something important to contribute on the economic side.' Neither Prime Minister nor Chancellor wanted to hear it.

About this time Tony embarked on another passionate love affair. *Match of the Day* entered his life and stayed – nothing for it but that I come to terms with my rival. As the match was usually a replay, Grimbarians, newsagents, any living soul he was likely to run into on a Saturday was alerted that on no account must the outcome of the match be revealed. The children or I turned on the television and waited until the players were actually on the field. Only then did Tony feel it safe to go into the so-called dining-room where the rented set stood. If he'd been out earlier in the evening for a Labour Party meeting and missed the beginning of play, he strode straight from front door to dining-room, confident that the black and white set would be tuned in, always touched at the sight of the ashtray and whisky-and-soda waiting on the table in front of the set.

Match of the Day had everything for him: he admired professionalism above all else; emotionally he was moved by teamwork; and, as football had nothing to do with his own work and talents, it was total relaxation.

If we entertained on a Saturday evening, everyone usually staying at the big Victorian table in the kitchen to talk after dinner, Sheila or Ellen-Craig, slightly pink-faced, came in and said: 'Tony, the red telephone in your study kept ringing, so I answered it. The Prime Minister wants to speak with you.' Tony politely excused himself from the table. I knew *Match of the Day* was over when he came back and said: 'Sorry. The telephone call turned out complicated. Where have you got to?'

He was determined to keep alive separate facets of his nature rather than compress them. He was aware of a special danger for politicians, perhaps most of all on television: they adopt a public

persona, which can become so much second nature that there is no
'real person' there any more. Tony wanted to maintain the con-
tradiction that he was a human being finding himself at the same
time that he was directing the lives of others.

In any case, he was extremely loath to accept that television had
become an expected link between politician and public. 'If I must,
I must,' he said glumly, grudging the time.

'The trouble with you on television, Tony,' said his PPS, Chris
Price, 'is that you look so bored.'

'How can I help it? They don't do enough homework and then
ask these footling questions.'

There were bursts of self-improvement. He asked that a BBC
recording be played back to him and Fred Goshawk, the civil
servant who was Diary Secretary in Private Office. Mr Goshawk
was a lifelong socialist.

'I wish to God I didn't sound like that, Fred.'

'Like what, Secretary of State?'

'So bloody lah-de-dah.'

Mr Goshawk thought the Secretary of State's full-bodied voice
was marvellous. 'People much prefer to hear someone talking with
an educated voice.'

Tony still didn't like the way he sounded, though he never tried
to change what he was, Mr Goshawk observed.

Civil servants worry about the drinking habits of Ministers,
concerned that things always be done 'in the right way'. All this
psychological metering makes some Ministers drink more, having
a quick one in their room before attending some function in case
they're overly nannied there. Tony, Frankie Donaldson used to
say, was the only Minister she knew who drank far less after he
entered government, her other friends stepping up their intake
after elevation and its accompanying stress.

The Department of Education was notoriously mean with
Government Hospitality funds, releasing the sherry bottle only if
they considered a meeting was of real importance. When delegates
came to see the Secretary of State too late in the day to give them
tea, he paid for any drink he offered them. Mr Goshawk, having
worked out that the Croslands weren't rich, decided that Government Hospitality should help out. He took up the cudgels, put the
matter to another civil servant, who was horrified. The request
went up from Assistant Secretary to Deputy Secretary, at last
reaching the Permanent Secretary who decreed that the odd couple
of bottles could be provided for the Secretary of State to dispense

on Departmental business. These stood inside a cabinet on one shelf, the Secretary of State's private stock on another.

For six months after Tony had infectious hepatitis, his shelf was stocked with Coca-Cola. Drinking Coke instead of whisky didn't change his nature, which Mr Goshawk pointed out to those civil servants who had decided the Secretary of State was an alcoholic when they learned he sometimes had a whisky at his desk before his sandwich lunch. 'They never took into account what they drank when they went to the Reform Club for their lunch. He didn't like clubs,' said Mr Goshawk. 'When his GP told him it was OK to drink again, the Secretary of State said on the whole he did prefer whisky to Cokes and resumed his natural habits.'

What Mr Goshawk liked best was walking into the Secretary of State's room at seven at night when most of the Department had been shut for an hour, seeing him sitting there working with a large Scotch beside him. Sometimes he'd say: 'You're working late, Fred. You'd better have a drink.' After eleven hours in an office you're very jaded: a nice size Scotch does wonders for you, was Mr Goshawk's view. He helped himself from the bottle paid for by the Secretary of State and took it back to his own desk.

Private Office knew that the Secretary of State regarded 'contraptions' as quite unnecessary. In his room at the House of Commons a new safe with a combination lock was installed. 'Take it away.' He wanted one with a key.

Security insisted that it be a combination. He said he wouldn't be able to remember the combination. 'Here was this remarkable intellect,' said Mr Goshawk, 'who could have remembered any combination if he chose to. He couldn't be bothered. Finally he said, all right, if the combination could be somebody's birthday – which was against all regulations – he could remember it. Even with that, he once phoned me to say he was sending the car back for me to come and open his safe.'

One evening when I took soup and a sandwich supper to have with Tony in his room at the House, I found the Scotch was locked in the safe. He couldn't remember the combination. 'You'll have to ask Fred Goshawk to tell you. I must go and divide,' he said, departing his room to the clangour of the division bells and the bawling of DIVISION by policemen assigned to make sure Ministers are not asleep in their rooms. He created this blockage to be perverse, in Mr Goshawk's view, though the Diary Secretary didn't say so at the time. Instead, talking on the private line between the Department and Tony's room at the House, Mr Goshawk broke all rules and told me the combination. I opened the safe. Mr Goshawk then arranged for the combination to be changed at eight o'clock the following morning. In the end the Secretary of State had a safe with a key.

He felt free when he was walking on his own. 'You have kept me cooped up long enough. I shall have twenty minutes doing what I want to do.' Private Office would ring through to the front door of Curzon Street: 'Tell Davis to take the car away. The Secretary of State will be walking to his meeting.'

There was a series of official visits through the Lake District, for which an enormous car was provided by a mayor. Halfway across the Peak the Secretary of State said to the driver: 'You drive on a couple of miles and wait there. I'm going to walk.'

The No. 2 Private Secretary, not long in his job, said: 'But Secretary of State, we're due to call on the mayor in forty minutes.'

'Everyone else is allowed to walk in the Lake District. I intend to do so.'

It was rare when he didn't manage to carve out some time to do exactly what he liked in whatever part of the world he was. Had the regional visit included York, Pevsner would have been in his dispatch case, the Minster his treat. The No. 2 Private Secretary, however, felt uncomfortable finding himself alone in the back of this huge vehicle, the Secretary of State walking a couple of miles behind. Mr Goshawk thought it had something to do with the wartime training. 'If you're trained to that standard, you can't chuck it just like that,' he said when his still uneasy colleague got back to London.

At Education they all knew he was an exacting master, but he wasn't harsh. He drove them, but they saw him driving himself. When things went wrong he invariably said afterwards: 'You'd better come in. We'll have an inquest.' If you were to blame, you got a rocket. But he didn't bear a grudge.

Mr Goshawk never knew him to be unfair except to Mr Davis, his Government driver. Everyone else called him Len or Davis, but to the children and me he remained Mr Davis. Whatever the rank of a civil servant, he was rarely addressed other than formally by me. Tony wanted home and office to be kept separate.

Over the nine years in government he had two drivers. Both were subjected to his being unfair; something about being fenced in by the government car first thing in the morning triggered off irritability; he improved as the day went on. Having left home as late as possible and then run into heavy traffic, he would say: 'You mustn't let this happen again.' It was hard on Davis. Everyone knew of the Secretary of State's fetish about time. He made a point of never being late for official business. He might get there ten seconds before he was due, but he was always there: if he set a time, he meant it. Mr Goshawk girded his loins and went into his master's office to put Davis's side of the case. It was accepted.

Possibly the Diary Secretary in a Minister's Private Office performs the most demanding task yet devised to test man's spirit. Mr Goshawk quickly observed that I failed to grasp the importance of punctuality in official life. The principal reason why the car is sent for a wife – normally not expected to set foot in it – is to ensure she is on time. He knew I had a job of my own – wasn't just waiting for tea and cakes at No. 10. But he felt that as he sent me my copy of the weekly Diary, I shouldn't have taken on things that interfered with it. Bad lapses already put me at a disadvantage when he rang just before I was due to step into the Princess. I was drying my hair, crouched by the bed on which I'd stood a fan heater designed to warm an entire room. Mr Goshawk said: 'The Secretary of State would like a word with you.'

Tony came on the line: he did hope that I was about to leave. 'You make life difficult for all of us when you cannot keep to a schedule.'

As my hair was still wet and I was naked, defensive instincts rushed forward: I was *not*, I said, at the beck and call of some bloody Diary Secretary who has nothing to do but sit at a desk all day. There was a little click. The Secretary of State chuckled. 'When you do get here you'd better come up to my room. I know you'll want to say good evening to Mr Goshawk. He was on the line when you referred to him just now.'

Thus I learned that any telephone call placed through Private Office is monitored. Nine times out of ten when Tony spoke to me from the Department, it was about the Diary. Mr Goshawk would listen long enough to discover if he was needed. If the conversation was personal, he got off the line: civil servants have enough to do. The system saves time, but this was the first I knew of its existence.

I improved, lapsed, improved again, lapsed. Tony had a dinner with educationalists after which he was going to a small reception at No. 10, solely because wives were invited and I'd seldom been to No. 10. He arranged to have a brisk walk between these engagements, the Princess collecting me from Lansdowne Road and

meeting him at an agreed spot in Hyde Park. The night turned
bitterly cold. He reached the spot on the minute agreed. The
Princess and I reached it a quarter of an hour later. He got in
without a word.

'Good evening,' I said.

There was no reply.

'Is anything the matter?'

'I wonder if any other Cabinet Minister is compelled to stand in
the middle of Hyde Park on a winter's night, with no overcoat,
waiting for his own car to collect him.' No trace of amusement was
detectable.

'Perhaps I'm late because for once I didn't have to hurry, and so
I lost track of the time.' I felt distinctly uneasy.

'When you actually put your mind to it, you succeed in being
the most inconsiderate woman I have ever known.'

We may have looked like a couple as we went up the broad
stairway to the first floor of No. 10, but he still hadn't addressed
another word to me. Nor did he while we were there, except to say,
after twenty minutes, that it was time for us to leave. Back we
climbed into the Princess which I tried to persuade myself was the
cause of this difficulty. Mr Davis drove to Lansdowne Road with
unbroken silence behind him – pleased, I suspected.

I improved.

To the chagrin of officials, Tony used outside advisers – experts
committed to Labour – who would come to Lansdowne Road in
the evening so he could pick their brains and test their arguments
against those of his civil servants. It irritated him that Education
had become too insular, too apart from the central economy. So
economists as well as educationalists came to our house.

Inside the Department a civil servant who was invaluable was
Wilma Harte – in charge of the reorganisation of secondary schools.
She was one of very few officials who talked with the Secretary of
State over a drink in his room after most had gone home. Unlike
many civil servants, she understood the feelings of people in schools
and local authorities, had what someone described as 'searing
common sense'. She and Tony were on the same wavelength.

When he first arrived at Curzon Street, the Robbins Report was
on the table. Robbins held that higher education was synonymous
with university education. Other forms of higher education were
beyond the pale. Tyrrell Burgess, whose writing on education was
respected by Tony, characterised the Robbins view as 'a kind of

club with the universities as full members, the colleges of education as associate members, and regional colleges on a gratifying waiting list.'

Toby Weaver was now the senior official concerned with higher education. He proposed the binary policy to Tony. Tony seized it, amended it, made it his own. Near the end of April 1965 he made the famous Woolwich Speech – putting in some offensive remarks bound to upset people. 'Let us now move away from our snobbish caste-ridden hierarchical obsession with university status,' was one.

The next thing was to determine where to move from there. With the help of Weaver and others, he invented the polytechnics as a makeweight to the universities – 'which took courage, was revolutionary, and was right,' Weaver said.

Tony had to struggle for the intellectual cohesion with which he defended the binary policy to democratise higher education; he succeeded in altering the terms of the debate: the Robbins attitudes lost their dominance. The polytechnics – related to the needs of technology and industry – were to stand alongside the universities, not inferior but different. In 1966 thirty polytechnics were created.

Much later Tyrrell Burgess blamed his polytechnic colleagues for failing properly to react to what Tony was trying to achieve; too many of them aspired to the traditional posture of university lecturers instead of developing their own distinctive stance.

-»-18-«-

A Knock on the Head

Few Cabinet Ministers go in for much private social life. How they handle official invitations varies with temperament; Tony accepted the absolute minimum. Prime Ministers, having less leeway, contrive their own methods of survival; conversation at dinner is exceptionally draining when conducted through interpreters perched cheek by jowl. At No. 10 dinners for a visiting head of government, Prime Minister Wilson looked off into space throughout his guest's after-dinner speech, not even feigning interest, peacefully emptying his wine glasses one by one. (A subsequent prime minister, James Callaghan, turned teetotal late in life, adopted a different method. He would converse pleasantly with his neighbour for a few minutes, asking about this and that in her life, then lapse into silence, gazing before him, benevolently presiding and resting at the same time.)

Once Tony had committed himself, he had a nice sense that it was the only time most people present would be dining in, say, Hampton Court Palace and put himself out for them. He felt less concern for those plainly familiar with official high life, especially when his table-partner sought to engage him in that form of chitchat which roams between '*Do* tell me, Mr Crosland, what you think about our economic situation,' and complaints about standards of domestic service these days. He developed something approaching obsession about ambassadors' wives; it all stemmed, he said, from an overseas visit when one such lady asked him whether she should send her daughter to Cheltenham or Roedean.

'What I find impertinent is the way these Tory jumped-up middle-class women assume that because one is middle-class, one must deep down share their attitudes,' he said to me. 'Extraordinary their husbands don't brief them on what is appropriate conversation with a Labour Minister.'

In time he accepted these tribulations more philosophically, though moments recurred when I grew conscious of a baleful eye fixed upon me from across the table. I learned to avoid meeting it, fearful its meaning would be evident enough to the lady's husband seated beside me. I may have worried unduly. One such gentleman said: 'Your husband is still very much in love with you, Mrs Crosland.' 'Why do you say that?' 'He's been looking at you throughout dinner.'

Unless he was the official host, Tony regarded his duties as finished at the end of the meal. A No. 10 factotum came up when I was chatting in the Pillared Room, made a bow and said: 'Your husband wants you to know, Mrs Crosland, that there is no reason for you to hurry away. But when you are ready to leave, you will find the Secretary of State in the drivers' room near the front door. He is looking at a football match on television and has asked me to tell you he is very content.'

All sorts of difficulties were made over protocol connected with Royalty. What was the point of having a Private Office if they couldn't get him out of these arrangements? He saw his dealings with the Royal Family as semi-comic. At a reception where he was host and Princess Margaret was the regal guest, the two proceeded around the room, smoking as they went, he trying to hurry Her Royal Highness along. At another official do where Princess Margaret was present, Lord Kennet, a junior minister at Housing and Local Government, found himself talking with Herself after Tony had moved away.

'I say, he's awfully crawss, isn't he?' she said.

'Who?'

'Your Mr Crawssland.' She thereupon produced a small cigar of her own and gave an imitation of Tony smoking – '*phyfft, phyfft*' between words. (When admonishing others about the folly of smoking, he maintained he didn't inhale deeply, and certainly as soon as he drew in on his small cigar he at once exhaled in dismissive little 'phyfft, phyfft's', for convenience the cigar generally remaining planted in the middle of his lips until the ash needed tipping off.)

For some reason he agreed to go to a Buckingham Palace garden party. We set off in the Austin Princess and his braces broke. He decided this was a sign; furthermore, neither Mr Davis nor I had a safety pin. He returned happily for a full afternoon's work in the office. This kept him in a good mood for days.

He was interested in the quality of what a person said rather than the sayer. In Nuffield College's Common Room, Professor Beloff thought he should have Tony's attention. A student said something that interested Tony more, and he turned his full attention on the student. The student was startled. The professor was miffed. Tony either didn't notice or didn't care.

He was surprisingly shy, gauche even, at 'passing the time of day'. Two representatives from further education somehow persuaded Private Office that a confidential talk at the Café Royal would be productive. Toby Weaver accompanied the Secretary of State and never forgot it. 'Dreadful evening. Tony was at his most unco-operative, couldn't understand why he had to spend his evening like this. They thought that's how the great behaved.' At other times he engaged all right, but in a way that made you uncomfortable. Like an Oxford don, he was capable of taking some small remark and examining it in a way the speaker hadn't intended. He would change the rules of the game: you were having an idle conversation and he suddenly took you up on it and then dissected you.

As dining out was the most hazardous, he devised a system to improve the success rate: preliminary telephone calls between hostesses and me (or Diary Secretary) established size of proposed assemblage, identity of other guests, position of eating (i.e. sitting down or standing up). A few hostesses took offence, I believe, when instead of having their invitations simply accepted or declined, they were submitted to a questionnaire. One newspaper editor took umbrage and thereupon withdrew his invitation to the Croslands. On the whole, however, Tony's system reduced strain all round. ('Why should anyone object if I prefer to stay in my own home?' he said.) Sometimes I went along to these dinners, gleaning nuggets to take back for gossip, he thus getting the best of both worlds.

With one thing and another, we decided that instead of going to other people's houses, it would be better if they came to ours. At Lansdowne Road he could orchestrate the conversation. Creative tension – the keynote – was impossible, he maintained, until people finished eating. 'No one wants second helpings, Susan.' Guests unfamiliar with our household rituals sometimes looked wistful. The children, acting as waiters, bore away the plates for second helpings. 'No one ever pays the slightest attention to my wishes,' he said.

At Curzon Street the momentum never slowed. Meetings didn't run into the sand: the Secretary of State always summed up, even if it was only to go on to the next point. Progress of some sort was made. But everything was overhung by Britain's balance of payments problem, and all Ministers of spending departments knew July would be rough.

July is traditionally a bad month, the Commons end-of-term in sight, Ministers weary. On top of everything else, the Public Expenditure Survey Committees of Cabinet engage in the critical annual tussle – PESC: in a nightmarish and seemingly interminable series of bouts, each Minister of a spending department tries to wrest from the Chancellor a larger slice of the Treasury's cake. When Maurice Kogan was writing *The Politics of Education*, he asked Tony how a Minister gets enough resources out of the Treasury. 'By persuading, arguing, cajoling, exploiting his political position, being a bloody nuisance in Cabinet,' Tony said. 'Above all, by being persistent. Obviously success depends on a whole mixture of factors, a lot of them a matter of luck – your relations with the Chancellor; your standing in the Cabinet; the way the rest of the Cabinet feels towards the education service; whether you can exhaust your colleagues before they exhaust you. It's an endless tactical battle which requires determination, cunning and occasional unscrupulousness. In an ideal world it would all no doubt be settled by some omniscient central unit, but this is the way it happens in our crude democratic world.'

In July 1965 the exercise began with Callaghan announcing the Treasury's view that the entire cake must be reduced in order to protect the balance of payments. Tony and the other spending Ministers fought for their programmes in the knowledge that they had to give up something; he won for Education a larger portion of the shrunken cake. During PESC there was a run on the pound, and a further deflationary package was presented to Cabinet. The three men at the top still set their faces against the alternative – The Unmentionable.

Near the end of July, the Tories used their three Supply Days to put down censure motions. One was that in the Labour Government's nine months of office it had failed to carry out its election pledges for a five-year programme. The Prime Minister opened the debate. Tony wound up for the Government. He was concentrating on the economic policy argument dominating Cabinet and grudged spending time on what he saw as mere ritual; remembering how easy his previous winding-up speech had been, he assumed a grasp of subject was sufficient. He put aside twenty minutes to prepare the speech.

I had rarely been to the House but decided to drop in that evening, mounting the stairs to the gallery to an increasing din.

This baying – it really does sound like hounds – came from the chamber, where Iain Macleod was well into the Opposition's winding-up speech, returned to his old form, waspish, savaging. Tony never got his speech off the ground. From the moment he took his place at the dispatch box the Tories jeered and shouted, stamped their feet, slapped their thighs, rocked back and forth in a manner alarming to one unfamiliar with the House of Commons. The Labour benches sat packed and silent. When the hand of the clock over the Speaker's chair somehow, eventually, reached 10, I went down to Tony's room to wait for him. Bill Rodgers came in.

'Tell Tony that nobody could have done any better in the situation. It is everyone's nightmare that they'll be caught in just such circumstances. Harold opened the debate in his most brilliant form, and he had lifted our backbenches into euphoria. The Tories were sunk in depression until Macleod fired them. After that they had no intention of letting Tony get the House under his control.'

Dick Crossman stopped in to send much the same message. So did Douglas Jay, who hadn't spoken to me for two years: adversity can effect reconciliation. They'd left when Tony appeared, poured a drink for each of us and began the post-mortem:

'The thing could be controlled at least 20 per cent by turning it into a shouting match. It's sheer technique: learning to switch from one gear to another.' The more the technique became clear to him the more regret he felt.

'Why didn't anyone on your side make some noise and try to help? Do they sit there like lumps out of a mixture of schadenfreude and genuine curiosity about how their comrade will extricate himself?'

'I didn't deserve support, the speech was so abysmal.'

Over breakfast the next morning he glanced at the papers. 'That's a good knock-on-the-head to begin the day.' He tossed me the *Daily Telegraph*; he was outclassed and there was no room at that level for an elegant lightweight, it said.

The next day, Saturday, Evelyn and Alan Taylor came for a drink. How would Alan have avoided the débâcle?

'Why do you call it a débâcle,' I asked, 'when on Thursday night it seemed to me a distressing incident?'

'It *was* a débâcle,' he replied. His self-confidence was badly shaken. Alan said that even when he was speaking five times a week and on top of his form, he still found it hard to change gear. Tony found this interesting but remained subdued when we were alone.

He discussed it with Roy Jenkins who was now becoming a

master of the art of addressing the House of Commons, bringing it under his control however adverse the circumstances.

'I think of it rather as if I were in a bullfight,' Roy said. 'I try to feel the House, to play the House, like a matador playing a bull, for if you slip, it's very difficult to get up again. On a major speech to a full House I like to go on the 20:1 ratio – allow twenty times as long for the preparation of the speech as the speech itself will be.'

On Sunday night we took the children to see the Beatles in *Help*, and for a few hours Tony forgot his humiliation.

On Monday night he was preparing for a confrontation in the next day's Cabinet.

Tuesday night he came home with his self-confidence restored: Cabinet had shown that he had got that technique under control – something he'd doubted several months earlier. The main item on the agenda had been whether George Brown's National Plan could still be published after Callaghan's Statement on his deflationary package the week before. Tony asked the Cabinet, Crossman told his diary, 'how we could talk about a plan based on a 4 per cent average increase of production each year when we now knew perfectly well that for the next eighteen months at least, production wasn't going to rise by anything like that – in fact when the Government was actually cutting back production by its deflationary measures. Crosland is the only member of the Cabinet who comes right out with these honest-to-God economic judgments. He then went on, "We are launched on deflation and I know I shall have to rewrite the whole of my chapter in George Brown's National Plan. It makes no sense any more." '

Wednesday morning he grumbled about domestic matters for the first time since The Débâcle, frowning fiercely at his poached egg. 'Egg whites are much too large these days. Never used to be like that.' His mortification had evidently run its course; he was himself again.

That night he walked up and down in the study as he went over recent decision-taking in PESC. At Thursday's Cabinet, the Chancellor argued for increases in the price of coal. 'Before anyone else could speak,' Crossman told his diary, 'Tony Crosland intervened. "I've got to go away to answer a Question," he said. "But before I go I want to say that Callaghan, of course, is absolutely right. If we are going to have a policy of deflation – which I don't agree with but which we have accepted – then we ought to have these price increases now. But," and here he paused, "we ought to have seen them as a part of last week's package. As it is, we have got to accept them in addition to the package." '

Tony then suggested that all Cabinet Ministers write to the Prime Minister on Monday and give their individual views on the devaluation question. He left for the House.

'The Secretary of State for Education and Science has muddied the waters,' the Prime Minister said to the rest of his Cabinet.

You could tell a Labour Government was in office because Parliament was still sitting on the Glorious Twelfth, Tory MPs fastened to the Commons benches while the annual slaughter of the grouse began. On 13 August Parliament rose for the summer recess. We rented a house near Sandwich for our first August holiday *en famille*. We were to travel down separately, the children and Clea – the Siamese cat – and I converging at Charing Cross Station to catch the train for Kent. Tony would drive down later in the Sunbeam, which was stuffed with suitcases, books, my typewriter, the sewing machine, gramophone, hundreds of Beatles records.

At Curzon Street Mr Goshawk looked at the Diary and brooded. He knew that the children and I had second-class reservations for the 2.10. He knew we had to take the livestock. He knew I had an early lunch interview with Margot Fonteyn in the Charing Cross Hotel restaurant. He was fond of the children, who usually answered the telephone at Lansdowne Road. The Secretary of State was having a sandwich lunch in his room, so his driver was free. Mr Goshawk said to Mr Davis:

'Len, let's pick up the children and take them to the station.'

Clea was in a basket with the lid strapped shut. Arriving at Charing Cross with plenty of time, Mr Davis left the Princess in the car park. A woman who'd come along from the secretariat took the children off for a soft drink. Mr Goshawk and Mr Davis went to a pub.

Twenty minutes later they all met again by the car. The basket was in ruins: Clea was gone. Kidnapped. Ellen-Craig began to howl. Sheila kept asking Mr Davis if he'd locked the car. Mr Davis began dismantling the Princess. Finally he removed the back seat: Clea was found.

Mr Goshawk and Mr Davis went back to the pub to get an empty whisky box. Possibly they had another quick beer. Then they marched into the stationmaster's office. The stationmaster gave them a ball of twine that must have been ten inches in diameter. I insisted on getting into the first carriage and walking through the train to reach an empty compartment, anxious that the train would depart early. Above all, I must not be late. I carried the box with Clea in it; Mr Goshawk walked beside me wrapping twine around it; Mr Davis walked behind carrying the enormous ball of twine; behind him came the children. Mr Davis dropped the ball and we kept walking with the ball left behind us, leaving this growing tail as we filed through coach after coach. Mr Goshawk had the impression that the other passengers thought we'd got loose from an asylum. When he and Mr Davis got off the train, neither had ever wanted a cigarette so badly.

It turned out to be a good family holiday, though before its end, Tony and I agreed there was much to be said for the children's and my August visit to our American family, his setting off alone to the continent to read and walk and indulge his love of architecture. Extreme conjugal intimacy, in our view, was assisted by periodic recharging of batteries.

19

Odysseus

'A decision on election-timing is a lonely one,' Harold Wilson wrote in his personal record: 'Whatever the consultations, it is one man's decision and if things go wrong he is as likely to be criticised for missing a favourable tide as for plunging in too early.'

At the beginning of 1966 the Government's overall majority of six had shrunk to two. It was widely believed that the Prime Minister would go for a March election if Labour did well in the Hull North by-election; the Labour candidate won a majority of 5,351 votes – a swing to Labour of 45 per cent. The Prime Minister called the general election for 31 March.

At the end of the second week of the campaign, the children and I joined the Labour candidate in Grimsby, they for a weekend, I to stay. He met us at the station, and we walked over the level crossing to the County Hotel. The four-hour journey had taken five. I hoped we could have a quiet supper and not start charging about until the next day.

'Someone is bringing you coffee and biscuits,' he said as we went into the bedroom. 'You ought to get some food inside you.'

'Aren't we going to have supper soon?'

'Something has come up. Let me get the children settled in their room and I'll tell you about it.'

On returning he poured an outsize shot of whisky into the tumbler that stood on the washstand. He was a great believer in travelling with a half-bottle for contingencies. 'Have a big swallow of this,' he said. I did so with pleasure. 'Tonight's going to be a strain that none of us expected. When I mentioned this to some doctor friend of Muriel Barker, he said it'd be a good idea for you to take a couple of these pills. No point in getting unduly exhausted as soon as you get here when there's a heavy week ahead.'

'What are they?'

'Please take them.'

As there wasn't a second glass, I washed the pills down with another swallow of whisky. What on earth could we have to do that evening that he should brace me like this, girding himself as well?

'Let us sit down on the bed,' he said tenderly. 'And have another swallow from that glass. I must tell you something you don't want to hear. I must tell you that your father has died.'

A little later he went across the corridor to the children's room. There was the low sound of his voice, the light murmur of a child's voice, a child crying. After a while he came back to our room.

The following day he drove all of us to Heathrow. We decided that whatever headmistresses' views of schoolchildren 'electioneering', Sheila and Ellen-Craig would be less disoriented if they were with him and friends in Grimsby. Just before I went through Passport Control, Ellen-Craig asked Tony for some money. She returned with her purchase and handed it to me. She knew Flake was my favourite chocolate, always gave me a Flake for family occasions. I caught the plane for Baltimore. They drove back to Grimsby.

My parents' marriage was exceptionally close. My sister and I were very anxious about our mother making the three train journeys required to reach the ice-locked shores of Lake Champlain where my father was born. The *Baltimore Sun* dealt with that by giving us their directors' light aircraft to take my father's ashes north. On the previous day, several New England cousins had cut a path through the frozen drifts that blanketed the family burial ground and chopped out a deep hole. During the night snow fell and froze again. My mother held the box of ashes against her while one of my cousins knelt on the icy ground with an axe. A little later my mother and sister and I climbed into the aeroplane and returned to Baltimore. It was about two years before I could speak of the fact that my father was dead.

In Britain the Prime Minister had got his election-timing right. Labour was returned to office with a majority of 110 over the Conservatives, an overall majority of 97 seats. Towards the middle of April I rejoined Tony and the children.

When Wilson became Leader, most Labour MPs accepted the fact, some with deep reluctance. On becoming Ministers, a very few tried strenuously to influence him in the direction they wanted a Labour Government to move. This was largely a doomed effort: whether Left, Right or Centre, few felt in communication with the Prime Minister. Tony was never certain that Wilson took a great interest in equality.

Though he remained popular with Labour supporters outside London, in Fleet Street and Westminster Wilson's honeymoon was long over. With Labour's new healthy majority, backbenchers saw no excuse for his continued policy of deflation rather than devaluation. His refusal to withdraw from 'east of Suez' was pretentious and costly: why didn't he accept that days of Empire were past and spend the money on social programmes? Britain no longer had real military influence in the Middle East, even Defence enthusiasts agreeing that some of the Defence budget was wasteful.

More and more he seemed influenced by his cronies – the 'Kitchen Cabinet', whom he trusted. It wasn't evident that he trusted many people. Finally, what should have been a triviality produced extraordinary results; he was obsessed with the press. He read every newspaper before midnight every day. One of his advisers, Lord Goodman, later Chairman of the Newspaper Publishers' Association, told Wilson above all to ignore the press: complaining would only incite them further. Wilson would not listen. Where Harold Macmillan knew how to handle journalists (he claimed that he never read newspapers), Wilson once summoned the editor of the *Observer* to No. 10 to reproach him for Nora Beloff's column.

Everything combined chemically to make the press – and a growing number of MPs – focus on Wilson's *style*: they found it offensive. He relied on the Paymaster-General, George Wigg, to keep him informed of what was being said. There was no way realistically to oust a prime minister who had just been endorsed by a large majority of Labour supporters. Yet Wilson's obsession with the press and plots against him did as much as anything to fuel a plot.

At this time Roy Jenkins, now the Home Secretary, became the hero of the liberal press. Older Right-wingers in the PLP and a number of young revisionist backbenchers looked to Roy as the only Cabinet Minister who could replace Wilson. Roy's championship of libertarian rights caught the mood of the 1960s. Under his direction, reform of outdated laws was given priority – abortion, homosexuality, criminal justice, and other important liberal Bills were brought forward. He had developed into a superb House of Commons orator, in advance wringing his hands in an uncontrollable mechanism of nerves, then rising to his feet and delivering a performance that lifted his backbenches to bellicose rapture. He had style.

Apart from the Prime Minister, it was very unusual for a Cabinet Minister to have a personal public relations officer. Not only did Roy Jenkins have one: John Harris was far more adroit in dealing with the press than was the PM's PRO. Cabinet Ministers took no great pleasure in reading newspaper versions of private meetings and events gone slightly askew in the telling. The Prime Minister took even less pleasure in reading that he ought to be replaced by his Home Secretary. Dick Crossman was delegated to approach Tony on the matter. Could his old friend Roy be persuaded that John Harris's press campaign was poisoning relationships and would in the end do Roy no good?

As he hardly saw Roy these days, he was not in a position to counsel him, Tony replied.

Over gossip that night he said: 'I'm not used to someone running back and forth between George and Jim and Harold in constant intrigue and self-promotion.'

'Did you say that to Dick as well?'

'Of course not. Since the press has built up this great rivalry between Roy and me, I'm the last person who can speak candidly about him. Still, nothing unusual in these feelings. Denis has practised his brand of gamesmanship on Dick Crossman for twenty years, gradually undermining Dick's self-confidence and morale; George's rivalry with Jim never gets below simmering, more often on the boil. What's unusual is that Roy's and my friendship has survived at all, though it's going to be a little tried if one can't open a newspaper without reading what a paragon he is.'

The Prime Minister by this time had reason to believe people were plotting against him, but he often saw conspirators where there were none, in and out of Cabinet. Tony lacked the temperament of a conspirator. Moreover, during some crises that faced the Government, whatever his antipathy to aspects of Harold Wilson, he had a detached regard for the man's nerve. An early instance was in November 1965, the night before Rhodesia declared UDI, when Tony was at Downing Street for a six o'clock appointment, made days earlier, to discuss an education problem in the Prime Minister's constituency.

'Surely it would be sensible to fix an appointment for another day,' he said to Marcia Williams, at which point the Prime Minister popped out of his room, genially insistent.

'Come in, come in. Of course I want to discuss my constituents.' For the next twenty minutes he chattered amiably and utterly relaxed as if he hadn't another care in the world.

'Quite remarkable, really,' Tony said when he came home that evening.

At other times his predominant feelings were stoical acceptance that the workings of the Prime Minister's mind must remain a

mystery, deep regret for what he regarded as shoddiness. The
Government was stuck with him. Publicly Tony defended the
Prime Minister. Privately he made clear his aversion to plotting
against a colleague and was particularly irritated by conspirators
who had supported Wilson for the leadership.

'You were right, Tony. He's nothing more than a shabby tactician.' Two young MPs were having a drink at Lansdowne Road.

'Oh, I've come round to your earlier view,' Tony replied, instantly recalcitrant. 'I may think one thing, Harold may think
another. Harold knows best. Harold is a bastard, but he's a genius.
He's like Odysseus. Odysseus also was a bastard, but he managed
to steer the ship between Scylla and Charybdis.'

When our guests had departed, I asked: 'How much of that did
you actually mean?'

'Don't know. But after all the balls-aching stuff about Harold's
great white heat of technology revolution which we used to hear
from those young men, I don't intend commiserating with them
now. I meant the Odysseus analogy.'

Inside the Cabinet Room, the Secretary of State for Education
persistently opened his contributions by saying: 'You know, Prime
Minister, that I am not in agreement about a fundamental issue.'
Colleagues thought Tony had isolated himself by banging on about
The Unmentionable.

When the Big Three made their original first-night decision
against devaluation, the Permanent Secretary of the Treasury – Sir
William Armstrong – was happy enough. If he had second
thoughts, he saw no point in expressing them: 'My temperament
is to say spilt milk is spilt milk. I'm not going to cry over it. I detest
that,' he said. 'But the Labour economists wouldn't forget it. They
went on chewing the fat.'

Foremost among them were Tony, Robert Neild, Nicky Kaldor,
and belatedly Tommy Balogh – the Prime Minister's personal
economic adviser. They talked at Lansdowne Road, Balogh always
arriving on his own. Tony expected Tommy to repeat their conversation to his employer: that was the point. The meetings were
not a conspiracy against an individual: they were attempts to bring
the Government to reconsider economic strategy. In July 1966
George Brown had finally come round to the necessity of devaluation. Callaghan had not.

'Robert and Nicky were surprised that I didn't try to stop them
seeing Jim,' Armstrong said when talking about it afterwards. 'I
didn't mind.' Because he and other Treasury officials would have

the last word, knowing they could count on the Prime Minister? 'If you want to put it that way.'

Relations between Callaghan and Brown got worse and worse, any concordat between their economic departments hard to detect. 'Harold was unmerciful in his divide-and-rule,' said Armstrong in his non-committal manner. 'If he got some story about Jim from George, he would tax Jim with it. If he got some story about George he would say: "We don't need to bother George yet. Perhaps you could ask him to look in after dinner." It was meant to sound an innocent remark, but he knew that George would be incoherent by then.'

On 12 July 1966, Cabinet's long-awaited discussion of productivity got off to a terrible start: the Chancellor announced he must lop a further half-billion pounds off public spending. Dick Crossman said to his diary:

The meeting only really got going when Tony Crosland said that whatever happened he didn't want a repetition of the July 1965 crisis. He didn't want to see us once again combating inflation by cutting public expenditure. I chipped in and said to the Chancellor '... The public sector is not too big now – it's far too small. There can be no question of a cut-back.' At this point the Chancellor woke up and said that he must tell Cabinet frankly that he didn't know how we were going to get out of the mess. We had totally failed to reach our objectives, we were drifting into devaluation in the worst possible conditions and he didn't know how he could retain his position as Chancellor.

On 13 July, the Prime Minister heard a suggestion that Callaghan was considering The Unmentionable and summoned him. Armstrong was present. 'Harold browbeat Jim. Jim retreated,' he said.

Three days later, displaying his usual nerve, the Prime Minister flew to Moscow for a weekend visit, hoping thus to counteract spreading international rumours that Britain's stricken economy was failing by the hour. He flew out of Heathrow on Saturday. By Sunday night at least a score of meetings had taken place in London between certain Ministers and economic advisers. The agenda: could Callaghan at last be persuaded to devalue or float the pound? If so, which course was now the better? If not, how could George Brown be prevented from resigning? – for, having seen the light on his way to Damascus, George took up devaluation with ardour. If he left the Cabinet it would be an enormous loss: he had imagination as well as ability. And, in Tony's view, the

Cabinet was overweighted with Oxbridge graduates: George was one of the few men governing the country who had first-hand experience of how the majority must make do without a privileged education.

'At moments of crisis,' said Robert Neild, 'people are caught in characteristic poses. Roy is at a grand country house. Nicky is rushing back and forth between Cambridge and London. Tony is at home with his wife and family.' It was still Sunday morning, and Robert had just arrived at Lansdowne Road. He went up to the study, followed a few minutes later by Nicky Kaldor. It was sure to be a crisis if Nicky didn't stop to kiss me.

Roy rang from the country, having read the Sunday papers and become very miserable at being out of things. George Brown had rung him the day before, saying he was going to resign and that Roy should resign too. This naturally made Roy angry.

At the morning's end, Robert and Nicky departed, and Tony drove to the Browns' flat in Carlton Gardens. George was calm. Contrary to one of many rumours, no one had been dispatched to Moscow to hand the Prime Minister a letter of resignation. 'I shall wait and decide after Cabinet on Wednesday,' said George. 'If Harold perseveres in his Tory policy, I shall then resign.'

At two o'clock Tony returned to Lansdowne Road. A few minutes later Robert and Nicky walked through our front door.

Eventually we had our sandwiches alone and I heard the day's gossip so far. Then Roy arrived from the country and went up to the study. Then Tony went to No. 11 to see Jim. Then he and Robert and Nicky met again. Then Tony went back to George's flat. The Sabbath was not observed.

On Monday afternoon the Secretary of State for Education left Curzon Street to work in his room at the Commons where no Private Secretary would be present when he was visited by the Prime Minister's economic adviser. Then came Dick Crossman, then Roy, and so on. By evening the corridor of Ministers' rooms was like ring a ring of roses, faces disappearing from one room to bob up in another.

Throughout his short visit to Moscow, the Prime Minister stalwartly faced the gruelling succession of state occasions. There was not a single break without Private Secretaries bearing messages of crisis upon crisis at home. On Tuesday afternoon, he went straight from Heathrow to chair a Cabinet which lasted nearly five hours. Before its end he was forced to make important concessions: if the Government could survive the present ghastly situation, The Unmentionable would be discussed; a small committee would be set up to work out economic strategy.

On the urgent issue – devaluation or floating *immediately* – he kept his grip on a majority of Cabinet; Ministers concerned with foreign affairs agreed that to alter sterling at this moment could undermine confidence in the Government; the 'weak Ministers' supported the Prime Minister as usual. The following morning the Cabinet met for a further four hours, formalising the Government's statement. That evening George Brown resigned.

Any acknowledgment of the Prime Minister's jetlag was out of the question. An evening of utter turmoil began, typified by Bill Rodgers, George's junior minister, rushing about the House of Commons with a great piece of paper, which he exhorted MPs to sign, begging George to stay on. The Prime Minister had to decide something, so he decided not to inform the Queen that her First Secretary had resigned. At the next morning's Cabinet, the First Secretary was in his place as usual.

The ensuing fortnight found Cabinets excessively strained, the Prime Minister nagging his colleagues about leaks to the press. Dick Crossman told his diary:

(4 AUGUST 1966) Harold again mentioned the danger of leaks. At this Tony Crosland barged in and said: 'Of course we don't mind that kind of thing being said by the Prime Minister, but we all know that most of the information goes to the press either from No. 10 or from the environs of DEA.' There was an awkward silence and I think this has cost Tony dear in his relations with Harold. Still, he had the courage to say it. This is the fourth Cabinet running in which he has played an active part, talking not just as a departmental Minister but as somebody who understands economics and rates himself equal with the PM, George Brown and James Callaghan, somebody who has forced his way into their stratosphere.

A week later the Prime Minister announced a small reshuffle of his Cabinet. George Brown's 'resignation' – his public disassociation from Government economic policy – made his position at DEA difficult. The Prime Minister swopped him with the Foreign Secretary, Michael Stewart, who now became First Secretary. In Wilson's record of those years, he wrote that when making the appointment he doubted that George Brown had the right temperament for Foreign Secretary.

Next the Prime Minister acted on the concession forced from

him by Cabinet: after nearly two years in office, he set up a Cabinet Committee to co-ordinate economic strategy. He had fulfilled his promise. He then instructed this committee not to discuss devaluation.

'Oh dear,' Dick Crossman said to his diary, 'it is a panjandrum committee – the Prime Minister, First Secretary, Foreign Secretary, the Minister of Defence, the Minister of Labour for some reason, myself. Of course, none of the people who really wanted to be on it – Tony Crosland, Roy Jenkins, Barbara. It's just the top people, sitting around without briefing and without officials.'

20

A Disturbed Holiday

1967 began. The balance of payments problem still overhung everything, but at least the distribution of the Treasury's cake had changed. When Tony went to Education in 1965, its portion was much smaller than that of Defence. After two years of PESC contentions, Education's share had increased, until its budget equalled that of Defence. In Curzon Street morale was high. Educationalists thought his capacity to administer reform was as important as his ideas. He had clear views on the purpose of a Cabinet Minister. 'That's not for me,' he said, waving away whatever it was he couldn't be bothered with. 'Let one of my junior ministers deal with that.'

Most Ministers' schedules are outside their control, but how early they start and how late they go on working can be adapted to their nature. Tony Benn liked breakfast meetings. Tony Crosland was an owl, getting up as late as possible and working into the small hours. If divisions chained him to the Commons at night, he worked there in his room. Cabinet Ministers, unlike other MPs, each have a big room at the House, so he had space to prowl back and forth when he was thinking something through. It was there his Ministers of State and other junior ministers came to see him individually. 'Seeing them all together, which sounds the obvious way of going about things, is always rather a shambles. What they really want is for one to be their psychoanalyst,' he said.

Some MPs came about education problems in their constituencies, some about personal problems. He stressed his belief that no one could advise another about marriage or a career: 'All one can do is help put the pros and cons in order.' If anybody talked to Tony about a private crisis and asked him not to tell me, he didn't tell me. (I learned about it only if the person told me, as occasionally happened years later.) He was rarely 'seen around the House' – in the tea room or in Annie's Bar. He was accessible in his room.

Following the nights when he'd been at the Commons for late

divisions, Private Office went over to collect the boxes he'd worked through and left locked in his room. They couldn't remember another Minister who after finishing one day's work could in the evening throw himself so completely into the equivalent of a second. He was more systematic under pressure than anyone Mr Goshawk ever served: 'When he relaxed, he relaxed completely. When the time he'd given himself was up, he'd eat something at his desk and have a cup of coffee and focus on work again. He knew how to pace himself. He was immensely strong. After he left Curzon Street, I followed his career. I wasn't at all prepared for what happened.'

We failed utterly to devise a system to make ministerial mornings less hateful to him: he detested having to leave home at 9 a.m. 'Do you realise that half of Britain has been up for at least two hours?' he would say in self-encouragement. He nevertheless so disliked looking out of our bedroom window upon the official car waiting to bear him off that he instructed Mr Davis to park outside someone else's house. He then had the brief illusion of freedom as he strolled the fifty or so yards from our front door to the Princess. People walking down Lansdowne Road to the tube station thought the Minister lived farther up the street.

He had bouts of obsession on this subject of starting the day. He would open his Monday-morning meeting with his civil servants: 'I have read the papers. The first four suggestions won't do for these reasons: A ... B ... C ... D ... We are left with suggestions five and six which we shall now discuss.' At the end he summed up, and they were departing when suddenly he asked: 'How much sleep do you need? How do you wake up in the morning?'

Assorted methods were tried. For a period he lurched straight from bed to lie in the big old-fashioned bathtub, enveloped by warm water. Then there were weeks when he started directly on his RAF exercises, doing pushups with his eyes still closed. Someone told him about an electric kettle with a clock on it. By nature Tony was an optimist. He described the marvellous kettle to me.

'The tea makes itself. All one has to do is reach over to the bedside table and pour it out. If one has the first cup of tea while looking through the morning papers, waking up isn't so trying.'

I rashly invested in this machine, which at the appointed hour began to sigh and murmur, eventually emitting the sound of boiling. It was a bit like having a third party in the bedroom.

'Why must it be on my side of the bed?' he asked after three mornings of this.

'Because I don't drink tea. I don't read the morning papers until I'm in bed at night. Under this new system I'm not meant to wake up all the way until you shave and I go make breakfast.'

A week passed.

'When I come home tonight, we must have a serious discussion.' His voice was sombre. That night he said: 'We haven't money to throw around. You went to trouble to find that machine. But there is something oppressive about its presence right beside my pillow. It makes me feel claustrophobic.' The paper boy had been late on two mornings, so there'd been no newspapers to read anyhow. A week later I unplugged the marvel and gave it away.

After my father died, my mother felt she must leave the house where she'd lived all those years. The burden of responsibility for what followed fell on my sister. My annual visits to Baltimore were now scheduled by factors other than the calendar.

In June of 1967 my mother crossed the ocean to stay at Lansdowne Road until August. I came home from an interview late on a Friday to find Tony and my mother in the drawing-room. He was sitting in a chair near her. Each had the look one sees on people who have just given way to deep emotion. Soon after I joined them, Tony said he supposed he'd better go upstairs and do some work. After a few minutes my mother said: 'Dear, you should be with your husband.' I went up to the study. Tony said: 'You should be with your mother. She broke down when I walked in half an hour ago. She said she'd been looking out the window on to the garden square, thinking how happy your father would be that our home is the way it is. Then she saw he was standing under the acacia tree. She said she knew with her mind that only barbarians imagine such things, yet she had watched him for some minutes as he stood there.' I went downstairs again.

Ten days after my mother returned to Baltimore, the children and I went to Barley Cove, Ireland. On vacation I liked to stay in one place, lie on the sand, swim far out into the bay. 'Why do you swim so far? We couldn't see you,' the children said.

Meanwhile Tony was touring Cyprus. I never volunteered – nor was asked – to take part in planning these solitary sojourns. Sylvia Littlejohns, his personal secretary, was paid for her strivings. During the months before his August holiday, at one side of his chair a neat pile grew: hotel brochures, railway timetables,

Mediterranean ferry timetables, international and airline timetables, P & O sailings, car-hire listings, all systematically examined
and whittled down when he was relaxing. He entrusted the booking
arrangements to Sylvia, but he alone meshed the timetables.
'Women can't read timetables,' he said. The relevant books on
architecture were taken down from the shelves, the theme of the
holiday refined as his imagination was seized.

He mixed method and inspiration in a manner that could reduce
less hardy spirits to despair. The previous August holiday a vessel
with only a dozen staterooms, most of the ship taken up by cargo,
was specifically instructed – and agreed in writing – to provide an
armchair in an otherwise unprepossessing stateroom. On entering
it Tony said: 'Where is my armchair?' Then followed feverish
logistical and physical efforts by men brought up from the boiler
room, all trying to manoeuvre an armchair from the saloon through
a door patently too narrow for such demands. Inexplicably the
thing was accomplished, the armchair inside the stateroom when
the passenger returned from his lunch.

If friends were renting a house in the area he was exploring, his
day could include lunch with them. When a British official relegated
to an out-of-the-way post was certain to know a Cabinet Minister
was around, Tony made the effort to call on him. But interruption
of his solitude was rare: he wasn't bored when alone; he liked
reading over a meal; he needed respite from the sound of the human
voice.

The only time he made systematic entries in his Labour Party
pocket diary was on his August holiday. Alongside whatever he'd
done, he entered a letter indicating whether it had been good, fair,
bad, so he wouldn't forget if he wanted to do it again. A number
was entered as well: this represented the cheroots he smoked that
day. He liked to cut back on them during holidays, though I failed
to see the point of this: he resumed heavy smoking as soon as the
holiday ended. 1967's notations included:

11 AUGUST		12 AUGUST	
Fly Athens:		Nicosia	
Athens–Nicosia	G	sightsee Old City	G
dine High Commissioner	F	lunch	
19		sleep	
		cafe c. view, dine	G

20 AUGUST
  Famagusta:
  a.m. Kantura Castle
      lunch Kantura   G
  p.m. bathe, Old City, walk
      dine cafe   G
    4

23 AUGUST
  Boat:
  6.15 pass thru Dardanelles   F
  lunch c. Captain   v.B.
  2.30 drive back Istanbul
  sightsee
  dine Consul-General   G
    8

25 AUGUST
  Istanbul:
  a.m. Topkapi Palace
  c. Director   F
  lunch c. Erten,
  Minister of Edn.
  sightsee, dine cafe   G
    3

27 AUGUST
  Famagusta:
  a.m. tel. calls c. H.W.,
  and trying to reach S. in
  Ireland   v.v.v.B.
  lunch, walk, bathe, dine F
    20

28 AUGUST
  a.m. drive Famagusta-
  Larnaca   v.G.
  sightsee & lunch Larnaca
  drive Platros:
  stroll, dine
  talk c. Cypriot gp.   G
    3

The next four days varied from F to v.G. and the number of cheroots settled at two. He was determined that tel. calls c. H.W. did not spoil the end of his August holiday.

When an international operator tracked him down on 27 August, a Sunday, he was just setting off on his day's sightseeing. In the Scilly Isles, the British Prime Minister was playing golf, his walkie-talkie accompanying him. A telephone connection between golf-links in the Scillies and a hotel bedroom in Cyprus is not what many of us would choose to discuss a complex matter. Most of the Prime Minister's words were lost in bursts of crackling, but their gist was clear enough: he wanted to bring Tony into the economic team to grapple with the balance of payments; Education had been set on the right road and someone else could now carry it on; with DEA being run down, it was important that the third economic department, the Board of Trade, be invigorated by someone who had both a wide grasp of economics and drive; he wanted Tony to become its President. If Tony agreed to this, of course he would be brought into the Cabinet's Steering Committee for Economic Policy.

Feeling this an unsatisfactory way to make major decisions, Tony said he would have to reflect before giving an answer. The Prime Minister resumed his golf. The Secretary of State for Education reflected. He'd been in a happy frame of mind when he went on his August holiday. His policy on comprehensives had gone so far as to be irreversible. He was getting the polytechnics established. He'd liberalised the government of the education colleges. He'd created the Social Science Research Council. He'd set up the Council for Educational Technology. The intractable problem of teacher supply was at last under control. He had just taken up the Plowden Report's recommendations for a large-scale building programme in educational priority areas. And the Public Schools Commission was due to report to him in the coming year. He was in sight of accomplishing many, not all, of the things he had set his heart on.

On the other hand, he wanted to be in a stronger position to influence central economic policy. He'd always dreaded being landed with the Board of Trade. Yet he knew he'd be far better placed there – and on the Steering Committee for Economic Policy – to press the devaluation issue and influence the economic strategy on which Education and every other domestic spending department ultimately depended.

A second telephone communication was established between the bedroom in Famagusta and the golf-links in the Scillies, and the man in the bedroom gave his answer. He was no longer happy.

Douglas Jay was even less happy. Summoned from Dartmoor where he was quietly enjoying his own holiday (Douglas nursed suspicions of 'abroad'), he met the Prime Minister in the stationmaster's office at Plymouth railway station, where he was told, in a kindly manner, that his services as President of the Board of Trade were no longer required. The Prime Minister then reboarded the train to continue the journey from Penzance to Paddington. He offered Douglas Jay no other job in Cabinet. 'Understandably, he took it badly,' Wilson wrote in his record.

Meanwhile, what remained of Tony's Sunday morning vanished in his vain attempts to make telephone communication with Barley Cove, Ireland.

That Sunday evening a Post Office messenger delivered a

telegram to Barley Cove (followed half an hour later by a reporter and photographer from the local paper, these agencies having mysterious links):

FAILED UTTERLY TO GET THROUGH BY PHONE RE-SHUFFLE TO BE ANNOUNCED MONDAY NIGHT MIXED FEELINGS BUT ON BALANCE MUST BE RIGHT I DO NOT REPEAT NOT HAVE TO RETURN EARLY PLEASE TELEPHONE CURZON STREET ASKING NOT TO TELL PRESS EXACT WHERE-ABOUTS SAY VAGUELY SOMEWHERE IN TURKEY WISH YOU WERE HERE LONGING TO SEE YOU FRIDAY ANTHONY.

I wondered who, struggling with Famagusta's telegraph service, had signed his name Anthony.

When the travellers reconvened at Lansdowne Road he was cheerful, though I knew he was depressed. Over the weekend the Callaghans came to dinner, the Board of Trade's Principal Private Secretary brought briefings, the Grimsby agent – in London for the day – stopped by for a drink, we went round the corner to see the Benns. On Monday morning the Princess set forth as usual, but at Curzon Street, instead of turning left, it continued to the end of Victoria Street where stood the Board of Trade. Later in the day I called in for a sandwich lunch with the President. The curtains hanging in his room appeared to have shrunk considerably when last cleaned. I failed to interest him in this aspect of his new department.

⇥ 21 ⇤

The Unmentionable

On joining SEP, as the Steering Committee for Economic Policy was known, the President of the Board of Trade ignored the Prime Minister's ban on discussing The Unmentionable. Towards the end of October 1967 he was invited to lunch in the Wilsons' flat at the top of No. 10. Tony hadn't previously visited the flat. Outside Cabinet he had practically no relations with the Prime Minister – though if it came to that, George Wigg and Dick Crossman and Tommy Balogh, Harold's closest collaborators, never had a meal in the Wilson home, wherever it was.

'What did you have for lunch?' I asked that evening.

'Far too much. Badly cooked. Marcia served the lunch. Mary popped in once or twice. Harold explained that the Douglas-Homes had preferred to live among the State Rooms.'

'But what did you eat?'

'You will insist on my trying to remember culinary detail. Pork chops. Lots of veg. Harold had a second pork chop.'

'Perhaps they were well-cooked and you just have a thing about pork chops because I've given you so many.'

'No, they were extremely badly cooked. Everything was. No one could say that Harold is the most elevated conversationalist. You're interested simply because he's Prime Minister. We don't all agree with Roy that Prime Ministers should be elegant and erudite. But one *did* have to drag him back to serious conversation: he was constantly breaking off with a fresh anecdote. Really all he wants to do is chitter-chatter. He's not interested in anything else.'

But he was. The motive for the cosy lunch at last emerged – this matter of Tony's raising The Unmentionable at SEP. Harold was not, he said, convinced of Tony's view, but he had 'an absolutely open mind'.

'You mean all those statements about his being against devaluation may not be true?'

'The trouble with Harold is one hasn't the faintest idea whether the bastard means what he says even at the moment he speaks it.'

A secondary motive for the lunch might, Tony thought, be that he was fairly alone in making no effort to talk with Harold outside Cabinet, and this made Harold at some point want to break the log-jam.

Early in November 1967, a decisive struggle took place in SEP. The President of the Board of Trade put the case for devaluation. The Prime Minister repeated what he'd said at the lunch: he had an open mind. He and the Chancellor would take the ultimate decision about devaluation, he said. The President of the Board of Trade argued that the decision must be taken at SEP. Reluctantly, the Prime Minister agreed.

The next evening, Tony was at home. After dinner Roy called in and went up to the study. As Home Secretary he was not a member of SEP. Conscious that momentous things were happening about which he knew nothing, he was nervous, glum, feeling left out.

The following Monday evening the Prime Minister made a much-heralded speech at the Guildhall, all about technology in Europe. 'Harold is mad, of course. That's the other thing about him,' Tony said over gossip. ' "A European Technological Community"! Good diversionary tactics when the economy is sinking round us. But nonsense, utter nonsense.'

On Tuesday morning the Princess left Lansdowne Road and headed in the wrong direction, Tony still not understanding why Private Office couldn't get him out of these engagements. By Royal Command the President of the Board of Trade had to be at Heathrow to see the Queen off for Malta. He then went straight to No. 11 Downing Street at 11.15 as requested: the Chancellor wanted to see him before they were caught up in talks with the Belgian Prime Minister whose visit to London rather unfortunately fell that week. What Jim wanted to tell Tony was that he and the Prime Minister had agreed to devalue.

At 11.30 the meeting with the Belgian Prime Minister and his colleagues began punctually, the visitors unaware how preoccupied were the minds of their hosts. The British Prime Minister passed two notes to the President of the Board of Trade. The first said: 'Happy?' The second: 'It is terribly important nothing be said to *any* colleague. A few of us are meeting today (including you of course), but *others of SEP* will not be there. We have to keep things very tight. H.'

Lunch at No. 10 followed the talks, afternoon meetings on various subjects that came under Trade, a working dinner with the

British Airports Authority, home. He asked for my gossip first. Then I asked for his.

'It's happening on Saturday.'

'Are you excited?'

'After three years it's somewhat anti-climactic.'

The people who had talked with the Prime Minister that afternoon were to be known simply as the Special Committee until their function was concluded: Jim Callaghan, George Brown, Tony, Denis Healey, Michael Stewart, Peter Shore, and George Thomson who as Commonwealth Secretary had to supervise those countries' notification. They met again at 9 a.m. on Wednesday and again that evening, secrecy essential lest speculators began a run on the pound before devaluation was announced. The Lord President of the Council, Dick Crossman, rushed hither and thither saying how scandalous it was that in this economic crisis there was no inner group set up, sublimely unaware of the existence of the Special Committee.

On Thursday morning the rest of Cabinet were told that sterling would be devalued on Saturday. Then the Prime Minister and his colleagues went ahead with their scheduled engagements as if nothing out of the ordinary impended.

Because Civil Aviation came under Trade, the President had access to a six-seater executive jet when departmental business required it. For forty-eight hours he zigzagged round northern England, ending up with an address to a Regional Conference at Washington, Co. Durham. When the jet landed at Heathrow on Saturday evening, he was met by his Permanent Secretary and Principal Private Secretary who filled him in on what had been happening while he was away. At our front door they parted company, and at 9.30 we listened to the BBC's announcement that the Government would devalue sterling. We took the telephone off its hook. When *Match of the Day* was over, I restored the telephone. Much later we got round to gossip.

'Jim may resign at the end of next week.'

'Oh no. Not so soon.'

'Well, perhaps not. But I think within two weeks, though all these feelings can change.'

On Sunday morning Jim's personal secretary rang. Would I ask Mr Crosland if he could join the Chancellor at No. 11 that evening to listen to the Prime Minister's television address to the nation? Jim also wanted his old cronies, Merlyn Rees and George Thomson, with him at this bitter end of his chancellorship: he intended to resign soon after the announcement that spelled the failure of his policy. When Tony got back to Lansdowne Road he broke the news gently. 'Merlyn said Jim should resign on Wednesday immediately after the Devaluation Debate. Merlyn is a nice man but a bloody fool when it comes to political judgment. If Jim were given some time, I think he could be persuaded to take another job in Cabinet. At the moment he is too knocked about to think straight.' He got out of his chair and walked up and down the study. Then he said: 'I think I should tell you that Jim talked in front of the others about my being Chancellor in a week or so. He says that he and Harold have agreed that the odds on this are 95:5.'

I had the grace to get out of my chair and kiss him. 'Congratulations.'

He was perfectly aware of my dismay.

It was five years since our last celebration of Hugh Gaitskell's birthday, a festive lunch for four, produced by Dora at Frognal Gardens. The two men took me off for a post-prandial expedition: I'd never visited Karl Marx's grave in Highgate Cemetery. The gates were locked, my skirt cut too narrow for me to scale the fence. The younger man dealt with the problem by picking me up and chucking me over the barrier. The older man laughed and flushed at the same time, observing the approach of more-sedate Sabbath strollers. 'Tony, I wish you would remember that I am Leader of Her Majesty's Opposition. I do not want to read in the *Daily Express* that my friends are hurling one another into Highgate Cemetery.'

At tea Dora said: 'Now that you have committed yourself to being a politician, Tony, what is your greatest ambition?'

'As every social objective I believe in depends on getting the economy right, I suppose one would like to be Chancellor of the Exchequer.'

At first I thought it was the prospect of moving into 11 Downing Street that dismayed me. We'd been married only three years; Lansdowne Road was the first complete home the children and I had known for some time. They could bring schoolmates back for lunch on the days Mrs McGovern made soda bread. In principle Mrs McGovern came in the mornings to do housework. In practice she was a family mainstay: by now Sheila and Ellen-Craig were both in the throes of adolescence. Edna Healey had told me that their move to Admiralty House, when Denis became Defence Minister, had blighted their younger daughter's childhood: 'As far as she's concerned, she has no home.' There was a second – no doubt ridiculous – anxiety that played round the edges of the mind: as Tony's public responsibility increased, how much more of our private life would slip away?

'If I do become Chancellor,' he said on Monday night, 'we won't move house. It would be absolutely wrong for the children. I could simply have a pied à terre at No. 11 – come home virtually every night.'

'I don't want you not to be Chancellor. I just wish it could be postponed for a couple of years.'

'I know,' he said. It was a domestic dilemma, not an argument.

On Tuesday he opened the Commons debate on devaluation. Dick Crossman recorded in his diary on 26 November: 'The officials are preparing a white paper under the direction of the Chancellor and the President of the Board of Trade ...' By Wednesday I was feeling ill most of the time. I would go to sleep at night and wake up an hour later thinking all over again about the ramifications of moving into an official residence.

'Wish I could stop you worrying like this,' Tony said. 'You're making yourself ill. It may not even happen. Though I have to tell you that Jim is now talking in front of Armstrong and Harold Lever about how I will have to deal with the gold problem next week.' He produced various thoughts to bolster morale. One was: 'It would encourage the Owen–Marquand–Price generation as evidence that scheming isn't necessary for success in politics.'

Thursday morning he went off to Cabinet. I went into the bathroom to be sick. Having got myself together, I arrived at the lunch for the Canadian Prime Minister's wife a few minutes before everyone moved into the dining-room. I went straight to Audrey Callaghan. Her husband's career in ruins, she was dignified as always, discussing with Mrs Mulley something sensible like curing dry rot.

'How are you, Audrey? How can you get through a week like this?'

'I can't sleep. I wake up and I can't make my brain stop. I would never advise Jim on politics, but I can't make my brain stop.'

'I'd hoped experience would make it a little easier to deal with terrible anxiety.'

'It gets much worse, because his responsibility increases.'

Edna Healey was at the same lunch, and I drove her back to Admiralty House. Among Labour wives there is more empathy than perhaps is imagined.

'How's Tony bearing up this week?' Edna asked. I said that he was so busy he hadn't time for introspection, but that I was sick in the loo a couple of times a day.

'I spent yesterday in bed, I felt so sick,' said Edna. Until then I hadn't realised that Denis, also, was wondering whether he would be Chancellor. 'Why don't you come in for a few minutes, Susan?'

'Thanks. I really just want to go home.'

'I know.'

That night when Tony came back he said that he'd again told Jim not to make up his mind yet to retire to the backbenches. Jim said he hadn't slept for two nights. Tony said to him: 'For heaven's sake. Don't make up your mind this week – go to the country this weekend and get some sleep and then decide.' In telling me this he added: 'If I find next week that I've talked myself out of the job, it will feel very odd.'

Jim went to his Sussex farm for the weekend. When he returned to Downing Street he discussed things afresh with the Prime Minister. In the end Jim decided not to go to the backbenches, and it was agreed that there was only one high office which could be made available and where he could move with dignity. That was the Home Office. The Prime Minister made a straight swop.

That same afternoon I was doing a long interview for my newspaper, returning home late in the day. The telephone was ringing as I opened the door. It was the Principal Private Secretary at the Board of Trade.

'The President is in a meeting, but he has asked me to let you know that the six o'clock news will announce the appointment of Mr Jenkins as Chancellor. I understand that you expected the President home for dinner, but because of today's changeover, he's been asked to deputise for the Chancellor at the OECD meetings in Paris. He'll be taking the 7.30 flight this evening and will be away for two nights. He'll have only a few minutes at Lansdowne Road on his way to Heathrow. He should get to you soon after 6.30. Could you very kindly have his overnight bag ready for him?'

Questions of Morality

The Board of Trade was a peculiar economic department, always had been, a ragbag of things that didn't relate to one another. Any Bill that wouldn't fit into any other department was dumped on Trade: shipping, textiles, civil aviation, tourism, films, British Institute of Management, Patent Office – interminable.

Tony's dominating concern was whether devaluation was going to work in pulling the balance of payments round. He was in charge of external trade. He and the Chancellor were looking for export growth – what the Labour Government had been seeking since 1964. It took much longer than anyone had expected for this to come through, though by the end of his period at the Board of Trade, the trade figures had come very right indeed.

He wanted a professional applied economist to supply detailed assessments of alternative economic policies – to harden his impact on SEP. He recruited Professor Wilfred Beckerman, a Fellow of Balliol College, Oxford, as his personal economic adviser. The two men had the unusual pleasure of starting a close friendship in middle age.

In most departments morality and objectives are married. Redistribution of wealth, central to Croslandism, scarcely arose at Trade where morality is only indirect – affecting other people's jobs which could be lost.

'Can you do something about the President?' a senior official asked the second Wilfred at Trade, one of Tony's Ministers of State, Wilfred Brown. 'He says he's not going to see the Greek Minister when he comes on a visit this week.'

The Greek colonels were then in power. The Commercial Minister knew his protocol: he couldn't see the Foreign Secretary, but he could see the President of the Board of Trade: the Department was involved in efforts to sell power stations to Greece. Tony had not been long at Trade.

Wilfred Brown was made a life peer before Labour came into government. He had a foot in both camps: business management and the Labour Party. In 1965 he was in New York running a seminar on industrial reform when he was rushed away to take an urgent telephone call from London. Events that followed were reported to me subsequently by Wilfred Brown, in his distinctive style.

A voice came on the line: 'This is Harold Wilson.'

'If you're Harold Wilson, I'm the Shah of Persia.'

'Stop it. This is the Prime Minister. I'm very busy. I have a job for you to do. I expect you at nine o'clock tomorrow morning.'

Lord Brown flew back to Heathrow, went to No. 10.

'I want someone to advance new ideas on export. You're to be Minister of State at the Board of Trade.'

Lord Brown had never done a public job and didn't want to. The Prime Minister walked to the end of the room, came back, stuck his pipe in Lord Brown's face. 'I accept that you don't want the job. Are you prepared to refuse me? You have accepted a peerage.'

'Well, all right.'

Lord Brown now prepared himself again. Without knowing the President well, he felt he understood Tony. Here was a man intense in his enmity for people like the Greek colonels: his emotions objected. How to make his intellect grasp? To take up a moral stance that achieves nothing is hypocrisy: that was the thought to implant. He went to the President's room.

'I'm not going to see the fascist bastard.'

'Look, Tony, you're going to Portugal next week for EFTA. You're going to Brazil. Do you think they're any better? You're not at the Foreign Office. You're at Trade. A large number of countries have different mores and morals from your own. If you start considering Trade on the basis of your morals you will simply put people out of work. Everything about Trade is in a sense immoral – deals, competitors trying to bust each other. You can't suddenly introduce morals into it unless you want to inflict unemployment – not on yourself – on others.'

There was something hypnotic about the President's eyes; Wilfred Brown had noticed it before, thought it might have to do with the paleness of the irises. He concentrated on what he had to say.

The President stood up, paced to the window, returned to his desk. 'Wilfred, you're a bloody fascist. I'll see the bastard. Damn you.'

That afternoon there was a meeting in his room with the head of the CBI and others. 'Gentlemen, I don't know if you know

Lord Brown, our local fascist.' Wilfred liked mordant humour. It bothered some people.

In Tony's first month at the Board of Trade, out of the hodgepodge two decisions were immediately taken. One concerned the third airport at Stansted – an elaborate blueprint painstakingly drawn up by civil servants and nodded through by the previous President, Douglas Jay. The new President said that the case for Stansted had not been made, and he reopened the whole issue. 'I shall never forget the row of black faces!' he said to Maurice Kogan afterwards. 'The officials thought they had finally got Stansted sewn up, and were enraged to have the whole wretched matter reopened. They thought I was mad and wrong. My relations with that group of people were pretty bad for some time.' (Most of them looked back on the decision as correct. 'Had the policy he found at the Board of Trade gone ahead,' said a senior official involved, 'we would have incurred immense expenses ten or fifteen years in advance of the need. Existing major airports can cater into the 1980s. If at the end of the day Stansted is concreted over, the case for doing so will have been intellectually examined, not just allowed to slide through.')

The other decision concerned, of all things, the *Queen Elizabeth II*. Instead of being launched nine days later by the Queen, it looked like being scrapped: Cunard was running out of money. In his diary Crossman begins the story when he 'went round to No. 10 for an impromptu emergency meeting'. The PM felt that urgent measures were required:

Tony at first held out firmly and said that he didn't see why we should spend a lot of money putting Cunard to rights. Let them go bankrupt and afterwards the Government could buy up the remains cheaply. However, others felt that this would be unfortunate for the Queen; and Harold Lever had come up with an ingenious new scheme. He is obviously the latest wonder boy of this Cabinet ...

At that time Lever was Financial Secretary to the Treasury but not yet in the Cabinet, brought in only on special occasions. He took up the tale:

'It was the kind of thing,' he said, 'where economics and politics come into focus in the mind of the public: who was going to rescue *QE II*? Tony asked me to come to Lansdowne Road on Sunday. He had two officials there from the Board of Trade; I had one official from the Treasury – all three there to give their advice to the President. He said: "Let's ask the Financial Secretary for his advice. He knows more about this kind of thing than anyone." None of the officials looked very pleased.'

On Monday the Financial Secretary had coffee with the President in his room at the Board of Trade. They stitched up Lever's scheme. Tony took it to Cabinet and it was approved, the *QE II* and a few other things saved without costing the Government a penny. The end of the story is what Lever liked best when it got back to him from others in Cabinet: the Prime Minister said they were all deeply grateful to the President of the Board of Trade for this swift and competent action.

'Very little to do with me,' replied the President of the Board of Trade, one hand waving it away. 'Whole credit belongs to the Financial Secretary.'

'If any other Minister behaved with that generosity, it has escaped my notice,' Lever said acidly when he'd been in the Cabinet for a few years.

It was early 1965 when Tony first put the question to Cabinet: 'Why can't a Labour policy-making body be formed?' Towards the end of 1967, the Prime Minister formed an inner group. It met for the first time at Chequers, two days after Christmas.

'It wasn't much of an inner Cabinet,' Dick Crossman observed to his diary, 'because as I expected there were ten of us there apart from the PM ... We all suspected it would be a fair waste of time as we stood about outside the Cabinet door. Tony Crosland came in his sports clothes and took off his waistcoat and said it was very stuffy and it was a cursed nuisance coming back from his cottage.' We had driven to Sandwich on Boxing Day to spend the rest of the Christmas break in two adjacent flats which we rented, Tony and I in one, the children with schoolgirl friends in the other, the great bleak sea crashing on to the pebble beach below our windows.

1968 commenced with the new Chancellor presenting the previous Chancellor's economic package for more cuts. The Prime Minister saw there would be difficulty in 'interpreting' his colleagues' consensus view: one or two were ostentatiously keeping their own tally of which way Ministers came down. The President of the Board of Trade was especially awkward: he was trying to discover the Treasury's reasoning behind the decision that nearly one billion pounds should be taken out of the economy. Why was Cabinet asked to make separate detailed cuts without any primary assessment of overall economic policy? He could get no answer. The separate decisions proceeded.

The most dramatic confrontation was over Education where Patrick Gordon Walker, returned to the Commons in 1966, was put in charge when Tony moved to Trade. An odd situation now existed: Education's case was argued not by its current Secretary of State, who was largely silent, but by his predecessors, Stewart and Crosland. The key issue was the Chancellor's proposal that Education make cuts by putting off Labour's manifesto pledge to raise the school-leaving age to sixteen.

Tony made the case against postponement. Then Stewart, George Brown, Gunter spoke brilliantly and with emotion, Tony said, against postponement. Crossman, supporting the Chancellor, asked the President of the Board of Trade just who would be affected by postponing raising the school-leaving age.

'Only 400,000 children. But they're not our children. It's always other people's children. None of us in this room would dream of letting our children leave school at fifteen.'

The Foreign Secretary, George Brown, said to the Secretary of State for Education: 'I want a straight answer to a straight question. If you had to choose between these 400,000 fifteen-year-olds and university students, which would you help?'

'If I had to make such a choice, I suppose I'd help university students,' Gordon Walker replied.

'May God forgive you,' said George Brown. It was very effective, Tony told me that night.

When the Cabinet next met to vote on the issue, the Prime Minister had got most of the way round the table. The spending Ministers had had their say: the tally was nine to seven against postponement. Then came the Secretaries of State for Scotland and Wales and the Lord Chancellor, and the vote shifted the other way. It now hung on the Secretary of State for Education. He said he felt it his duty to support the Chancellor and accordingly voted to postpone raising the school-leaving age. Considerable contempt was silently displayed. Dick Crossman ascribed the unexpected victory for the Chancellor's side to 'the tiddlers always sensitive to changes in the wind'.

'Makes one disheartened about democracy,' Tony said when he came home that evening, depressed, 'except it doesn't really, because no one can think of anything better. Also makes one wonder about Gordon Walker. In fairness, he has now lost his nerve. Even so.' (A few months later, the Prime Minister asked

Gordon Walker to stand down and promoted the Postmaster General, Ted Short, to Education.)

Only one of those who voted for postponement puzzled Tony. That was the newest head of the fading DEA, Peter Shore. 'He's the only one that is un-understandable. Harold must be the Iron Prime Minister, Roy the Iron Chancellor. Dick Crossman is so crazy. Denis simply takes the vulgar view. Dick Marsh is becoming a total reactionary: he's a selfmade man who's kicked the ladder out under him. The others are simply unsound or second-rate. Still, we mustn't brood about it indefinitely. It was a democratic decision.'

He nevertheless brooded further. 'Pakenham says he'll resign. George is threatening to. He feels passionately about it – says it would have made all the difference in his life.'

Later on, lying in his bath, he said: 'I'm going to have one more try. It has to come up once again. I'm going to ring Roy over the weekend and try to swing him, make him see that on *political* grounds this is the one decision that is *wrong*. The trouble is he's probably made a bargain with Harold: he'll support some cuts if Harold will support others.'

Later still, this time I in the bath, he came in: 'I've thought of the lever. There was another issue where the vote was within one.'

'Which was that?'

He answered a bit crossly. 'You ask about Cabinet as if it were a cocktail party. It's irrelevant which it was. The point is there was just this one vote that made the difference. That particular item has to come up a second time. I shall tell Roy that unless he switches his vote on school-leaving postponement, I'll switch my vote on the other.'

'You mean simple blackmail?'

'Only partly. I shall tell him I'm only willing to risk selling a certain number of beliefs down the river to save the present economy. I suppose it is blackmail, really.'

Roy wouldn't be swung: on the other issue, never identified to me, another member of the Cabinet switched his vote, cancelling out Tony's. George stayed on in Cabinet. Frank Pakenham – better known as Lord Longford – resigned in protest over the school-leaving-age postponement. 'If I'd had some important departmental job,' he said, 'I might have stayed on to do it. But as my job was to commend Government policies to the House of Lords, I felt it was time to go. I felt if I swallowed this, there was nothing I wouldn't swallow. The trouble with resigning is you can only do it once. A few months later people came up to me over the Kenya Asians and said: "I hope you're going to resign over this." "I can't," I said, "I already have."'

Frank Longford was replaced as Labour's Leader in the Lords by Eddie Shackleton, son of the Antarctic explorer, as good a background as any for the job.

Government Car Services were changing over to Rover saloons instead of limousines. Len Davis wanted to drive a Rover: it was more powerful and reliable than the ageing Austin Princess. The Principal Private Secretary, Roy Croft, put the matter to the President, who mistrusted it: how would he have sufficient leg room? The Board of Trade took a Rover on trial. The President confirmed that there wasn't enough leg room. The next day Len Davis was behind the wheel of the old Princess; one day it would break down he was sure. Then someone observed that the Chancellor had managed to get a Daimler. (The Prime Minister, typically, preferred a nice modest Rover.)

'What do I have a Private Office for if it can't ensure that I have a car with as much leg room as the Chancellor has?' the President said to Roy Croft.

A Trade visit to Moscow began, the President to meet up at Heathrow with Roy Croft and the senior officials involved. The Princess stood waiting in Lansdowne Road. Tony and I hadn't finished a conversation. I was still in bare feet when I walked out to the car with him.

'You'd better get in, Susan. Otherwise it will be six days before we can polish off this subject. Len, you don't mind dropping my wife off on your way back? I'm afraid there isn't time for her to get her shoes.' We finished our conversation. The Princess broke down on the M4. Time had been cut as neatly as usual. Mr Davis stood by the carriageway headed towards Heathrow. Tony stood on the dividing verge, hands on hips, surveying the carriageway headed back to London. He hailed a taxi. It crossed the verge. Barefoot I jumped out of the Princess and into the taxi, waved goodbye to Mr Davis.

Outside the VIP lounge, Roy Croft was biting his nails. I stayed in the taxi because of my bare feet, and in any case, it being twenty minutes to take-off time, no one lingered. On the return journey I looked out of the taxi window to the opposite carriageway and saw that the Princess had now been joined by a police car and breakdown van. Mr Davis got to drive a Rover, the President muttering each morning that there wasn't enough leg room.

Sometimes I accompanied Tony on official visits abroad, depending on children, my job, whether the host country had invited the wife. Once she gets there, she is the host country's guest, her functions twofold. She is shown aspects of the foreign country to feed back to her husband; naturally she is shown what her hosts want her to see, but one would like to think wives bright enough to perceive other aspects as well. And she is to convey to her hosts, tactfully one hopes, the virtues of democracy, and information about life in Britain. The burden of virtually non-stop concentration falls on the Minister. All the same, I was usually white with fatigue when we met in our room for a brief break – Tony reflecting, making notes; I stretched out on the bed, grateful for stillness.

That's all by the by for the British taxpayers. What they want to know is: who pays for the wife to get there and back? She does when travel is by commercial flight – which ordinarily it is. The President and his officials sat together in First Class where Government boxes could be opened, briefs read. If one is carrying a Government box, the British taxpayer foots the bill. As I hadn't a box, I sat in Economy. Before lunch a glass of champagne would appear with the Secretary of State's compliments. From time to time he ambled back to make sure I was content. When we reached our destination, I nipped up front and we descended together to the welcoming committee and the bouquet for me.

The Crosland system seemed sensible to us: we wanted to do other things with the money, and during most of the flight Tony was working anyhow. The concept so troubled one high-ranking Board of Trade official that he insisted on leaving First Class to wedge himself on one side of me in Economy, which that day was like a boiler-room. Having made his courtly gesture he felt obliged to maintain it all the way from Kiev to Heathrow. Sweat flowed freely.

In March 1968 the British economy faced a new crisis – rumours about the price of gold threatened further devaluation of the pound. On the evening of 14 March, an all-night sitting in the House began. The Prime Minister was at No. 10. The Chancellor was at No. 11, moving back and forth through the connecting door. Wilson's record says that around 11 p.m. the Governor of the Bank of England arrived. American bankers urgently asked that the London gold pool be closed down. This meant declaring the next day – Friday – a bank holiday in order to close the stock exchange. That in turn required a Privy Council meeting with the Queen, no matter that it was now approaching midnight. A quorum of three Privy Councillors was needed. Where was the Foreign Secretary – the Deputy Leader – who would ordinarily have made up the threesome? Wilson's record implies heavily that George Brown was unavailable:

... I asked the Clerk to the Privy Council to go ahead with the Council for 12.15 a.m., or as soon afterwards as possible. At this point, having heard that George Brown had surfaced, I sent a senior secretary over to the House to tell him what was happening. A few minutes earlier Peter Shore, who had heard rumours that something was afoot, had telephoned to ask what was going on. I could not tell him anything but, realising we should have to assemble with all speed a quorum for the Council, sent a message asking him to come over. It was an afterthought with cataclysmic results.

In fact Peter Shore had called in at No. 10 earlier in the evening and was there throughout.

Prime Minister, Chancellor and the (last) head of DEA, Peter Shore, set out for Buckingham Palace. The Privy Council was held.

In the House of Commons at about 1 a.m., George Brown heard what had happened and erupted. While most MPs went on with their all-night sitting, irate Cabinet Ministers assembled at No. 10. There, while the Chancellor was explaining the precipitate Privy Council, George Brown made a terrific din: no one had tried to find him, and the Prime Minister had Peter Shore with him from the outset, George said.

Tony was angry that the Prime Minister had not consulted his Cabinet colleagues who were only five minutes away: endless recrimination was pointless, the thing was done. But he thought it a scandalous way to take major decisions, and wanted an assurance that there would be no repetition of it. ('There was no earthly reason why on Thursday evening Harold shouldn't have quietly permitted Burke Trend to organise a meeting of all available members of SEP or of Cabinet, including the Deputy Leader,' Dick Crossman said to his diary.)

The Prime Minister, trying for conciliation, pointed out to his colleagues confronting him in the small hours that he'd been in a situation without precedent. George Brown kept up his din. He was outraged by suggestions that he couldn't be found because he

was under the weather from drink. He resigned. Later he said that
Tony tried to stop him – told him to get some sleep and then
decide. The Cabinet returned to the House, where at 3.20 in the
morning the Chancellor took command and made a magisterial
statement about the economic crisis and the fact that a bank
holiday had just begun. At 10.30 that morning Cabinet met at
No. 10 to review the night's events. The Foreign Secretary was
not present.

According to Harold Wilson's record, he had prepared for this
moment six months earlier when he moved Michael Stewart from
DEA and gave him a co-ordinating role: 'It could only be a matter
of time before one of George's late-night resignations stuck and I
would want Michael back at the Foreign Office.'

Bill Rodgers, one of George's junior ministers and very close to
him, told Crossman that George waited in his flat all day Friday
for a call from No. 10 enabling him to withdraw his words. No
message came. At the end of the afternoon he had no choice but to
write his resignation letter. The Prime Minister accepted it and
made Michael Stewart the Foreign Secretary.

Though George Brown stayed on as the Party's Deputy Leader
for the rest of the Parliament, he was out of Labour's Cabinet for
ever. He always remembered what Tony said to him: 'The piano
will never play the tune the same. It has lost one of its legs.'

·-· 23 ·-·

Ups, Downs, Out

Civil servants thought the inner Cabinet a joke. Be that as it may, Tony was excluded from it – probably in April 1968, though I have no recollection of the expulsion. Dick Crossman, however, recorded his own conversation about it with the Prime Minister on 10 April:

I then got on to the subject of the Parliamentary Committee [inner Cabinet] which now consists of ten members, with Peter Shore in as the tenth and Tony Crosland out as the eleventh. 'He has to be punished for what he has done. What he did was very wrong.' 'What on earth has he been doing?' I asked. 'He's been negotiating, talking, intriguing in the Foreign Office with George Brown and George Brown has got a tape of what he said, I can tell you that.' This absolutely bewildered me and bewilders me still but I'll let it lie at the back of my mind until I can find something which makes sense of it.

Dick and Tony clashed at different times in their lives, but each had a good idea what made the other tick. Two days later Dick's diary reports again on the puzzle, this time raised in conversation with Roy:

... he repeated the story about Tony Crosland's 'crimes' and the tape-recording George had made. I said to him that since Roy knew Tony so well he can surely talk to him about it. But I don't think that he can and it looks as though Tony isn't as close to Roy now as some people believe. But certainly the impression Roy gave me is that Crosland and Healey are right out on a limb as the men whom Harold sees as the chief conspirators against him. Roy had asked Harold about the inner Cabinet and ... had pleaded for a smaller group, possibly meeting informally once a week and spelt out the names of the five he would like – the Prime Minister, Barbara, Dick [himself], Denis Healey, Roy Jenkins. I think that's as good an inner group as you can select, though I doubt whether Harold will ever keep to it.

At this point Dick seems to have abandoned all effort to untangle the mystery of Tony's 'crimes'. As for Tony, his expulsion was not a great grievance – there being no sign that the inner Cabinet was grappling with strategy – but he thought Harold an ass to keep him out.

Lansdowne Road runs along the middle of Notting Hill's western slope, hence our terrific sunsets. Further down the hill lies the village, Clarendon Cross. Before everything changed for our family and we moved away, the gentrification of the village was nearly complete – greengrocer, butcher, general store where spools of thread were sold, replaced by young men and women 'into' eastern carpets and hand-painted blinds – though bookie and newsagent and cobbler still survived. The cobbler's activities included feuding with the newsagent next door, each deriving the pleasure of an old dog growling daily at another, bereft when the other is no longer there to provide diurnal jousting. That the cobbler's lathe produced a frightful racket was undeniable, but much of the time, the cobbler said, he was quietly trimming soles. The newsagent's deep freeze, on the other hand, had to keep its lollies in shape night and day, Sundays included, humming unremittingly through the connecting wall. The cobbler lived above his shop, hadn't a moment's respite from his neighbour's hum.

Neither cobbler nor I thought to roughen Tony's newly re-soled walking shoes with a knife or sandpaper. Loading the boot for a family weekend with friends in the country, he turned and slipped on the wet December leaves, came down on the cement on his elbow. I was still in the house, and when first he walked in and said 'I've hurt myself,' I thought he was joking. I never thought of him as physically vulnerable.

In Outpatients at Westminster Hospital, the polite young registrar regretted that X-ray showed the elbow to be smashed to pieces. ('I'm sorry to read about the accident to your elbow,' wrote one well-wisher whose letter of some length indicated he read the *Daily Telegraph*, 'as I should much prefer it had been your head.') A delicate operation was required.

Waiting for the surgeon to arrive, Tony sat up in bed reading the *Financial Times*, I reading the *Guardian*. Half an hour before the operation a nurse shot the pethidine, intended to make him doze, into his thigh. He was halfway through the *Economist* when she looked in twenty minutes later. She hurried away with puzzled brow. When the orderlies came to fetch him and he was lying on

the trolley, covered to his chin with a white sheet, still alert, he
decided to mime what was expected of him, winked at me and
closed his eyes, looked solemn. Instantly he brought to mind those
recumbent statues in churches. As they rolled him from the room,
I played a morbid game – Getting in Practice – and found it so
disagreeable that I smartly curtailed it.

In the patient's absence, contingency preparations went forward
– an oxygen tank was trundled in, a machine for extracting phlegm
from the throat if the patient failed to come round from the
anaesthetic, and so on. I grew restive. The twentieth opening of
the door at last ushered in the trolley making its return journey.
The patient raised his head from the trolley and said to me curtly:

'You heard what happened?'

'No.'

'They did the wrong arm.'

I must have looked horrified; the orderlies and nurse certainly
did. He laughed. They didn't. I half did, still nervous.

Sitting up in bed again, he gossiped with me about this and that,
wondered when he could have a smoke. He used to refer to his
resilience as that of an old ox. Just before Christmas he came out
of hospital and in January we had a week in Italy – not quite as
good as it would have been had he not had one arm in a sling, but
at least it was his left arm. He hated physical constraint.

During the same period, Barbara Castle and her officials at
Industry were working on *In Place of Strife* – her attempt to reform
the trade unions. In January 1969 Tony returned to Whitehall and
got wind of it. He was incredulous. Although he found Barbara's
need for empire-building 'frivolous', he agreed with her on issues
about 70 per cent of the time; but to contemplate a policy like this
late in a Parliament was mad. It was primarily a tactical disagreement: Barbara's proposed Bill wouldn't work: you couldn't make
it work. As Chancellor, surely Roy would help persuade the Prime
Minister of the folly of putting through a Bill you could not enforce.
Tony would speak to Roy. Before he could do so he learned that
the Chancellor was on the Cabinet Committee which had already
discussed *In Place of Strife*, and Roy supported it.

Treasury officials had great respect for Roy as Chancellor. 'We
had a natural rapport,' said Sir William Armstrong when explaining
to me how the Treasury preferred to function. 'I don't remember
anything where we were across each other. And once you were
together with Roy, you knew you had the PM behind you. Each
needed the other. Roy had a group of Right-wingers supporting

him, but there weren't enough of them: he couldn't make a go of it without Harold: there was much of the Centre and the whole of the Left which only Harold could deliver. Equally, Harold needed Roy. We saw the two of them as a kind of centaur, which is a Treasury man's dream of bliss – the Prime Minister and Chancellor locked together.'

To the Treasury it seemed as if the Prime Minister had never accepted either Callaghan or Brown as his right hand, playing one off against the other. 'Harold seemed to us,' said Armstrong, 'gratefully to accept Roy. Once Roy was his Chancellor, Harold didn't feel threatened by him. He knew the Jenkinsites went on plotting, but he was convinced it didn't matter.'

With Prime Minister and Chancellor behind her, Barbara Castle couldn't imagine that In Place of Strife might not reach fruition. Disliking Jim Callaghan, she underrated him. Jim was in almost open rebellion, acting outside Cabinet, holding his own meetings with trade union leaders. 'Jim is behaving now like a caricature of an old wheeler-dealer. Sometimes it's difficult to stomach,' Tony said to me. In Cabinet, he firmly supported Callaghan's opposition to In Place of Strife, as did Dick Marsh.

In May the Prime Minister created a slightly smaller inner Cabinet – formally named Management Committee. Here Callaghan was alone in his opposition to Barbara's Industrial Relations Bill. A fortnight after Management Committee's inception, Callaghan was ousted. 'I'm sorry to tell you that your colleagues no longer have confidence in you. So I'm afraid you can no longer be a member of the inner Cabinet,' the Prime Minister told Callaghan.

Jim had never had a humiliation like this. Several of his staff at the Home Office said he should resign. Jim swallowed his humiliation, knowing if he went to the backbenches he was finished. 'Ups and downs are simply part of a politician's life,' he said stoically.

The battle over In Place of Strife – not too aptly named – was moving towards dénouement. In June hostilities began to tell on the Prime Minister's nervous system: self-control was replaced by petulance. While leaks poured out from his own office, he opened Cabinet with a ritual complaint about others leaking to the press; one morning as he said it, he looked at the President of the Board of Trade who at once broke in: 'This time, Prime Minister, you provoke my patience beyond endurance. We all know the principal source of these leaks.' The Prime Minister skipped away from the subject as he often did when openly confronted. Tony talked indiscreetly about his opinion of people, but he did not approve of leaking to the press a correct – or distorted – account of a confidential meeting.

By now the Cabinet was meeting four or five times a week, sometimes twice a day. 'Harold will assemble us only to spoil Roy's dinner party and Fred Peart's evening at the Levers' and my evening at home with my wife,' Tony said over gossip. 'His unspeakable nature is one of the great facts of our political life. That's why I get impatient at having to defend him against illegitimate attacks. There are legitimate attacks that are quite sufficient.'

Before that particular week was out, the Prime Minister's behaviour at Cabinet had grown more than odd. It was so uncontrolled as to be embarrassing, over the hours calling on Ministers by name, threatening them in an hysterical way: 'All right, Dick, I supported you last time, but next time I shan't.' Alternatively he threatened to resign. After one Cabinet Tony and Dick Crossman discussed the disturbing thought that the Prime Minister was cracking up. A day or two later he had recaptured his 'Churchillian' aplomb, and it was apparent that his extraordinary resilience would see him through.

Rejecting the view of the inner Cabinet, the Cabinet came down against introducing Barbara's Bill. The Prime Minister capitulated with a grace that insured he need not resign. *In Place of Strife* was scuppered. Barbara Castle was shattered.

The Prime Minister said to Armstrong: 'Poor Barbara. She hangs around like someone with a still-born child. She can't believe it's dead.'

'It's Jimmy,' Tony Benn always said when he rang Lansdowne Road. 'Jimmy' was his family nickname; he and his former teacher never gave up its usage in their friendship which continued to the end. A natural mimic, sometimes he'd pretend to be somebody else, imitating whichever accent was appropriate. We were listed in the telephone book: unknown souls rang from time to time to vent their feelings. After some such diatribe was cut short by its recipient, Tony said: 'I wonder if that mad farmer was really Jimmy?'

In conversation with others, Tony applied a dual standard when Jimmy was the subject, a habit of his where friends and family were concerned. He could say what he liked in private, employ any hyperbole that took his fancy. But anyone who indiscriminately attacked Benn was told: 'Won't hear a word said against him. I'm devoted to Tony Benn. Nothing the matter with him except he's a bit cracked.'

Elsie, Tony and Evelyn

On leave in Rome, 1944

Addressing the Oxford Union, 1946   (*International News Photos*)

Election victory at South Gloucestershire, 1950, Dougie Atkins on the new Labour Member's right   (*Bristol Evening Post*)

With Hilary, on their wedding day, 1952 (*Universal Pictorial Press Agency*)

Carol and Tony Benn and their son Hilary return home after re-election in Bristol South-East (*Central Press Photos Ltd*)

Hugh Gaitskell
(*Sunday Express*)

Susan Catling in London,
November 1956

The Catling Family

With Roy Jenkins, canvassing in Grimsby in the 1959 election
(*The Observer*)

With Ian and Dobs Little at the wedding lunch at Hobury Street,
February 1964

The Secretary of State for
Education takes time for
reflection in the Eames
chair, 1965
(*Sunday Times*)

Roy Hattersley confronting a
deputation of Birmingham
teachers outside the House of
Commons in March 1970
(*Press Association*)

Michael Foot, Tony Benn, Peter Shore and Barbara Castle at an
Anti-Marketeers' press conference during the run up to the EEC
referendum held on 5 June 1975   (*Guardian*)

China, May 1976: visiting a People's Commune

The Bicentennial celebrations in July 1976: Susan Crosland smiling for the television cameras minutes before she fainted

Dr Kissinger bows out after Republican defeat in the United
States; informal farewell at Lansdowne Road, December 1976
(*Sunday Times*)

Adderbury in North Oxfordshire

March 1977: scattering the ashes at sea off Grimsby
(*Grimsby Evening Telegraph*)

Leaving the Service of Thanksgiving at Westminster Abbey
(*Keystone Press Agency Ltd*)

Tony Benn had an engaging, unEnglish way of making occasional calls late on Sunday morning, uninvited, unannounced, nearly always welcome, his ancient bicycle parked at the kerb. Sunday afternoons at Lansdowne Road, however, were sacrosanct. The front door was kept on the latch to minimise the bell ringing when the children's friends called after lunch. They endeavoured to close doors without the usual reverberation as tea mugs were conveyed to and fro between kitchen and drawing-room where Hugh Dalton's gramophone resided, this last suppressed to lowish decibels under Sunday restrictions.

On one such afternoon the adults of the household were reading the Sunday papers prior to siesta. 'Shall smoke one more Mannikin and come to bed.' I departed the study for the bedroom alongside it, nearly colliding with Tony Benn as he rounded the top of the stairs, bicycle clips fixed to his trousers.

'How do you spend your Sunday afternoons, Jimmy? If you'd walked in five minutes later, Susan and I would have been in bed.'

'My dear chap. I didn't think. I shan't stay. There was something I wanted to talk to you about.'

'Do you mind, Susan, if we put things back half an hour?'

It was all right with me as long as I could take the newspapers into the bedroom. As I closed its door and someone closed the study door, Jimmy raised his voice in fury, three times invoking the Prime Minister's name. ' —— Harold. —— Harold. —— Harold.' The Prime Minister took some pleasure in teasing Tony Benn, raising and dashing his hopes.

'Harold Wilson was a nicer bloke on 16th October 1964 than he was on the 17th,' Sir William Armstrong said, when he thought about it later. The 17th was, of course, Wilson's first full day as Prime Minister, a species viewed by Armstrong with dispassion. 'Absolute power did corrupt him, but not in the normal sense – bribes and so on. I mean *folie de grandeur*. The man who had it in a big way was Harold Macmillan. And of course Winston stayed on too long. Attlee avoided it. The sign of it is when the PM says to a Minister: "I'll take this on" when the Minister knows better how to do it, but the PM thinks his charisma will be enough.'

Prime Minister Wilson's sense of his own importance suffered a severe knock when *In Place of Strife* was defeated. Heads must roll. During the summer, speculation mounted that Callaghan, Crosland, Marsh would be sacked. Tony thought this was Prime Ministerial wild talk late at night: it was not politically possible to get rid of all three. Roy Jenkins wasn't so sure.

Then during September Roy wrote a surprisingly pompous
letter to his old friend. It concerned the trade figures the President
had just announced to the House. The figures were very good, but
Tony added a cautionary note about viewing them too compla-
cently. (There were shortly to be setbacks.) The Chancellor complained that the President's comments had caused a restraining
effect on the day's foreign market 'for reasons of which you are
probably unaware' and admonished him for doing this sort of
thing. The letter the Chancellor received in reply left him uncomfortable. He then feared, he told Tony later, that if Tony
did get the sack, he would think Roy in pique had helped to
engineer it. Tony thought nothing of the kind, however chilly their
relations.

'Despite our mutual malice on some things, there is a limit to
Roy's self-centredness. He might hope I would be demoted within
the Government, but he would always say at the end of the day:
"I think you're mad if you drop Tony." Roy would actually say:
"It would be *wrong* as well as foolish." '

Public discussion of impending Government changes grew so
intense that a few days before the President of the Board of Trade
was to make an official visit to Japan, he wrote an analytical letter
to the Prime Minister setting out his views on the machinery – not
personalities – necessary for effective use of the economic departments. His Permanent Secretary advised him against sending it.
He sent it. 'I agree it may simply irritate Harold, but I'm too old
not to speak my mind.' Tony always said this as if up to that
moment he had behaved differently.

The Prime Minister asked him to come to No. 10 the following
day, 23 September. Although his ministerial colleagues knew
nothing about it, the Prime Minister explained, since July he'd
been working with civil servants to restructure various departments, creating two vast new empires, at the same time reducing
Cabinet by two members. DEA was to expire altogether. The
Board of Trade would be diminished. Parts of both would go into
a new department which he wanted Tony to head. This empire
would embrace Housing, Transport, Local Government, Regional
Planning. It hadn't yet a name.

'What do you think of it?' I asked over gossip.

'Don't know. Harold always makes things sound better than
they turn out to be. I've not become cynical – just world-weary. I
couldn't bring myself to ask him about the status of the job.' At the
centre of him was an inability to 'place-seek'. Some regretted that

he was unable to do this, even when they understood why he couldn't.

The other enormous new department at least had a name: it was an expanded Ministry of Technology, and was to be headed by Tony Benn, with two ministers of Cabinet rank to assist him – 'double-banking'. On personal grounds I was glad of his promotion. People made fun of Tony Benn. In Government he would not go farther than this. And he worked so hard.

'The thing about Jimmy is that he creates endless crises. I'm sure he works very hard, but that's a separate point,' Tony said.

No announcement was to be made of the Prime Minister's latest arrangements until after the Labour Party conference at Brighton, which coincided with British Week in Tokyo. Tony flew off to the latter, the visit cut down to five days because of the impending change. He and his officials stayed at a hotel. Before his overseas visits, Private Office engaged in intricate manoeuvring so the President could escape certain obligations expected if he stayed at the Embassy, as most Cabinet Ministers did. On the last night in Tokyo there was an end-of-term feeling: after the official functions were over, Tony went off to a nightclub, his Principal Private Secretary, Roy Croft, returning to the hotel to discover that a wretched senior official, trying to get a decent night's sleep before the return flight to London, had been dragged out of bed at one in the morning by the Head of Chancery who had a telegram for the President from the Prime Minister. Roy Croft opened the telegram, wondering in which nightclub he might have to seek out the President. 'I'VE BEEN THINKING ABOUT A TITLE FOR YOUR NEW JOB EVERYONE HERE HAS BEEN TALKING ABOUT IT WHAT ABOUT SECRETARY OF STATE FOR THE ENVIRONMENT,' said the Prime Minister's telegram. Roy Croft put it away and went to bed.

As no one uninvolved knew about the new job, 'everyone' was talking about something different. Within hours of Tony's return from Japan on 4 October, the *Sunday Express* carried a great banner across its front page: 'NO. 10 CLIFFHANGER – CROSLAND GOING?'

The following day's *Daily Express* carried another headline over a picture of Tony and me laughing: 'WILSON PICKS "TWO SUPERMEN": Crosland Regional Overlord; Benn Industrial Overlord.' The Prime Minister always enjoyed confusing the press.

'In the evening came the news of this famous reshuffle which had been dominating Brighton,' Dick Crossman told his diary as he started on the new week. 'What do we see when we compare it with Harold's great talk of July and early August of removing Callaghan,

Marsh and Crosland? Callaghan is exactly where he was, stronger than ever as a result of Ireland. Crosland is promoted to the gigantic job of running Housing and Transport, with Tony Greenwood under him. The only man who is clean out is Dick Marsh.'

Dick Marsh had been kept on tenter-hooks. Late Saturday afternoon the Minister of Power still knew nothing of his future. His Permanent Secretary had told him, with embarrassment, that he, the official, knew what was happening, but that he couldn't tell his own Minister. Dick rang Roy Jenkins and Denis Healey, both of whom said they knew nothing. Tony was en route from Tokyo. On Sunday, jetlagged, nothing yet announced publicly, he rang Dick Marsh to see how things were going with him. He'd just heard he was out. They talked a long time, Tony urging Dick to be philosophical about ups and downs and so on. Feeling bad for Dick, Tony rang him a second time to say the same thing. Then we went to bed.

When I went downstairs later, Tony not yet awake, Sheila said the Permanent Secretary at Housing had rung and would ring back at 5.30. A man rang at 5.30 and said the Permanent Secretary was already on his way to Lansdowne Road and would arrive in fifteen minutes. He did so, joining Sheila and her long-haired friends in the drawing-room with their mugs of tea. I took coffee up to the bedroom. After the six o'clock announcement on the news, things became hectic.

The next morning at 7.30, Tony was shaving in preparation for an all-day jaunt to Balmoral, muttering about this use of his first day in a new job. The Queen, unlike practically everyone else, turned out to be extremely well briefed.

Later in the week the Prime Minister sent a couple of notes down the Cabinet table to the *S. of S. L-G, Regional P.* (Instead of Environment, the Department began under the name Local Government and Regional Planning.) One of these said: 'In case I omit to mention it when we meet, I'm re-forming the Management Cttee, so-called Inner Cabinet. I hope you will join it. Our job is of course much more political strategy, including Parlty. strategy, than day to day Govt business. HW.'

'Funny man, Harold,' said Tony. That evening he was home for dinner *en famille*.

'What's that noise?' asked Sheila.

'Don't hear any noise.'

'You must hear it.' There was, now that one listened, a faint rhythmic sound emanating from somewhere round the table, rather a rusty sound. 'Tony, it's your chest.'

'You're not to be rude about my chest, Sheila.' He patted it respectfully. 'It's like a machine from the early Industrial Revolution – creaks, needs to be oiled from time to time. As it's obsolete, the parts can't be replaced, but there's no point in getting rid of it either: it does the job very well.'

In that same autumn of 1969, the Prime Minister and Mrs Wilson travelled to Grimsby to open the Labour Club in Crosland Road, part of a new housing estate. The Prime Minister excelled on grass roots occasions. He told everyone present that he and Mary would sign their programmes if someone would get them to No. 10. This was duly organised. Weeks passed. Tony's constituency secretary asked why Grimbarians had not received back their programmes. Embarrassment at No. 10: the programmes were now signed and packed for return to Grimsby, but only the Prime Minister had signed them. 'Mrs Wilson didn't have time.'

1970 began. In preparation for the Chancellor's spring budget, a PESC exercise was held in March, tempers fraying as Ministers argued against the Chancellor's proposed cuts. Roy and Tony were in sharp disagreement over money for Housing.

'It's up to me as Chancellor to decide.'

'On the contrary. It's up to the two of us to decide, as it's my Department that is under discussion.'

The Prime Minister interceded in his mollifying way, and the Chancellor amended his attitude. A few minutes later he was rude to the Secretary of State for Social Services, Dick Crossman. Over gossip Tony said: 'Because Dick's a bully, he doesn't know how to stand up to another bully. He just makes faces and shrugs and is silent instead of answering back.' Probably this PESC was no more fractious than most.

In the May local elections, Labour did marvellously well. The success was, in part, the result of competing for seats which had been lost in a period of acute unpopularity. In part it was a brief reversal of a deep-laid trend. Expecting the improvement to continue, the Prime Minister called a general election for 18 June. Labour was confident of victory.

'It's a funny thing. I've always said I wanted to be Chancellor. I find I'd like to keep this job. It includes all the things that now interest me most,' Tony said.

Throughout the count at the Town Hall in Grimsby, the Tories were glum as they saw the Labour candidate's lead piling up before their eyes. But they had spectacular consolation: news was already coming over radio and television sets, passed by word of mouth into the room where the count went on: the rest of the country was likely to return a Conservative Government. After Tony's victory speech of thanks to his supporters, we went back to Muriel and Jeremy Barker's and watched the results as they appeared on the television screen. After a time I went over and sat on the arm of Tony's chair as, mesmerised, he watched the screen bear home its message that Labour was out.

A few hours later the alarm clock went off. That particular bedroom at the County is long and narrow, not much more than six feet wide, single beds set head to toe. I shoved clothes into a suitcase before waking Tony. He was dead asleep, lying diagonally across the other bed; he was taller than it was long. He was face down, one arm flung out.

On Saturday evening several old friends attended a wake at Lansdowne Road, most of us still in shock. When both Benns said: 'We've never been happier,' I imagined they had to be putting on a front, despite one of Carol Benn's attractions being her wisecrack candour. And it was true enough that Tony Benn saw himself as the left-wing answer to Enoch Powell calling in the wilderness. 'Enoch has had more effect on the country than either Party,' Jimmy said, adding that he himself intended making a major speech every three months.

'On an occasion like last night when everyone's been cast down, why did the Benns act as if they weren't in the slightest bruised?' I asked next morning.

'They weren't acting,' Tony said. 'He *is* happier in Opposition. There's no other time he can make his move.'

'Do you think he genuinely believes things can be manipulated so one day he's Leader?'

'Certainly. We all know he occasionally lies, but no one doubts his sincerity in seeing himself as a Messiah. The trouble with fanatics – why one should never underestimate them – is they're so assiduous.'

'Do you think he'd ever succeed?'

'Over my dead body.'

24

A Normal Life Begins

My high heels clattered gaily as I tripped down Lansdowne Road. 'I'm free. I'm free.'

When first I came to London fourteen years earlier, I imagined I'd be homesick and was puzzled – felt a little guilty – that I wasn't. Letters flew back and forth across the Atlantic, and for a month each year I returned to my close extended family. But in my anonymity in London I found a constraint removed which until then I hadn't known was there: a sense of obligation, in part self-imposed, to do what was expected of me, at any rate publicly.

Why now did I feel the same exuberance of stepping free from constriction? 'What's it like to be a Minister's wife?' begins to affect the psyche. One observes that in a subtle way one is regarded differently: everyday personal relations, never entirely simple, become less straightforward. We are told that the rich suffer from not knowing whether they are liked for themselves or for their money – or disliked if it comes to that. The analogy, though not exact, will do. As we became 'figures' in the neighbourhood, I grew diffident. If meat that should have been tender was tough, I could hardly bring myself to mention his failing to the butcher lest I seem to be behaving like the Colonel's lady. This inhibition was now removed.

Did I miss the grand occasions of ministerial life? Well, no. We'd not gone in much for these (apart from compulsory affairs, only those which promised entertainment) and one doesn't want to do that sort of thing for ever. Curiosity was satisfied.

The most dramatic change was the most welcome: when he hadn't to be at the House of Commons, Tony now worked at home. 'Although she would never admit it,' he said to Dick Leonard, his PPS in Opposition, 'Susan was rather glad we lost the election.' I was conscious of putting private life before public welfare. But I hadn't brought about this state of affairs: the electorate had. The children and I happened to be beneficiaries.

How much Tony felt the upheaval – for which he'd not prepared himself – it was hard to gauge. He was robust in vicissitude, but few men sacked or retired are spared initial disorientation. Too much is put on Ministers, while at the same time they are coddled with assistants, secretaries, the car and so on, without which they simply could not carry their burden. Overnight both burden and coddling disappear.

For six years, other than occasionally at weekends, Tony had not dialled an ordinary telephone. The frustrations of this activity he now rediscovered, felt keenly when halfway through dialling a number the instrument rebelled and resumed its dialling tone. Alternatively, he succeeded in completing the dialling only for deathly silence to ensue. He sighed. 'You're quite sure the telephone was always like this?'

He supposed in Opposition he would get an outside job: his earnings were cut by two-thirds overnight. My earnings from my profiles for the *Sunday Times* helped. But our income was inadequate. He pondered. Why *had* the Labour Government disappointed its supporters? Why wasn't more achieved? The huge spectrum of progress he'd worked out in *The Future of Socialism* had never been practised because of the central economic failure. But he had to ask himself: Was economic growth – one of his primary tools for greater equality – impossible to achieve? Which of the others could be used to more effect? He would rethink the whole argument. He wouldn't take an outside job. He would write articles, another book. Our income would remain inadequate.

In his main job as an MP, he would do two things: literally be a Shadow Minister; also have time to reflect. 'The secret of leadership,' he once wrote to Hugh Gaitskell, 'especially for an intellectual without a staff-system, is time to think.'

He disliked Tory-bashing for its own sake. It was observed that he felt real hatred of Tory policies. Within six months of being cast down, he had shaken off defeat and written a Fabian pamphlet. It spelt out that you had to keep adapting to a changing world; but the pragmatic approach to politics was not enough: you not only must decide afresh the priorities in the struggle to reach the goal but must also be seen by Labour supporters to have your sights trained on the goal. It was a coherent statement of democratic socialism for the 1970s – his own manifesto for Labour.

Six years after marriage we faced domestic adjustments that most people encounter in their first year. At no time were we beset by that potentially lethal affliction – 'getting on each other's nerves'. But with Tony at home so much, more points of view had daily to be taken into account. He quite enjoyed confrontation with others,

but not with me. We both hated rows. 'The pleasure of reconciliation isn't worth the misery that precedes it,' he taught me early on.
Even when I knew I was at fault, he usually had to take the
responsibility to clear the thing up before we went to bed: 'Someone
has to look after a relationship. It doesn't look after itself.' If a
row hung over, the next day was bleak, something to be got
through until he came home again and said: 'We'd better have a
talk.'

Petrol, of all things, presented itself as source of grievance.
During the six years that I had sole use of the Sunbeam during the
week, clearly it was my duty to put up with the tedium of the petrol
station. Couldn't this now be shared? The precedent, however, had
been established. 'You do know you're taking risks with this marriage,' he said when I raised the matter.

I applied my mind. In a relationship, one has two mental funnels,
I decided – an intellectual one where you argue things out when
necessary, an emotional one where you enjoy whatever roles suit
you both; one funnel needn't impinge on the other. I made notes
on a bit of paper so I wouldn't be thrown off course, and made a
date for discussing the petrol station. On Saturday morning – at
the appointed minute – I went into the study with two cups of
coffee and my notes. He looked at his watch, laid aside the housing
file on which he was writing, glanced at my piece of paper. If there
had to be an argument with his wife, it helped if she approached it
systematically. He fixed his attention on me.

After my first point, I stopped for comment.

'I see,' he said, drawling the words, drawing on the cheroot
planted in the middle of his lips and breathing out almost simultaneously – *phyfft, phyfft*. Next point?'

I put my second argument.

'Interesting concept. I'll think about it. How many more points
have you on that piece of paper?'

'One.' I deployed it with care.

'Is that all?'

'Yes.'

He looked at his watch, leant forward to take up the housing file,
put on his reading spectacles. 'You'll want to get back to your desk.
Each of us has a lot to do.'

That day's sandwich lunch was unrelaxed, no reference made to
the earlier conversation. Once he gave a matter his attention and
you had made your case, it was imperative to rest it there: repetition
was counterproductive, made him feel nagged. Who goes to the

petrol station – for weeks devouring my soul – was never mentioned by me again. He simply started sharing the tiresome task.

In Opposition, not only did the children and their step-father have more access to one another: the overnight disappearance of Establishment symbols made a difference to Ellen-Craig in particular. She had developed profound hostility to the Austin Princess and its successor, mortified by such a presence in our road. In her first year at Holland Park Comprehensive she was a model pupil, top of her class, active in team sport, wearing correct uniform though it was not compulsory. In her second year, noticing that some girls in her class eschewed the plain blue or white shirt recommended, she put on a striped one. 'Who do you think you are?' asked a teacher. 'Just because your father is Minister for Education is no reason to think you can do anything you like.'

'I didn't realise they even knew about Tony's job,' Ellen-Craig said when she came home. 'Anyhow, he's my step-father.' The next day, in addition to striped shirt, she wore a sweater of non-recommended hue. Though her mother and step-father were not 'permissive' parents, I felt sufficient moral stands already existed without getting embroiled over non-compulsory uniform.

In Government, Tony's knowledge of the children's crises had usually to be secondhand during weekdays. Sometimes they resented the concept that they should wait for the weekend to produce their thoughts. On marriage I'd acquired the English custom of cooking a joint for Sunday lunch. This I now renounced, mood at table too unpredictable to warrant much culinary effort. His opening question to his step-daughters as we foregathered – 'What have you been up to this week?' – might well receive the answer 'Nothing', intended to irritate, always succeeding.

Now they could get to him – at him – more regularly, to please, provoke, seek understanding when none came from me. By this time the throes of adolescence were acute, uncontained emotion surging through the house on some days, on others a sullen silence prevailing. To my surprise, he liked being more involved in all this.

He never sought to ingratiate himself with his step-daughters: from early days they had to defend their views. He could be uncomfortably blunt if one of them made a sweeping statement in favour, say, of censorship because *Clockwork Orange* so distressed her that she had to leave the cinema halfway through.

'You're perfectly capable of reading reviews, Sheila. That film has been described in every national newspaper. No one forced you to go to it. I haven't the faintest desire to see *Clockwork Orange*.

That doesn't mean others shouldn't see if it that's how they want to spend their time.'

On some subjects, having brooded, the children discovered an answer to his case. Sheila would then re-raise the thing, confront him back, so to speak. Ellen-Craig, being younger, had not yet developed the technique. 'The trouble is, Mama, I can never think of the answer when Tony is there. It's only afterwards, and then it's too late.'

'It's not too late. He'll be impressed. Go knock on the study door, say you know he's working now, but could you make an appointment to see him later for twenty minutes as you now have the answer to his argument. For heaven's sake, write it down and take your notes with you. Otherwise you may lose the thread. Also, when he sees you have a piece of paper with your points, he'll want you to win the argument.'

Of the two children, Sheila was less inclined, thankfully, to volunteer information certain to be horrendous. She was now at Kingsway College of Further Education where she was allegedly studying for her 'A' levels. At home she sat decorously at her chessboard in the drawing-room window, quietly intent on defeating the young Kingsway suitor hunched in the chair opposite. Her rather ethereal beauty concealed a fierce determination.

Notting Hill has more than its fair share of creeps. When one of these – sometimes popping out not far from our tube station – exposed himself to Sheila, this wraithlike nymph swung back one high-heeled boot, gave him a tremendous and certainly painful kick, and almost without losing stride moved silently on her way. When people bemoaned violence increasing in London – 'There's nowhere today a woman can walk alone at night' – Tony replied: 'Well, that isn't our experience in Notting Hill. Both our daughters walk home perfectly happily after dark. They wear boots. If any man approaches them they simply give him a bloody great kick in the crotch.'

Because four or five people in public life had children at Holland Park Comprehensive, it was fancifully described by hacks as something approaching a finishing school. Its catchment area included Notting Hill and North Kensington and swinging Ladbroke Grove. Invited to a private meeting of middle-class parents more permissive than ourselves, I was asked if my refusal to let fourteen-year-olds smoke pot in our house was based on the fact that my husband would be embarrassed if they were caught.

Ellen-Craig was attractive to many, though it seemed to her

mother that her effect on lame ducks was positively magnetic. There seemed no reason why I should ever answer the doorbell and not find a policeman standing there. Did we know the whereabouts of a fourteen-year-old girl who had run away from home? She was a classmate of Ellen-Craig Catling. A youth had been picked up a street away on suspicion of intent to commit a crime. He said he knew our family, was a friend of Ellen-Craig Catling. A vicar, observing a healthy young girl and three wrecks sitting quietly smoking, minding their own business, on the bench in the entrance porch of his church, got it into his head that they were bent on stealing the church silver; he called the police. The healthy young girl was Ellen-Craig Catling. Endless.

Tony, though sterner, was calmer than me under much provocation. Looking back we reckoned that adolescence was a three-year tunnel. With three years' difference in the children's ages, as Sheila emerged from one end, Ellen-Craig disappeared into the other. It was six years' slog.

'I know how much you minded at the time,' he said, 'but the luckiest thing that ever happened to us was your losing that baby. I'd be sixty years old when it became an adolescent. I don't think I could go through all this again when I'm sixty.'

Towards the end of the first year of Opposition, forced by bronchitis to take to his bed, he submitted an arm to the visiting GP for the routine strapping and squeezing by the contraption that measures blood pressure. Thinking the first reading must be wrong, the doctor repeated the process. To his surprise, the patient had developed high blood-pressure. Not having the least desire to shorten his time on this earth, Tony submitted the whole of his body to a specialist in these matters, a sophisticated man who said high blood-pressure was a common side effect of political responsibility.

'Why then didn't one have high blood-pressure during the six years in Cabinet?'

The doctor thought it possibly had been building up and only manifested itself when the adrenalin stopped working overtime. We would be astonished, he said, if he told us the names of foremost medical consultants who had high blood-pressure. He did himself, keeping fit by the simple routine of daily tablets. Who could blame the human body for protesting at such unreasonable demands put on it, particularly by a man living the life of a Cabinet Minister with this constant anxiety about national, international affairs?

'Nothing to do with the nation's affairs. If anything is responsible for altering my blood-pressure, it's my wife's children and their friends, most of whom, as far as one can make out, are deranged or delinquent - often both.'

↠ 25 ↞

The Charge into Europe

For some years dormant, the matter of the Common Market erupted in 1971. Prime Minister Heath was determined to take Britain into Europe. The Tory Party was divided by the issue. The Labour Party looked like being irreparably torn. Emotions ran high.

When a united Europe was conceived by Jean Monnet after the war, Tony was instinctively in favour as an internationalist. Time passed; the situation changed. He analysed the new arguments being used by both sides. He concluded that membership of the Market would be on balance of advantage to Britain. But only on balance. He thought the Market largely irrelevant to key issues facing ordinary people – growth, inflation, housing, education – and that it would be an act of political folly to allow the Market to endanger the unity of the Labour Party. Nor could he see any morality in acting in such a way as to keep Mr Heath's Government in power. It really mattered to him that under a Tory Government, the worse off were being made still worse off, the better off cushioned.

By July 1971 the Market struggle had turned into religious war. Most of the media presented Labour's pro-Marketeers as the men of principle. Tony pointed out that the principles involved in the dispute were neither simple nor self-evident. Pressure brought to bear on individuals by opposing factions was terrific. In some constituencies, particularly London ones where the changing population made it easier for unrepresentative activists to move suddenly upon a local Party, pro-Market MPs were threatened with rejection at the next election if they voted against the local Party's wishes. Other threats were more subtle, emotional coercion applied: If you don't stand up for our side you are a coward – that sort of thing. 'I do rather wish Bernard Levin – Roy when it comes to that – would stop proclaiming we must all stand up and be counted as if one hadn't been stating one's position as plainly as possible for the past twenty-five years,' Tony said.

He expected – rather liked – assaults on his philosophy and

policies. The assault on his integrity delivered by erstwhile friends was something else. It was his most unhappy period in politics.

'If I thought a little less, I might be able to accept the claptrap being expounded by my pro-European friends,' he said. He found their extremism irresponsible and told them so.

It was no good supporting something unless you supported it with enthusiasm, Roy Jenkins said to him.

'I have always supported something with enthusiasm if I felt enthusiastic. I do not support things with enthusiasm if I do not feel enthusiastic. You may like this or not. That's the way I am,' Tony replied.

He found the arguments of the anti-Market lobby equally facile – and unattractive to boot. He drafted a speech stating his position – that he was still pro-Europe, but if it became a question of keeping Mr Heath in power by voting for Europe, then he would not do so. Europe remained lower on his list of priorities than the egalitarian policies which only a Labour Government would undertake. Whether he would abstain on the European vote he hadn't yet decided.

He showed the draft speech to several pro-European MPs. All asked him not to deliver it: 'It is logical from your viewpoint, but you admit that you don't feel strongly about Europe, and you will damage the European cause about which we feel passionately.' With deep distaste he allowed himself to be persuaded that, on this issue, if he spelled out his position publicly it would be largely in his own interest.

Grimsby's Labour Party, itself divided on the issue, were clear that they couldn't pressurise their MP, even if they could agree how they wanted him to vote, but they had to mandate a delegate to the constituency section of conference. The speech Tony reluctantly agreed not to make publicly he made privately to his General Management Committee. It was accepted as reasonable, and an unfanatical pro-Marketeer was sent as delegate to conference. At the same time that Tony was speaking to his GMC in Grimsby, part of his draft speech was leaked in London by one of the pro-Europeans he'd consulted earlier in the week. What caused the most resentment was his use of the word 'élitist' to describe their more fervent attitudes.

'It's ironic,' said Tony to one of the extreme 'pros', 'that by the democratic process of consulting and then taking advice, I have ended up not giving the speech publicly and having it leaked in the most damaging way by a consultant.'

'You've been too long in this game not to have known that would happen,' said his colleague.

The truncated version of the Grimsby speech shared headlines with an announcement made the same day by Denis Healey who, a few weeks earlier having written an article in favour of Europe, now said he was against it and would vote with the 'antis'. Denis, the Jenkinsites said, boasted of being opportunist, so his opposition did not matter; they were aiming at the intelligentsia. Tony was known as an honest intellectual; when *he* qualified their case, he became the threat.

Things became entangled in people's minds: 'We never thought of Tony as an opportunist until we read yesterday about him and Denis.' Some thought Tony had said he would vote with the antis. In any case, he had harmed their cause. Of that the pro-Europeans were certain. They set out to wound – a lot was at stake – and for perhaps six months they succeeded, their choice of verbal weapons – 'expedient', 'temporising', 'turncoat', 'apostasy' – reminiscent of language associated with the Christian fanatics from whom Tony separated himself when a boy.

When she was in her seventies, his mother was visited one evening by three elders of the Exclusive Brethren. At a previous Sunday meeting, a member of the Brethren was driven out for some deviation from doctrine, denounced as a moral leper, son of Belial. Mrs Crosland refused to join in the denunciation. The elders came to her flat, where she lived alone, to persuade her to accept their judgment. She refused. So they chucked her out too.

'It was very unpleasant sometimes,' she recalled when she was in her nineties or thereabouts. (She was vague about her age. Only after her death was it discovered from Somerset House records that not only were the family wrong about the year of her birth but celebrated it on the wrong date.) 'I'm glad now, because the Brethren since then have become Taylorites – that American, you know. They've gone downhill. But at the time it happened, I was sometimes very unhappy.' On Highgate Hill when she met members of the Brethren whom she'd known most of her life, they put their hands behind their backs.

Originally the Common Market wasn't a Left-Right issue, but in the Labour Party's struggle in Opposition to clarify its future direction, the Market became polarised. The issue, moreover, became hopelessly enmeshed with a separate question: could Roy Jenkins replace Harold Wilson as Labour Leader? Since the 1950s

Roy had advocated the Common Market. Gathered now round his banner were pro-Europeans. Shoulder to shoulder with them stood Right-wingers whose chief interest was Roy Jenkins, their concern for the Market less pressing. Roy, least of all, could unsnarl these two different issues.

Bill Rodgers threw his energies into organising both groups of pro-European MPs into a body that would put 'principle before Party'. In a committee room at the House, he held periodic meetings to keep up morale – meetings by invitation – so you could see there were at least fifty of you. A certain amount of self-righteousness was bound to grip you as you rode together under the banner of principle, perhaps risking your career, urged on and acclaimed for heroism by political commentators (no matter that many of these had little objection to the Labour Party being rent). Tony's PPS, Dick Leonard, was among the horsemen – partly from obstinacy: his London constituency's GMC had tried to pressurise him to vote against Europe. At one stage he had doubts that he could vote with the Tory Government, but he resolved them and said he would vote with the group.

Roy's influence on Labour's pro-Europeans was crucial: if he'd told them to abstain in the initial vote on accepting the terms for entry, they would have abstained. Abstention is heartily disliked, but it is far less flagrant an affront than total opposition to policy accepted by the PLP. At a meeting of Roy's group, David Owen put the case: 'It would be better to have many abstaining than a smaller number voting with the Tories.' His argument was brushed aside.

When Tony heard of this he said to Roy: 'It's irresponsible for you not to allow abstention to be seriously discussed by your group. You could make your European stand without voting with Heath. You might reflect that in the long run you are damaging yourself as well as the Labour Party.'

It was nothing to the damage Tony had done himself by his 'indecisiveness' on this issue, Roy replied. 'We', Roy said, knew only too well how Tony had to analyse and analyse before taking a stand.

'Your view is that it is better for a group to be strong and wrong. I disagree,' Tony said.

'I now realise it's typical of Tony,' Roy Hattersley said to Dick Leonard. 'His nerve gives out. I shall ring him and tell him so.'

A few weeks earlier Tony had rung him about something else. Hattersley was being subjected to abuse for writing an article –

which some thought opportunist – in the *New Statesman*. Tony telephoned him to say that, while he thought it a mistake, we all make mistakes and it certainly didn't affect his feelings for him. Tony liked Roy Hattersley.

Now the two men encountered one another going through the division lobby. 'I thought you were going to ring me yesterday to tell me my nerve gives out,' Tony said.

Hattersley was slightly taken aback by this confrontation, then righted himself. 'No, that's not why I was going to ring you. What I was going to say was that for a long time you've wanted to dissociate yourself from our group. And by God, you have.'

'At any rate,' Tony said, 'I've not so far in my life dissociated myself from anything for the sake of £50 from the *New Statesman*.' Tempers were not good.

An informal supper club called XYZ had existed among Labour supporters since Hugh Dalton's day, meeting at the House, spouses invited once a year. That July Tony and I decided to attend. We all met before dinner in a small room. I was only acquainted with Dick Taverne and his wife, but I'd known Silvia Rodgers for years. When Tony and I walked in, they turned their backs upon us. There was something comic about the little phalanx of backs. We laughed. The unpleasant part was to come.

From Tony's standpoint, some who thought of themselves as Gaitskellites had moved so far to the Right that they disappeared from view. From their standpoint, this once most outspoken of all critics of the extreme Left was now courting it. Roy Jenkins had pressed for his supporters to get jobs in government, sometimes succeeding. Tony, when asked by Bill Rodgers to do so, replied that he did not see his role as promoting a coterie – he preferred a representative team of all shades of opinion in the PLP.

When something occurs that people dislike, they often hark back and reassess their previous view. Now that they thought about it, the Jenkinsites said, Tony's character had changed when Labour came into government in 1964; since then he had been calculating for his personal advancement. That's what he was considering when he declined to fight for a Europe in which he really believed, whatever he said. He was simply a careerist.

Meanwhile Harold Wilson was wrestling with the central problem, and Harold Lever had many discussions with him – trying to persuade the Leader to take a position more favourable to the Common Market, while retaining Party unity. Lever's record as a champion of the Market was probably the most pure of all in the

Labour Party. He went to see a leading Jenkinsite and said: 'We must try to persuade Wilson that if he loses his allies amongst the Left antis, the pro-Europeans can't overthrow him even if they want to, and they don't. Wilson still thinks I don't understand these matters and that you'll cut his throat.'

'Of course we'll cut his throat.'

Lever then gave up trying to persuade Wilson to support the Europeans. 'I don't cheat,' Lever said. He now felt that the caballist nature of the Jenkinsites was actually hindering the ideological purpose they professed to serve.

⇥ 26 ⇤

'We Must Punish Him'

The Common Market wrangle inside the Labour Party gave me a sustained illustration of in-fighting. Moreover, it was the classic situation: not only does each side think its case eminently reasonable, but when the opposing cases are set out, the onlooker can see how they slot into one another.

By late October 1971, with the great European vote imminent, how many Labour pro-Marketeers would go into the lobby with Mr Heath? Who were heroes? Who were villains? Most of the PLP were overwrought or worn down. Tony was depressed when he came home from the House the night before the final debate, so we started with my gossip. I was considering a commission to write a biography instead of the profiles I'd been doing for the *Sunday Times*.

His own gossip was largely political that evening. The day seemed a long time ago. 'Can't remember who I had lunch with. Oh yes. Harold and Jim. Some time I must think about Harold's intellect. Don't know what's the matter with it. I told Jim I'm going to abstain on the vote tomorrow night. He said it was a terrible mistake: however mixed my feelings about Europe, I should establish myself in people's minds as a Party man, forever distinct from the Jenkinsite Right.'

Abstaining on a major vote was hard for Tony to stomach. So far as I know he'd never considered it in any previous circumstances. 'The only place where I've been cowardly', he said, 'is in not admitting how much I've altered my mind since last spring's economic figures – when I realised the case for going into Europe is even weaker than I have said. I didn't admit it because I thought in the present climate nobody would believe me.

'So I'll abstain tomorrow night. It's more consistent with my expressed view than anything else, I think.'

The following morning the chairman of his local Party, Ivor Hanson, rang from Grimsby. There were other things to sort out, but inevitably the Common Market arose. Ivor said his parents had said that if Tony abstained they'd stay away from the polling booth in the next election. Tony said he was going to abstain. Ivor received this amicably enough. 'But I'm sorry to disappoint them,' Tony said as he gathered up his housing papers before setting off for the Commons.

About 5.30 that afternoon, he walked through our front door again. 'I put myself practically beside Harold during his speech, so everybody knows I was there and am not sick and am abstaining because I want to abstain. So I don't see why I should sit through all the speeches this evening. I do hope that the next crisis in my life is about a subject in which I feel an emotional involvement.'

I switched on the television soon after ten to hear the results and then went up to the study to tell him. The Government won its pro-Europe proposal – 356 in favour, 244 against. Sixty-nine Labour MPs voted with Mr Heath, giving him his victory. Nineteen Labour MPs abstained. I returned downstairs to watch some of the interviews. Bill Rodgers, his face etched with nervous strain, was trying to explain how the Labour pro-Marketeers, having voted with Mr Heath, could with any consistency vote against the Bill as it was debated in the coming months. Tony remained in his study working through two housing files.

'He's behaved like a shit and we must punish him,' Bill Rodgers said to Dick Leonard. It was a few weeks after the Common Market vote, and the PLP was preparing for the elections it holds annually in Opposition. Harold Wilson was re-elected Leader, Roy Jenkins re-elected Deputy Leader. (Callaghan never stood for the deputy leadership, preferring to establish himself as No. 2 without contending for a title which he thought had little significance.)

The sixty-nine Labour pro-Marketeers were anxious, naturally enough, to win places for their group in the Shadow Cabinet. For some of them there was also a vendetta to be pursued. Dick Leonard heard the Jenkinsites were making a concerted effort to get Tony out of Shadow Cabinet. Dick confronted Bill Rodgers in the angriest conversation the two friends ever had.

'If this is true, it is ludicrous. The only result will be to put someone in Shadow Cabinet with whom you disagree a great deal more,' Dick said.

'He's behaved like a shit,' Bill repeated. 'He's got to be taught a lesson.'

I seldom went to the House of Commons, but I was writing a profile of the Lord Chancellor, Lord Hailsham, and was next door in the Lords for one of many interviews with him. I decided to call

in at Tony's room. He disliked the claustrophobia of this room –
not much more than a cubicle in a row of similar cells allocated to
Shadow Ministers. He wasn't there. I sat down to wait. Bill Rodgers
appeared at the door.

'Will you give Tony a message?' he said. As Tony walked in at
that moment, sat down at his desk, offered Bill the third chair in
the cubicle, the message was delivered directly. 'You know I will
vote for you, Tony, but I think you should know that there is this
group of fifteen or twenty votes that will not go to you if you vote
for Reg Prentice.'

Though the ballot was secret, most MPs assumed that if you
said you were going to vote for someone, you did. Tony intended
casting one of his twelve votes for Prentice. (Strange as it seemed
a few years later, in 1971 Prentice was a middle-of-the-road Labour
MP, dedicated to comprehensive education and overseas development. He was an anti-European at that time.)

Having given Bill his attention, Tony closed his eyes slowly and
then opened them.

Receiving no further acknowledgment, Bill went on: 'We
thought you were petulant at last week's 1963 dinner.' After Hugh
Gaitskell's death in 1963, his supporters from CDS days met
informally from time to time. The 1963 Club was now engrossed
in twin causes: Roy Jenkins and Europe. Tony turned up at the
dinner and told them that if they would vote for him only if he
made his decisions in a particular way, he didn't want their votes.
He added that they really must decide whether they intended to
remain The Sixty-nine Apart or to ask some others to join these
CDS dinners and themselves rejoin the Party.

'We were glad, Susan,' said Bill, turning to me, 'that you used
your influence to stop Tony writing us the letter he had planned.
At least what he said was less petulant than what you stopped him
writing.'

Tony and I glanced at one another. He winked. How, I asked
myself, did this extraordinary group imagine they knew what Tony
and I discussed in the privacy of our home? In any case, what I had
actually said to him was that so far as I cared, they could all stuff
themselves.

Bill reiterated his warning, the wording this time a bit heavy-
toned. He would be glad to 'deliver', as he put it, these fifteen or
twenty votes to Tony if Tony would agree not to vote for this
anti-European. The intense emphasis on the delivery seemed to
me scarcely warranted by the substance.

'I see,' Tony said, drawling the words. 'It's courteous of you to let me know.'

Years later Bill told me how impressed he was by the way I didn't leap in and take Tony's part. There weren't many wives, he said, who could have kept detached like that. In fact, during this bizarre scene my mind was occupied with other reflections. These were: (1) Is Bill Rodgers deranged? (2) If he's not deranged, what has happened to his judgment for him to think this a fruitful approach to someone of Tony's personality? (3) Did a long-ago American B-film, possibly about gangsters, have a subliminal influence on Bill's personality?

For the third time Bill made his threat, now unmistakably sinister in undertone. Tony closed his eyes and opened them. Bill departed.

'Has he come unstuck?' I asked.

'I think it's more the gang mentality. They are a bullying little clique. Dick Leonard tells me that Bill and Hattersley now say: "Oh well, Tony is indecisive again." As far as I know, the Common Market is the first issue on which I've been indecisive - because I don't care terribly about it. But it's the same point that Roy made to me. A legend grows rapidly; Bill is now acting on the legend.' In those days 'Roy' was always Roy Jenkins.

In the Shadow Cabinet ballot, Tony dropped from his previous place, third, but he wasn't knocked off. He came eighth. Denis Healey dropped from second place to twelfth.

Tony agreed to dine with Roy. Despite their ever-increasing differences over the years, the two men could still enjoy one another's company when alone. This was not one of those evenings. Roy had a proposition to make. He was the good political tactician. Tony was the good political thinker. If he would join Roy's group, Tony would attract to it a number of people who could then build it up to a majority of the Labour Party. Michael Foot had changed personality and now wanted power, so if Harold was run over by the bus, Foot and Roy would beat Callaghan on the first ballot. Of course, if Jim could survive the first ballot, he would win (as Tony believed Jim would have won if he'd survived the first ballot in the 1963 leadership election). But with Roy's group so well organised, and Michael now becoming organised, Jim would be knocked out on the first ballot. Tony was necessary to Roy's group and would play the second major role in the group if he could 'only be decisive enough' to join them.

All this Roy set out. Tony thought that halfway through, Roy sensed he had played it badly. The answer would have been the same however he had played it.

In his championship of Europe, Harold Lever went on working alongside Roy's acolytes and was not too comfortable. He was reminded of his army days, when he was in OCTU attending tutorials under a Major, he told me: aspiring officers would dissent from the Major's argument simply to suck up to him, draw attention to themselves, invariably indicating as the tutorial approached its close that the Major was right and they were wrong. Lever had the greatest difficulty in banishing this image from his mind when attending meetings between Roy and his group.

The group saw themselves as motivated by the highest principles. They were held together by tight bonds of intellectual, ideological, personal affinities, devoted to the purpose of making Roy Prime Minister, when his supporters would stand on the topmost rungs.

Lever observed with interest the behaviour of his recently acquired colleagues: when Tony refused to join them and take the advisory role, he was felt to represent a menace to the prospects of the group. Wherever Tony's independence manifested itself – the Common Market above all – that feeling was sharpened. When you're in a gang, you believe in good faith that anyone who disagrees with you has an ulterior motive – wants the power that you want. Feelings were further sharpened by there being no point in sucking up to Tony: at the end of the day the only advantage would be that he'd be more aware of your possibilities than otherwise. But he wouldn't say: 'Well done, my good and faithful servant. The Treasury is yours.' That's how Lever saw feelings among the Jenkinsites.

Not a man who uses language sparely, Harold Lever confronted two of Roy's lieutenants. When he later told me the discourse he had delivered, like anyone who knows Harold I did not doubt it. Were he a painter, he would have been happy in the Baroque School. 'I must tell you,' he told the two lieutenants, 'that I understand your dedication to Roy. If you're going to have a leader, you want to be sure the guy has an obsession with becoming king of the castle. Roy has always had a conscious design to end up being PM. Tony, when he was younger at any rate, had a vaguer idea of himself: politics? don? drink and screw? He has not followed a systematic course in his personal life. So Roy's ambition was made of sterner stuff and earlier. I accept all that.

'I accept that perfectly honourable men can create a self-serving fantasy about another man as you are doing about Tony. I understand that. But I disapprove of it. In your heart of hearts you must know that Tony's character has not suddenly changed in some abominable way. I don't agree with his stance on Europe, but that's nothing to do with integrity. It has to do with standards developed outside politics which he brought into politics with him. He is under the control of his own principles, a dangerous thing in a leader, I accept. The meaner, more squalid elements of politics he despises. I must tell you that I despise them too.'

That was all very well, they said, but Tony's rejection of their group was bound to weaken it. He must be seen to pay for what he had done.

'Do you mind if I think out loud?' Tony asked. He'd turned into the almost empty dual carriageway that leads to Winchester. We liked to go there alone sometimes, staying in a hotel overlooking the Cathedral.

'I can see how the Jenkinsites look at the thing,' he said. 'They make three points. They feel I am sulking in my tent. They do not accept how far from mine their political values have moved. They believe I could bring them enough centrist MPs to tip the balance.

'I think they're deluding themselves. The danger of seeing only members of your group is you begin to think more people are likeminded than is the case, think your convictions are the only authentic convictions.

'I ask myself: do I not join them because of vanity, pride? That has to be a factor. Certainly I would find it demeaning. But I don't *think* that's my main reason for refusing. Their idea of a Labour Party is not mine. Roy has come actually to dislike socialism. Even if I was prepared to chuck my own values and strengthen their group, they still couldn't win over the Party – shouldn't win it over. The most that would happen is that the Party would be split for a generation. It is Roy's misfortune that because of his father, he's in the wrong Party. As a Liberal or Conservative, he might make a very good Leader.'

We drove in silence for some miles.

'Thank you very much,' he said. 'I wanted to clear my mind once and for all. Why don't you reach into my briefcase and get out Pevsner? Shall we go to Norman Cross tomorrow? If you don't feel like walking through all those muddy fields, you could take the car, and we could meet by the almshouses. I'll bet you've only brought shoes with heels at least six inches high.'

Though sometimes aggravated, he wasn't again wounded by the Jenkinsites. Having satisfied himself that his former friends actually believed what they were saying about his character, he stopped minding, became prone when encountering them in the House to inquire after the state of their principles: he hoped these remained unsullied.

Nearly seven years later, Bill Rodgers wrote me a letter giving his assessment of what happened between the group he called the Gaitskellites and Tony:

(17 OCTOBER 1978) I don't think that any of us who were critical of Tony in the later stages of his career ever qualified our regard for his intellectual distinction or doubted his integrity or lost our affection for him ...

... While Hugh Gaitskell was leader, he, Tony, could be a maverick, challenging the conventional wisdom, but with no personal responsibility for policy-making. After Hugh's death, and more particularly from October 1964, he saw his role change. He became devoted to the business of Government with more than an eye to the opportunities of rising to the top.

I would be the last person to despise his application to running a great Department of State. His achievements, particularly at Education and Environment, were significant and lasting. But he seemed to lose his capacity for taking an independent overall view of the Government ...

I understand Tony's views on the Common Market. Odd as it seems, I substantially shared them. We joined the Labour Committee for Europe (or whatever it was then called) at the same time and joined a delegation to see Hugh Gaitskell to explain our anxieties in the autumn of 1962. But his subsequent actions, in 1971, seemed less because of doubts about membership and more designed to avoid being type-cast in the PLP. It was political calculation (so uncharacteristic of him in his earlier days) as much as political conviction.

At Lansdowne Road we were, mercifully, just about through the tunnel of adolescence. Family meals at the weekend were no longer locked in silent, gruelling contests of nerve; communication lines across the table were reopened. This day Ellen-Craig was chirpy. 'At Holland Park they're still talking about you, Tony – Big T. breaking up a fight in Notting Hill Gate tube station.' The children's friends referred to him as 'Big T.', though not when he was around.

One of Ellen-Craig's schoolfriends had been among the evening rush-hour crowds pouring on to the Circle Line platform at Notting Hill Gate, making for home. This flow of humanity altered course when it reached the spot where something distinctly unpleasant was taking place on the platform, moved to one side and then forward again, as if it hadn't seen.

There was no three-line whip that night, so Tony was in the crowd decanted from the Circle train. He'd been in the last coach where life was marginally less congested, took his time while the crowd thinned out, saw what was taking place. Three youths had encircled a fourth who was curled up on the platform, shielding his head with one arm, his stomach with the other. The standing ones were concentrating on kicking him. They wore the heavy shoes favoured by those who like kicking people.

'What in the fuck do you think you're doing?'

All three desisted from their occupation, together turned and faced him. When he was outraged, the pale eyes actually did look like ice. He just stood there. The assailants, whose expressions did not proclaim overwhelming intelligence, may have thought he'd materialised from thin air. They moved back a little, hesitated, mumbled, turned and slouched together towards the Way Out sign, one of them looking back over his shoulder before they disappeared round the corner.

'You all right?'

The downtrodden youth was uncrumpling himself, getting to his feet. He wiped his mouth with the back of one hand, looked sullenly at the blood on it.

'Yeah.'

A thin, pallid girl appeared from somewhere and stood beside the youth. Tony resumed his path to Way Out. Ellen-Craig's schoolfriend, not much given to anything so ordinary as smiling, permitted himself a half-smile as he concluded his account. 'That was a good scene,' he said.

After family lunch Tony said to me: 'My poor old ego must still be a little battered: I found myself very pleased when Ellen-Craig said they're still talking about that.'

27

Teamwork

Mr Heath's Government could last up to five years. Then Tony expected Labour to win again, himself to be at Environment where housing would be his primary subject. No one had ever come to grips with housing. It was a finite subject that affected his Grimsby constituents. 'Know nothing about housing,' he said and immersed himself in it. The British system, always quaint, then provided no assistance whatsoever for Shadow Ministers expected to question and criticise Government Ministers backed by legions of civil servants. Shadows had to find their own experts. Soon after ten in the morning, the doorbell began ringing, the first of a battery of housing specialists – Shelter administrators, economists, people from tenants' associations, Labour councillors, Transport House advisers – mounting the stairs to the study.

The Tories implemented several major pieces of legislation proposed by the new Department of the Environment, DOE. Tony decided it would be the Housing Finance Bill on which he would lead the Opposition through the Committee stage. Today virtually all Members are on Standing Committees. When Tony began as a backbencher, Committees were smaller; fewer demands were made on MPs by the Whips and presumably he resisted them. This was his first experience of a Commons Committee. Imagining it would be a bore, he was soon intrigued, flung himself into it with a passion at odds with the still prevailing view of him in the House. Backbenchers discovered the difference between him and many intellectuals – his pleasure in working in a team. The Housing Finance Committee became entwined with his affection for the Labour movement. He understood the Labour Party to an extent perhaps it never appreciated, and he was glad to work with cross-sections of the Party to fight a Bill that was anathema to all of them. It was also a chance to fight a snobbery that he detested – the paternalist snobbery of the Bill. And it related to Grimsby, to ordinary people. Everything made it genuine to him.

It was a very scratch army to start with – seventeen or eighteen Labour MPs who had had little to do with one another. (There were more volunteers from London Members than places for them, several very upset at not being on the Committee: they had horrific housing problems in their constituencies.) He forged them into an effective unit by being prepared to muck in himself. He was older than most of them, and they expected him to play the strategic role, leave the dirty work to others, go home early. Instead he stayed all night. The rank and file were surprised to discover how well they got on with him. He in turn discovered they knew more about the nuts and bolts of politics than he did; most of them had been local councillors before entering the House. Pleasure was felt on both sides.

Dennis Skinner was one of the Left-wingers on the team. The 'Beast of Bolsover', as he is styled by the press, never could endure pretension. He was down the Derbyshire pits that surround Clay Cross when he won a miner's scholarship to Ruskin; he determined that an Oxford education would not alter his mores. He never 'paired' at the House, attending every vote regardless of its importance. He declined all-Party invitations, whether to play tennis in Bermuda or visit South Africa to observe fascism first-hand. Jaunts of any kind were suspect in his mind. He was a practising puritan.

'You really mustn't get yourself an ulcer,' Tony said. He had developed a soft spot for Dennis Skinner, enjoyed the mordant humour, liked the way Dennis behaved in character.

Skinner had learned to distinguish between those who feign a background, and those whose background is foisted upon them, as he put it: 'Tony was from the greener side of the hill. The people I can't stand are the ones who switch on a regional accent to accord with fashion, find a convenient great-grandfather who lived near a pitshaft. There are lots inside the Labour Party. Tony didn't fit into them. In a goldfish bowl like the Housing Finance Committee, living together nearly six months, you learn about people. Some feel they have to pretend to be puritans. Tony Crosland didn't know that problem. He had this combination of being totally involved in the argument and also having a drink or two. He had this loftiness – dismissed the peripheral argument very quickly, got to the central question. To people on the outside, he looked as if he was coasting along; they took him at face value. When you worked with him, you realised he was pulling more than his share.'

The Committee stage of the Housing Finance Bill was the longest in Commons history, often meeting twice a day, running on into the night, sometimes locked together until late the following morning. Between sessions Tony would say to the team: 'Let's meet for a quarter of an hour to go over the tactics of the thing.' He consulted rather than laid down the law, then led. It was chance that none of his Government departments had been associated with legislation, and MPs were now observing for the first time what had been known for six years in Whitehall. Though they worked as a team, he was the one who exposed the divergence between the stated object of the Tories' Bill and what it was actually going to do. Not even the Tories realised this until the leader of the Labour team discovered it. MPs watched the faces of Housing civil servants present who were impressed as well as discomforted. Halfway through the Housing Finance Bill, the Tories' Minister of Housing, Julian Amery, was switched to the Foreign Office. Peter Walker, in overall charge of Environment, was switched to Trade. It's unusual for this to happen in the middle of major legislation, and it was widely assumed that Heath heard that these two Ministers couldn't cope with the Shadow Minister.

Several nights I drove to the House to watch this rather moving example of team spirit. Committee rooms are small, half-a-dozen chairs for visitors placed against the wall opposite the man who serves as referee (whom parliamentarians prefer to call 'Mr Chairman'). The several rows of MPs opposing one another were separated by little more than a yard or two. On the Labour side some had removed their jackets. There was a strong sense of ideological combat and camaraderie.

One night Tony rang Lansdowne Road to ask me to bring his overnight bag – a small, brown canvas thing with a zipper (later to puzzle the Foreign Office by its prosaic character: I think it had been my father's 'kit bag' from his own journeys in the Second World War). Would I put in it a bottle of whisky and his carpet slippers? 'The whisky will be good for our morale, bad for theirs. Also, if we're going to be sitting here for two days, it would be bliss to get out of one's shoes for a few hours.' When I perched on a visitor's chair and unpacked the bag, an MP stepped over to collect the contents, setting these out in front of Tony who was concentrating on the Tory leader's speech. Some time in the small hours they all took a twenty-minute break. Tony's whisky was shared out among the Labour team.

Meanwhile, having sat on my visitor's chair for a couple of hours, I realised I was going to faint, made for the door rapidly, rounded the corner out of sight of the policeman on duty, and lay at the top of a helpfully draughty staircase, waiting for the oxygen to return to my brain. I was glad no one climbed the stairs while this Stranger reclined on the floor. (*'Hats off, Strangers!'* is probably the most charming of commands when issued in a colossal bellow by a policeman as the Speaker's Procession tramps through Central Lobby.)

On a February afternoon in 1972, as Tony walked through a passage in the Commons, smiling to himself over the latest ploy just devised in the meeting of Labour's housing MPs, he came on Bill Rodgers in conversation with another Labour European.

'What are you smiling about?' asked Bill.

Tony told him.

Bill indicated that no one should be able to smile after the Labour Party's united vote against some stage of the European Bill. Tony indicated that he was more interested in housing than in Europe. Bill reacted furiously. 'No man of your intelligence could actually believe that,' he said, turning on his heel and stalking off.

'But Bill has known that for ages,' I said to Tony over gossip that evening.

'Perhaps I stated it in a more extreme manner.' Ah yes. I could see the picture clearly now.

The sixty-nine Labour Marketeers were no longer in good heart. Having voted with the Tory Government in October on the principle of joining Europe, they were now voting with the rest of the Labour Party against the Bill as it moved through its various stages. The press began calling attention to cracks in images. Bill Rodgers and Dick Taverne urged Roy Jenkins to resign his posts as Shadow Chancellor and Deputy Leader. John Harris and David Owen urged him not to resign, Shirley Williams and Roy Hattersley sharing their view. Five or six of Roy's principal lieutenants advised him daily, proffering conflicting advice. Anyone would have been emotionally strung up by all this. Hattersley, for some time not on speaking terms with Tony, now approached him in the Commons. 'You're the only person I know who isn't caught up in this insanity. We must meet.'

'Let's give it a miss. I'm involved in housing.'

Roy Hattersley had entered the Commons in 1964. I remember his coming to Lansdowne Road a couple of times and looking surly when Tony referred to him and me collectively as 'you children'. When in his twenties, Hattersley had been chairman of housing on Sheffield City Council and was unaccustomed to this form of address. 'How do you put up with it, Susan?' he said. (Having been called Child throughout my life by Southern members of my family, I thought nothing of it.)

Despite insult and other tribulations, both Hattersleys became friends of both Croslands some time late in the 1960s. Unless one was skilled in bearing grudges, it was hard not to enjoy Roy Hatt when he was in ebullient mood, flourishing on plots and counter-plots and the farce that accompanies them. 'The thing about Hat-tersley's personal ambition is he's entirely open about it,' Tony said. 'And unlike most of that group, he's an egalitarian. Very big political potential there.'

Eventually it was fixed that the Hattersleys would lunch at Lansdowne Road one Sunday in March. That weekend Roy Jen-kins delivered a much publicised speech on poverty; the press reported it as Jenkins's Bid for the Leadership.

'Congratulations on a brilliant political coup,' Tony said when Roy Hatt and Molly walked in. They broke into wild laughter, assuming, wrongly, that Tony was being sardonic.

'What is so maddening', said Roy Hatt, 'is that the whole group had decided *not* to stress in any way the leadership bid. We wanted headlines saying: "Jenkins Makes Breakthrough on Poverty". We've all worked for weeks on this speech. And now nobody is even going to notice its content because it's being treated as a political bid.' He was in one of his morose moods.

'But surely,' Tony said, 'this is the only year between now and an election when Roy can make his bid.'

'Yes, perhaps, but he won't make his bid. Roy, we all know, is superficially daring but fundamentally cautious. If the Labour Government comes back, Harold will stay PM for only three years. If we can build Roy up, he can then get it by default. That's why we're all working to get him associated with things like poverty and equality.'

Tony laughed. 'Roy will get impatient, rightly, and not want to wait another six years.'

Hatt began to laugh. 'It's a long campaign, you may well say. It's gone on six years already. My relation to Roy is a purely professional one. Bill Rodgers has a real personal affection for him which I do not. Bill will be having lunch or dinner with him today and talking to him in that emotional way.' He lapsed into his earlier mood. 'It really is very irritating that we should have spent the last ten days briefing the press on the importance of this speech, and now nobody is noticing its substance. However, you might like to know that we plan for his next speech to be on education.' He brightened at the thought. 'There will be passages in it that you may find strangely familiar.'

Later that afternoon, Tony and I strolled in the square behind our house. 'I can't say I enjoy knowing my own preserve is being usurped in this way,' he said. 'It'll be put right in twenty years' time. But meanwhile, it's like an intelligent and original author seeing his ideas plagiarised by a pop writer. This I *do* feel.'

In the event the education speech was not delivered. It was the Easter recess. Tony was in Tokyo for an environmental conference. Sheila was in Dublin working part-time as journalist, part-time as barmaid. Ellen-Craig was in Cornwall visiting a schoolfriend's family. On Monday, 10 April, I finally got down to writing a profile of Kenneth Tynan, confident of no interruption. The telephone rang.

It was Dick Leonard. He had just learned from David Owen that Roy Jenkins and Harold Lever and George Thomson were resigning from Labour's front bench that evening – in protest against the Shadow Cabinet's decision that when Labour was returned to office, a referendum would be held on whether Britain should stay in the Common Market. Shirley was not resigning. Roy Hattersley said he was not going to do anything so dramatic as resign himself, but he'd just stop being there.

Owing to the Japanese difficulty in pronouncing 'r', the telegram received by Tony read:

LEONALD ANXIOUS YOU KNOW JENKINS THOMPSON LEVEL
LESIGNING FLONT BENCH TONIGHT STOP DICK AGLEES
JEPAN IDEAL PLACE NOW LOVE SUSAN

28

A Deputy Leadership Contest

Dick didn't agree for long. Nor did some others. Roy's resignation left two jobs to be filled – Shadow Chancellor and Deputy Leader, the former the more important. Our telephone entered a manic phase. This time the voice belonged to a Labour friend inclined to twenty sentences where two would do.

'Where is Tony?' he asked.

'Tokyo.'

'My God. Has Roy taken leave of his senses? Harold Lever wanted to resign and fight for the Market from the backbenches last October, but Roy's group said that would weaken the cause. What on earth is the point in resigning over the referendum? If John Harris had been here instead of in the United States, this wouldn't have happened. I think perhaps I should ring Jennifer and discuss the thing with her.'

I always liked Jennifer Jenkins. 'I shouldn't do that,' I said.

'You think I shouldn't?'

'That's right.'

'When did Tony go to Tokyo?'

'Two days ago. He'll be there for ten days.'

'Why didn't anyone alert Tony to Roy's resignation? Anything can happen to the Party before Tony gets back from Japan.'

Just when I was giving some thought to going to sleep Monday night, a Labour activist rang for the third time. 'Don't you think, Susan, Tony should have the chance to say whether he wants to return or not?'

'OK. I'll ring him. Does anyone know the time difference?'

'I do. When it's midnight in London, it's eight o'clock tomorrow morning in Tokyo.'

Midnight in London fast approaching, I copied out the digits required to ring Tokyo direct. In his hotel room, woken from innocent sleep at one minute past eight in the morning, my telegram patently not yet received, Tony displayed no pleasure on hearing my voice.

'Something has happened to one of the children.'

'No no. We're all fine.'

'Wish you wouldn't alarm me like that, Susan.'

'We're absolutely OK. But there's been a slight political happening.' This I explained.

'I see. I'm delivering my speech to the conference later today. Could you ring me right after that? Meanwhile I'll have time to think. Bugger it. Hope I don't decide to return to London: the conference is fascinating.'

At the appointed time I rang Tokyo again.

'How long did it take you to get this call through from Lansdowne Road?'

'However long it takes to dial all those digits and listen to some whirring sounds.'

'Extraordinary. It takes me twenty minutes to get on to the Embassy or BOAC, and they're only a few streets away. Perhaps Benn's got something in his technology after all. What day is it in London?'

'Tuesday. It's morning here. Dick Leonard says that the Shadow Chancellor will be appointed later today. He says there's talk it will be you or Peter Shore.'

'Oh, God.' He was silent for a bit. 'I suppose there is nothing for it but to ring Harold. Peter Shore is a nice man but his economic theories are not what one wants at this moment. Could you tell Dick to tell Harold I'll be ringing him at 2 p.m. your time? Something the matter with me and Tokyo. The last time I was here their beautifully arranged programme was cut in two because Harold was springing Environment upon the nation. Good thing the Japanese are stoical.'

It was getting on to three-thirty in London when he rang me back, still riveted by Benn's technology. He sounded cheerful. 'Perhaps it's because I've decided to drink whisky alone in my hotel room. It's nearly midnight here. Or it may be I'm not sufficiently ambitious. Actually, it's very depressing – Harold was at his worst, evasive, rattled, all over the shop, saying: "You understand there are many permutations, and I have to fit three people into two jobs, etc." I said I didn't understand and wasn't interested in the permutations and just wished it to be clear that I wanted the job and thought I would be best at doing it.'

That Harold had been evasive was not surprising: Denis Healey had already asked for the Shadow Chancellorship and got it. Jim Callaghan, the third person in the permutations, had already been given the job being vacated by Denis – Shadow Foreign Secretary.

Shirley Williams had replaced Jim as Shadow Home Secretary.
Roy Hattersley, who had been Deputy Foreign Affairs spokesman,
was in the process of becoming Shadow Defence Secretary.
The last appointment took the longest to complete. Hattersley
was summoned to the Opposition Leader's room at the House and
sat himself upon the sofa. Harold offered him the Shadow Defence
post. Hattersley leapt off the sofa, paced back and forth.
'What's the matter?' inquired Harold.

Hattersley said what was obviously the matter – his dislike of
seeming to let down his European friends. He'd be replacing
George Thomson who had resigned. He'd have to go away and
think about it, he said.

'You mean you want to discuss it with George,' said Harold.
'That's all right. But you must give me your answer in an
hour.'

George Thomson urged Hattersley to accept. An hour later he
was back in Wilson's room. Yes, he would take the job, but he
voiced his misgivings. The next bit of the anecdote was what Roy
Hatt liked best to recount.

'Why don't you voice your misgivings in a letter,' said Harold.
'Then tomorrow you'll be acclaimed by the press for being tough
with me. The day after tomorrow they'll denounce you. And you'll
have a bad time in the Sundays. But these things are forgotten and
are not important.' When life was going well for Harold, he was
more realistic about the press. The new Shadow Defence Minister
wrote his letter, gave it to the press, and events transpired as Harold
foretold.

Between Tokyo and London, Benn's technology was actively
employed. With the Shadow Chancellor job allotted, the next
question was put to Tony: shouldn't he return to stand for the
vacated deputy leadership? Spending probably less time than almost any senior politician in weighing up his personal future, when
a personal contest actually presented itself, he tossed his hat in the
ring. It was something to do with 'challenge' – like the red rag to
the bull: the word had only to be uttered for me to know what
would follow. On the first flight available after his conference
speech had been delivered, he flew out of Tokyo.

In England it was still Wednesday when Dick Leonard and I
drove to Heathrow to meet him. We were not alone. Press photographers stood round the steps rolled up to the aircraft. The first
passenger we recognised was Tariq Ali, who paused, scowled
fiercely at the photographers below, possibly annoyed by their lack

of interest in him: since his days as a revolutionary student – a mature one – Tariq Ali had ceased to excite the media. There was no sign of Tony, but this was because he felt disobliging and concealed his presence by walking down the steps behind an enormously fat man, causing at least four other passengers to break into applause.

Finding Dick and me plus journalists inside the terminal, he was surprised to learn how far the deputy leadership contest had advanced. Dick had already drafted a statement for him to make. 'Did I really tell you, Susan, I was interested in standing?' Tony said, agreeing he probably had. He wasn't delighted to see Dick, yet was intrigued by the situation, uncertain whether to be impressed by Dick's enterprise or irritated by his presumption. Mildly jetlagged, the returned voyager was determined to sleep on it before making his final decision. In any case, the decisive forty-eight hours had already elapsed since Roy Jenkins's resignation: Harold had made his appointments, and the Jenkinsites had concentrated on rounding up the Right and working on the Centre to commit them to elect Ted Short as Deputy Leader. Michael Foot was the Left candidate. The only thing odd in any of this was that Ted Short had not only abstained with Tony in the emotive October vote on EEC entry, but had also cast the decisive vote in Shadow Cabinet in favour of the referendum, and it was Roy Jenkins's objection to the outcome of this vote that had led him to resign. On the referendum issue, Tony and Roy had been on the same side. No matter. Ted Short, the Jenkinsites said to one another, was a nonentity; if they could make him Deputy Leader, he would keep the seat warm for Roy, step down when asked. (They misjudged Ted Short's character.) If Tony got it, they argued, he would be a strong Deputy Leader; he wouldn't be a caretaker who would move aside if Roy wanted the job again. The Short bandwagon was rolling long before the plane from Tokyo landed at Heathrow.

Tony liked Ted Short personally, but so irrational is human nature that the gang quality of the Jenkinsites' lobbying elicited defiance. It was further nourished when Shirley Williams rang Lansdowne Road from a callbox at the House to say: '*We* think you shouldn't stand.'

'Who's "we"?' Tony said.

Shirley was evasive. Later her PPS, knowing Tony pretty well, said: 'As soon as Shirley told us she was going to ring you, I knew it would be counter-productive.'

At the House, Tony saw Jim Callaghan. 'I think you'll get fifty votes at the most. I don't think you'll help yourself or hurt yourself. How you make up your mind is a matter of temperament,' Jim said.

Out of courtesy Tony went down the Shadow Cabinet's corridor to see Ted Short and tell him he was standing. Ted said he thought Tony should have waited and stood for the leadership instead. But it was a friendly conversation.

Any fan of Iris Murdoch's arabesque convolutions should go into politics. 'Tell me,' Tony said to David Owen, 'do you not find something illogical in Roy's group supporting for Deputy Leader the very man whose vote tipped the balance in favour of the referendum which led Roy to resign?' Tony was in good humour.

David was acutely uncomfortable. The group had held a meeting at which he argued that they should support Tony. The majority were adamant that Tony should not benefit from Roy's resignation, and the established rule was that the majority vote was accepted by all; David very reluctantly agreed to their ruling. He could not refer to this meeting. 'We think on balance that Ted behaved better than you,' he said.

'How?'

David didn't answer the question. He advanced a separate argument. 'Ted doesn't stand for anything. If you were Deputy Leader, you would strengthen Labour's leadership. We think the essential thing is to weaken Harold. If Ted is Deputy Leader, we can beat Harold.'

'That's no doubt an interesting line, though it's a different one,' Tony said. 'I don't feel any great grievance, but why won't you acknowledge the hypocrisy of the group's argument that their concern is for the Labour Party and only Ted Short can keep Michael Foot from being Deputy Leader? Either Ted or I could do that, and you know it.'

He issued his statement saying he was running on a non-sectarian ticket: the deputy leadership should become a positive post: while the Leader of the Party is concerned with the day-to-day dramas, his Deputy can get on with the job of creating policy: a radical, egalitarian, socialist programme. Time was running out.

Just before midnight the telephone rang once more. Tony held the receiver away from his ear so I could hear the disembodied voice droning on. The voice said he was a Post Office engineer, had heard Mr Crosland on the news, just wanted to congratulate him. 'I think it's Jimmy,' Tony whispered as the voice went on. So it was. When Tony Benn reverted to his normal voice, he said that of course he would be voting for Michael Foot. The two men talked for a while before saying goodnight. Tony Benn had stood in the previous deputy leadership contest, coming third with forty-six votes.

The next night when the candidate came home from a meeting with his small, independent-minded band of supporters, he announced: 'I have set my helm irreversibly for disaster. If Bill Rodgers could see our organisation, he would fall out of bed laughing.' He lit a cheroot. '*Phyfft, phyfft*. You mustn't worry unduly about my feelings: there's entertainment as well as tension in my unpromising position. Must be why some people go in for horse-racing.'

When I took breakfast up to our bedroom the following morning, vociferous groans ensued. 'I refuse to get out of this bed. I cannot get through another day.' Fairly soon, however, the adrenalin began to flow and he was touring round in his dressing-gown, muttering that he would *have* to write things down for the future: 'Never take a decision at an airport.' I was addressed as 'Jennie' in reference to Jennie Lee's aggressive role in Nye Bevan's career. (Ordinarily if Jennie Lee was mentioned, Tony would remark: 'Thank God I do not have a political wife.') Finished shaving, he emerged from the bathroom in scarlet underpants I'd bought him, assumed a semi-crouched position, and dog-trotted back and forth across the confines of our bedroom, propelling himself in imitation of Groucho Marx, explaining as he doubled back: 'I'm limbering up for the deputy leadership race.'

Over the weekend the Hattersleys came for a meal. Neither was happy. There were two reasons. Roy doggedly repeated the view that only Ted Short could defeat Michael Foot, but his heart wasn't in it. The second reason for depression was the rough time he was being given by the Jenkinsites for having taken promotion in the Shadow Cabinet after Roy Jenkins resigned. (Shirley had done exactly the same thing as Hattersley, but she wasn't vilified.)

'Do you think I've committed a heinous crime?' Roy Hatt asked Tony.

Somebody once complained that if I was present when a question was put to Tony, he turned to me and gave his answer. It was his teacher role with me. He turned away from Roy Hatt and said to me:

'The more I read history, the clearer it seems that all successful political leaders have accepted three rules of conduct: (a) keep their Party together; (b) hold the middle-ground against ultras of Left

or Right; (c) shift and adapt to changing circumstances, whatever
the cries of betrayal. Reputation for vice or virtue depends on style
and supposed motives. Lincoln chopped and changed over emancipation, Cavour over Italian reunification. Twists and turns are
morally acceptable if they're not motivated by purely personal
ambition.'

The first ballot for the deputy leadership was announced two
days later. Ted Short came top with 111, Michael Foot got 110,
Tony Crosland 61 votes.

Some years afterwards Roy Jenkins spoke about the election to
Dick Leonard, who had the firm impression that Roy wanted to set
the record straight. Roy said that he had kept Tony from becoming
Deputy Leader. His group had managed the forty crucial votes
that went to Ted Short. The Jenkinsites certainly did not see
themselves as playing what he called the spoiling role. If Tony had
been willing to help them, Roy could have become Leader. Roy
didn't blame Tony for feeling as he did: at Oxford Tony was the
prominent figure. But circumstances conspired to give Roy more
clout than Tony. And then Tony spoiled things for Roy. That's
how Roy said he saw the matter.

At the Shadow Cabinet's first meeting after Ted Short was
elected Deputy Leader, Wilson was absent, Ted in the chair. His
briskness was welcome: Harold had a tendency to meander. There
was a general air of comradeship that hadn't existed for a long time.
Labour colleagues found it agreeable to call in the Deputy Leader's
room without having to pass by John Harris's portals.

My profile of Kenneth Tynan was at last delivered to the *Sunday
Times*. The Housing Finance Committee was finally brought to an
end by the guillotine, Tony making the Opposition's closing speech
on a Bill much dented since first presented by the Tories. It was
May. Early one evening the Labour Committee on the Housing
Finance Bill came to Lansdowne Road for drinks. All trooped
down to the garden, where Ellen-Craig and Dick Leonard had
made a fire on which the Bill was thrown, page by page going up
in smoke as everyone sang 'The Red Flag' (its tune the same as one
used for a different song of loyalty on which I was raised: 'Oh
Maryland, my Maryland'). Neighbours in the house adjoining ours
leant out of their windows. 'Sing it again,' one woman cried. We
sang it again.

·· 29 ··

The Coffee Pot

I used to think that disorganised people were more spontaneous, had more pleasure. Tony taught me the contrary – that organising your life allows you more freedom to seize opportunities; however short the play periods, he maximised them – whether reading, rapt by *Rosenkavalier*, exploring yet another Early English transept, having a siesta. He enjoyed things for their own sake. He was moved by Pasternak's phrase 'the poetry of the trivia of married life'.

As anyone who has ever lingered in a kitchen can testify, separate sounds – emanating from frying pan, running taps, chopping of parsley, conversation, portable radio possibly adding Beethoven's 7th for good measure – together combine to make it virtually impossible to hear any sound outside the kitchen.

'What's that noise?' asked one of Ellen-Craig's friends, replacing his teamug on the kitchen table as he listened intently.

'It's only Tony calling Mama. Mama, Tony's calling you.'

He had perfected a call which could reach from the first-floor bathroom and penetrate the sound barrier at the kitchen door. This call was very like an American Indian warwhoop. He produced it by putting his index finger between his lips and vibrating the finger, emitting a sustained tenor note at least an octave higher than his natural baritone.

I turned off the gas under the frying pan and mounted the stairs to our bathroom. He looked content and comfortable: it was a capacious bathtub, long and deep enough so he could lie with everything between chin and calves submerged.

'Is something the matter?' I asked.

'I'm so happy. I just wanted to tell you.'

Some of this happiness derived from his having only an hour's gentle work to do that evening. I wondered if he remembered that earlier in the week he'd said he would put aside part of Sunday evening to read through the fourth draft of the profile I was completing.

After supper I appeared in the study bearing my heap of typed

pages. He slumped his shoulders. 'I thought you'd forgotten,' he
said. 'How many are there?'

'About forty.'

'Well, if I said I'd do it, I must do it. Hand them over.' He was
an editor manqué, but after two and a half hours, patience waned.
'You always do this, Susan. You've given it to me a draft too soon.'

'It's the best I can do.'

'Nonsense. Anyone can see that pages 30 and 31 are in the wrong
place. Also 31a, 31b, 31c, 31d. I do wish you'd number your pages
less dishonestly.' He looked at his watch. 'Nothing for it but to
plough on. *Why* you will invert adverbs I shall never understand.'
Again he made an S-curve. He drew a sharp red line across three-
quarters of the next page.

'What's the matter with that part?'

'Boring. Doesn't add anything.'

'You don't think that it's worth keeping for its own sake?'

'You have asked for my opinion. You can accept it or reject it.
But for God's sake let's not argue about it.' He looked at his watch.

Three and a half hours later, I left the study with my manuscript,
no trace of his happy mood detectable. Sombrely I prepared for
bed. He appeared in the doorway. 'It's extremely interesting. I
learned things I didn't know before. But *please* couldn't you next
time give it to me one draft later?'

A new figure entered our landscape. Most of the fortune made
from Rowntree chocolate is used beneficially. During 1972 five
'chocolate soldiers' were funded as assistants to Shadow Ministers.
One of the beneficiaries was the Shadow for Environment.

'D. Lip marvellous,' Tony said after only a few weeks. 'How did
I do without him before?'

David Lipsey, just turned twenty-four, set about becoming a
housing specialist. One or two mornings a week he worked at
Lansdowne Road, Tony often appearing at my desk shortly before
lunch to ask: 'Any possibility of the boy having health soup and a
sandwich with us? Seems a little hard not to invite him.' (After
memorising the list of stuff that people with high blood-pressure
are not meant to eat, I had concocted 'health soup' – tasted good,
allowed variation, was nourishing.) David was the easiest of guests,
keen on Women's Liberation. Tony began a dossier to demonstrate
that despite his upbringing in a different ethos, he too was prepared
to 'turn into a male maid', helping remake the bed at weekends,
clearing away glasses and coffee cups after a Saturday lunch party,

taking a long turn at the kitchen sink. When I drove his aged mother home after lunch with us, I'd get back to Lansdowne Road to find cutlery washed and dried, neatly laid out, waiting to be observed and put away.

The children's departure from home having deprived Clea of accustomed companions, she stationed herself outside our bedroom door, intoning a dirge of exceptional melancholy. 'That cat may break up this marriage,' Tony said. A few nights later, however, he was bending over to put a wedge-shaped object in our bedroom doorway, allowing Clea silent passage. 'I'll bet those youths like D. Lip with their talk about Women's Lib don't do half the work round the house that I do,' he said.

On a Monday in January 1973, D. Lip had departed early. Tony, unusually, was lunching out so that I could concentrate on preparing for an interview at T and G headquarters with its General Secretary, Jack Jones – not the easiest of subjects for a profile. I went up to the study to ask one more question. The telephone rang. Tony's side of the conversation was brief. When he put back the receiver he said: 'That was the BBC. I've been mentioned in the Poulson case.' He gave a small, unamused smile.

'Who *is* Poulson?' I had a sketchy impression of a bankruptcy case involving corruption of several officials.

'Evidently a disreputable contractor. Do you remember anything about a coffee pot presented to me when I was at Education?'

'Yes. I've forgotten which comprehensive you were opening, but I remember being surprised when you didn't bring home another set of wooden bowls.'

'Do you think it could possibly be worth £500?'

'Good Lord no. Why?'

'The Prosecuting Counsel has just stated in court that it's worth at least that. Where is it?'

'Let me think. Has to be somewhere.'

He looked at his watch. 'I'm running late. When you get back from seeing Jack Jones, could you try to find it?'

On my way back from seeing Jack Jones, I passed an *Evening Standard* placard bearing Crosland's name in large letters, stopped and bought a paper in which I read that he was alleged to have accepted an antique-silver coffee pot from this Mr Poulson whose firm had built a comprehensive school in Bradford. Few presentation mementoes have monetary value; if there is doubt, civil servants have the thing appraised to make sure it's worth no more than £50. None the less, here was the Prosecuting Counsel, a Mr

Muir Hunter, QC, stating in court that it must have cost more than
£500. As I neared our house, I saw a large contingent assembled
by the two squat pillars that flanked our front path. Equipment
dangled from necks and shoulders. This untidy brigade appeared
to be waiting for someone. I went to a neighbour's house instead.

'You'll never guess what's happened,' I said to my neighbour,
Val Arnold-Forster. 'Tony is alleged to have been involved seven
years ago in petty graft.'

Val started to laugh. She couldn't stop. She had to sit down.

'I can see its comic side, Val, but meanwhile there is this assemblage outside our front door. I refuse to give them the pleasure of
taking my photograph as I say "no comment". When you can stop
laughing, I don't suppose you'd be willing to walk round to Lansdowne Road, make your way through all those people, let yourself
in our front door, then let me in the back?'

This she faithfully did, closed the curtains before turning on the
lights, answered the ringing telephone and then left it off the hook.
I looked out from an unlit upstairs window.

At the House of Commons, friends offered advice. Some said
Tony should keep his head down and wait for it to blow over. He
didn't. He was outraged. When I turned on the television news,
there he was, facing the thing head on, sad as well as angry.

A relation, visiting us, let herself in our front door. 'I'm Mrs
Crosland's cousin,' she said to the newsmen, closing the door upon
them. The Japanese who lived with his wife in the downstairs flat
came home from work. 'I dwell below,' he said, going down to
his separate door. The lodger, who had taken over the bedsit-
kitchenette once used by the au pair, let herself in the front door.
'I live upstairs,' she said to the gathering outside.

About 11.30 I recognised the Sunbeam's motor as Tony returned
from the Commons. A shout went up from the pavement army. He
walked through them cheerfully, said he'd give them a statement
in the morning when he knew what the damned thing was worth,
let himself in the front door and closed it. Neither of us was happy.

Eileen – who was now our daily, spending her weekday mornings
as general factotum – arrived promptly at 9 a.m. The siege hadn't
lifted: she was in heaven. The two D.L.s arrived. Dick Leonard
smiled. 'Accidents will happen,' he said. David Lipsey said: 'Surely
the civil servants at Education would have realised if it was that
valuable.'

Finally I found the coffee pot. We all gazed upon it. Sylvia
Littlejohns, Tony's personal secretary, who had also arrived, put

it in a Harrods shopping bag, went out our back door, crossed the connecting square, went in the Arnold-Forsters' back door, out the front, took a taxi to Sotheby's. In Lansdowne Road a policeman arrived to keep traffic moving. Sylvia rang from Sotheby's and put the silver valuer on the line. David wrote down what he said.

'Read it out,' said Tony.

David did. The coffee pot was a reproduction worth £40.

'Good. Ask Sylvia if she very kindly will wrap the thing up and send it directly to the Public Prosecutor or whoever wants it. I cannot remember ever seeing it before, and I wish never to see it again.'

Still in his red carpet slippers, he stepped out our front door and said much the same to the eager throng, bulbs flashing, reels whirring.

The episode gave some pleasure to civil servants who had been in Tony's Private Office when he was at the Board of Trade. 'He was forever telling us how marvellous his Private Office had been at Education: "You don't do it nearly so well." We had our revenge when this appalling letter to Poulson appeared. It was written at Education and went unnoticed through their Private Office. Also, how could anyone take it seriously? He was the least likely person to corrupt.'

Like many who do not give or want fulsome compliments, Tony's sporadic efforts in that direction were doomed. The appalling letter was in fact a postscript, added in his own fair hand, to a routine letter written by Private Office – one in a pile waiting for his signature. He'd opened the school in Bradford only a few days earlier, and the event was still clear in his mind: everyone had seemed pleased about the presentation gift that the contractor apparently had organised. Glancing through Private Office's letter of thanks, Tony thought it chilly to the point of rudeness. Incapable of adding an ordinary bit of flattery, he wrote: 'I tremble to think what it cost' and thought no more about it until seven years later.

It was then the turn of the Prosecuting Counsel, Mr Muir Hunter, QC, to be on the receiving end, criticised by MPs and press for using smear tactics. The coffee pot brought into focus the whole question of defaming an uninvolved third party.

Two years later when Labour was returned to office, Mr Muir Hunter was among a dozen people attending a meeting at DOE with Lord Goodman's new Housing Corporation. When the Secretary of State for the Environment entered the room, he went to each person standing round the table, looked at his or her place

COMMONS SMOKING ROOM.

POULSON COFFEE POT SENT BACK—

JAK

"Twelve coffees and a tea for Mr Crosland!"

card, engaged in a few civilised words. After examining one card, he paused, looked at the man who went with it, said: 'Oh, Mr Muir Hunter.'

The barrister gave a fractional bow. Silence followed, broken by Lord Goodman. 'Mr Muir Hunter is our unofficial legal adviser,' he said.

'Oh yes? He was also my unofficial publicity adviser a year or two back,' the Secretary of State replied, passing on to the next person at the table. Mr Muir Hunter's face – so D. Lip reported afterwards – became absolutely rigid. At the meeting's close, as the Secretary of State departed, he again spoke to each individual. Mr Muir Hunter gave a bow positively Japanese in its deference.

'What must have been most galling for that barrister', D. Lip said to Tony, 'was your having forgiven him for something he never thought he'd done wrong.'

In January 1973 through our letter-box came a photocopied invitation from *Socialist Commentary*. Did we want tickets for a dinner to commemorate Hugh Gaitskell, who had died ten years before? Mr Roy Jenkins would be speaking.

As the evening approached and press reports suggested that

Gaitskell's mantle was about to descend on his heir, etc., Charlie Pannell, an elder statesman in the PLP and supporter of Roy on Europe, grew very uncomfortable. He went to Dora. She rang Tony: it was quite wrong that he not be asked to speak and he must do so. The editor of *Socialist Commentary* then rang Tony: he was sorry not to have discussed any of this earlier, but John Harris had rather taken over matters.

Battling with my profile of Jack Jones, I made a day-trip to Oxford for a tutorial with Bill McCarthy on trade unions, returning in time to set off with Tony for the dinner. From the top table one looked over a gathering of London's intelligentsia and media figures. Roy, who had been extremely nervous, was not on form, and the speech, typed out word for word, went on an awfully long time.

Charlie Pannell delivered a funny, sharp speech, rather unexpectedly saying he was tired of hearing about 'men of principle'. 'It's easy for cold men to stick rigidly to a principle, but Hugh wasn't cold,' he said.

Tony's speech was the shortest – vignettes of Hugh as he was, some humorous, some poignant, ending with a quotation from the tribute Tony gave on television the night Hugh died. When we were all leaving, Bill Rodgers came up and put an arm round me – getting less than full response – and said: 'It was moving and magnificent and I nearly burst into tears as Tony was finishing. It brought back with total clarity the whole thing.'

Tony said to me: 'Roy set it up. I didn't. He chose the venue, the weapons. Then he was routed. It's a nice little cameo.' He fell silent. The weekend before, he'd got out letters from Hugh. There were certain memories of Hugh and gramophone records at The Boltons, Hugh and the children at Hobury Street, that Tony remained unable to recall with entire equanimity. Hard to believe ten years had passed since he'd said that night: 'Whether he was a sufficiently radical leader for a left-wing party is another question. But he was a leader. You trusted him. You knew absolutely where you were with him. Of how many other politicians in Britain at the moment could you say the same?'

One little tussle was still to come before Roy and Tony accepted that their battered friendship could just about survive if both acknowledged that their political priorities were irreconcilable. (Their social lives were always different.) Following a *Sunday Express* article suggesting they were not speaking, Tony likely to win the race, and so forth, Roy sensibly rang up and proposed a pre-dinner drink. He and Jennifer came round. The two men faced each other in armchairs either side of the fire, wives seated together a few yards away. I said I thought, considering all the pressures, it was to Roy's and Tony's credit that their relationship remained as good as it did.

Roy took sharp issue with me: all he and Tony ever talked about was country cottages. (We were, undeniably, curious about how others decided what they wanted in the way of a country cottage and how they managed to afford it.) Roy thought his and Tony's relationship was surprisingly *bad*; I was much too glib, he said.

Tony got up, sauntered over to the Yorkshire chest where the drink stood, sauntered back and said: 'Well, if you would like to have serious conversation, shall we begin now? Shall we begin with the two recent episodes which *have* worsened relations between us? The first is the Gaitskell dinner.'

Jennifer asked me how the children were. Roy sprang from his chair and said that as Jennifer and I were talking about something else, he and Tony could go over to the window to have their talk.

'Oh,' Tony said, 'I think it would be agreeable if we all four talked together about it,' and sat down again. Roy did likewise.

Roy said he hadn't discussed the Gaitskell dinner with Tony because he knew Tony didn't like dinner parties and would have discouraged having it, and if Tony was upset by first learning of it through a photocopied form, Roy was sorry.

Finding that kind of apology tiresome, I intervened. 'The only way I can see such situations is to transpose the names. Can you imagine any circumstances, Roy, in which Tony would have arranged such a dinner for Hugh without mentioning it to you?'

The second episode concerned Roy's recent speech berating Labour's collective leadership for giving way to the Left. Intense irritation was felt, Tony said, by those in the Party who were attending Committee meetings each week – in his own case, nine a week – to fight against the Left getting its way, while Roy stood on the sidelines and wrote elegant biographical pieces for *The Times* for a fat fee.

The subject then veered. Tony was to blame for Roy's resignation. 'You could have stopped me,' Roy said.

'How could I stop you when I was in Tokyo? In fact, your resignation cost us £50 in telephone calls.'

Two dogs with a bone came to mind. One of the children was home that weekend. I wanted to have a family supper. Jennifer and Tony and I rose to our feet, he giving a tug at the frayed tie that acted as a belt supporting the ancient army fatigues dyed bottle green. Roy sat fast. A little later, when I returned from the kitchen to see how things were coming along, the combatants were re-engaged on episode two. The last words I heard as I retired again to the cooker were Roy's: 'Well, you could resign too.'

The Jenkinses departed. Tony joined me in the kitchen, in a thoroughly good humour. 'Occasionally a little blood-letting is healthy,' he said.

When he and Roy met in a House of Commons lift for the first time after the dust-up, Tony said, 'We must have another of those conversations soon. Very enjoyable.'

Roy, surprised, immediately collected himself. 'I suppose that any bridge-building must be preceded by major excavation,' he said.

It was late Sunday morning. Tony Benn's bicycle was parked at the kerb. I was invited into the study – 'Susan will be interested,' Tony said. Jimmy addressed himself intently to his colleague, expatiating on the Levellers, Luddites, Chartists, and their historic relevance to Jimmy's aims for the Labour Party. Tony, practically horizontal in the Eames chair, his legs stretched out on the ottoman, kept his eyes fixed on Jimmy except to remove his cheroot and tip its ash.

'Do you disagree with any of that?' asked Jimmy at intervals. 'Wouldn't you agree that is true?'

Tony's replies were largely monosyllabic – 'Nope.' 'Yep.' – leaving me uncertain whether he was indicating assent, or acknowledging a point taken, or wondering when Jimmy would finish.

After he left I said: 'It's so odd. He has this astonishing command of language. He speaks in perfectly shaped prose. The history lesson was fascinating. Yet I haven't the faintest idea what his conclusion meant.'

'Not surprised. The conclusion was meaningless.'

⇥ 30 ⇤

'More Hated by Environmentalists than Any Man I Know'

One of the Heath Government's pet projects was Maplin – an extravaganza airport-cum-seaport to be built on the remote shores of Essex at Foulness. 'Heathograd' was one of several epithets applied to it by Labour's Shadow Minister for the Environment, who thought there were much higher priorities that should not be sacrificed to this lavish scheme. Economists, conservationists, transport experts, local councillors tramped up to the study at Lansdowne Road. He read virtually everything published on the subject. From the Opposition front bench he then declared: 'The choice of Foulness is totally wrong, on the grounds of damage to the environment, and particularly the coastline; on the grounds of destruction of homes for motorways; on the grounds of enormous additional cost; and probably also on the grounds of safety. I prophesy that Foulness if it is ever built will turn out to be the white elephant of the century, because airlines will not use it.'

Never an orator, his force of argument came from his first penetrating the subject and then presenting it with a clarity that frightened opponents. By the time Maplin's runways were actually completed, he said, planes with vertical take-off could be nearing production stage, a third London airport unnecessary. Outlying regions, starved of first-class modern airports, should get the money which any increase in air traffic demanded, rather than the cosseted South-East.

In this instance conservationists applauded him. It was not always so. 'The fact is that the man I want to see lead the Labour Party,' another Labour MP, Bruce Douglas-Mann, said to Tony some time in 1973, 'is more hated by environmentalists than any man I know.' Ironically, this hated man was a passionate supporter of most conservation and environmental causes. 'Greedy men,' he wrote, 'abetted by a complacent government, are prowling over

Britain and devastating it.' In the previous Labour Government, he stopped Stansted, reprieved Richmond Terrace and Norman Shaw's Scotland Yard, set up a uniquely thorough inquiry into the GLC's motorway proposals, established a Royal Commission on environmental pollution, published the first-ever comprehensive White Paper on the subject. He recognised that commitment to the 'environment' was not without its contradictions. The desire to preserve rural beauty spots, for instance, conflicts with the need to acquire rural land for over-spill housing. It was necessary to include all of the relevant factors in planning the use of land.

He loved uncongested countryside. Once, early on, he nearly finished me off when we climbed Cader Idris, familiar to him from Royal Welch training. 'Used to go up it twice a day.' In my innocence of what the second highest mountain in Wales entailed, I set off in tennis shoes, cheerfully eating an apple.

'Why your vanity forbids you to own a pair of decent walking shoes I shall never understand. You're going to regret it,' he said. Two hours later he discovered I suffer from ledge-phobia. Through the simple expedient of instinctively avoiding ledges since childhood agonies of terror, I'd forgotten about it. Having himself nonchalantly, though carefully, traversed a narrow shelf overhanging a nasty drop – something less than sixty feet, rather more than 'a few feet at the most' – he looked back to see his companion, halfway across the ledge, hurl herself prone, clutching at some miserable bracken that grew there, tears of uncontrollable panic pouring into the scrub.

'What is it, Susan?'

'I'm going to fall off.'

'Don't be silly.'

'I'm going to fall off.'

'No you're not. Don't move,' he said quietly, making his way back along the ledge. 'Just don't move. I'm coming to get you.'

I had no desire to move. Quite the opposite.

He gripped one of my wrists. 'Now let go those wretched plants.'

'No.'

'Look. Whatever happens, I'm keeping hold of your wrist. So you can release the shrubbery from that one hand.'

'No.'

'Just open the one hand. You can go on clutching the other shrub as long as you like. Rather hard on it, minding its own business, to be attacked in this manner.' Time passed. 'Good. Now let go the other shrub.' After a while he laughed. 'We cannot continue in this absurd posture for the entire afternoon: one's beginning to feel rather cramped. All you have to do is open your other hand and let go that shrub. Don't try to stand up. Don't look over the ledge. Just look at the path. Crawl along behind me. I'm not going to let go your wrist. Nice if we could complete this exercise in the next hour or two.'

When the ledge had been negotiated in this graceless manner and the ground immediately widened into a normal mountainside, we sat upon it for a few minutes.

'Wish you wouldn't do things like that, Susan. You nearly persuaded me that you actually were going to fall. Crossed my mind that as I had no intention of letting go your wrist, if you began thrashing about, we'd hurtle down together. Not that it would have done us the slightest harm. That drop can't be more than a few feet at the most. How long have you had this phobia?'

'Always.'

'You might have told me.'

Where Tony parted company from the environmentalist lobby was over their basic hostility to economic growth and their indifference to the needs of ordinary people. 'This obsessive conservationist attitude is (a) morally wrong when we still have so many pressing social needs that can only be met if we have economic growth; (b) self-defeating since without growth we shall never find the huge sums of money which we desperately need to cure pollution and improve the environment.' He argued that most of our environmental problems are legacies from the past: slum housing, polluted rivers, ancient factories belching filth. Without economic growth, there was no chance of righting these wrongs.

In the early 1970s, Friends of the Earth, Doomwatch and suchlike were in fashion and made a tremendous impact on the media, inveighing against the evils of economic growth. One of their more famous figures, Professor Mishan, concerned about disturbance caused by night charter flights, proposed holiday towns where only horses and horse-drawn vehicles would be admitted: a ban on all international air travel would produce 'an enormous reduction in the demand for foreign travel', he said.

'Yes, indeed,' Tony commented in a Fabian pamphlet. 'The rich would proceed in leisurely fashion across Europe to the Mediterranean beauty spots where they would park their Rolls-Royces and take to a boat or horse-drawn vehicle. As for my constituents, who have only a fortnight's holiday, let them eat cake and go back to Blackpool.'

The heart of his dispute with the environmentalists was that their attitudes, in his view, were anti-democratic, springing – probably unconsciously – from a common enough middle-class and upper-class bias (he threw in princely bias while he was about it, Prince Philip's in particular). They were often, he said, kindly and dedicated people, but were usually affluent and wanted to kick the ladder down behind them. Compromise must be reached between despoiling the land and keeping it the preserve of the fortunate few.

On a television programme that was instantly notorious, he and Professor Wilfred Beckerman put the case for economic growth to a studio audience carefully picked to articulate the environmentalist lobby's anti-growth case. First, however, a fifteen-minute propaganda film was shown, made by this same lobby, designed to demonstrate that growth is a pestilence which will destroy mankind, and so on. Immediately the film ended, the television cameras turned to the Shadow Minister for Environment in his chair on the platform. Before he could open his mouth, a woman in the audience asked a question:

'How can Mr Crosland judge the case when throughout the film he was asleep?' Jacky Gillott was a writer and broadcaster of some distinction.

'I was not asleep,' he replied. 'I have seen that film four times, and I thought this a good opportunity to rest my eyes.'

When he came home that evening he said: 'Afraid that cheeky young woman came out on top in our little exchange. Never occurred to me that anyone would notice poor Toto resting his weary eyes, let alone use it to score a point. Cunning of her.'

I suppose he knew as much about architecture as any politician. He was moved by architecture. Outings invariably had some building as their focal point. The National Trust has, of course, been highly successful in preserving some of Britain's heritage – acquiring some of the finest country houses on the understanding that they be opened to the public, at the same time enabling the residents of these ancestral mansions to live there without paying upkeep. When Tony – relevant volume of Pevsner's *Buildings of England* in hand – would arrive at the gateway to the anticipated pleasure only to find it barred to the public except for a few days a year between 1 p.m. and 4 p.m., a sharp letter would be dispatched to the National Trust: 'I should be glad if you could explain the reason for preserving our nation's heritage if the nation is not permitted to see it.' (Having been bombarded with these missives, embarrassing to them, the National Trust may have been surprised to receive £2,000 in his will.)

Having reached a great age, Tony's mother died. For several years her body had troubled her – increasing aches and pains – and she felt the indignation of those who have been inordinately healthy. The fact of being well into her nineties when overtaken by these afflictions did little to lessen her annoyance. She refused to let lifelong Christianity – or the initial stroke that preceded her end – inhibit a tart tongue. During one of my visits to the nursing home, an uninvited do-gooder appeared, asked if Mrs Crosland remembered her, fluttered a bit over the bed before departing.

'Who was that?' I asked my aged mother-in-law who now lay waiting for God to take her.

'A bore,' she said.

That Saturday Tony and I drove to Grimsby together: Sunday's Mayor-making was the big annual civic celebration where Tony's speech was the now traditional high point of the reception. (As it was a non-Party occasion, he always emphasised that the entire Council of Grimsby was responsible for the previous year's lamentable failure to preserve a crumbling church, convert an old mill to a current need.) We had just gone to our room at the County Hotel when the manageress knocked on the door to say that Mr Crosland's sister was on the telephone. He went down to the public callbox, and early Sunday morning we made the drive back.

His mother's death was in no sense a tragedy, but Grimbarians would have been surprised if he had stayed to deliver his speech. Neither they nor we had been raised in the tradition that The Show Must Go On.

Because his father died at sixty, his mother at ninety-six, in a childish way we thought in terms of his striking a happy medium. He didn't much want to be seventy-eight, but seventy-four would be OK. At this time he was fifty-four, so we had a sense of twenty years left to us, longer than we had known one another so far, really rather a lot of time when one thought of it like that.

Towards the end of 1973 we were in the study when just after midnight the telephone rang. Tony answered. Nasal tone and rhythmically inverted cadence announced an international operator. 'Will you accept a collect call from John in America?' she asked.

'No. I don't know any John in America,' he said, replacing the telephone. An unlikely statement.

She rang back and said the collect call was from John Conroy – one of my multitudinous northern cousins who live on a farm near the Canadian border. Tony accepted the call, listened, began to laugh. 'Hang on, John. You'll want to talk with him, Susan. He's rung to tell us that Sheila is engaged to Pete.'

A year earlier I'd opened the front door at Lansdowne Road to discover Pete Conroy standing casually, knapsack beside him, clearly intending to stay. Having returned from Vietnam, one leg the worse for shrapnel, otherwise intact, he made his next venture marriage to Sheila. The wedding was to take place on Boxing Day in an ice-locked little community beside Lake Champlain, Tony to give the bride away. He was deeply touched by her insistence that he take this role.

As the day approached, he alone was well organised. Mr Heath's Government had reduced workers to a three-day week, and those of us who worked at home did so after 4 p.m. by means of a 40 watt bulb or candles. On 20 December I was still finishing a profile of Jeremy Thorpe by candlelight. Ellen-Craig was camping at the American Embassy, having found her passport was out-of-date.

When we returned, 1974 had begun, the three-day week still in force, miners on strike, Mr Heath in a fury that his authority should be defied. He must reassert it in terms none could question: he called a general election in February. 'So soon?' I'd counted on the status quo lasting longer, Tony being able to work at home for half the day, us having lunch together. 'Do you really want to win – only to govern an ungovernable mess?' I asked.

'Oh I want Labour to win. However appalling the economic situation, there *are* things we can do. We did before. Why else were the Tories so anxious to reverse our decisions? And this time I'm much more experienced – could see that more was done.'

'Suppose Labour loses? Engraved on my memory is that picture of you lying on the bed in Grimsby in that exhausted sleep. You didn't moan about it, but in some ways you were stricken for a couple of months. I don't want you to feel like that again.'

Later when he came to bed he said: 'I've been thinking about what you said. This time if we lose I shan't be stricken like that. I am feeling serene about the whole thing, whatever happens. If we win I'll be less intense than last time. If we lose I'll not feel any bitterness. I've just been reading Wilfred Beckerman's new book and re-reading Tyrrell Burgess: I've contributed something intellectually and something politically. If I don't contribute anything else, I shall be satisfied.'

31

Socialism Now

The result of the election held on 28 February 1974 took longer than usual to become clear. Labour won only five more seats than the Tories and had no overall majority. The Prime Minister refused to concede. Harold Wilson behaved with dignity, marking time. Over the weekend Mr Heath invited the Liberal Leader, Jeremy Thorpe, to No. 10 for private talks. The Liberals had won twelve seats. Could not their two Parties join forces to keep Labour out, the Tories in? Mr Thorpe declined Mr Heath's invitation.

On Monday afternoon, 4 March, Labour's Shadow Cabinet met again, marking time. That evening Mr Heath capitulated, went out the back door of No. 10. Prime Minister Wilson went in the front. Until he could safely call another election and get a workable majority in Parliament, the Government was hamstrung.

For Tony and me there was a curious lack of exhilaration. Nor, happily, was there to be the sense of personal inhibition that sometimes circumscribed us during the 1964–70 Labour Governments. We tried to account for this. Was it because we were ten years older? Or because this time we knew Labour couldn't achieve what the incoming 1964 Government had believed possible? Or simply that we'd been down this road before?

'Second time round, what?' said the Duke of Edinburgh when he and Tony met not long after Labour's return to office.

'Impertinent fellow,' the new Secretary of State for Environment said to me.

A month after Labour's victory, *Socialism Now* was published. In the title essay, Tony reassessed his own argument:

First, then, where stands the revisionist thesis in the light of the last ten years of experience? There is, at least, no need for revisionists to revise our *definition* of socialism. Socialism, in our view, was basically about equality. By equality, we meant more than a meritocratic society of equal opportunities in which the greatest rewards would go to those with the most fortunate genetic endowment and

family background; we adopted the 'strong' definition of equality
– what Rawls has subsequently called the 'democratic' as opposed
to the 'liberal' conception. We also meant more than a simple (not
that it has proved simple in practice) redistribution of income. We
wanted a wider social equality embracing also the distribution of
property, the educational system, social-class relationships, power
and privilege in industry – indeed all that was enshrined in the
age-old socialist dream of a more 'classless society' . . .

Of course we can endlessly debate the concept of equality . . .
What, for example, are the most crucial causes of inequality –
inherited wealth, inherited I.Q., home circumstances, hard work
or luck? What are the most important inequalities? Are they of
income, capital, education, housing or industrial power? Or are
they between the sexes or between races? Or are they perhaps of
privacy, sunlight and access to unpolluted beaches? . . .

A practising politician in the Britain of the 1970s, not cerebrating
in a monastery cell but living day by day in the thick of things, is
not required to answer the stern examiner's question: how much
equality ultimately? He has plenty of harsh, specific and unmerited
inequalities to combat in the next ten years; and a decade is my
time-span, not eternity.

But revisionism was about means as well as ends: in *The Future of
Socialism* he had argued that socialism could be pursued within the
framework of a mixed economy – public ownership only one of a
number of means. A major tool – growth – had proved far more
difficult to achieve than anyone expected in the 1950s. Did world-
wide changes mean the 1970s revisionist should adopt different
routes to the goal? To answer the question he first examined the
record of the 1964–70 Wilson Governments:

It is now the fashion to . . . write it off as a total disaster, or at least
to exhibit a selective amnesia in which the successes are forgotten
and only the failures remembered.

Nobody disputes the central failure of economic policy . . .
Growth was consistently sacrificed to the balance of payments, notably to the defence of a fixed and unrealistic rate of
exchange.

This central failure bedevilled all the efforts and good intentions
of the Labour Government . . . And it has made it hard for Labour
to claim in future – or, rather, it would have done but for the
far worse mess which the Tories are making of the economy –
that we can manage things more efficiently than they can. Yet

despite these constraints, solid progress was made on a number of fronts.

Health and social security benefits, education, housing, libertarian reforms, regional policy, and so on. The achievements 'must have meant something for equality if the Tories are so anxious to reverse them,' he wrote. Yet:

... the performance (and I must take my share of responsibility) did not live up to the hopes ... The lessons of this experience are not entirely palatable ... extreme class inequalities remain, poverty is far from eliminated, the economy is in a state of semi-permanent crisis and inflation is rampant ... Do these setbacks to our hopes demonstrate that the revisionist analysis of means and ends was wrong, and the Marxist analysis which it sought to rebut was right?

He then analysed the current power structure, the current relationship between equality and public ownership, the current economic performance and social behaviour. He asserted once again that 'with the managerial revolution, there *is* a vacuum in accountability', and set out methods to remedy this, noting:

Not all nationalised industries have flawless records on safety, the control of pollution or even incorruptibility. The British Government is itself the largest single employer of low-wage workers ... Experience has shown that the mere fact of public responsibility does not immunize the state against the age-old instincts of greed and personal gain ...

I see no reason to abandon the revisionist analysis of socialism in favour of a refurbished Marxism ... public ownership remains (along with taxation, legislation, government controls, trade union action and so on) one of a number of means to achieving our socialist ends – and a means which, in the light of the improved performance of the public sector, can now be used more freely.

He listed his own five priorities for public ownership – land 'overwhelmingly first' and private rented housing second – but warned that one should not raise expectations of miracles to follow:

British society – slow-moving, rigid, class-ridden – has proved much harder to change than was supposed. Looking back with hindsight, the early revisionist writings were too complacent in tone; they proposed the right reforms, but under-rated the difficulty of achieving them in a British context. We were optimists then, though we soon learned our lesson; after the 1959 election defeat I wrote in near-despair that 'a dogged resistance to change now blankets every segment of our national life.'

Admittedly Conservative administrations have been in power for the greater part of the last two decades. Yet much more should have been achieved by a Labour Government in office and Labour pressure in opposition. Against the dogged resistance to change, we should have pitted a stronger will to change. I conclude that a move to the Left is needed, not in the traditional sense of a move towards old-fashioned Clause 4 Marxism, but in the sense of a sharper delineation of fundamental objectives, a greater clarity about egalitarian priorities and a stronger determination to achieve them.

The priority for overseas policy should, of course, be a sharp increase in aid for developing countries. The six priorities to be ruthlessly selected and pursued in the domestic field were reducing poverty, enabling everyone to have a decent home, taking development land into public ownership, redistributing capital wealth, eliminating segregation in schools, extending industrial democracy. Yet the present mood towards a programme of reform was one of pessimism, he acknowledged:

The intelligentsia, always prone to the liberal rhetoric of catastrophe, has adopted an apocalyptic mood, denying (against the facts) that reformist progress can be made and believing in any case that ecological disaster is just over the horizon. Industrial militancy in on the increase, but often with competitive and sectional rather than socialist goals in mind. The stability of democratic society and the possibility of peaceful reform seem more and more threatened by angry workers, students, squatters and even middle-class amenity groups ... Even the rule of law is challenged by some Labour councillors and trade unionists, though historically – and let no socialist ever forget this – the law has been the means by which the weak obtained redress against the strong ...

But this mood of discontent, though often (and naturally enough, given the fact of inflation) selfish and negative rather than radical and positive, makes it more essential, not less, to strive for a more just and equal society ...

... An increasingly educated public, with higher aspirations in all directions, makes more and more incompatible demands; government is asked to perform marvels, though the achievement of one marvel often rules out the possibility of another ...

Socialists must be unapologetic about this ... We shall require higher taxation of the whole better-off section of the community, which now includes some trade unionists (for example, in the docks, engineering, printing) who believe more strongly in differentials than in equality.

If Britain had a faster rate of growth, socialist advance would be far easier, but it was never the only revisionist means to the end: 'whatever the rate of growth, we can, and must, mount a determined attack on specific social evils and specific inequalities.'

The other essays in the book set out a coherent egalitarian strategy for a Labour Government to pursue. 'Diffusion of effort is the enemy of social progress. Only if we concentrate our effort will we make a significant advance towards greater justice and equality.'

Socialism Now was reviewed favourably. The Professor of Government at Essex University, Anthony King, went so far as to describe Crosland as the most important socialist writer Britain had produced. The Professor concluded his review by saying: 'A major test of our new government – and not least of Anthony Crosland, philosopher/king – will be whether the fit between aspiration and performance is closer than it was last time.' The thought did not occur that halfway through the government Tony Crosland would disappear from the scene.

He had actually drawn up the blueprint for the giant Department of the Environment just before Labour's 1970 defeat. In March 1974 when he arrived in Marsham Street at that huge concrete heap that is the DOE, he found it was a good Department, politically very sophisticated. The officials had made themselves familiar with his writing as well as with Labour's manifesto, had a good idea what he would want to do. Two of the priorities he'd set out in *Socialism Now* came under Environment – housing and the public ownership of development land – and there were important manifesto commitments to freeze rents, give security of tenure to tenants of furnished privately-rented homes, give more help to the inner-city areas. He'd worked closely with Transport House on the housing part of Labour's manifesto.

On his first day at DOE he said to Sir Idwal Pugh, the Permanent Secretary who dealt with Housing, that he wanted to freeze rents. Would the officials give him the means to do so in four days' time? Rents were frozen at the end of the first week. In the second week the programme for increasing council housing began.

Next Maplin was given the chop.

But some decisions required Parliament's approval. One was waiting on his desk when he arrived at DOE: the distribution of the Rate Support Grant. The Tories' proposal for the coming year favoured the mainly rural areas. Tony had to decide whether to accept it or reject it. He rejected it. The burden on the hard-pressed metropolitan areas should be lightened, he argued. This meant the burden on the more rural areas became heavier. The latter were represented not only by Tory MPs: Grimsby would suffer as a result of his decision.

With no overall majority it was anybody's guess whether a highly controversial measure could be got through Parliament. In the Commons the Tories agreed a concerted attack on the 'arrogance' of the Secretary of State for the Environment. Nor were all his own backbenchers pleased by this egalitarian decision. From the Strangers' Gallery I looked down on another raucous winding-up debate. Labour MPs whose seats – like his – were adversely affected added their complaint to Tory tumult. When Tony was not at the Dispatch Box answering critics on all sides, Michael Foot sat on the Front Bench immediately beside him. Tony was back at the Dispatch Box, in command but under terrific bombardment, when someone sat down beside me on my front bench in the gallery. It was Michael. He wanted to congratulate me, he said, on my profile of Jeremy Thorpe. I knew his real purpose in joining me was to lend moral support.

'Are we going to win this bloody vote?' I asked him.

'I don't know.'

'Have you noticed that each time a Minister does anything socialist, half the Party objects? Not always the same half either.'

Michael smiled. 'Tell Tony I enjoyed his socialist defence of his rates decision at the PLP meeting. He delivered it in exactly five sentences. Socialist and succinct.'

The vote was won, but only just. On my way out I met Dennis Skinner. Non-metropolitan areas that would suffer included his Derbyshire constituency.

'We Left-wingers always thought Tony had long-term judgment, Susan. This decision is bad for his reputation. It is worrying, because though I disagree with him on a lot of things, he is the only one I could imagine being Leader – accepting that no one on our side of the Party can get it. Harold isn't going to live for ever. Tony must think more in terms of this.'

'There's nothing to be done about it, Dennis. He makes decisions on the merits of the case. This may be a strength or a weakness, but that's the way he is.'

'I didn't mean that Tony should see everything in terms of the leadership, but he should see perhaps a fifth of everything in that light.'

A few months later, during his August holiday, Tony included among his reflections on government: 'Now clear: redistribution of R.S.G. [Rate Support Grant] morally and socially absolutely right, but politically definitely wrong. Good and socialist policies *not* electorally popular.'

However, there was nothing new about that. He'd been defeated in Shadow Cabinet when he proposed that an incoming Labour Government 'equalise' benefits for home owners and council tenants by lowering tax relief on the home-owner's mortgage. He had long argued that the middle classes got more out of the welfare state than they put in. He saw his proposal as morally and intellectually unassailable and thought if it was carried out early in a Parliament, the people who would hate it would get used to it. It was overridden by his colleagues on the grounds that it would be much too unpopular.

To most civil servants Anthony Crosland seemed austere: the intellectual discipline, the economy of effort – no time to be wasted talking about things once you have got as far as you can, meet only if you have to meet, better to have it distilled on paper. So vast was the Department of the Environment that it required four Permanent Secretaries. Sir Idwal Pugh (later to be the Ombudsman) dealt with Transport as well as Housing. A blunt Welshman, Sir Idwal found the Secretary of State's leadership remarkable, believed its effects would be lasting. But the man himself puzzled Sir Idwal: 'He was always very relaxed with senior officials and showed us the most impeccable courtesy, but his reserve allowed no indication of what he was feeling. Early on I made up my mind simply to know him on paper.

'The ideal relationship between a Permanent Secretary and a Minister is when you meet late in the evening over a whisky or a cup of tea and talk about this and that. I never did with Mr Crosland. You can work with a Minister either way. You become less committed if it is done more formally. I felt he didn't look on civil servants as his real advisers on fundamentals. He had a full life outside the office with advisers he respected. He looked on civil servants as people who are naturally conservative. He presented a closed front. "This is what I want to do. Tell me how to do it." We always talked about business on the basis of an agenda. It was all very *proper*. We would go into his room and sit on our side of the table. He'd say: "This is the subject. These are the points." We'd go through them. "O.K." We'd depart.'

Sir Idwal had no way of knowing that his straight blunt manner was liked by Tony. Nor could he know that few of the outside advisers had personal relations with Tony. Some felt he used them like books.

'This is what I'm interested in at the moment. What can you tell me?' he would say. '*Phyffi, phyffi.* Very interesting.' Or, 'That's not what I need. I understand that already.' They felt they were always on trial. Sometimes they produced what he wanted. Sometimes he put them back on the shelf. Sometimes they didn't know what the purpose was.

'You don't tell a book your purpose, you rifle through it,' said Bill McCarthy, an outside adviser who understood this utilitarian approach to brains. 'And you don't look for the kind of people Tony wanted unless you're intellectually very secure. Most people say they want you to level with them, and it takes a while to realise that what they want is for you to agree with them: they want to be supported. Tony didn't want that. He wanted *facts*.'

'The most exciting thing happened to me today,' he announced on his return to Lansdowne Road. 'Twice I was proved wrong.'

When he thought a brief well argued, even if he didn't agree with the recommendation, he'd ask Private Office to convey to the official his appreciation of the clear concise presentation. Occasionally he wrote a note himself. When the draft was too long, however, he waved it away. 'Not my job to reduce this rambling stuff to something coherent. Send it back.' He was not short-tempered with junior civil servants who were obtuse, but he was intolerant of senior officials whose minds should have kept up with his and didn't.

'You were driven to produce the highest quality,' Sir Idwal said. 'You used your best men to do so.'

Even with that, the Secretary of State brought in a colleague to help him. Tony wanted to keep mortgage rates down. The Chancellor, Denis Healey, said they must go up. Tony said they couldn't go up: they must be subsidised by the Government. The Chancellor of the Duchy of Lancaster, Harold Lever, said both men were right, both men were wrong; he knew a way to keep mortgage rates down without costing the Government a penny.

Tony invited Harold Lever for coffee in his room at DOE. Then the Secretary of State invited his officials to join them. 'The Chancellor of the Duchy of Lancaster knows more about finance than anyone,' he said. The officials looked pretty grim to Lever – this interloper who said he could negotiate a deal with the Building Societies and get the subsidy through them.

'There is no possibility that they will accept your suggestion,' the Chancellor of the Duchy of Lancaster was told by a high-ranking DOE official.

On the contrary.

The civil servants who make up a Minister's Private Office are uniquely placed: double agents, their loyalty is divided between political master (transient) and Permanent Secretary (non-transient). The able Private Secretary who will talk with intelligent indiscretion is invaluable to a Minister – a shortcut to discovering strengths and weaknesses in his Department, which civil servants lower down the hierarchy have facts wanted by the Minister to further his policy, and so forth.

'Mr So and So,' the Secretary of State, looking past the senior official present, would say to some lowlier soul seated well down the conference table, 'I believe you hold a view on such and such. I should like to hear it.' This could be awkward for the junior official. Private Office would then arrange to by-pass the senior chap, the junior man coming alone to the Secretary of State's room to have his brains picked.

When Tony first went to Environment in 1974, his Principal Private Secretary was Andrew Semple. Having previously had Geoffrey Rippon as his Minister, Andrew woke abruptly to the fact that he now had an immensely methodical Minister with intense concentration and a puritanical view about the use of time: time for work, time for relaxation ('though when it was time for relaxation, I felt that work was looking over his shoulder,' Andrew told me later). Tony minded very much his loss of privacy, this endless Diary. If there had to be all these arrangements, they had to be precise. On the dot. He would state the exact time his prosaic meal was required at his desk. If it was two minutes early it was rejected. If it was two minutes late he buzzed Private Office: 'Where is my sandwich lunch?'

Andrew devised a system with Les Pugh, the Secretary of State's personal messenger. Andrew could see Big Ben from his desk and would wait for the actual moment. 'There it goes, Les. You can go in.' Les marched in with the sandwich lunch.

Permanent Secretaries would congregate in Private Office for a meeting with the Secretary of State and the relevant minister – John Silkin when the subject was land. They'd see Private Secretaries begin to look strained. 'Fifteen seconds to go. Where is John Silkin?'

David Lipsey, like the five other chocolate soldiers, was now translated into a temporary civil servant, his job that of political adviser, an innovation that worked more smoothly than anyone expected. D. Lip was assumed to be available at shortish notice. His office was four floors down in that monstrosity which perversely houses the Department of the Environment. His telephone would ring.

'The Secretary of State wants to see you in two and a half minutes.'

D. Lip thought this time thing was mostly to make sure people didn't start slipping. There was also an element of tease, but that did not prevent his walking into the Secretary of State's room exactly two and a half minutes later, slightly breathless as all the lifts had been at least ten floors away when he received the summons.

'Ministers are under unbelievable pressure,' Andrew said. 'They show it in different ways. Some shout at their officials. Some stamp their authority by being rude. With Anthony Crosland it was his rules. On a good day he could tease us. If he lost something in Cabinet or Cabinet Committee that he didn't care about, he could joke about it. If he lost something he minded about, he came back in a very bad mood indeed. Then he'd be particularly exact about his rules, the twenty-minute nap after lunch. He was a man who didn't hide his quirks.'

'I think of Private Office as family,' Tony sometimes said to them after he had been difficult. What he meant, they believed, was that with them he could show himself: he didn't mind if they knew he was vulnerable, though there was still a great deal of privacy and reserve about him. He talked to me about them as individuals, felt personal concern for them. But the terms of the relationship were defined. And the terms were set by him.

'It is presumptuous of me, Andrew,' said the Secretary of State, 'but I think I should speak to you seriously about something.' Andrew, though an easy-going product of Winchester and Cambridge, braced himself. 'It is your handwriting. It is unformed and illegible. You really must think seriously about it in the light of your future career.'

I rarely rang the Department. On doing so one day, I was mildly surprised when a Private Secretary answered the telephone and said: 'Tony Crosland's office.' About this time Anthony Wedgwood Benn had indicated that in future he wished to be addressed as Tony Benn.

'My wife tells me,' the Secretary of State for Environment told Private Office, 'that one of you says this is Tony Crosland's office. There is no such person here. Other people may choose to make their names more plebeian. That is for them. As far as you're concerned, I'm Anthony Crosland.'

More capable than most of self-analysis, he was the first to recognise his own shyness. ('How can Tony say he's shy when he walks across the road like that?' asked Ellen-Craig, looking out on Lansdowne Road from a bedroom window, uncomfortable as her step-father stood before the house opposite where a gramophone was still going strong at ten o'clock Sunday morning. '*Oi*!' he called. 'Anyone alive in there? What about turning down the sound?' An unseen hand did so, and he strolled back.) But he liked to maintain that his was an uncomplicated personality, really very simple. 'I ask for very little,' he said. In a way, true. Yet I thought of Milne's verse about the wistful king whose breakfast – simple enough – sent queen, maid, dairymaid, cow, I forget who else, into a frenzy of activity.

Andrew thought him a most complex man. 'Great layers of complexity. You never quite knew how he was going to react – to people, to situations, intellectual problems, his surroundings. You learned some of the rules, but you never learned them all, never knew why some days he was disproportionately irritable, other days were sunny.'

Andrew accompanied the Secretary of State to Blackpool where he was to address UCATT (the building trades union). D. Lip was with them. They had a slightly scratchy journey: the train ran late.

'I wonder, Andrew, if you would be kind enough to ask the driver why the train is late,' he said as they waited at Preston. 'Does he not know I have an important engagement in Blackpool?'

Andrew climbed out of the compartment on to the platform and set off towards the front of the train which was more than twelve carriages away. He returned. 'The driver says he will do his best, Secretary of State.' Andrew suspected the Secretary of State knew he hadn't actually walked the full length of the train to ask the driver.

After the speech and lunch was over, the sunny day began. Their car passed the Kalamazoo factory. The Secretary of State began to sing: 'I've Got a Gal in Kalamazoo.' He sang them every verse, totally relaxed and happy.

When his mother died the previous year, some confusion attended her burial, uncertainty as to just where J.B. Crosland was interred in the huge cemetery in north London. This, coupled with the time required for Tony to go through her affairs, determined him to make life as simple as possible for his own survivors. In any case, once a year he culled his papers, throwing out all that was now irrelevant. He suggested that he dictate a note to Sylvia so that the children would not have to fret about what to do with our bodies. At the hotel that overlooks Winchester Cathedral, we had a pre-dinner drink in our room and considered the matter. Once or twice we felt tearful. Over the second drink the thing was settled.

First choice: if we came down together in a plane crash, both lots of ashes would go to the Watson burial ground on the shores of Lake Champlain. He made a face. 'God! You were determined to show me that bleak little graveyard however the blizzard raged. I suppose one has no posthumous responsibility to admirers of democratic socialism: they're not going to find it easy to traipse through all that snow to gaze upon my tombstone. I liked the way one of your forbears married first one sister, then another sister, then the housekeeper. Clearly preferred a settled life.'

Second choice: if we died separately, Tony's ashes would be scattered from a Grimsby trawler, mine eventually to go to the Watson burial ground.

'Suppose I die first?' I asked, resisting this chronology.

'You're being frivolous,' he said.

32

Grimsby

London and other large cities present special problems for MPs: their constituents are often transient, making a quick blitz on the local Party by an unrepresentative caucus easier than elsewhere in Britain. In most of the country, the attitude of constituents to their MP rests largely with him. If he becomes a Cabinet Minister and his job leads him to neglect them, they resent it; if he maintains his relationship with them, generally they're proud to have a national figure in their midst. Despite the public pastime of ridiculing politicians, few people faced individually with a Cabinet Minister treat him in an offhand manner.

When the Member for Grimsby wanted to see the Humber Bridge, then half-completed, everyone assembled on the site was apprehensive: as Secretary of State for Environment, he was in charge of Transport. He looked up at the tower.

'My God. I wouldn't go up there,' he said.

'But you were a paratrooper,' said the Mayor.

'Oh yes. I joined the paratroops to cure my vertigo.'

He maximised the use of his time in Grimsby. He would end up on Saturday with six packets of Castellas; he would need them during the week, so he bought them from six different shops. His constituents knew how much he talked publicly about Grimsby. They heard that other national figures groaned: 'Oh no. Not Grimsby again.' But Grimsby liked it.

Most of all they liked the fact that he promptly took up any matter brought to him in his surgery or in conversation or correspondence. They saw the results and not many griped that often they saw him no more than one weekend in four – the weekend that his General Management Committee met. This was his constituency pattern, in or out of office.

In what turned out to be seventeen and a half years as Borough Member, he hoisted his majority from the mortifying 101 to 8,000. His abilities and the nature of Grimsby led him sometimes to be short on sympathy for MPs who found themselves ousted by militants: 'How could Reg Prentice *let* his management committee get in such a state?' If the London media got a bee in their bonnet, and dozens of familiar names signed another letter to *The Times* – 'into' ecology, say, and zero-growth – yet in Grimsby there was no echo of their preoccupation, he ridiculed the crusaders of London SW1 and NW3 as trendies. He looked to the people of Grimsby to keep him from becoming remote in high office. The whole ambience of Grimsby had a gut effect on Tony. Grimsby was reality.

He and members of his GMC had their differences – over capital punishment, abortion, homosexuality, the EEC and so on. 'Look,' he said, 'I'm your MP, but I'm not your delegate. I'll take note of what you say. But I'm the one going through the Division Lobby. If you want a delegate, you have the wrong man.'

His GMC accepted this. 'You don't join the Labour Party just to tear up your card every time there's a difference of opinion,' was their general view.

When he first came to Grimsby some of the railwaymen imagined he was another public school academic come to teach the lads socialism. Then they met him and discovered he knew the problems better sometimes than they did, even though they were the ones who lived with them. His personality struck them more than the Oxford accent. They knew he didn't jump on bandwagons: he had joined the Labour Party when he was sixteen. He'd been in the army, knew how to get on with people. He was a bloody big man. He liked a pint. He could sling stuff back at them. The difference in accents was then forgotten: they didn't hold his academic advantages against him.

His methods of encouragement were various, as Alec Bovill discovered. A railwayman uncertain whether to engage in the Labour Party and local government, Alec was influenced to read more seriously when Tony suggested books that were interesting. That was one tactic. Another was that when you were doing a job for him, he noticed what went right, what went wrong. 'If I'd organised something really well,' Alec said, 'when we were having a pint alone he'd say: "There's officer material here, young man." He guyed both of us. He didn't often thank you directly; he thanked you by his manner. I don't know *why* it was right the way he did it, but it *was* right.'

Another tactic was to batter you verbally. Sometimes this was meant to provide solace. Sometimes it was intended to remedy a fault in you that he exaggerated by insult, thus removing any possibility that he was preaching. Some people took years to understand what he was about. It was apprehended more quickly in Grimsby than in London.

After his surgery on the one Saturday in four, Tony and Alec were in the Crest Hotel having sandwiches before going to see The Town play at home. The sandwiches were topped with cress and cucumber. Alec looked at the greenery. 'There's something in etiquette about whether you eat it if it's outside or in,' he said.

'We've come here to talk about housing during the one hour we have before the match, and you're concerned whether to eat the bloody lettuce,' Tony said. 'If I'd asked you that, you would have gone up in the air about people raving over etiquette.'

Alec knew Tony said it to show him that eating or not eating the cress and cucumber didn't matter an iota; he knew that Tony was annoyed by this concern for trivia. He'd only made the remark as a break between sentences as he leant over to pick up the sandwich. *He* felt annoyed. Tony realised this and they got back to housing.

'Most academics are so bloody superior they make me sick,' Alec said later, thinking it over, 'but Tony never patronised you. He sort of confronted you. "Are you pleading again for railwaymen's wages? I suppose you've just bought another 1600." You took it from him because you knew he didn't mean it – that he talked like that because he was at ease with you. We knew of Tony's great desire to have *real* equality and a society in which men could enjoy life. But because he was of such a complicated makeup, no one will ever be able to describe him as he was.

'He used to call me Bovill when he knew he'd bloody well won the argument and I couldn't answer back. At other times he'd call me Alec in that beautiful rounded voice. He could have altered his accent. He could have smoked cigarettes instead of cigars. We liked him because he didn't pretend to be other than what he was.' (In fact, Tony smoked cigarettes for most of his life, switching to those small cigars only when convinced by medical evidence that cigarette-smoking and cancer are linked: he was in no hurry to pop off.)

Part of his housing policy at Environment was to favour modernising old houses instead of pulling them down. When Alec Bovill became Grimsby's housing chairman, he and Tony discussed what to do about Harold Street where tin baths stood in backyard sheds. Alec wanted to knock the whole row of houses down. 'If we start afresh, the houses can be more compact, people can have more grass in their backyards – the kind of house they want,' he said.

'How do you know that's what they want?'

'I know because I've talked to them.'

'Well, I've just talked with six poor buggers in Harold Street you didn't talk to, Bovill.'

Someone at a meeting would tell a long rambling story. The Borough Member (as Grimbarians call their MP) rested his elbows on the platform table, his back to the 'No Smoking' sign, puffing at the cheroot planted in the middle of his lips, attention fixed on the speaker. Then he took the cheroot from his mouth. 'Your problem is such and such.' He got to the essence.

Grimbarians might have an argument with the Borough Member, but they admired his self-assurance. 'He had a shyness at times which you would only recognise if you were that way yourself,' said Councillor Ivor Hanson, himself not widely noted for shyness; 'but what I saw most of the time was the magnificent arrogance of a man who knew his subject, never fell down on the job. Of course, Tony irritated me sometimes.'

Especially irritating was the running battle over the Council's desire to demolish what few attractive remnants of earlier centuries still stand in this industrial town. When the Borough Member was at Environment, he slapped a preservation order on the handsome, empty Yarborough Hotel just before the bulldozers moved in, then 'requested' the Council to find a use for the building. (Some years later, pleased with themselves, they accepted an application to develop the Yarborough as a hotel, with its Victorian structure and detail as features.)

The Member noted with pleasure the Council's conversion of a disused mill into a riverside theatre. More often, however, he stood up at his GMC and rebuked those who were councillors: 'You're being irresponsible with our architectural heritage. I had a look at that church today. Nothing the matter with it that any small builder worth his salt couldn't put right in a week.'

'It's a bloody rotten old church,' said Councillor Hanson who was in the chair. 'Let's take the sodding thing down.'

'Disgraceful! That church makes a dramatic finish to the street.'

To those who disagreed with him, he became perhaps a little too self-assured about what should happen to Grimsby. 'Before the chairman opens the discussion,' he would interpose, 'I'd like to say such and such,' settling the vote before there'd been any discussion. Sometimes Ivor Hanson was driven to declare:

'I'm ruling as chairman that the Member shall not speak on what is a local matter which concerns only the Council.'

The Member had to accept this, but he muttered audibly.

A regular feature of Tony's Grimsby weekend was going back to the Barkers' or Franklins' home when all else was finished. Jeremy Barker and Jack Franklin were local businessmen; Muriel Barker and Florence Franklin were teachers – all four heavily involved in Grimsby Labour Party affairs and local government. When Derek and Ruth Gladwin returned home to Grimsby, they were usually to be found at the Barkers'. That's where Derek, a senior national officer of the General and Municipal Workers' Union, began his friendship with us.

'Tony knew he could relax at the Barkers' whatever mood he arrived in,' Derek said, thinking back on it all. 'He could behave exactly as he liked because the Barkers and Franklins could look after themselves. He'd walk in ebullient, everything gone well during the day, to find Muriel tired and Jack moaning about the local Party. "It's your bloody Party," Tony would say, irritated by the letdown: "Do something about it if you don't like it." That irritated Muriel. The fur began to fly.'

Alternatively, he arrived fed up about a piece of his Grimsby weekend gone wrong. Immediately he charged Muriel and Jack with being slack in the local Party. Muriel, having looked forward to some discussion of national affairs, gave back as good as she got. If it was a Saturday night, Tony took a large glass of his host's whisky and retired into the breakfast room to watch *Match of the Day*. When it was over he returned to the sitting-room and the row resumed. When Derek was there he poured the oil around, as he put it. If he was in his own home in Woking, he rang Muriel on Sundays to learn the local news. 'I've had that sod here again,' she said. 'Next time he can bring his own whisky.'

Derek saw the other side of the coin as well: 'When Tony and I were alone, he showed his affection and admiration for Muriel in the way he talked about her, his concern for her health, asking me to try and get her to do less. For her part she really enjoyed the stimulation of his visits, however exasperating and arrogant she found him.'

It was Muriel who one winter afternoon would stand in Grimsby's handsome Perpendicular parish church giving an address simultaneously restrained and emotional. It was Derek who read the Lesson from a pulpit in Westminster Abbey.

With an autumn election virtually certain – only six months after the earlier one – July Cabinets had an exceptional number of subjects coming to the boil. Terrific pressure was applied so that what normally would take two years could be done in several months – the White Paper on Devolution and two DOE Bills: the repeal of the 1972 Tory Housing Finance Act and the White Paper on public ownership of development land. Civil servants at Environment could recall no period of greater strain, though at least they could go home at the end of the day; the Secretary of State, like his colleagues, was at the Commons most evenings: the Government's lack of an overall majority meant continuous running three-line whips. It was fairly hellish.

'I thought things were going to be less intense second time round,' I said.

Months earlier Tony had worked out his three-week holiday, this one in France, to begin on 1 August, I to depart for my US family the following day. It became plain that the Cabinet would be meeting in August. Hearing that the Secretary of State was refusing to alter his plans, one of DOE's Permanent Secretaries asked to see him.

'You're one of the leading members of Cabinet, Tony. You're its most profound thinker. You must be present at these Cabinets,' Sir Robert Marshall said.

'Not interested in Devolution. Have no intention of wrecking my August holiday simply to hold a fatuous discussion about another White Paper. Tell Sir J. Hunt that every other member of the British public is permitted a holiday. I shall have mine.' Sir John Hunt was Secretary to the Cabinet.

As the holiday date drew near, Sir Robert conferred with Tony's Private Office daily. He needn't have fretted. 'As my August holiday is mucked up, why shouldn't those responsible stew a little?' was Tony's view.

His reflections on government written during his mucked-up holiday included a long sentence on his and John Silkin's Bill for the public ownership of development land: 'Land: terrible suspicions, but not shared by me: I think many officials genuinely (and reasonably) alarmed by enormous complications and implications, and rightly felt had to express alarm: but main troubles were lunatic speed and Silkin's maddening and purely oral methods of work – "I suddenly had a new idea in my bath this morning."'

Tony then went on to a donnish appraisal of his own term's work: 'Suppose my main achievement in June–July was getting Land White Paper thru – tho' what it will look like in end, time will tell. Otherwise? Building Societies again, but credit entirely

H. Lever's. Nothing on transport, because have left to Mulley.
Housing: mainly in train already. Excellent programme of legislation, but others did all the work. With Denis' help (and
otherwise impossible) have killed rates, and set up 1st-rate Cttees.
Doesn't seem much! Perhaps main thing is having presided over
vast and politically sensitive Dept. and avoided cock-ups!'

Halfway through September the Prime Minister called the
second election of 1974. In Grimsby, even in September, the biting
wind off the North Sea makes canvassing more taxing than ever.
Party workers returned to committee rooms, got out of their coats
to sit down for a cup of tea. In strode the candidate from his own
canvassing. He clapped his hands. 'Up and away. No sitting round.
We must be getting on.' They didn't mind for long because he
never asked them to do anything he wasn't prepared to do.

Six of them went out to canvass one of the rougher estates,
broken glass scattered on communal staircases. Jean Hanson was
wearing sandals. She cut her foot. Blood poured out.

'Look, Tony,' she said.

'Dreadful. Dreadful. Who can deal with Jean's foot? We must
be getting on.'

He expected the local Party to provide efficient organisation and
would take advice when off his own patch. 'You know the area.
Where do I go? Right.' At the end of each day's canvassing there
was a post-mortem at Party headquarters before the evening meetings began. He had a list of about five things that were good. Then
he had a longer list: 'We mustn't do this next time, mustn't do that.
Do keep a record of this. We don't want a cock-up again, stuck
outside Birdseye with that bloody megaphone and no one there.'
Everything itemised.

During the national campaign, the Tory Shadow for Environment, Mrs Margaret Thatcher, made an election pledge: a Tory
Government, she said, would reduce mortgage rates from the
current 11 per cent to 9½ per cent. Labour's Environment Secretary
dismissed her claim as frivolous. Voters prefer to be told the truth
brutally and frankly, he said: the next two years would be years of
national austerity.

Mrs Thatcher then enlarged her promises to include abolishing
domestic rates. But the biggest bribe remained her 'unshakeable'
intention to reduce mortgage rates to 9½ per cent. The only thing
to be said for Mrs Thatcher's sordid contribution to the campaign,
Socialist Commentary observed, was that it occasioned the more
frequent appearance of Tony Crosland at national press confer-

ences. 'Mr Crosland's appearances were invariably stunning –
striped shirts, cigarellos, flamboyant yellow braces, and that unique
mix of olympian intellect and seething passion. Though Denis
Healey first mentioned the word "lies", apropos of the Tories, he
did it jokily, but Tony Crosland, when he turned on Mrs Thatcher,
really meant it. He spoke of moral outrage. Few politicians dare
use phrases like that, and be completely convincing. Mr Crosland
was.'

While he was about it, he wrote off Lord Chalfont and another
Labour peer who had just defected – 'these delicate souls who flee
for the Liberals at the first sound of Tory and Fleet Street
grapeshot.' The House of Lords, he told a Middlesex meeting
where he was speaking for another candidate, 'appears to have a
curious effect on the political judgment of a few of the Labour
Members. Losing all touch with reality, they fall hook, line and
sinker for the absurd canard that the Labour Party is dominated by
leftwing Marxists.' He challenged those who accuse Labour of
extremism to name one single policy of the *Government* which was
unacceptable to any convinced democratic socialist. 'The smear
that Labour is immoderate is levelled for one and one reason only:
it represents the last-ditch stand of the immoderately rich and the
immoderately powerful.'

Back in Grimsby on eve of poll, the traditional Labour cavalcade
began. 'Always a cock-up somewhere,' Tony said. Our car was led
up a cul-de-sac. He jumped out, doing his big steps as he canvassed
three more people, others having to reverse two cars and two vans
out of the cul-de-sac.

During the third week of the campaign, he and Alec Bovill
arranged to meet outside our hotel at 11.43 to go to the fishdocks
for midnight landing. Given it was the middle of the night, why
the three minutes were specified is not clear. It had been a long
day. Alec fell asleep at home. Having stood for twelve minutes in
Brighowgate, braced against the North Sea gale, Tony returned
briefly to our room. 'Last time I say anything about officer material.
Bovill hasn't shown up. If he does, tell him I've gone to the
fishdocks.'

After Tony's victory was announced on Thursday night, we all
went to the Labour Club in Crosland Road. In his speech to his
supporters, the re-elected MP gave his indirect form of thanks:
'Only one slight technical hitch stands out from our campaign.' He
spoke of the housing chairman's failure to turn up for the midnight
landing.

'One bloody hitch after trudging for fourteen ruddy days,' Alec Bovill thought to himself.

Then Tony clasped the microphone to his chest, assumed the mien of an opera singer in the pause before his great aria. The rest of us had no idea what would follow. It was 'Lili Marlene'. He sang with grave, unhurried resonance. During the Italian campaign he'd grown sentimental about 'Lili Marlene'. On this occasion he changed a few words. Everyone except Alec began to laugh. After a little, his annoyance changed to pleasure, and he started laughing. Some years later, by which time he was Labour Leader of the Council, Alec could visualise the scene as if it had just occurred.

'He did it absolutely deadpan, in that deep baritone:

> "Underneath the lamppost,
> Waiting in Brighowgate,
> Waiting for Bovill
> As usual bloody late ... "

'He went on for five stanzas taking the mickey out of me. He always had his own way of showing appreciation. When do you suppose he had made up all those verses?'

·· 33 ··

The Rule of Law

The second election in 1974 was on 10 October. Four days later Tony returned to his desk at DOE. Clay Cross was waiting for him.

In his commonplace book he devoted one sentence to Clay Cross: 'C.C. wretched bore: but someone had to do it – only option was to resign.' Others described it differently: Clay Cross created a sensation. The fracas went on a long time. The Conservative 1972 Housing Finance Act legislated to force councils willy-nilly to adopt a rigorous timetable for increases in council rents. During its Committee stage, Tony had denounced the Tory Government's politics of confrontation, warning that to legislate in this way – without consent, without consultation, and with no willingness to compromise – would invite councils to defy the law. The councils that did so, he argued, were rarely under extremist control: they were peaceful, law-abiding men and women to whom it would never occur in normal circumstances to break the law. He could not condone, let alone encourage, defiance of the law. But democracy was a two-way affair: the Government has an obligation not to make laws that leave large groups feeling outside the system, that offend against the basic sense of natural justice.

The Bill was passed and became the law. Hundreds of councillors up and down the country defied it – refused to put up rents. The penalty for refusal to obey was automatic disqualification from council service and a £6,000 surcharge 'fine'. Most Labour councillors eventually complied, but even then they were liable to the penalties because they were late in implementation. In this country you don't bankrupt and jail hundreds of ordinarily law-abiding councillors. Somehow they had to be let off. Almost certainly a Tory Minister would also have had to declare a general amnesty.

Meanwhile public attention became fixed on the councillors of Clay Cross, the Skinner family's redoubt: they never implemented the Act. Their loud and total defiance made them modern Tolpuddle Martyrs for much of the Labour movement.

At the Party's 1973 conference, a composite resolution was put forward to commit a future Labour Government to help the Clay

Cross councillors. To the general astonishment of the Shadow Cabinet and parliamentary colleagues, the Deputy Leader, Ted Short, endorsed the resolution to help elected representatives who defied the law. When the words came out of his mouth, wild applause burst among some delegates. Others audibly drew in their breath. Tony beetled the brow, pressed the lips.

'You made him Deputy Leader to stand up to the Left, I seem to recall,' he said when he and Roy Jenkins ran into one another; 'I trust you are giving your hero full support.'

And now in October 1974 something had to be done about Clay Cross.

'Why can't the Deputy Leader deal with this shambles?' some MPs asked.

'Tempting,' said Tony, 'as Ted has said not one further word about the shit he's landed us in. But frivolous. It comes under my Department. Can't weasel out of it.'

It was another watershed. Was he, or wasn't he, prepared to dirty his hands?

'I never before really understood that expression about sullying one's hands in the marketplace,' I said. 'As you believe a Labour Government is highly preferable to a Tory one, I suppose you shouldn't be so fastidious that you won't soil your hands in the interest of Labour.'

'Quite. That doesn't mean I shall enjoy it.'

Private Office watched him carrying it through as a duty. He argued that the concessions to this 'miserable promise' be the absolute minimum. He was prepared to take the stick, but Private Office knew he was very unhappy that he, Anthony Crosland, was the one who had to see it through.

With the Clay Cross councillors established as martyrs, it was impossible to win the PLP's approval for legislation which did not also help them. And so when Tony proposed a general amnesty for councillors who had been late in implementing the Act, he extended part of the amnesty to the Clay Cross councillors who continued to break the law: he lifted from them the automatic disqualification from council service, though he did not lift the £6,000 fine that went with it.

Under the heading 'In Memoriam—A. Crosland', a *Daily Telegraph* leader writer reported the anguish he personally suffered at watching 'the finest intellect and what was the finest sensibility in the Labour Party, reduced to mouthing things which others may believe to be true but he must know to be false.'

'First time I can remember the *D. Tel.* extolling your intellect and moral sensibility,' I said as we glanced through the newspapers I'd taken upstairs with our breakfast.

Moral censure was not limited to the Tory press. Tony's feelings were quite different from when the pro-Europeans assaulted his integrity – when he felt morally in the right. Over Clay Cross an unpalatable deed had to be done, and when he was criticised for doing it he felt there was some substance in the criticism. So it stung. The comment he minded most was in the *Sunday Times* where Harold Evans, always expert at finding the epithet most offensive to the individual under attack, used the very phrase – turning it round – that Tony had used. 'The Cabinet's decision to reprieve the Clay Cross councillors is an evil mistake,' said the *Sunday Times*; 'Mr Crosland's words were, frankly, weasel words.'

Introducing a Bill to sweep away the Tories' detested 1972 Housing Finance Act, which he also did in November, gave him satisfaction. Housing was the subject on which he was focused. He wanted to make councils understand the importance of diversity in people's lives: society was damaged in all kinds of ways by herding people into estates built to standardised specifications, often appallingly managed by a remote and insensitive bureaucracy. Old properties should be redeveloped, not bulldozed, wherever feasible, allowing the tenants more choice (and often saving money for the council). Councils should be persuaded to buy from private developers, creating mixed estates in which those renting were not branded as socially apart from home-owners. Tenants would be helped to form co-operative management – decide for themselves their priorities of maintenance, what colour they wanted their front doors, what pets they could have in their rented homes.

Tony had been better equipped than most Shadow Ministers with outside advisers plus D. Lip, but once again he discovered that Opposition simply hasn't the resources to prepare detailed policy. He set up the Housing Review – the widest ever undertaken. It would enable ministers and civil servants for the first time to grasp the result of their interacting separate endeavours. He took charge himself.

Some think a politician's role is above all to be seen to act. He thought it criminal to take decisions without the case for them being made intellectually: 'I daresay thinking is a minority occupation among Ministers, though I've always found it helpful.'

Two years earlier a Tory minister for the Environment, Peter Walker, reorganised local government, destroying communities' sense of identity and loyalty – the worst domestic decision in many years. Presumably Walker hadn't seen how the results of his policy would affect one another.

The Housing Review took a long time to get the answers. Tony didn't go into detail in the nit-picking way: it was a relentless process: the whole thing had to be solid. He felt he had to spend time on this. Another might say: how can a great office-holder find that amount of time, especially one committed to giving a lot of thought to Labour's overall political policy? It was possible through concentration and through cutting out other things. Environment's PRO had to cajole him to see the press. We had little social life.

Once he made a decision, that was it. He could take decisions entirely from his own judgment: politically he felt his flanks were protected. 'As long as Harold is Prime Minister, I can't be other than I am now – in a key position. He can't give me anything less, though he'll be damned if he'll give me anything more.'

At Lansdowne road, matrimony had entered that phase which commences when children go off – Sheila to marriage, Ellen-Craig to a bedsit near Camberwell School of Art in south London. Adolescent tribulations excepted, they were distinctly agreeable children, curious about ideas, conscious that intellectual weapons are needed to stand one's ground, lending support to any member of the family currently in a bad patch. Their visits home gave mutual pleasure. On the other hand, a different pleasure undeniably exists when parents – assuming they enjoy one another's company – have more time not subject to interruption. It must have been about then that Tony, if he was at home for an evening, began coming into the bedroom after dinner to say: 'Why don't you read in the study? I'm not doing work where I have to be alone. Nice if we were in the same room.'

On one such evening I persuaded him to come to bed early in preparation for a thirty-six-hour official visit to East Anglia which meant getting up at 7 a.m. Shortly after 11 p.m., contemplating the exotic experience of an early night, we prepared for bed. The telephone rang. I answered it on the bedroom extension. Callbox pips ensued, followed by a continuous dialling tone through which I could just make out the voice of Ellen-Craig's friend, Nick South. He sounded as if he were speaking under water thousands of miles away.

'The craziest thing just happened. Ellen and I and Richard and Robin have been at a pub for a perfectly ordinary evening. We were riding back to Camberwell on top of a bus when some police rushed up the stairs and took Ellen and Robin away.'

'That dialling tone makes conversation a strain, Nick. Let's get a better line. Give me the number of your callbox.'

We both hung up.

'What is it?' Tony asked. I told him. 'Don't ring back yet. Let's stop and think.' We thought. 'You *have* told me, haven't you, that Ellen-Craig is no longer interested in marijuana and so on?'

Having waited for two minutes, Nick rang back. Tony took the call. From his concentrated expression, I knew the continuous dialling tone was overlaying all communication from that particular callbox.

'Had the police a reason, Nick, to take them off the bus?'

Nick – I learned a few minutes later – said there was no reason, and he thought it was disgusting and was about to go to East Dulwich Police Station to say so.

'As you've had a fair bit to drink, it would be more useful to keep away from the police station. Why don't you go to Ellen-Craig's place and see if the police have sent her home? Then ring us back.'

He put down the telephone. 'We may as well go back to the study. I knew your idea of an early night was too good to be true.' He returned to the Eames chair, stretched out his legs on the ottoman, lit a cheroot. '*Phyffi, phyffi.*' He began to laugh. 'Expect one's identity won't improve matters.'

'In what way?'

'Most police are conservative working class – heartily dislike our liberalising the law. Can't really blame them if they take a little pleasure in picking up one of our children. I suppose Ellen-Craig wasn't smoking pot?'

'If that's what she wants to do, why would she go to a pub? She's told me about this huge pub where everyone knows plainclothesmen are present.' I was not at all easy in my mind.

He dialled the number of East Dulwich Police Station. 'May I speak with the Duty Sergeant? This is Mr Anthony Crosland, Secretary of State for the Environment.' A second person must have come on the line. 'Good evening. This is Mr Anthony Crosland. I have a somewhat garbled message, but I gather you've taken my step-daughter off the top of a bus.' His voice was courteous and good-humoured. 'I see. Where is she now? ... I see ... Yes.' He chuckled. 'Yes. I can imagine the scene. Well, let me ask your advice then. Should I ring up my solicitor?' After listening to the answer he chuckled again. 'That sounds quite reasonable. Well then you'll ring me back in half an hour . . . Good.'

He put back the telephone. 'They're holding her on suspicion of using illegal drugs. After she and her friends left the pub, the police examined cigarette butts on their table and "had reason to suspect marijuana had been smoked". She's refusing to take a saliva or blood test. Apparently she has the legal right to refuse. He says her language is rather "pink". They're waiting for the CID to arrive before they decide about charges. He says if I'm going to wake up my solicitor at ten minutes to twelve I might as well wait another half hour and wake him at 12.20.'

Briefly we switched roles; I said lightheartedly: 'As she's your step-daughter, perhaps you'll get a sympathy vote at the next election.'

'Not in Grimsby,' he said, unamused. 'I can see the *Evening Telegraph* now. I can imagine every word of it.' He turned to the sports page of the *Evening Standard* to read about football. 'Bloody fool,' he muttered once.

At 12.25 the telephone rang. He answered, easy-tempered, but confirming several times: 'You'll be sending her home tonight.' My interest in Tony's predicament almost equalled my interest in Ellen-Craig's. When things were going smoothly, he tended to refer to his step-daughters as these bloody children he'd landed himself with, adding a little 'tccht'. In crisis he expressed his love for them more directly.

He put back the telephone. 'She still won't take the saliva or blood test. But they're going to send her home some time tonight. We'll learn in the morning whether or not they've charged her.'

The telephone rang. It was Nick South in the callbox with the perpetual dialling tone.

Tony put back the telephone. It rang. From my chair across the room, I could hear Ellen-Craig's voice weeping. 'Tony, Tony . . .'

He sounded neither critical nor sympathetic. Afterwards I asked if he had assumed the police were listening on another line, and he said it was probably in his subconscious. 'Yes, I know you're there. I've talked with them several times. Didn't they tell you? . . . Well, are you sure you also are not being beastly to them? . . . Well I know that. You're pissed as a fart. But *were* you also smoking pot? . . . My sympathy is divided between you and the police. They think if you're telling the truth, there's no reason not to take the saliva and blood tests. I think they're being reasonable here . . . None of us like needles in us. You're nearly an adult and you must decide whether it wouldn't be simpler to take the tests and clear the matter up in ten seconds and go home. Are you sobering down at all yet? ... All right. Then say you'll take the saliva test. If you're co-operative, things could be simplified ... Good. Well let us hear from you soon, as everyone in this house is quite curious, to say the least, as to what has been happening.'

He put back the telephone. Ten minutes later it rang. Ellen-Craig was in the callbox with the perpetual dialling tone. I noticed that it was two o'clock by now. Tony sounded pleased and asked if she'd like to talk with me.

'Hullo Mama. I didn't have to take any test. They let us go because they hadn't anything to charge us with. I'll tell you about it tomorrow.'

Tony said: 'Ask her if the police raped her.'

I asked her.

'No. Though a huge policewoman got me to strip. Do you want to know why they thought I'd been smoking pot, Mama? I'd been crying in the pub and my eyes were red.'

Once more we prepared to retire to our bed. Four hours later the alarm clock went off. Tony began his ablutions prior to the East Anglia tour.

Towards evening, perhaps six weeks later, Ellen-Craig was washing her hair in her south London bedsit when someone knocked at her door. She opened it to two policemen. They inquired if they could come in, sat down on the two upright wooden chairs, asked her a bit about life at art college. They'd come to return the things taken from her at the police station, they said. Lipstick, used Tampax, crumpled handkerchief were handed to her in a small plastic bag fastened with two staples.

'The Party's Over'

'I can't go on like this,' Tony had said over gossip during the earlier years of governing. 'There is nothing further to say and he still stands there. Everywhere I go he's at my shoulder. Shouldn't be the least surprised to be quietly peeing one day, my mind on other things, and turn round to find him standing behind me. I'm sure he means well, sees it as part of his job. But it makes me feel claustrophobic.'

Success or failure as a Principal Private Secretary is important to a civil servant's career. Over a drink in his room Tony said to his Permanent Secretary: 'I'm sorry to have to raise with you a matter that has nothing to do with competence. He hovers. This might suit another Minister very well. It drives me mad. It would be grossly unfair to put a black on this man's record because of my idiosyncrasy. When he can be moved without the slightest question of opprobrium, will you arrange this?'

A week or two later a new Principal Private Secretary appeared, the one who hovered continuing his ascent in a different section of the Department, record unsullied.

At DOE Andrew Semple had skilfully completed the heavily mined course. He had to be replaced. Sir Ian Bancroft was consulted. Bancroft had been a Principal Private Secretary at the Treasury when Labour came into office in 1964. Just over ten years later he was Permanent Secretary of DOE, soon afterwards head of the entire Home Civil Service. He and Tony overlapped at Environment. They got on well and met once a week in Tony's room for a drink and indiscreet conversation. Previously, Bancroft knew only the formal aspect of the Secretary of State's presence. He was surprised at the 'colourful language' employed in private. Early in their relationship Tony told Bancroft that he didn't like characters who seemed always to agree with him or had only a superficial knowledge of facts. He wanted civil servants with sharp edges – not only intellectually able but who could stand their ground. Bancroft thought Terry Heiser was the man for this particular Minister.

He was – but in his first six months, the new Principal Private

Secretary felt resentful. Like many civil servants, he was overawed by the style and the intellect, though he had glimmerings that the Secretary of State was, rather surprisingly, a shy man. This realisation did little to diminish Terry Heiser's resentment. Clearly the Secretary of State did not relish new faces in quarters as close to him as Private Office: he presumed – found immense pleasure in – the support and loyalty of a familiar few and certainly did not want to spend his psychic energy on establishing another relationship.

One day Terry Heiser woke up to realise that he admired and was fond of the man. He accepted the idiosyncrasies. He wondered about the shyness and the deeply-felt emotions Anthony Crosland did not care to parade. Did all this, coupled with an uncompromising intellectuality, produce the reserve that seemed like arrogance?

The first six months were made worse by the Secretary of State's being already acclimatised to the No. 2 in Private Office, David McDonald, a young Ulsterman. Like others for whom Tony developed strong affection, D. Mac had bad days.

'All civil servants knew he was the thinker of the Labour Party, and to most of them he was an enigmatic figure. His air and manner quite frightened people initially. As he became more familiar with them and they with him, they discovered he wouldn't bite. Because his own Private Office saw him every day, the process of coming to love him took place more quickly. Sometimes I hated him.'

On David McDonald's first day, the Secretary of State came in, said good morning to everyone, looked at the new face with considerable suspicion, and went into his room. Half an hour later he buzzed. David McDonald went in.

'You have a photographic memory.'

'I'm sorry, Secretary of State?'

'You do not have a notebook.'

The novice left the room at once and came straight back with a notebook.

'Unless your memory is infallible, always take a note of what I ask.'

Later that day he buzzed again. David McDonald went in. Five questions were hurled at him and he scribbled them down. He was asked to get the answers in ten minutes. He returned in ten minutes, thinking he'd done bloody well. 'I think I have the answers to your five questions.'

The Secretary of State had both hands placed like blinkers either side of his face, elbows resting either side of the papers on his desk,

enclosed in concentration. 'Then you shouldn't be here,' he said
without looking up.

'I'm sorry, Secretary of State, I don't know what you mean.'

'If you only think you have the answers to my questions, why
are you here?'

'Sorry, Secretary of State. Bad drafting. I *do* have the answers to
your questions.'

He was always demanding perfection, couldn't tolerate sloppy
presentation. Private Office would unlock the box he'd worked
through the night before. Written on the front of the folder would
be: 'D. Mac. This is sloppy. Do not show me things in this form
again.' He did not mention it after that. Sometimes the insistence
on perfection was wildly irritating.

Whatever the pressure, he never raised his voice to Private
Office. What was devastating was his expression of disappointment.
'How could you possibly have let me down like this?' He would
withdraw, become entirely detached, not actually discourteous, but
unrelaxed with them, in his shell. This withdrawal was much worse
than being shouted at. Then it was over – no sign that for a day or
more this black cloud had overhung them all.

Where one sits at the Cabinet table is determined by job rather
than whim. In a previous manifestation, Barbara Castle and Tony
were neighbours. 'I notice he has an odd habit when sitting next to
me of shaking his foot violently ...' she observed in *The Castle
Diaries*. Swinging the leg, we are told, can indicate anger, anxiety,
insecurity *et al*. With Tony it meant patience was near its end.

December 1974 stretched on. Beneath the Cabinet table, one
man had his right leg crossed over his left, the right one swinging
in an ever-widening arc. Why on earth didn't Harold move the
discussion along? Had he nothing to do? Barbara had already made
her case; remorselessly the Secretary of State for Social Services
pounded the table. The Foreign Secretary pushed a piece of paper
across the Cabinet table to the 'S of S for Environment'. It said:

'*Party game to be played during Barbara's Speeches*. Speculation
for 1975: How many of us will still be here in Dec. 1975 & who,
and on what grounds, will leave? ANSWER:–' A line bisected the
rest of the page, the left-hand column for Tony's answers, the
right-hand for Jim's. They did only the Leavers. Tony guessed:
'Ted Short – I.B.A.; R. Prentice – resignation over rule of law; Bob
Mellish – resignation because of general sulks; Benn, Shore, Foot:
?? resign over Europe.' Jim guessed: 'Michael Foot because he

Party game to be played during Barbara's [?] ure
Speculation for 1975 :

How many of us will still be here in Dec. 1975
+ on what grounds + who, will the be others
who will leave ?

ANSWER :-

Leavers

Ted Short — I.B.A. ✓

R. Prentice — resignation over
                      rule or law ✗

Bob Mellish — resignation :.
                      general sulks

Benn ⎫
Shore ⎬ ?? resign over
Foot ⎭   Europe

① Michael Foot because he can't
   stand the strain of anyway
                                    NO

② P. Shore because we recommended
   staying in EEC.

③ Shirley W because the
   Referendum goes against us.

④ Ted Short to a Public Bd

⑤ R.J. to edit the Times

⑥ A. Benn if he sees a
   chance of grabbing the
                      leadership

can't stand the strain of saying "No"; P. Shore because we recommend staying in EEC; Shirley W. because the Referendum goes against us; Ted Short to a Public Bd; R.J. to edit *The Times*; A. Benn if he sees a chance of grabbing the leadership.'

Tony Benn's brainchild – the referendum on whether Britain would remain in the EEC – dominated the first half of 1975. In Shadow Cabinet three years earlier, Tony Crosland had voted against the referendum. In 1975 he supported it, believing that the unabated controversy would be settled in no other way. Benn's purpose was twofold: to get Britain out of the EEC and to be hailed by the people for doing so. He felt confident they would vote to withdraw from the Common Market.

The referendum campaign began. At the first press conference of the Labour Committee for Europe, David Ennals and Tony Crosland were thought particularly effective speakers because they were the least committed to the extreme 'Pro' position. In Tony's case, he was intent that this time his stance be unmistakable. In the past, he said from the platform, he had been rather more agnostic about Europe than some of his colleagues: he had never believed Britain's entry would perform miracles that justified splitting the Labour Party. The situation, however, had changed since 1971 when he abstained in the vote on whether Britain should enter the EEC. Britain was in, and as a consequence nearly all the Commonwealth countries had made new trading agreements; if we now came out, it would be to total isolation, and Britain depended on trading. 'Moreover,' he said, 'to withdraw now would create in this country a mood of poor man's inchoate chauvinism, reviving old dreams of Empire and special relationships that have had such disastrous effects on British policy-making since 1945.'

Roy Jenkins, leading the all-Party Britain in Europe campaign, said to Tony: 'For an agnostic, it's interesting that you made the strongest statement of any of us.'

During the rest of the campaign, Tony's speeches received little coverage. He put this down to chance. 'The non-zealots have a useful argument to contribute. I should have liked to be able to put it more widely,' he said to Dick Leonard, still an ardent pro-European.

'You are mistaken in thinking it largely chance that has led the media to concentrate only on Roy and Shirley and Reg Prentice speaking for the pros,' Dick said. 'The campaign has been very carefully calculated as a means to put Roy back in the political race, and at each and every press conference, several Jenkinsites – usually John Harris, Bill Rodgers, David Marquand – are there in the back row to brief the press.'

On 5 June the British people voted to stay in the EEC. The result was, clearly, a setback for Tony Benn. Nor did Roy receive the accolades. These – to general surprise – went to the Prime Minister. For the first time in his life, Harold Wilson was hailed by the British media as a statesman: his viciously denigrated zig-zagging had been vindicated. Britain was not withdrawing from Europe; Labour had not split.

Having established to the world that he was a statesman who would retire only when he wished to, the Prime Minister began to amuse himself, rearranging his Cabinet in cat-and-mouse spirit, taking particular pleasure in teasing Benn. 'I decided several weeks ago to use Tony Benn to display my sense of humour,' he said.

For days no one knew what the Prime Minister was up to as he raised the hopes of would-be members of Cabinet, caused needless anxiety to others. At DOE, as the Secretary of State was leaving the building one Friday in June, his personal messenger said to him: 'I'm going on a week's holiday, Sir. Will I ever see you again?'

'Why shouldn't you see me again, Les?'

'The newspapers say you'll be changing jobs with Mr Benn, Sir,' said Les, demonstrating the effect that a single news-story can have on the human psyche.

'Enjoy your holiday, Les. I expect you'll see me when you return.'

That evening Tony was detached about a man he would never understand. 'In all this, Harold is largely absorbed with his own mischievous pleasure in making his arrangements. I don't entirely blame him. He's put up with hell for the past fifteen years, and now he doesn't care and is going to enjoy himself. It's irresponsible, but one has a certain sympathy with him.'

Finally Tony Benn was told of his demotion from Industry to Energy.

Meanwhile, as inflation accelerated in the first months of 1975, the Treasury had presented a huge package of cuts. One Minister walked up and down the study floor at Lansdowne Road, thought, made notes, walked up and down some more. He then wrote what Whitehall believed to be an unprecedented letter to the Prime Minister. As far as anyone knew, Tony consulted nobody about what became known as the Chequers Letter, which made the following points: why can't we stop thinking purely in terms of our departments? Shouldn't we look at the *net* effect of all decisions we take, and *then* make the individual decisions? When there is the most economic pressure, it is even more crucial to choose priorities. The CPRS should be put to work discovering the effect of separate departmental decisions on each other so that Cabinet can see how to achieve the greatest benefit in line with Labour objectives, even if one's own department gets less as a result.

He thought expenditure at DOE had been lax on roads generally, so cuts there were less painful. The restriction of local services, however, pained him greatly. Housing, which he ringed in the letter, stood as his No. 1 priority. At a meeting of Ministers at Chequers he handed the letter to the Prime Minister. On Monday copies were circulating throughout Whitehall.

'Extraordinary letter,' DOE officials remarked, not entirely with pleasure: it was plain that the Secretary of State was more interested in policy-making than concentrating all his attention on *their* Department.

My weekend 'beauty cure' entailed lying in the bath for perhaps an hour, giving myself a manicure and a pedicure. Tony had just finished a Housing file when he paid his first visit to the bathroom. Ten minutes later he was back again.

'My restless mind is now thinking about Transport,' he said, watching with some interest as I removed week-old pink pearlised varnish from my toenails. 'If I stayed in this bloody job for another two years, I could actually *advance* something. Not solve it. You can't solve anything. But start things moving in the right direction.' He surveyed the debris floating on the bathwater. 'How is it that your bathwater ends up so much dirtier than mine?'

His third visit concerned a file he'd just come to in the red box. 'It's a really excellent paper produced by the CPRS – discussing *policy*.'

'I can never remember what those initials stand for.'

'Why should you? It's the Think Tank. The paper is about the effect of the social services on one another. Says several times that this approach was put forward by the S of S for Environment. It's what my Chequers letter was about. The paper is an excellent beginning. The civil servants wouldn't have done it without a political push.'

That was in April. The surge of local government spending under the Tory Government had continued through the first year of Labour's return to office. Tony accepted that local authorities were certainly spending more than the country could afford, but he argued that the Treasury was cutting back too hard and too generally. The Chancellor only somewhat moderated his demands for cuts.

The overall reining-in was far from pleasant for a man who believed high public expenditure was morally right. The rate of increase in inflation had to be slowed, stabilised, then reduced. He must preside over this. He made his announcement. For the future, he said, the Labour Government had not lost sight of its priorities, it had not given up its goals. Meanwhile, the British people must experience the first real decline in living standards in a generation. 'We have to come to terms with the harsh reality of the situation which we inherited. The party's over.'

He did not in the least mind being attacked by the extreme Left outside Parliament. 'Of course Communists and Trots want Labour to fail.' Disappointing his own people's aspirations was something else. He created the Consultative Council on Local Government Finance – a meeting place for Ministers of the domestic spending departments (Environment, Education, Home Affairs, Health) and the leaders of local authorities. As chairman he frequently had to talk the latter into accepting a view that he regretted. His officials watched the process.

'There would be a *huge* conglomerate of different departmental Ministers, civil servants, representatives of the local authorities, forty of them sitting round the table and masses behind them.' David McDonald described the scene. 'He would walk in and often with a jocular manner assume control. The local authority representatives knew he knew his subject inside out. They respected him. He acquired respect for them. He made the process of consultation work.'

Precisely when Tony developed a soft spot for Michael Foot it's hard to say. Certainly by the early 1970s I can remember his saying, 'Sweet man, Michael', minutes after they'd debated opposing views at a conference fringe meeting. Except when Michael came to Lansdowne Road in response to my asking his help with a profile, neither man ate in the other's home. But when I took supper to Tony's room in the House, it was not unusual for him to say: 'Let's step across the corridor and see how Michael's getting on.' Sometimes he found it nearly impossible to recall the vitriol with which he and Michael Foot had assailed one another when the Left of the Party was trying to destroy Gaitskell.

On Labour's return to Government in March 1974, after years as a backbencher, Foot became Secretary of State for Employment. The appointment was regarded as one of Wilson's best – bringing into the centre the romantic left-wing orator while at the same time encouraging the unions to believe – rightly – that they'd receive a sympathetic hearing, whatever the Government's final decision on their claims.

No sooner had the referendum dust settled in 1975 than the National Union of Railwaymen threatened strike action because the Government resisted their pay claim. Tony had been brooding about a 'state of the nation' speech and decided to make it now. Michael asked him not to, believing it would simply antagonise union leaders. Tony brooded further and sent a message saying he was going ahead. He stated categorically that the present scale of pay and price rises meant Britain was 'on a suicide course'. He ruled out a statutory wages policy because it had been shown time and again not to work. The Government's second possibility – increasing the level of unemployment – he described as a policy of despair. 'I doubt that it would work – certainly not quickly enough. But the real objection is one of principle. For high unemployment represents more than a squandering of our most valuable resource: it is a social evil, which would be utterly alien to the philosophy of any Government in the modern world.'

Instead, he put a detailed case for tightening the Social Contract. The Government could not protect employment if workers did their best to price themselves out of their jobs. 'The National Union of Railwaymen must be clear on that point. Principles of social justice should determine the distribution of our national wealth. But all Government efforts to increase social justice are lost in the crazy haphazard lurches which characterise pay settlements under conditions of such rapid inflation.

'The most extraordinary thing about this situation is that most wage and salary earners agree with everything I have said. Opinion polls consistently show large majorities in favour of tighter re-straints on pay. Yet workers are understandably fearful of acting on this belief and showing restraint themselves, lest some other less altruistic group should steal a march on them.'

Michael Foot was angry, very angry. A few days later, however, the two men were working in harness: with the Prime Minister and the Chancellor they met at Downing Street on a Saturday evening to negotiate with the NUR executive. 'Whoever would have thought', said a usually bumptious member of the railwaymen,

'that I'd be here at No. 10 with the Prime Minister?' He was excited
by it, as the Prime Minister intended when deciding the venue for
this stage of negotiations.

'This time Michael and I were together, which is a pleasure,'
Tony said. 'He was masterly.'

A couple of nights later he reverted to the subject of Michael
Foot, intrigued by the new manifestation. 'Everyone was wrong
about Michael. He said to me last night: "I'm not going to make
up my mind about this until I've discussed it with my
Department." He says his civil servants see it like a chess game:
"They've been playing the game for thirty years, so they must have
got fairly good at it."'

'Does that mean you'll be together on the railways pay decision?'

'No. I'm more hardline than Michael. Michael's Department is
a softline one: they always want to avoid strikes.'

~·35~·

Not Fenced In

Ministers vary enormously in how much they take to Cabinet, self-confidence an important factor. One Minister used simply to read out his civil service brief. 'The whole thing was underlined in red ink. Absolutely extraordinary,' Tony said of this approach to governing. He took to Cabinet as little as possible of his own departmental decisions. Ministers also vary in how they see their non-departmental role in Cabinet. Shirley Williams, who first entered Cabinet in 1974, viewed the thing quite differently from Tony.

He was fond of Shirley. For a number of years she and Bernard Williams and their daughter joined Sasha and Michael Young and their children for Christmas Eve dinner and carols at Lansdowne Road. Sasha and Shirley sang the soprano and contralto parts with poignant purity. Michael and Tony were a team – taking turns reading and miming 'The Night Before Christmas'. Shirley and Tony's friendship was badly bruised during the early 1970s: she was an extreme pro-European. Europe took its toll on friendships. Theirs recovered. He was glad when she entered the Cabinet, despite their running disagreement on methods of governing. (Shirley had been one of his ministers at Education.)

He shared Attlee's view that the great thing in Cabinet was to stop people talking; no self-respecting Minister should have to use time explaining detail to colleagues who won't have properly mastered the issue. Unless policy or the economy or a subject on which he was expert was concerned (or one in which he took a special interest), he might say nothing.

Shirley complained about this to people outside Cabinet: there were times when she *knew* Tony agreed with her, and he didn't say anything. Roy, she felt, was readier to back her. When she asked Tony to support her on something or other – Africa, say – he might well reply: 'I'm not interested in Africa at the moment.'

He, in turn, complained of Shirley: '1 Spends her time on detail that a civil servant should be handling when she ought to be applying herself to *policy* decisions. 2 Takes far too much to Cabinet. Why can't she make decisions by herself instead of having to be reassured? 3. Has some deep psychological need to show she's familiar with every subject under the sun, knows the name of the Foreign Minister of every underdeveloped country. *Finally* Harold is winding up Cabinet after four and a half hours, everyone longing to get back to their own work, and Shirley says: "Prime Minister, there's just another tiny point I'd like to raise." Enough to make one weep.'

By 1975, whenever the subject was public spending, the Prime Minister called on the Secretary of State for the Environment to speak immediately after the Chancellor, thus ensuring that the argument would be put against the Treasury before the Prime Minister committed himself. Once Prime Minister and Chancellor have voiced agreement, they are almost unbeatable. It was well known on the Whitehall circuit that senior Treasury officials had grown 'obsessed' with Anthony Crosland: they wanted to get at him directly, try to convince him he was wrong. He was so assertive in Cabinet that they always expected personal unpleasantness between him and Denis Healey, but there wasn't – though the two saw little of each other outside Cabinet and the Commons.

In these overriding PESC struggles, DOE civil servants gave their Secretary of State little help. Of course they provided figures and drafted what they were told to draft. But Tony sometimes felt they could have done more had they not been protecting their traditional relationship with the Treasury.

As July wore on, Ministers showed their need for a holiday in different ways. Tony wanted a briefing on a major subject coming up at Cabinet on Thursday morning. The papers weren't ready the night before. David McDonald rose at dawn on Thursday, took his own car to pick up the official concerned with the subject, got to Marsham Street at 8 a.m. to collect the papers, from there rang Lansdowne Road to say he and the official would be outside No. 10 to meet the Secretary of State before Cabinet to give him the papers and brief him.

'David,' said the Secretary of State, stepping out of his car as it pulled up in Downing Street, 'what have you been up to? You didn't warn me that the British Library was on today's agenda.' The British Library – a minor item on Cabinet's agenda – was one of his interests. He would have asked for a special brief, had he realised in time that it was coming up.

'But Secretary of State, I did tell you earlier in the week. You ticked it.'

'This will not do. You must warn me in advance when you know I'm interested in a subject.' The brief on the major subject was practically snatched from D. Mac's hands, and the official concerned was never asked a thing about it.

After Cabinet the Secretary of State returned to Marsham Street. 'David. A word.'

D. Mac had prepared his ground: while the Cabinet met, he had dug out the papers from earlier in the week. He handed over one which included the fact that the British Library would be on Thursday's agenda. Alongside it in red ink, written with the Secretary of State's birthday present from Private Office, was a tick.

'Well, clearly you did tell me. But you didn't make me aware of its importance.'

During the rest of the day, grievance surged through D. Mac's breast. 'That bastard,' he thought to himself. 'That ungrateful bastard. Quite unreasonable.'

Yet on his good days, the Secretary of State could be so charming that D. Mac almost forgot that a few days earlier he'd been bloody impossible. They shared an addiction to cricket. The rest of Private Office – like Tony's family – wasn't interested in cricket. Sometimes during these July weeks, when he had no Cabinet Committee or meetings in the afternoon and he hadn't to be at the House, the Secretary of State would come out of his room. 'David. Cricket.'

Part of the charade required D. Mac to bring papers with him. The Secretary of State poured himself a drink: 'I suppose you can have a teeny weeny drink, but I'm not going to pour it for you.' He'd sit at his desk. D. Mac would sit at the conference table. Both had a good view of the television set. 'Right. Sound on for ten minutes. After that, sound off unless something exciting happens.' They'd both glance up from time to time. 'What *appalling* batting.' An hour might pass. 'Right. Enough of this idleness. You're not actually working, and I'm not actually working. Back to your room. I'll get on with this.' The ritual never altered.

Parliament at last rose in August. His three-week holiday in France began. The commonplace book reflects diverse curiosity, Kingsley Amis sandwiched between Keir Hardie and François I. Though Keir Hardie's personality was patently very different from Tony's, the description of the Labour Party is strangely familiar. '... Temperance major factor in his life: & even more a sort of mystical inchoate Christianity ... If anyone thinks L.P. badly split & quarrelling now, far worse in early yrs. 1906–14: terrible sectarian battles, jealousies, mutual suspicions in I.L.P. Personal relations never trusting, continuously fluctuating, often tense. Plus ça change: 1907 L.P. Conf.: motion to bind PLP to Conf. resolutions were "opinions only". Hadn't realised K.H. was major internat'l figure, & also int-minded, in what was then almost completely insular Party ... Life ended in tragedy when in 1914 almost whole Lab. Mov. & w.c. [working class] rejected his profoundly-held pacifist views ...'

Instead of making my August visit to my American family, I was at Adderbury. Private life had taken a remarkable turn: we'd found the country cottage.

Two years earlier, in a spurt of inquiry, we followed up an advertisement for a converted mill. Adderbury is three miles south of Banbury. The Crossmans lived three miles north of that ancient market town. We lunched with them one Sunday, then drove in two cars to Adderbury – four Crossmans and two Croslands. A For Sale board hung outside, but no one was around. The six of us climbed over a five-bar gate into the garden. 'As soon as I saw it, my heart turned over,' Tony said that evening.

I rang the estate agent in the morning and was told the mill had been sold the previous week. Whenever we were sightseeing in north Oxfordshire, Tony would say: 'Do you mind if we go a little off our route and have another look at the mill in Adderbury?' I would stay in the car reading Pevsner on the village where we were headed for a pub lunch, while he walked round the footpath which partly encircles the mill. 'Each time I see it,' he said when he got back in the car, 'my heart turns over.'

Two years later it came back on the market. I went with Ellen-Craig to look inside the house, described it to Tony that night. Ellen-Craig rang him in the morning. 'We *must* buy it. It's like something out of a dream.'

There wasn't money for a downpayment: the whole lot would have to be borrowed. 'We've talked about a country cottage for ten years,' he said. 'If we don't do it now, we never will.'

Acquiring Adderbury – 'buying' seems hardly the apt word – shook our solicitor. Only half the mortgage on Lansdowne Road was paid off. The Labour Government had legislated against tax relief on mortgages for second homes. Yet here we were taking out another 'first' mortgage, something called a second mortgage, plus two insurance policies on my life. Because of the age and sex difference, by insuring my life instead of Tony's, payments could be spread over a much longer period. (A little over eighteen months later, an accountant said to me: 'Too bad Adderbury was not in your husband's name and the insurance on his life.' The accountant was wrong: had Adderbury been paid for by that means, I could never have stayed there.)

Only two of the Crossmans were to visit Adderbury again. In the two years since we first saw it together, Dick died from cancer, Patrick – at seventeen – from suicide. Though we'd not previously seen a lot of one another, after that Tony said from time to time: 'Shall we see if Anne Crossman and Virginia would like to drive over for lunch?' Anne's stoicism was staggering. She and I talked of various things. After Dick's stomach operation, he had resumed his biography of Weitzman, finding it more complicated than he had expected. As the months went by and he slogged away on research, Anne thought to herself that he didn't act like someone who knew he had terminal cancer. Yet she believed the doctor had indicated this to Dick immediately after the operation. It turned out Dick didn't know. Having used up a year in the research on Weitzman, he discovered he had three to six months to live. He was furious, absolutely furious. 'Why on earth didn't someone tell me?'

What Anne always found so strange was that a man as intelligent as Dick should not have asked what the operation had been about. After his initial rage of discovery, he shoved Weitzman aside and hurled his energies into editing his diaries, though he hadn't time to complete them. When I told Tony this, he found it a terrible story, completely sympathised with Dick's anger. 'If you knew I had a fatal illness and you didn't make *absolutely certain* I knew, I should never forgive you. One would want to put one's affairs in order.'

It was about this time, I imagine, that he made a list which I later found in the top drawer of his desk. 'If pop off, where to go for money.'

One column listed assets and debts. The other column was 'Who to approach.' The assets – Lansdowne Road – didn't look too good compared with the debts, so he topped up the assets: 'Eleemosynary payment from Queen for services to country: £1,000,000.' The one to approach was the Duke of Edinburgh 'thru Willie Hamilton'. Although Tony didn't share Willie Hamilton's intense anti-Monarchist emotions, he enjoyed Willie's general eccentricity. Searching my dictionary, I thought of the MP who once said at the back of a hall where Tony was speaking: 'I *do* wish Tony wouldn't use these words I can't understand.'

For nine years – since my father died and our family home in Baltimore was sold – Lansdowne Road had been stuffed with early American furniture waiting for the country cottage. 'Tony, as we've borrowed so much money, do you think we could find some more? It was ten years before I got Lansdowne Road finished. If I could get Adderbury right at one go, then we'd be able to enjoy it completely the weekends we're there. I'd buy haircord carpet.'

The last thing I wanted was him anywhere near Adderbury while it was being transformed. Since the war Tony displayed resolute antipathy to any form of camping, however romantic the setting. He went to France for his three-week August holiday. Sylvia and Eileen and Ellen-Craig took turns helping me at Adderbury. It was unbelievably exciting. Unable to accept with grace British hostility to a standard-size electric plug – to say nothing of the custom of selling goods without anything attached to make them work – I was jubilant when I screwed the last of the manifold plugs in place. The rooms were sparely furnished, but each of them was ready. The pale carpet throughout – haircord though it was – seemed, curiously, the most exciting of all.

The Friday after Tony was back in England, I drove with Clea to Adderbury. Late that afternoon he departed Marsham Street. He travelled by train, the better to savour what lay ahead – his first time inside the mill. I met him at Banbury station.

'Incredible,' he said, as he walked slowly from room to room, through the garden, surveyed the millpond. 'It's actually happened. Absolutely incredible.'

The following morning, soon after waking, he began to breathe heavily. There was also, from our open bedroom window, the distant but unmistakable sound of lorries toiling up a hill. Over breakfast – at Adderbury we ate breakfast downstairs – he looked grim. 'Something unfortunate has happened,' he said. His voice was hoarse, issuing in a bronchial wheeze. (This wheeze was hard for one to judge, sometimes genuine enough, other times brought into play when he was out of sorts – especially when he felt put upon. After a succession of late-night sittings at the Commons, when he was finally permitted to start for Lansdowne Road, it was his Government driver, Chris Green, who as usual bore the brunt. Directly behind him would commence this alarming sound, rather like violas warming up. Sometimes Tony would maintain it until he'd reached the top of the stairs outside our bedroom, when normal breathing would resume.) 'We must have a serious discussion. Shall we have it over mid-morning coffee? 11.45?'

At 11.45 I took our coffee into the sitting-room, where he worked in his armchair. I sat down.

'I think we've bought the wrong house,' he said.

'Oh.'

'It's two things. You didn't tell me there was all that sound of traffic.'

'Sometimes when the wind is blowing the wrong way you hear a distant humming, but it's never been like this morning. It must be because the other main road out of Banbury is blocked for repairs and everything is pouring along the one road. I'm sure it's temporary.'

'The other thing is my weak chest. I know you've spent ten years looking for a country cottage with water beside it. Neither of us considered that as water flows through a hollow – in this case actually under the house – the air is bound to be damp. If I'm going to get bronchitis every time we come here, I don't think Adderbury will prove a success.'

'I do see that. Anyway, as so far not a penny has been paid for it, I suppose one shouldn't have expected it to last for long.'

'You always carry things to extremes. I'm not suggesting that we sell it immediately. I'm asking whether we have got carried away with the idea that Adderbury is a fairy-tale come true. How would you feel if it was not the ultimate home we'd intended – if one day, we decided there was somewhere even better than Adderbury? Neither of us likes moving, I know.'

'Supposing we thought of it as our penultimate home?'

'Your saying that makes all the difference. What I minded was feeling we'd made a mistake and were stuck with it for the rest of our lives. Now that we can think of it as our penultimate home, I'm happy again.' His voice had lost all trace of bronchial symptoms. He no longer felt fenced in. Thenceforth, not only did his 'weak chest' not suffer at Adderbury: I was the only one who noticed the sound of traffic when the wind blew the wrong way. 'Penultimate' and 'ultimate' became our shorthand for a less than perfect weekend and a perfect one.

That autumn he made a week's visit to Central America. When the General Secretary of the Socialist International was asked by the President of Costa Rica who should lecture there on democratic socialism in Europe, he mentioned two names: Bruno Kreisky, the Chancellor of Austria, and Anthony Crosland. Tony was invited and accepted: D. Mac went with him. To learn more while they were about it they visited Venezuela as well.

Unlike Costa Rica, in Venezuela the British Ambassador was in residence. He gave a party for the Secretary of State. The Secretary of State talked to the appropriate people. Then D. Mac noticed he'd gone. The Ambassador's wife said: 'Where is the Secretary of State? There are all these other people who have not yet been able to talk with him.'

He was sitting on the patio outside his bedroom in the darkness, looking at the moon shining on the swimming pool, a whisky in his hand. As soon as he heard D. Mac's footsteps he said: 'Yes, I know, David. You're going to tell me I'm failing in my duty. Give me five minutes and I'll come back.'

And he did. He gave them his undivided attention. Then having done it, he looked at his watch.

'What would you most like now?' he asked D. Mac as they went to their rooms.

'I don't know.'

'I'd like to be instantly home with my wife.'

Still Have a Vision

He returned to his wife and the voracious demands of DOE, Cabinet, a Parliament with frequent all-night sittings – a familiar enough combination of interests. The steady, painful cutting back of local services was accepted reasonably well by local authorities because of the good will engendered by the Consultative Council he'd created. But rumours coming from the Treasury were terrible.

The danger, he wrote in his reflections on government during his August holiday, 'is that the inevitable disillusionment will go too far, as in '68–70. What must therefore do is: (1) choose & *announce* limited number of priorities; (2) create sense that still have a *vision* despite constraints – haven't given up long-term goals.'

At home he walked up and down the study late at night. On the last day of October he wrote again to the Prime Minister, enclosing a copy of the long systematic letter he had just written to the Think Tank, setting out his relative priorities for public expenditure – low, middling, high – and the reasons for his categories, where subsidies should be restrained if politically possible, where investment would certainly have to increase.

In the short covering letter to the Prime Minister he wrote:

PUBLIC EXPENDITURE: I am enclosing a letter which I have written to Dick Ross [a member of the Think Tank] in reply to a query from him about social policy.

My letter (which I fear may cause offence in some quarters) is an attempt to bring the question of priorities in public spending out into the open. We have had one helpful discussion about this at Chequers. But I fear that in the pressure of events interest in this may wane unless someone now revives it – and in concrete and specific terms. This I have sought to do, and to do in a non-departmental frame of mind; two of my three big spending categories appear as 'low priority'.

I hope you may think that other Cabinet Ministers might be

encouraged to set out their (*non*-departmental) priorities in the same way.

I am copying this to all members of Cabinet and to Sir John Hunt.

A.C.

High priorities were: overseas aid – 'A test of a Labour Government's conscience'; urban aid – 'Now an utter shambles because totally unco-ordinated. Needs more money and a change in the machinery of government'; social service cash benefits – 'Direct help to less well-off'; housing – 'I cannot do better than quote the comments of Gordon Oakes, a (non-Housing) Minister in my Department.' Among his comments, Oakes stressed the wider social effects of homelessness: 'In my experience bad housing, overcrowding etc. is the greatest single factor in broken marriages with inevitably resultant social service expenditure on single-parent families ... The review might well consider ... to what extent increase in housing expenditure will reduce social service expenditure as well as the significant reduction in human unhappiness.'

Labour's Chief Secretary to the Treasury since 1974, Joel Barnett, has written in his account of those years, *Inside the Treasury*, that Tony was 'the Minister who had the greatest impact on Cabinet decisions on most issues.'

However, the impact seems to have been psychological rather than practical: Cabinet paid lip service to his strategy; individual Ministers then declined to put the strategy into effect. 'Each time a spending Minister argued with the Treasury,' Barnett told me, 'except for Tony, not one of them offered to sacrifice a low priority for the sake of a high priority.'

In November 1975 the Chancellor announced that up to a further £3¾ billion must be cut from public expenditure. The Secretary of State for the Environment led the resistance: the Treasury had not made its case. His strongest ally was Barbara Castle; they came within two votes of defeating Denis Healey.

'As usual on PESC,' Tony said to me, 'the Chancellor has a built-in majority: PM squared beforehand, two ex-Chancellors parading their wounds, and eight people – as always, the Lord Chancellor, Lord Privy Seal, Wales, Agriculture, etc. – too timid to resist talk of the pound and international confidence etc. etc.'

With December came the bilateral struggles between the Treasury and each spending department. Barbara and Tony fought very rough battles indeed. Tony volunteered to accept the Treasury's cuts in roads and some other environmental services, but he wouldn't budge on housing. When the tussle reached Cabinet he had to yield a little, though he salvaged most of his programme – 'but only after slamming my papers together in a gesture of resignation and scaring Harold,' he said. 'A cut in housing investment *would* have been a resigning issue, coming on top of – in my view – an over-large total of cuts.' It was the only time he got close to resigning.

Until the end of 1975 he had carried out his Transport responsibilities, but with some detachment. He'd spent ages in Opposition developing a socialist transport policy – chairing a group whose report was set out in *Socialist Commentary*. When he became Secretary of State at DOE he made it clear that this policy should now be taken into account. One of the Permanent Secretaries, Sir Robert Marshall, had never heard of *Socialist Commentary*. Private Office gave him his copy; Sir Robert engrossed himself in it, other Southern Region commuters peering at him uneasily over the top of their *Daily Telegraph* and *Financial Times*.

Yet during his long preoccupation with Housing, Tony said more than once: 'Transport is a great bore.' Having got Housing under control, at Christmas he took all the Transport briefs to Adderbury, spent much of his holiday reading through an immense intricate document compiled by civil servant specialists. 'Had forgotten Transport was so interesting,' he said. 'Right.'

On his return to Marsham Street in January 1976, he summoned all the officials concerned to tell them what had come to him after reflecting on the huge review they'd been beavering away on for years.

'We've never had a Minister who took a subject apart like this, re-thought it and re-presented it in this way,' said Sir Idwal Pugh.

A new pattern began: each morning before leaving Lansdowne Road, Tony would ring the Private Office official who dealt with Transport, D. Mac. 'I want to know the following things.' He'd have thought out and rewritten the previous night's draft. He wanted the new information and then wanted to think it out again. He was systematically applying first principles.

Some Ministers take four boxes home regularly – because they want to feel in touch with every bit of paper that moves, or they can't delegate, or they feel lonely without a lot of boxes. Tony adamantly refused to be smothered by masses of papers: 'They cramp vision.' He could rarely be induced to take home more than one box. When Private Office opened it in the morning, they simply photocopied whole pages with his writing in the margin.

'It was a fairly unusual way of doing business,' Sir Ian Bancroft said to me. '(1) Raw material was presented by the Department. (2) Written comment was made by the Minister in his own fair hand which (3) formed the agenda for discussion which ended up in (4) the Green Paper – with his personal imprint on it.' Tony's enumeration habit was catching.

The aim was to produce a practical, socialist transport policy. Priority was to be switched away from building more motorways mostly used by better-off business travellers. Railway passengers would have to pay more: he wanted to move away from the regressive policy of subsidising the better-off who could afford to live in country comfort and commute to London. More money was to be allocated to coach and to local bus services. Road tax would be abolished and replaced with higher petrol tax, on the principle that working people who use their cars largely for weekend family visits should not have to pay the same tax as those who use the roads daily.

Every major point of the entire roads programme that the officials had assembled was called into question. Things became tumultuous among them, one very senior official shouting at another: 'Jesus Christ. You know better than that.' What he meant was that they must produce what the Minister had asked them to produce.

What threw a number of them was his capacity – in the middle of concentrated argument – suddenly to make unexpected statements. 'We need worse roads in the UK, not better. On the continent roads are so bumpy that you can't fall asleep at the wheel.' On the drive from Marsham Street to Adderbury, he regularly remarked to Chris that while it was all very well for him, the M40 was underused. To his officials at Marsham Street he said: 'The M40 is a beautiful piece of engineering. But it has no traffic on it. How absurd.' Everyone could see the Transport man blanch.

Some civil servants wondered whether it was a game. 'In fact it was a device,' D. Lip said, '(1) to show people round the conference table that he was not inclined to take the roads man's advice: others should speak; (2) that it's important to observe with one's eyes and take personal factors into account: a politician should not be a purely rational animal, whereas the civil servant's ethos depends on looking at problems from pure logic; (3) a way of challenging assumptions.'

Often asked if Anthony Crosland was not arrogant, Bancroft preferred the phrase 'self-sufficient'. 'In areas like Housing – later Transport – he was the alpha plus expert and he knew it. He hewed his own course a great deal. What I found most intriguing were all those corners he had. His interest in politics, international, national, Party. His immense preoccupation with family; it was never overtly mentioned: it was just evident. Grimsby. Football and all that. His writing. What he showed not the slightest interest in was social life: he'd been through that.'

Late one night in March, working at home, Tony completed the final draft of the Transport Review. When he strolled into our bedroom, he was exhilarated: another of these colossal subjects was pointed in the right direction. He would now oversee its progress through Cabinet and Parliament. That's what he thought when he came to bed and shaved in the morning.

That particular morning, 16 March 1976, I left Lansdowne Road for King's Cross station before he was awake. Except for special occasions – Mayor's Sunday – and elections, I went by myself to Grimsby. This had come about through Tony's belief in maximising time: if I went separately I wasn't trailing round behind him. I had my own relationship with Grimsby. On these trips I stayed with Florence and Jack Franklin who had my schedule waiting.

Jack was at the station to meet me. 'A *Grimsby Evening Telegraph* reporter and photographer are waiting at the Victoria Street café, Susan. It's just been announced that Harold Wilson has resigned. They want to talk to you about the leadership contest. Let's stand here for a moment while you think what you want to say.'

At this time Jeremy Thorpe's leadership of the Liberal Party was in its last spasms. I thought Jack Franklin had mixed up the names.

'No,' he said. 'I'm talking about the Prime Minister. He has resigned.'

When I reached Lansdowne Road again late that night, Tony said that when Harold made his announcement at Cabinet they were transfixed.

►►37◄◄

The Leadership Contest

Not many weeks before, at an official dinner given by the Foreign
Secretary, James Callaghan, I sat one side of Jim who conversed
amiably for a bit and then sensibly gazed ahead, resting from the
day's pressures. On my other side sat an MP who lectured me on
the need for Tony to 'gather troops' against the day when Harold
would resign. 'Tony never once has invited me to his room. He
hasn't invited me to an official dinner. This is the third dinner that
Jim has invited me to.'

I began to laugh. 'DOE doesn't actually go in much for this sort
of occasion. Tony is accessible in his room at the House if you want
to see him.'

This subject of 'gathering troops' was first registered by me, I
think, in the latter years of Opposition when people were fed up
with the emotionalism of the extreme pro- and anti-Europeans,
some of whom had become positively embarrassing. Why should
the Party's political theorist not lead it one day when Harold
eventually went? A woman activist summed things up: 'The trouble
with you, Tony, is that you give everyone the impression that you
don't care whether you get to No. 10 or not.'

'How can I help it?' Tony said. '(a) As long as Harold is there,
it doesn't arise; (b) I'm not sure I'd be willing to give up more time
with my wife and family, whom I happen to enjoy. And can you
imagine the sheer bloody boredom of having to turn up regularly
for Prime Minister's Questions two days a week?'

'He can't really mean that, can he?' Roy Hatt said to me in frank
disbelief.

He did. Tony had a deep ambivalence about the leadership.
Most politicians have conflicting feelings, though the balance varies
greatly. Some think almost all the time of climbing the ladder. In
others the ladder is a dormant consideration.

Dick Leonard, his PPS in Opposition, did not share this ambivalence. His and Tony's differences over Europe hadn't altered
their friendship. Tony felt deep affection for Dick and Irène Leonard, they for him. Dick nagged away with patient good humour

on this business of gathering troops. Periodically he produced a fresh dossier showing Tony's current listing in press speculation about prospective Leaders.

'All this conjecture really is fatuous when you think about it,' Tony said to Dick. 'Except for the Roy phenomenon – when he alone seemed the potential successor – there have always at any given moment been four or five decent middle-aged gentlemen, anyone of whom would make a perfectly acceptable Leader. Don't you agree?'

'Perhaps,' said Dick. 'But you're the only one of them who could view it with that detachment.'

Dick left Parliament in the February 1974 election. He went on nagging. His successor as Tony's PPS, Peter Hardy, a Yorkshireman, joined in. Sometimes they gave Tony a bad conscience. 'I'll tell Peter that I'll eat in the Members' Dining Room tomorrow night instead,' became a regular preamble when he rang me in the early evening from his room at the House. 'But tonight it would be absolute bliss if you could bring health soup and sandwiches here so we can have an hour together and catch up on gossip.'

At some point he worked out a fantasy. 'I've solved the problem: I can satisfy my loyal handful of supporters and still have some privacy with my wife. The fantasy goes like this: I continue to divide my energies as usual. That means not gathering troops,' he added, knowing my wariness of this subject, 'even supposing there are any to be gathered. Yet despite no troops there is mounting demand within the PLP for Crosland to assume the Leader's mantle. When demand reaches a point where it cannot be resisted, he says he will accept it, but only after consultation with his doctors. I then omit to take my blood-pressure tablets for several days, call upon old Sawbones for examination, that great man discovers my blood pressure has soared. A press conference is summoned and Crosland – flanked by GP and consultant – says he is deeply honoured but must decline the crown on the advice of his doctors. Having stepped down, I immediately start taking my pills again.'

And now Harold had suddenly resigned. Tony was forced to face his ambivalence. Did he still believe what he had said to Dick Leonard only a year or so before? The fact was that while Crosland revisionism was sometimes said to be the basis of two recent Labour Governments, it had never been put into practice.

Harold's resignation announcement was on a Tuesday. That evening as I returned from Grimsby, I looked out the train window for an hour. I had something to face as well. Having got as far as I could in that direction, I exercised will and took Iris Murdoch's latest novel out of my hold-all – a handy author to have around when one wants to take the mind off complications in one's own life.

When I reached Lansdowne Road at midnight, Tony asked me how I felt about it.

'On the train I was thinking that it's a bit like that baby. I failed. You never minded, and now I'm glad I failed. But if I hadn't tried, I might have always taxed myself in moments of depression – said "if only". That must be terrible. Perhaps the best thing would be to try – so you could never have regrets afterwards – and fail.'

'I think the best thing would be to come second,' Tony said, 'not that there is the slightest reason to think that likely.'

At nine o'clock on Wednesday morning Bruce Douglas-Mann turned up at Lansdowne Road. A backbencher on Shelter's board, he'd worked with Tony on housing. He'd come to discuss the case for contesting the leadership. Tony hadn't made up his mind. 'I'm not sure I even *want* to be Prime Minister. Though I'm perfectly sure I don't want to come bottom of the poll,' he said as he left home.

A little later on Wednesday morning in his room at the House, he met with a handful of MPs and the two DLs. Everyone present knew he didn't want to give up more of his private life. They also knew he was committed to social change. If he threw his hat in the ring, what were his chances?

'Unfortunate that it's come three years too soon,' said Gordon Oakes. Peter Hardy summed up: 'Probably you are most MPs' second choice. You are few MPs' first choice. What would become your vote in the second ballot will go to others in the first ballot. Were it a straight fight you could win. But it's very doubtful that you can get in that position: you're unlikely to get through the first ballot.'

Under the system then used in selecting the Labour Leader, only MPs voted. Successive ballots were held, each time the bottom man knocked off, until one candidate had a clear majority. Had Harold stayed on through the Government's likely term of office, it was generally assumed that Jim Callaghan would be too old to succeed him. By resigning in March 1976, however, Harold made Jim his likely successor. In the view of Tony's supporters, if he couldn't get through the first ballot, the votes would then be carved up between Callaghan and Foot.

Jim's base in the Party was deeper and more extensive than

anyone else's. He'd been operating for thirty years. Tony always
thought it was a natural part of Jim's character to do this, not cold
calculation: politicking was his life. When members of the PLP
elect a Leader, most have a perfectly natural interest in someone
who will give jobs to his supporters. Jim delivered the goods.

Tony – everyone agreed on this – was personally disadvantaged
by the jobs he held, no matter what was achieved in them. DOE
lacks glamour, nor can its administrator please people: he is usually
refusing councillors who find it convenient to blame him. It is
better to have a job with status that doesn't upset so many colleagues. He had no base.

None the less, if he stood he would be 'putting down a marker'
– he could both get over the message that he had a coherent vision
of what a democratic socialist Britain ought to be, and be seen
outside Cabinet and Whitehall to be the strongest fighter for egalitarian policies. And if he could get through the first ballot, everything would look different: he might then do well on the second
ballot. He was risking nothing except the humiliation of coming
bottom of the first ballot.

On the other hand, humiliation could not be entirely ignored. It
would be disagreeable for the man and for his supporters. And –
the argument had to be faced – would it diminish Tony's general
clout? The half-dozen men dispersed to take soundings among
their colleagues in the House.

As a Minister of State at the Foreign Office, Roy Hattersley
found himself in Bulgaria when Westminster's world erupted.
Frantically he was trying to reach Tony by international telephone.
DOE said that the Secretary of State had already left for the Palace.
Hattersley thought he was going mad until Private Office explained
that Prince Philip was giving a dinner to discuss a housing fund.
Roy Hatt was trying to reach Tony to implore him not to contest
an election that he was certain could only result, for Tony, in a
damagingly small vote.

Like most decisions, it was settled by temperament. Pride was
involved: could he stand back and seem to acknowledge that others
who had put their names on the sheet were better than he? Recklessness was involved. Stubbornness was involved. He threw his
hat in the ring. By Wednesday afternoon the candidates were:
Benn, Callaghan, Crosland, Foot, Jenkins. Denis Healey had not
yet decided whether it would be better to skip this round and wait
for another day.

Tony was clearly the dark horse. 'I expect to draw my support from those who are looking for the common ground which unites both Left and Right in my Party,' he said in his statement.

On Wednesday evening, his little band of supporters met again in his room, genuinely sad. Gordon Oakes put his hand on Tony's knee and told him that humiliation was his only prospect in this contest: whatever way they counted heads, they saw no possibility of his getting through the crucial first ballot. They didn't want to see him hurt. Peter Hardy said: 'Given the slim chance of success, there's something to be said for your withdrawing and supporting Jim. It wouldn't hurt your chance of a better job than the killing slog of Environment.'

Thursday brought fresh human factors into play. Tony's entry in the race had made Denis Healey's life more awkward than it was already. On Thursday evening Denis decided he'd better put his marker down too. This in turn made it psychologically even harder for Tony to consider withdrawal. It must have been about then that Roy Hattersley, unable longer to endure being on the sidelines in Bulgaria, cut short his official visit and returned to the smoke of battle in Westminster where he at once began to work actively for Callaghan. He called in Roy Jenkins's room to tell him. Would Roy Jenkins like to know why Roy Hattersley was not voting for him?

He'd be very interested, Roy Jenkins said.

Roy Hattersley told him why. His growing lack of sympathy with Jenkins's political position was reinforced by Jenkins's recent television broadcast saying that more than 60 per cent of national income devoted to public expenditure would lead to tyranny – quite the opposite of what Tawney and Crosland had written and Hattersley himself believed. Hattersley was supporting Callaghan for fear of 'splitting the vote' and letting Foot in.

Roy Jenkins said he quite understood and hoped this would in no way affect their friendship. The two men have had the most perfunctory of relations since.

Hattersley then called on Tony at DOE and repeated his intention of supporting Callaghan. 'Would you like to know why I'm not voting for you?'

'No. Fuck off.'

When the lift decanted Roy Hatt on the ground floor, he was met with a message to go back up again. 'Let's keep in touch,' Tony said. A drink over the weekend was fixed.

On Friday morning I set off for King's Cross station and Grimsby. It was the Friday for the Grimsby Labour Ladies' Spring

Fayre. Tony was waiting to meet me at King's Cross on Saturday morning. He was quite glad to see me again.

'How are you feeling?' I asked.

'Bruised and stubborn.'

Late Sunday morning, a handful of Labour-based supporters were working in our drawing-room when the Hattersleys arrived for a pre-lunch drink. Tony insisted on formal introductions. 'This is Roy Hattersley. He's going to vote for Callaghan and is going round forcing people to listen to the hard truth as if he were a member of the Oxford Movement.'

When the four of us were upstairs in the study, Roy Hatt's first words were that Tony must think him 'perfidious'.

'That is not a deserved description,' Tony said. 'You are career-minded, yes. I'm sorry that you're supporting Callaghan in the first ballot. But I certainly don't blame you. As for "perfidious", no. You've been entirely candid about your changes of allegiance.'

Shortly before the list for the first ballot was to close on Monday – not quite a week since Harold dropped his bombshell – Roy Hatt came to Tony's room with a message. Jim, he said, was in a particularly aggressive mood (the kind of mood he gets in when he's on the defensive, Tony recalled from Jim's pre-Devaluation days at the Exchequer). It was no good, Jim had said angrily, Tony coming along *after* the first ballot to offer his support; he must offer it before the first ballot or else Jim had not the slightest interest in him – or words to that effect.

'If nothing else would have confirmed my decision to remain as a candidate, it was that message from Jim,' said Tony. He also asked me to give the children and his sisters a ring and tell them not to be distressed on his account. 'Tell them I'll find it a little bruising, but only a minor episode.'

Monday evening produced a surrealistic touch. While those MPs who thrive on campaigning parleyed in the House, using every device to induce a colleague to vote for their man, at No. 10 the candidates – along with the rest of the Cabinet – were attending a farewell dinner for the departing Prime Minister, Harold Wilson.

'It turned out entertaining,' Tony said, 'despite the fact that at least six people present may from time to time have had their thoughts elsewhere. Tony Benn gave a riotous performance, reading out an obit on Harold which he'd been asked by *The Times* to write in 1953. Also, Jim – who was on one side of me – raised a notion that was intellectually engaging.'

Jim had said something on the lines of: 'I hear all of you think I couldn't have got a Second if I'd gone to Oxford.' Conscious of his lack of a university education, Callaghan – unlike George Brown – didn't carry it around as a chip.

Tony considered the remark and then replied that Jim could have got a First. 'The trouble is not with your IQ: it's that you don't allow yourself enough time for reflection. You read through a brief on economics, say, and take the points quickly enough, but you then don't take forty-eight hours to reflect on whether they are actually going to achieve what is intended.' Jim was attentive to this, and they discussed it a bit more. 'Another thing that pleased me about the dinner was the friendliness among the competitors. Mind you, that may not still be so by next week, but it was so tonight,' Tony said to me.

After the dinner, six of the guests made their farewell as rapidly as decency permitted and headed back to the House. The following morning the Cabinet met as usual.

The polls were united about one candidate: Crosland could not get through the first ballot. His little team remained dogged. So poignant did I find this that I wanted to do something too – at least make a gesture. I rang Ron Pollard, public relations director of Ladbroke's where Susan Barnes kept a not very active account for placing political bets: this meant we hadn't to put up cash for a £50 bet, which usually we won; if we lost, we had until the end of the month to settle. Ron Pollard was out, but his assistant said Ladbroke's was giving odds of 66-1 against Crosland winning the leadership. She put me through to a clerk who said the odds were 50-1.

'Ron Pollard's assistant just told me they were 66-1,' I said, determined to have the highest possible odds on this impossible undertaking. The clerk said to hang on. I heard him talk to someone else, then say: 'You must be joking.' When he came back to me, it was clear he had learned Susan Barnes's married name.

'You can have the 66-1 odds,' he said. 'Do you really think he can survive the first ballot?'

'I haven't the slightest idea. But isn't it correct that if I lose £100 on the first ballot, I can get it back by placing a more cautious bet on the next one?' That was correct, he replied.

At Lansdowne Road, the telephone was again in a hyper-active phase. One call later that day was from neither politician nor journalist, which at least made a change. It was Ron Pollard.

'Why did you do that?' he asked.

'Some sort of bravado.'

A similar emotion led Terry Heiser and D. Mac to walk round to a betting shop near Marsham Street where each placed £15 on a man they knew couldn't possibly win.

During the afternoon Tony rang. He was cheerful. He was at DOE with work that he enjoyed. And he'd been encouraged by the general political attitude of the younger Fabians he'd addressed that morning. An economist he respected, Maurice Peston, had chaired the meeting. Peston – like Dennis Skinner the day before – told Tony that he could not have done other than stand and that his only difficulty now would be the pain of the next night's humiliation.

I said: 'It seems quite wrong in terms of simple arithmetic that two people sharing the pain of one cannot halve it.'

Tony said: 'What you have done is alleviate it. I told Maurice Peston that I could get through the public humiliation because I have a happy marriage and we have just bought a country cottage.'

At the Commons that evening he was put in a good mood by George Cunningham who'd had a flaming row with him a few weeks before. George called in at Tony's room to say he'd be voting for him. 'I think you're going to poll more than the single figures that the other camps are saying is all you'll get,' he said, adding: 'Mind you, if the press knew the motley collection of screwballs and crackpots who make up your basic support, you'd be finished for good.'

When the divisions were over and he came home, he was tired and less cheerful. Instead of gossiping about our different days, he read my erratic diary's account while he unwound, made an addition with the red-inked pen from Private Office, handed the pages over to me so I could read them too. We talked for a bit. I asked how many votes he would find not too bad.

'10–15: disaster. 15–20: very bad. 20–25: tolerable. 25–30: good. 30–35: very good. Anything over 35: sensational.'

'What number do you actually expect?'

'This is the psychological factor. I'm always optimistic. That's the difficulty. So I think I will stick at the two DLs' figure of 23.'

On Thursday morning Cabinet met as usual. In the afternoon Tony led a Grimsby deputation to a meeting with the Secretary of State for Employment, Michael Foot: Grimsby was threatened with a closure. Next came a meeting with anxious representatives of the fishing industry. Finally, at 6 p.m., the PLP assembled in Room 14 of the Commons to learn the results of the first ballot:

Foot 90, Callaghan 84, Jenkins 56, Benn 37, Healey 30, Crosland 17.

'We were out to establish a position in the Centre of the Party. It is a foundation on which growing support can be built for Tony Crosland as a candidate of the Centre,' Peter Hardy said to the press.

'It's better than your opponents predicted. They said you couldn't get more than single figures,' I said to Tony.

'It's very bad,' he said to me.

Immediately after the results were known, Tony Benn announced his withdrawal, asking his supporters to vote for Michael Foot. Roy Jenkins's group met. Their man had polled 133 votes in the 1970 deputy leadership contest; his present vote fallen to 56, the writing was on the wall. David Owen advised Roy to go to the EEC: it need not rule out Roy's returning to British politics. Roy withdrew from the leadership contest, but he left his options open: if he could become Foreign Secretary, things might still be all right. Denis Healey stuck, refused to withdraw. This meant three ballots would almost certainly be required before Britain's Prime Minister was elected.

An hour or so after the results of the first ballot were announced, Tony got home. I took our supper upstairs. The fact that the low vote was expected did not lessen the humiliation. He took it very well, though there were moments of feeling down. While he was reflecting in the bath, the telephone, quiet again, rang.

'Susan, it's Roy Hattersley. How is Tony?'

'Oh he's all right.'

'Well . . .' He waited for some assistance from my end. 'I just rang to say hello and goodbye. That hasn't come out very well. What I'm trying to say is that I just wanted to make contact.'

'Oh.'

'Will you tell Tony that I'll be talking to him later this weekend?'

On Friday morning when the Secretary of State for Environment got to Marsham Street, he found on his desk a bottle of champagne and a note 'with sympathy and indignation', signed by everyone in Private Office. After Cabinet he came home for a sandwich lunch with me. Later we drove to Adderbury for a weekend convalescence, re-examined our beautiful half-acre of wild garden ('Let us look over our estate,' he said), entertained Beckermans and McCarthys to a convivial lunch, slept.

On Monday he returned to Marsham Street and its demands. That evening I went to a wake he gave himself in his room at DOE, his method of expressing thanks to Private Office – Terry, D. Mac, Noreen Bovill, Margaret Turner – who had been marvellous during the run-up to the first ballot.

On Tuesday I rang Ron Pollard again. I had to put £800 on Callaghan in order to recover my £100 bet on Tony and have a tiny bit left over. Good thing I had an account. Later that day at the PLP meeting in Room 14, the result of the second ballot was announced: Callaghan 141, Foot 133, Healey 38.

While waiting for Jim to win the third ballot and start making his arrangements, there was more than enough at Environment to occupy the mind. Tony loved DOE more than any other Department. At the same time he was compelled by the past fortnight to accept the much propounded view of supporters – in and out of Parliament – that he needed to have one of the three great offices of state that carry a clout all their own, no matter that in 1976 two of these wielded less real power than two lower-ranking Departments, DOE and Industry. The Home Office, at that time not caught up in cardinal moral and political issues, didn't interest Tony – though when people speculated that it could be offered to someone of his abilities only with an extra job thrown in, Ulster or Devolution for instance, and he said Ulster would be 'a challenge', my heart sank.

Even if Tony were offered Ulster alone, Peter Hardy told him, he should really not refuse; he could not lose by it. Tony replied: 'I see that, although I don't think Susan would be amused. Still, the Parachute Regiment might be there.'

He hoped for either the Exchequer or the Foreign Office, but he knew Denis Healey was unlikely to be moved from the Exchequer at that moment. Rather to my surprise, the Foreign Office began to appeal to him. 'My international reputation among socialist intellectuals is not being used by my own country. I'd like to be involved in international affairs for a while. I'm even prepared to put up with the boredom of all those ambassadors.'

For me, no news is unsettling, not good. No one had the faintest idea what kind of Prime Minister Jim would wish to be. I looked forward to the end of the third ballot so we could find out. To my erratic diary I said: 'If we end up with the bloody boring Home Office plus some impossible task like Ulster or Devolution, I shall quietly scream.'

When the result of the final ballot was announced on Monday 5 April and James Callaghan became Prime Minister, Tony wrote him a letter. He asked that two of his supporters be promoted. He was embarrassed when speaking about this to his PPS. He had not done it as patronage, he told Peter Hardy; he felt both men were qualified for promotion. (Neither was immediately promoted.) His own future remained unknown.

We slept late Thursday morning, and Tony was shaving when I answered the telephone at ten. Margaret Turner, his Diary Secretary, said: 'The Secretary of State has been summoned to Downing Street. He is to be there at 10.45.'

'Yep,' I said, my asperity produced by the 'summoned' bit, a word I disliked just then. Tony shaved more briskly and departed.

Some time after noon Margaret rang to say that the Secretary of State had asked her to let me know he was 'fairly cheerful' and would be back for lunch with me. Eileen was just leaving as he walked in the door. They chatted a bit before he came upstairs, changed into the red carpet slippers, poured himself a drink.

'Would *you* like a little drink just for a change?' he said.

He poured a token vodka into a miniature blue goblet kept in the study for that purpose. Ordinarily I don't like alcohol until the evening meal is in sight.

'What do you think it is?' he asked. I guessed DOE and was wrong. A fortnight after finishing bottom of the leadership poll, he was Foreign Secretary. After our sandwich lunch, we lay down to collect our thoughts, and then he returned to DOE.

When it was known in the afternoon that he was going, David McDonald could not face the goodbye. He went off to another floor to have a drink with the Transport minister. When he got back to Private Office, the Secretary of State had gone. It had taken him longer than usual to leave, the rest of Private Office said. He had opened the door which leads from Private Office to the corridor, and shut it again. 'I shall miss you all just like family.' A second time he opened and shut the door. 'I shall really miss you. I have come to think of you as family.' It took him five minutes opening and shutting the door before he went out and closed it behind him.

⇥ 38 ⇤

Learning to Live with One Another

On Friday morning, instead of driving to Marsham Street, Chris bore the Secretary of State to Downing Street West. Victoria's Foreign Office was built to display the Empire's power and glory, a grandiose double staircase ascending to a principal floor of inordinate splendour, colossal height. When I arrived for a sandwich lunch with the Foreign Secretary, I thought he had shrunk and Private Office was staffed entirely by pygmies. (I later realised that the Principal Private Secretary, Ewen Fergusson, was even taller than Tony, a rugby player to boot.) Tony said that when I walked through the door, it went through his mind that I had shrunk. Even the ingenuity of Tony Benn – who called on his colleague and whipped out his pocket-instant automatic camera – couldn't get the Foreign Secretary into focus and also show the height of the room.

At the same time as Tony and I were eating our sandwiches (presented on a silver salver) and prowling round this astonishing room, elsewhere two Principal Private Secretaries lunched together: Ewen Fergusson wanted to learn from Terry Heiser a little more of the Foreign Secretary's temperament. 'He's quite a disconcerting person if the first morning is anything to go by. We knew he was a very strong character but hadn't quite realised how little he bothers with the icing and lubricants of social life,' Ewen Fergusson said. He knew Anthony Crosland was from a not-very-different background to the public school products who make up the higher echelons of the Foreign Office: they must share at least some cultural interests. Ewen Fergusson knew a thing or two about twelfth-century stone carvings at Autun.

'That may be,' said Terry Heiser, 'but don't think things will be cosy. He has his extended family to which D. Lip is admitted. Don't you attempt to mix personal and official life.'

Almost the first thing Ewen had to do was arrange for a second member of the extended family to be transferred on a temporary basis from the Home Civil Service to the sacrosanct Foreign Service. The Foreign Secretary made it plain he had no intention of establishing a relationship with a new Diary Secretary. He was particularly fond of Margaret Turner. Called Maggie by herself and others, Tony used her proper name. 'Margaret's going hunting later today,' he would say when she appeared in trim culottes and fashionable boots. With quiet tenacity on his behalf she strove with the Diary.

It seemed to Ewen that the Foreign Secretary's next priority was bringing over DOE's Private Office for a farewell drink in his room at the House. I was there too. Tony wanted to hear what was happening at DOE, told them what hell the Foreign Office was. When this got back to the FO, they were disheartened. Also mystified. Except with D. Lip and Margaret, he drew a boundary round himself which the sophisticates of Private Office were very hesitant to cross.

Always disliking the first months in any job, this time the learning period was much worse because he was constantly travelling, fulfilling commitments made by his predecessor, aware that the Foreign Office was being run by the officials while he was away.

They, in turn, were resentful – amazed, really – that he should not be prepared to assume all the habitual burdens of being Foreign Secretary. He was particularly recalcitrant on the matter of ambassadors. 'It's footling to waste time like this when I ought to be learning. What's the point when I don't know what to say to him or understand what he's saying to me?'

Except for the Cod War and Rhodesia, he seemed uninterested in getting to grips with his job. Officials would recommend something. He would say: 'I don't understand it yet, so I don't want to be committed yet.' Sometimes he said: 'I shall *never* understand it.' Private Office rarely succeeded in getting him to take home more than one box. As Foreign Secretary, he was a member of more Cabinet Committees than when at DOE. Each of the red folders was a Cabinet Committee: to have all these in one box meant there would be no room for the dross which his officials felt he should read. He wanted time to think.

His predecessor at the Foreign Office, Callaghan, came to the job with experience: in Opposition he'd been spokesman on Foreign Affairs, and he also had the background knowledge of an ex-Chancellor. (Tony's successor, David Owen, had been a junior minister at Defence, wrote *The Politics of Defence*, was a

Minister of State at the Foreign Office before becoming Foreign Secretary.) Apart from international socialism, which he knew inside out, and international economics, Tony had engrossed himself for twelve years in Britain's domestic policy. As far as he was concerned, he didn't know anything about foreign affairs.

Learning something of this from D. Lip, Bill McCarthy understood it all. 'The FO isn't accustomed to having an intellectual as Foreign Secretary. They're used to people who simply try to master the brief and then take it to Cabinet. They don't know that when Tony says "I don't understand," underneath all this he begins to sort the thing out in his mind so that he can make a Crosland policy. We've all heard him say "I've not read anything about economics for years – don't know anything about economics." Rubbish. He can take in economics through his pores: that's why he plays the part he does in Cabinet. In Opposition we did a hell of a lot of work so he'd already *learned* about DOE when he got there. He was dropped from the skies into the FO.'

Meanwhile, across the Atlantic Ocean, Dr Henry Kissinger had turned his mind to southern Africa. Generally accepted as the most remarkable Secretary of State that the United States has produced in this century, Dr Kissinger's attention was drawn to southern Africa by the Cuban presence in Angola and its significance for the two power blocs. In the middle of April 1976, he made a speech in Phoenix, Arizona saying he was going to Africa to establish USA policy, particularly in relation to Rhodesia, South Africa, Angola.

In Downing Street West, FO officials had seen years of abortive attempts to negotiate with Ian Smith since he declared UDI in 1965. Wilson's *Tiger* hopes, Wilson's *Fearless* hopes, all UK hopes and enterprise had ended with Ian Smith pulling the wool over their eyes. In FO jargon, Smith was a slippery customer. Now the world's greatest global conceptualist was about to step on to the African stage. The FO intended full co-operation with him. He did not want advice from his own officials, but he accepted that it might be useful to have a briefing from the British, who knew the set-up. To that end he planned a flying visit to London before he began a gruelling fortnight visiting Kenya, Tanzania, Zambia, Zaire, Liberia, Senegal. He was to set out from Washington, DC on Friday, 23 April.

On that Friday, having spent a total of five days in Downing Street West since his appointment as Foreign Secretary a fortnight earlier, Tony set out from King's Cross station. It was the one weekend in four that his GMC met, constituency commitments tightly organised.

With so little time, the Americans hoped that the British could come to Heathrow to brief Dr Kissinger in his specially fitted plane. Here was he, the most important Secretary of State, making this detour to London. He was proud of his plane, thought people would be happy to drive to Heathrow to join him on his lovely plane. Instead he was told that the Foreign Secretary would be busy in his constituency, though Dr Kissinger was very welcome to join him for breakfast.

'It's his Grimsby weekend,' Private Office explained.

'Where is Grimsby?' Dr Kissinger asked.

Private Office said it was quite near an RAF airfield at Waddington in Lincolnshire.

'Naturally I am very grateful to Dr Kissinger for arranging to come to Waddington instead of us meeting in London,' the Borough Member said to the *Grimsby Evening Telegraph*'s chief political reporter and head photographer who accompanied him on Saturday morning to record the initial meeting of these two great men at the modest, rural airfield.

'Dr Kissinger is twenty minutes late,' his host observed as the gleaming blue and white 707 landed at 8.56 a.m. Dragged from their beds as well as Dr Kissinger were the American Ambassador, Anne Armstrong, a hundred assorted diplomats, international journalists, enough armed bodyguards to stop a revolution, only to find that the Foreign Secretary appeared to know nothing about foreign policy except for the Cod Wars – vital to Grimsby and Britain's other North Sea ports. Having elicited from Dr Kissinger the firm promise that US shipyards would not privately sell gunboats to Iceland, the Foreign Secretary asked questions about Rhodesia, then contributed little more. The Permanent Secretary of the Foreign Office, Sir Michael Palliser, noted that when this particular Minister did not feel in control of a subject, '*il est dans ses plumes*'. (Before Sir Michael became head of the Diplomatic Service, he was Britain's Ambassador to the EEC, used languages interchangeably.)

Two and a quarter hours later when Dr Kissinger and entourage departed for Africa, one or two journalists – still indisposed from the early rising – had taken the trouble to discover the Foreign Secretary's 'crucial constituency engagements in Grimsby' and were further aggravated on learning that these included watching

The Town play Gillingham while they were trying to catch up on their sleep en route to Nairobi.

'I like Kissinger,' Tony said when he returned to Lansdowne Road. 'He's just like all these New York Jewish intellectuals.'

The feeling wasn't mutual.

'At our first meeting in that hinterland,' Kissinger said a few months later, 'I realised he could master the subject. I didn't know if he wanted to.'

On 27 April, in Zambia, Dr Kissinger delivered his famous 'message of commitment and co-operation' setting out US policy on Rhodesia. 'We support self-determination, majority rule, equal rights and human dignity for all the peoples of southern Africa.'

He then went on to list his ten points, beginning with strong US support for British proposals for independence, conditional on majority rule being achieved within two years of a negotiated settlement. The message reflected almost word for word the discussion with the FO in the RAF officers' mess at Waddington.

Among his other points were two that would result in dramatic misunderstandings: the US would communicate to the Smith regime its view that a settlement leading to majority rule must be negotiated rapidly; and Dr Kissinger would consult with the Presidents of Botswana, Mozambique, Tanzania and Zambia.

In London the Foreign Office was trying to come to terms with the new Foreign Secretary. The Permanent Secretary had known from the outset that this was not an easy man to understand. 'It took me three years to get to know him,' Sir Michael Palliser said. They'd first met one another when Tony was at the Board of Trade. 'He was always extremely polite when we conducted business, but we were not on first name terms for a long time. The process of breaking the ice was slowish.' In the earlier days Palliser was 'a fly on the wall' in Cabinet. Just inside the green baize door separating the Cabinet Room from the Private Secretaries' Offices stood two chairs occupied by whichever Private Secretaries were relevant to the discussion, placed so that the Prime Minister could catch their eye to ask a question. By its nature, the Board of Trade overlapped with foreign affairs. Palliser had never seen Anthony Crosland other than in command of his subject, assumed his knowledge of foreign affairs was up-to-date.

'After his first few weeks at the Foreign Office, I realised he needed time to learn. He felt this process was impeded by things the Foreign Secretary is supposed to do – seeing ambassadors, etc., which are tedious chores but necessary.' A compromise was reached: instead of seeing the envoys individually, he met the whole lot at one reception, put himself out, was charming. I remember it because there were so many ambassadors and high commissioners and their ladies, all apparently wishing us well.

This latest transmutation had affected the Minister's wife: I felt like a seesaw. The Foreign Secretary's room in the Commons is on a different floor from most of his colleagues' and on a vastly different scale. To reach it, one must first go through an ante-room where sits a detective. I arrived there for lunch with Tony the Monday after his elevation, my own work altogether disordered. I bore health soup and sandwiches past the detective and into the Foreign Secretary's room, closing the door behind me. I found myself alone in a mausoleum.

The door opened again. Sylvia walked in, chirpy. She looked round her, then back at me.

'Not exactly cosy, is it. Are you all right, Susan?' Later she said that she'd never before seen me look daunted. 'You were really *down.*'

Only the Prime Minister, Foreign Secretary, Home Secretary and Secretary for Northern Ireland had detectives. Tony's were to prove so considerate and tactful that I grew to like them, but at the beginning they imparted a sense of privacy further constricted. It could have been much worse: Special Branch want to carry out their job of protecting the Foreign Secretary twenty-four hours a day. If he forbids this, not only can't they do their job, but they feel they'll be blamed if something happens in their absence. Foreign Secretaries deal with the matter differently – according to temperament, the size of their house, the current mood of terrorism.

When Tony came home, whichever detective was on duty walked with him to the front door of Lansdowne Road where they said goodnight, the detective then going off in the car with Chris. After walking to the front door of Adderbury, the detective was driven by Chris to Banbury, three miles away; Special Branch wanted him positioned at the nearest point. 'Absurd waste of the taxpayers' money,' Tony habitually said. The scrambler telephone at Adderbury was in a small so-called study where Tony went only when Government calls were necessary. When he became Foreign Secretary, the scrambler was adjusted so that if we needed help we could get straight through to the Banbury police, who would immediately pick up the detective and drive to Adderbury. The mill was to be wired with panic buttons. The police arrived one Monday to draw up a plan. Presumably Tony learned that panic buttons are notorious for being set off accidentally, because they were never actually installed.

Special Branch would have been happier had we moved into the official residence provided in Whitehall for the Foreign Secretary. On the one hand I was curious to see No. 1 Carlton Gardens, a maisonette of looming formality, officialdom's rooms immediately below. On the other hand, having seen it I fell into acute depression.

I called upon my GP, entered her office, closed the door, burst into tears.

'My dear girl, what is the matter?'

'I do apologise. Nothing is actually wrong. I suppose something good has happened. But I keep waking up at five in the morning and I can't get back to sleep.' Again I applied my handkerchief, so sodden that she offered me a tissue from the box on her desk.

'My dear girl, what you need is something to make you go back to sleep at five o'clock.'

She wrote out a prescription. I got some sleep. Tony settled the house problem.

'You don't want to leave Lansdowne Road. I know I used to say I'd like to live over the shop. What I didn't consider was that one would always be supervised – that the official residence is also intended for the convenience of officials.' Private Office were asked to state in words of their choosing that the Foreign Secretary had a perfectly good home of his own.

⊷ 39 ⊶

A Dangerous Line of Argument

May began. At Heathrow, we climbed into a VC-10 converted to ensure that the VIP arrives without backache. The Foreign Secretary and his wife were installed within a comfortable inner sanctum furnished with a table for four, whatever a sofa is called when it's screwed to the shell of a plane, a coffee table, and two berths behind curtains. During the next twenty-four hours I sat or lay down without regard to the hour as we sped into time a day ahead of usual. Our inner sanctum had two doors. Behind one was the crew, behind the other a score of FO officials and typists plus a regiment from the media – all sitting more or less upright.

Ewen Fergusson and the No. 2 from Private Office entered with some briefs.

'Who is this man Youde?' Tony asked while I was reading the extraordinary brief he'd just finished. The British Ambassador to Peking, Edward Youde, had distilled a complex mass of China's political history into lucid prose.

'He's a Welshman, Secretary of State. I think you'll like him,' Ewen said. 'And you'll find Mrs Youde rather different from the Ambassadress who turned the Secretary of State against her species. They both speak fluent Chinese – several dialects. They met in China before the Communist victory in 1949, Mrs Crosland,' Ewen added courteously in case I didn't know which year that revolution had taken place.

1976 was one of China's most momentous years. Outside contact remained extremely limited. 'Impact' – as distinct from 'continuous' – diplomacy was the purpose of the Foreign Secretary's six-day visit. No western Minister had been there since early April when Hua Kuo-feng became Prime Minister and heir apparent to Mao. Having achieved one of the few great revolutions – and ended with the insoluble problem posed by a cult of personality – Mao was dying, his wife dictator in his name. When we arrived in Peking the purge of the Vice-Premier, Deng Xiaoping, was in its sixth week. One of Deng's 'crimes' was his intention to open China from self-imposed isolation. What Hua intended was unknown. Tony's job was to try to find out.

Everyone was aware of China's obsessive hostility to detente between the West and Russia, but he needed to absorb first-hand any evidence of a shifting attitude to the major powers which might affect his view of Britain's relations with Russia. And he wanted to strengthen Britain's growing trading partnership with China; he hoped to return with a shipping deal among several others that would favour British exports. Politics and trade as usual were in tandem.

To these ends he had one exceptionally useful British ally, Youde, and one potentially strong Chinese ally – the able Foreign Minister, Chiao Kuan-hua. At Peking airport we were met by the Minister and his wife, who both spoke English and seemed genuinely friendly throughout the visit. (Had we arrived five months later, we'd have seen no trace of them: they were alleged to have been too close to the Gang of Four.)

Tony did not believe in the innate blessings of socialism regardless of whether people vote for it: he was not a revolutionary socialist guided by opportunity alone: he was a democratic socialist. *But* – and he had spelled this out in a letter to Philip during the war – 'where there is no democracy which can say yes or no to our Socialism, then we become revolutionary Socialists. The two conditions to be fulfilled are (1) that the general will is on our side, (2) that there is no democratic machinery through which the people can make effective their wishes.' The years had not altered his view.

The case for revolutionary socialism seemed to be met in China. What did he think of its results? He was pulled two ways.

Before he left a foreign country Tony always tried to make notes. His five concise pages on China covered the economy, culture, foreign policy, and, first and foremost, equality – the ends and means. On the plus side of the balance sheet were participation, equality between the sexes, and the determination to combat privilege, bureaucracy, remoteness. He was struck by the constant effort since the Cultural Revolution to prevent élitism. Unlike in Russia, equality in China seemed real.

When he turned to the totalitarian means, he found them repulsive. 'Total political control of every activity; total indoctrination from childhood onwards; the attempt at thought control,' he wrote on the other side of his balance sheet. 'Can they really change human nature?'

'God,' he said to me when our car stopped for a traffic light in the middle of Peking rush hour. I was spellbound by the thousands of bicycles waiting their turn to cross. There are four million people in Peking and two million bicycles. He was reacting to the loud-speakers fixed at the major crossroads, blaring the uniform phrases at the people on the bicycles, ceaselessly denouncing Deng, ad-mired a few months before, now 'the right deviationist', 'class enemy', 'chief unrepentant capitalist roader'.

'The last phrase is rather lovely,' Tony said, trying to cheer himself up as our interpreter resumed listing meaningless statistics.

We went to Peking University where with pride we were shown the wallposters, six lanes of them. 'The people are free to write or paint whatever they feel,' we were told. The texts written by all those hands were denunciations of Deng; the paintings depicting him as a monster varied only in artistic invention. Instead of talking to students the Foreign Secretary was harangued by one official after another. Tony closed his eyes, suddenly opening them when the final phrase was reached. 'Capitalist rodent! What is a capitalist rodent?' he asked.

In the clean, well-equipped school we visited sat alert, bright-faced children who twenty years earlier would have been illiterate peasants. In the English-speaking class, the teacher called upon a boy of about ten years to display his command of the language. Out of the child's mouth poured the phrases denouncing Deng. A girl was next called on. Out came the jargon. Several pupils raised their hands in excitement: their schoolmate had got a phrase wrong, and they were eager to correct her. I glanced sideways at Tony. He looked bleak.

And yet: compared with India, which has received vast volumes of foreign aid, Mao's economic achievement was markedly super-ior: everyone had enough to eat, was clothed, had shoes, had housing (however low the standard). No beggars were lying in the streets, Tony noted.

'Where is the music coming from?' I asked as we drove through mile upon mile of paddy fields between Peking and the Forbidden City, the Summer Palace, the Ming Tombs – fantastic testaments to a civilisation incomparably ahead of Europe until the eighteenth century. 'The people like to hear music while they are working,' said my interpreter just before the martial music broke off and the propaganda blared from loudspeakers scattered over the paddy fields. I was struck by how the Chinese made no attempt to divert us from their continuous effort to indoctrinate. In Russia, although we were told outright lies ('the Second World War began in 1941'), the propaganda methods were not blatantly displayed; the Russians showed an awareness of possible western responses.

Perhaps because I had visited Russia four times, had travelled across much of it by train, had at least some sense of that continent, in China I found myself often making comparisons in an effort to grasp a little from a canvas too large to deal with. Our Chinese hosts revealed, I felt, an ambivalence about the scale and richness of the testaments to their past achievements in the arts. It reminded me of the Russian ambivalence to the mother-country's treasures, preserved and cherished by the proletariat in museums that were once the homes of the Tsars. My Chinese guides proudly showed me yet another exquisite silk painting that adorned the imperial bedrooms, then added the litany about class struggle.

Like most government banquets, the Chinese banquets were lavish. Course after course appeared in an enormous bowl placed in the centre of each table for people to help themselves – though Mrs Chiao, on one side of me, or my interpreter, on the other, served me so that I had only to use my chopsticks to grapple with what was on my plate. My companions took great pleasure in my successes, clapping their hands when I'd done particularly well in negotiating the slippery beans. Tony, I noticed, used the knife and fork provided for the British.

Wives not being privy to formal talks, I was taken on a tour of the Museum of Chinese History while the Foreign Secretary negotiated with the Chinese Minister of Foreign Trade. At the end of two hours, agreements had been reached enabling easier movement for British ships and their cargoes in Chinese ports; deals had gone forward for British exports of aircraft, mining machinery, railway equipment, and so forth.

During the hour-and-a-half meeting when Prime Minister Hua and Tony were seeking some common ground between themselves and the countries they represented, I was happily shopping for blue-and-white china for Adderbury. Plates stood in piles on the floor of the narrow room; I squatted, looking for ones with clearly-painted patterns. (The 'perfect' ones were exported.) Large plates cost 5p each, small ones 3p. An old woman was the only other shopper. She bought one plate. She showed no hostility as my twenty plates were being wrapped.

It was outside Shanghai that we visited a commune. Central to the management of communist China, the communes ensure an exceptionally high degree of income equality. The Foreign Secretary was pressing in his questions about pay differentials between the sexes and was told there was none. The men and women we saw in the wheatfields and the small factories looked well-nourished on their simple diet – rice, beans, nuts, fish. The houses we saw consisted of two small rooms for a family – the back room for sleeping, the front room for everything else, cooking and other facilities at their most basic. Many Westerners are shocked by the living standards, but the British Sino-experts were in no doubt that most people's lives were materially vastly improved over what they'd known before.

When we were told that there is little crime in the communes, we had no reason to doubt it: there was little to steal and no way to sell anything stolen. Equality had produced security because everything was communal. The Commune Revolutionary Committee knew everything you were doing. There was no room for dissent of any kind. I watched Tony, this democratic socialist attached to the importance of private thought and individuality, trying to believe the benefit was worth the price.

'The Chinese are like the Russians in one respect at any rate,' he said to me that evening. 'They don't believe in conversation with foreigners – only interminable, boring, patronising, self-righteous, ignorant, inward-looking sermons.'

Although his method of interrogation was generally relaxed and good-tempered, at the same time it made plain his detestation of the conformity. And he was tired of being harangued. In Shanghai, home of the Radicals, stronghold of the Gang of Four, tension at one meeting grew so taut that the hundred representatives of two opposing ideologies seemed to be holding their breath. Two men on the platform were not. One was the Foreign Secretary, cheroot in mouth, attention fixed on a middle-aged spokesman for the People's Republic who was expounding on the twice-weekly meetings for political 'discussion' which every Chinese man and woman 'voluntarily' attends.

The Foreign Secretary took the cheroot from his mouth. 'The last thing my wife and I would want to do with a free evening is attend a political discussion,' he said amicably. 'Do all Chinese really do this *voluntarily*?'

After hesitation the spokesman repeated word for word what he had just said.

The Foreign Secretary rephrased his question. 'Just suppose your wife did not attend one of these evening political discussions. Would others notice her absence and criticise her?'

The spokesman said nothing. One felt intense unease in the

air and saw it on the British faces. Then the parrot words were repeated.

'Well then, let me put it this way. If for a perfectly good reason your wife didn't feel like going out that particular evening, would her neighbours treat her any differently the next day?'

The other person on the platform who was not holding his breath was the young, self-confident Vice-Chairman of the Revolutionary Committee in Shanghai, Hsu Ching-hsien. Tony was much taken by Hsu at the same time as not entirely accepting him. Hsu now dealt with what had become a nearly intolerable tension.

'Her neighbours *would* treat her differently the next day,' he said.

Hsu was fired by ideals, full of energy, clear on views, even cocky. And he was powerful enough to believe that when it was reported what he had said, he wouldn't suffer: he was above that kind of intimidation. Much involved in the struggle taking place for Mao's mantle, he was confident of the Radicals' success.

'People like Prime Minister Hua', one of the British Sino-experts said afterwards, 'would be briefed for that kind of session. But for people who had never been outside China, to be closely interrogated by a foreigner was a new experience. That was no reason why they should be spared.'

Some FO officials were not attracted by Tony's method. The Ambassador felt otherwise: he saw it as part and parcel of the man. 'Other politicians,' Youde said, thinking back on the visit, 'go to China concerned only with the interplay of power. Tony Crosland had a clear enough understanding of power, but his priority was different. He was interested in the restructuring of society – how society works at a deep level. He was not a man who deals off the top of the pack: he wanted to know everything about the thirteen cards in each suit, why they were there.'

A Sunday or two after our return to England, Ellen-Craig was having lunch with us at Lansdowne Road.

'What were your main impressions, Mama?'

'It seemed better than Russia. I used to hate the way our convoy of Government cars was driven through Moscow at eighty miles an hour, horns blaring, everyone else having to swerve to get out of the way. In China our cars crept along quietly. In fact, at rush hour I wondered whether we'd be engulfed by the sea of bicycles. In the markets, the produce was always arranged prettily – textures, colours – and while it was obvious that everyone could afford to buy only a little, they hadn't that terrible strained look of those women queueing in Moscow. The Chinese seemed more content.'

'China was far more horrifying than Russia.' Tony spoke sharply. 'How could you have been other than appalled by the lack of any privacy from the regime, the total lack of dissent?' He was angry. 'In Russia one can still express one's own thought, even if sometimes tortured for doing so. Unlike Galileo, I'd not have to be shown the torture instruments: they could simply be described and I'd recant on the spot, mouth whatever inanity was required. But my *thought* would still be my own.'

I said: 'But surely most Chinese never had privacy, and presumably few of them ever dared *voice* dissent. Since they all have shoes today, some sort of housing, on balance mustn't they be better off?'

He remained passionate. 'That's a dangerous line of argument. It's like saying that because people have been tortured for 900 years and you torture them a little less, they are better off. I found the Chinese forcing conformity on the privacy of human minds more abhorrent than anything I have seen in Eastern Europe, revolting as their methods also can be.'

A few months after our visit to China, the Gang of Four were overthrown. The new conformity at once replaced its predecessor. Tony asked for a note on what had become of Hsu, the intelligent and cocky young Shanghai Radical who had attracted him. When the note came through, he brought it home to show me. After the Radicals were deposed, Hsu was summoned to Peking. Like Chiao, the Foreign Minister, and his wife, he disappeared from view.

'*A Colossal Pain in the Neck*'

Because the officials who counted most judged the China trip a success, the FO had a short psychological respite from their trials. But if they were to be honest, they had not experienced any sustained pleasure for some time. They still had reservations about the Foreign Secretary. And they had not been all that happy with his predecessor, James Callaghan. The FO were prepared to see some faults in the EEC, but they retained the evangelist's faith: when Callaghan had gone to meetings on Europe and was even mildly critical of the EEC, the media were not discouraged from describing him as crass.

Dr Kissinger was a further trial. Backed by White House power, he so dominated international diplomacy that the FO's role in Rhodesia was inevitably hamstrung. What made matters most tiresome was that the FO suspected Kissinger didn't understand Rhodesian politics. Across the breakfast table at that airfield near Grimsby, the Permanent Secretary, Sir Michael Palliser, said, not for the first time: 'The crucial issue is to get rid of Ian Smith.' Instead of assessing how to get rid of Smith, Kissinger was taken for a ride by Smith. That's how FO officials saw it.

Nor were they surprised. With all his talents, Kissinger hadn't the skill, they pointed out, to get his policy through the US Congress. Furthermore, 'this German' had reduced his own professional establishment to robots: professional diplomats must be allowed some latitude if they are not to miss opportunities. Their attitude to Kissinger's 'flaw' was hardened, no doubt, when he ignored their advice as well. At the same time, some high-ranking FO officials liked the man himself immensely.

Kissinger was of course aware of the FO attitude to him. But this was offset to a large extent by the fact that Callaghan loved him. And Kissinger loved Callaghan. Each had what the other lacked. Kissinger was the intellectual who liked to understand the essence of the power struggle. Callaghan was the political-manager to the marrow: he liked to get the problem out of the way. He was glad to accept Kissinger's analysis of global dynamics. In turn, when Kissinger felt besieged in domestic politics, Callaghan could calm him down. They complemented each other.

Now Anthony Crosland had appeared on the scene and complicated matters. Kissinger was working himself into a position to say something to Callaghan. This Crosland was impossible.

UK and USA representatives sit beside one another at international meetings. In May 1976, the month after Tony became Foreign Secretary, he and Kissinger sat side by side when the OECD Ministers met at Luxembourg. Tony was taken by the originality of Kissinger's intellect and his humour, unconscious of his own effect on the US Secretary of State. Not for nothing was Kissinger a diplomat.

'Tony behaved abominably at the OECD meeting,' Henry Kissinger said to me a couple of months later. 'That is to say, he behaved sensibly but was so insulting to others. He absolutely refused to go along with convention. Meetings are meant to be of two hours' duration. You had to repeat yourself to keep the thing going that long. Each time a Minister repeated himself, Tony said: "We've already heard that. Let's move on to the next point." The meeting was over in half an hour.

'He treated me with great respect, that is to say, less disdain than the others. I thought of him as a colossal pain in the neck.'

'I may fall in love with Henry,' Tony said to me when he got back from Luxembourg.

Four days later they sat side by side in Oslo where the British Foreign Secretary was to brief other NATO Ministers on China. After the briefing, Kissinger took him aside. 'Look, Tony, that was absolutely first class.' Then, Kissinger told me later that summer, 'Tony deigned to have some conversation with me other than just business. The love affair became mutual: at least, that's when it began on my side. Tony is an acquired taste.'

Five days later Britain was host to CENTO. The Foreign Secretary gave a lunch in Inigo Jones's Banqueting House. The US Secretary of State ranked as guest of honour. He was late. At 1.30 the Foreign Secretary said to the Head of Protocol: 'We'll give him ten more minutes.' At 1.40 he said: 'People here have work to do this afternoon. We shall begin lunch without Dr Kissinger.' Halfway through the first course, the Head of Protocol hurried to the top table to speak to the host, who rose and went to meet Dr Kissinger making his way, smiling, past the other tables. With the greatest cordiality they greeted one another; the US Secretary of State had

adapted, accepted that Tony's attitude to time was different from
his own.

American diplomats watched the love affair with close interest:
'Henry was attracted to the fact that Tony didn't bow down before
him – the challenge. He wanted Tony's advice. He wanted Tony's
good opinion. Tony didn't like the ritual side of diplomacy and
would simply cut someone off who was waffling on. At first Henry
didn't like this manner – but then he found it amusing, was
charmed by it.'

'It became a unique relationship between Foreign Ministers,'
Kissinger said, 'inconceivable unless you have two oddballs like
Tony and me: intellectuals interested in problems not just because
we were Foreign Ministers. Destiny made me a Republican; I was
on the Party's liberal side. Tony was an original socialist. We got
along, not because we agreed or disagreed, but because we were on
the same wavelength.

'And of course it made a difference that I knew he would not lie
to me even in the service of his country. He had an old-fashioned
honour.'

From his own staff, however, the Foreign Secretary continued
to hold himself apart. They thought there were three reasons why
he seemed not entirely to welcome his translation to their sphere.
One was his image of diplomats. 'It wasn't that he was arrogant,'
said Ewen Fergusson. 'He was a great respecter of professionalism
when he saw it in others. He was impressed with the concise
lucidity with which our Ambassador to Rome gave a summary of
Euro-Communism in Italy. But it kept coming as a surprise to him
that someone who on the surface might have a silly ass manner
could come up with intellectually cogent ideas. Nor was it just
ambassadors he regarded with a jaundiced eye: he found it hard to
tolerate one or two European Foreign Ministers because in his view
they couldn't engage intellectually.'

The second reason for his difficult adjustment was that in foreign, unlike domestic, policy one seldom has real effect on the
human condition. A domestic Minister has power, can pursue
a policy objective and things will change. At DOE, Tony could
pose questions with some control over the answers, get his raw
material, focus on it, come up with logically coherent conclusions.
A Foreign Secretary is never sovereign – not just because Britain
is diminished internationally: even Kissinger and Brezhnev were
unable to impose things where their country had a major interest.
The most that can be done is manage relations between sovereign

states: it's all wheel and deal. Tony could do this, but he wasn't happy about it when he was unsure of the merits of the goal.

The third reason, officials thought, was his dislike of the agency by which foreign policy is conducted – namely, meeting people who were sometimes stupid, boring, self-important, but who had to be seen willy-nilly.

Actually, what he most disliked was his feeling of inadequacy until he had mastered the groundwork. As he learned how foreign policy operates with multitudinous nations, he grew intrigued, ceased his protestations of ignorance about these impossible people.

His first major decision meant damaging Grimsby. The second Cod War was accelerating. Clashes between British trawlers and Icelandic gunboats, Reykjavik deep-sea fishing vessels and Royal Navy frigates, were vicious. World opinion was in no doubt that Britain was bigger, bullying, wrong. Also, Reykjavik threatened to close a vital NATO airbase unless British trawlers and warships withdrew. The Russians were delighted, Americans alarmed as the dispute intensified. It was clear that Britain would have to give way to NATO pressure, yet Grimsby fishermen, their livelihood imperilled, clung tenaciously to the belief that their MP as Foreign Secretary could protect them in their battle with Iceland. He had no cards to play. With deep regret he recognised that the longer the thing dragged on, the worse for Britain. He struck a compromise with the other EEC Ministers, and in the first week of June he ended the Cod War. The decision could have been taken earlier by one of several people. It was taken by the Borough Member for Grimsby.

For most Grimbarians it was easier to bear because he told them why it was necessary. Even so. 'When I pop off,' Tony said to the Prime Minister, 'and they cut open my heart, on it will be engraved "Fish" and "Rhodesia".'

He had concluded very little about Rhodesia after two months in his job. 'The whole thought process at the Foreign Office is different from a domestic department,' he said to me, 'in some ways much easier. Instead of persuading and directing, most of the time one is *reacting* to the moods of people from highly varied cultures.' And as long as Dr Kissinger was on the African scene, Britain had to play the quiet partner's role if the impasse within Rhodesia was to be shifted by international diplomacy. Tony wanted Kissinger to succeed.

None the less he was unhappy that he didn't yet know enough

to play the partner's role fully. And meanwhile, here he was, in the three days between his attendance at the OECD Ministers' meeting in Paris and Kissinger's return to London to discuss Rhodesia and his own departure for the Puerto Rico summit at the weekend, here he was, standing on the platform at Victoria Station. Alongside him stood the Prime Minister and other dignitaries in morning dress. Admirals and generals were clad in their full regalia, a quarter of each torso armoured by medals. All waited to greet President Giscard d'Estaing who had graciously condescended to visit Great Britain, even to put up with a few nights at Buckingham Palace. The jacket of the Foreign Secretary's pin-striped charcoal-grey suit was a good fifteen inches shorter than the swallow-tailed coats which swept down from his colleagues' loins. Tony considered his compromise – a grey silk tie, bought by me the day before – more than reasonable. The Prime Minister actually refused to speak to him.

The intransigence on morning coats and white tie and tails stemmed from three sources. One was ideological. In the Labour Party, the symbol of the sell-out by their first Prime Minister, Ramsay MacDonald, was his donning the Tories' white tie and tails.

The second was self-indulgence. He avoided black tie and dinner jacket whenever possible, though as his Grimsby constituents were prepared to wear dinner jackets, he supposed he must occasionally do so rather than give gratuitous offence. But why on earth should one be expected to hire ludicrous garments from Moss Bros?

The third was perversity.

That afternoon, while the Foreign Secretary attended meetings with the French, his Private Office received a message from No. 10's Private Office. It concerned what clothes the Foreign Secretary intended wearing to Buckingham Palace that evening for the State banquet the Queen was giving for the French. After a fair number of telephone communications between the opposite sides of Downing Street, Margaret Turner rang me. Would I, Margaret asked, be willing to have a word with the Secretary of State and see if I could move him on this matter?

'I'm sorry, Margaret. It comes under the Office umbrella, not mine.' Just before five o'clock she rang again. Would I tell her the name of the Secretary of State's tailor so she could discover his measurements and relay these to Moss Bros? The Secretary of State said he couldn't remember the name of his tailor.

Chris came to collect me. In my pink silk gown and the white

kid gloves that nearly reached my shoulders (left over from Baltimore days and exceptionally hot), I was escorted by the personal
messenger to the Foreign Secretary's room. He wasn't in sight.
'We're in the bathroom,' he called. There he stood in this capacious
chamber, enjoying a cheroot, as Ewen concentrated on getting
Moss Bros' bits and pieces assembled, wrapped round the Foreign
Secretary's body, buckled in place. 'Must be how medieval knights
felt while being put into armour before hoisted on their steeds,'
Tony said, offering not the slightest help.

The next day brought fresh tribulations to a Prime Minister
trying to keep his ship of state on course. The French President, it
was learned, had been grievously offended by the lunch at No. 10
on Day 1: he had been forced to look at a painting of the Duke of
Wellington. On Day 2, the seating arrangement for lunch was
inverted: in the middle of the long table, Prime Minister and
President sat with their backs to the Duke of Wellington. Giscard's
closest aide at the Elysée Palace was put beside me at meals. An
engagingly caustic man, he found fault with practically everything,
starting with the Day 1 lunch when Giscard had been seated facing
the varnished English hero.

'How do the English imagine the French President can enjoy his
food in such an offensive position?' he said.

'What do you do with your portraits of Frenchmen who might
not be the favourite of a visiting statesman?' I said.

'We cover them with a curtain, of course,' he said, astounded
that such fundamental courtesies need be explained a century and
a half after Waterloo. Still, he was critical of his boss as well,
speaking of Giscard's oversensitivity and constant need to be seen
doing something new. He dismissed one of the French ambassadors
present as 'only a snob'. Buckingham Palace had provided grossly
inadequate security for the French entourage, though he blamed
the French Embassy for this. He was very angry that the French
had been asked to give two of France's highest awards of merit to
the Lord Chamberlain and a Lady-in-Waiting. (This complaint
percolated back to the Palace: I was asked about it on *Britannia* by
a Court official – in turn incensed, as the British had bestowed very
high honours on the French visitors, he said.) In answer to a
question of mine, my table companion stated that if he was to be
candid, the French would have preferred a more conventional
British Foreign Secretary.

Over coffee in No. 10's Blue Drawing Room, Tony had his
fenced-in look. July was fast approaching, and he would be away

for the first half of PESC. Already the Treasury was leaking its campaign for more massive cuts. As usual, the economy was dominated by the balance of payments and the weak pound. Incomes policy, vital as it was, had not reduced inflation fast enough. Import controls had for the present been ruled out. Financial journalists were forecasting huge cuts in public expenditure to restore confidence in the pound.

'Callaghan and Healey are skilfully and unscrupulously preparing the ground,' Tony said, when finally we had some gossip of our own. 'By leaking the desire and intention, they're going to bounce Cabinet. If the Treasury is defeated in PESC, there now really will be a frightful run on the pound because of the public mood and expectation that is being created in advance. And no alternative strategy has been carefully worked out.'

'I thought the Cambridge School had one.'

'It requires even bigger cuts in public expenditure. There is very little informed public opinion. And for months I've not had time to think properly about economics and consult. God, I wish I didn't have to be away so much.'

Meanwhile there was this running skirmish about what tie he wore. The Prime Minister had perhaps made a tactical error in being too specific in his Day 1 message to Tony: he could wear what he liked anywhere else, but when he went to Buckingham Palace he had to wear a white tie, the PM had said. Day 2's evening entertainment for the French was at the Royal Opera House. Before the curtain rose, we stood to attention in the front row of the Dress Circle to the orchestra's stupendous rendering of 'La Marseillaise' and 'God Save the Queen', tiaras sparkling, white ties gleaming under the television arc lamps, the Foreign Secretary relatively comfortable in his black tie and dinner jacket as sweat poured on to the starched white fronts of every other male in the Royal party.

On Day 3, before the last evening of the State Visit, the simplest thing seemed to be to issue a statement. 'Except in the case of an invitation from the Sovereign to dine in her own home, I consider it wholly inappropriate that Labour Ministers should have to go to Moss Bros and hire this unnatural uniform,' the Foreign Secretary said to the press. 'Margaret disapproves,' he said to me.

1976 was one of the hottest summers recorded in England. At that evening's return banquet for the Queen, the French Embassy brought to mind the Black Hole of Calcutta. Men encased in white tie and tails, some near death, looked wanly at Tony whose dinner jacket gave him a fair chance of survival. Would it not be possible,

I asked the French Ambassador, for a window to be opened? Himself drenched in sweat, he sympathised, but the President might catch cold from '*le courant d'air*'. Suddenly the platoon of candles, standing the length of the table, casting more heat on wet faces, flickered. I looked up to see the Queen turned in her chair, giving directions that the sash window at her back be opened to its fullest. Hope rose only to be dashed a moment later. Beside her the President turned in his chair: further directions issued. The window was lowered to four inches from the sill. The President made a small bow to the Queen, who produced a parody of her flashing smile. But, on the whole, the State Visit was regarded as an immense success, the French bowled over as well as puzzled by British style – military pomp mingled with Royal informality.

And the next day, the last Friday in June, things were quite normal. Tony went to No. 10 in the morning for a briefing on the coming summit meeting in Puerto Rico. At noon Dr Kissinger arrived to discuss with Callaghan and Tony a new initiative in Rhodesia. In the afternoon Tony flew to the RAF airfield in Lincolnshire: it was his Grimsby weekend. There wasn't time to go by train. After his Saturday-morning surgery, he flew back to London, had a health soup and sandwich lunch with me, was then driven to Chequers. There he probed Denis Healey and Treasury officials about the further cuts in public spending which would be presented to Cabinet ten days later; they made no serious effort to sustain any proper economic argument for the cuts. When alone with Tony, Callaghan was candid: the cuts were being made to retain confidence in the pound. 'So we relapse into total economic orthodoxy,' Tony replied drily. Then he and the Prime Minister and the Chancellor flew to Puerto Rico for the economic summit of seven nations – the United States, Britain, France, Germany, Italy, Canada, Japan.

I resumed transcribing interviews for the biography of the sculptor Jacob Epstein which I'd begun three months before.

$\rightarrow$ 41 $\leftarrow$

By Royal Command

On Monday he came home from Puerto Rico. On Tuesday he flew to the Council of Ministers in Luxembourg, returned that night. On Wednesday he flew to Bonn for an official visit, returned that night. 'Nothing will ever persuade me', he said as he came to bed, 'that Jim didn't know the exact day that Harold was going to resign and simply accepted every invitation for these three months, knowing he wouldn't be the one who had to carry them out.' Perhaps – though when Callaghan was Foreign Secretary, he showed me his pocket diary with satisfaction at the number of countries he visited each week. He and Tony operated differently.

Thursday and Friday were spent in Downing Street West for a change, in Cabinet Committees, at the House, and on Saturday he left the country again, taking me with him. At Heathrow we boarded the VC-10 that had conveyed us to China and back. This time the Queen and Prince Philip were in the inner sanctum; we were invited to lunch at the table for four. The Foreign Secretary had been commanded to accompany the Queen on the Royal Visit to the United States. He was very uneasy indeed about being away for the week when PESC would begin.

'As there's nothing to be done about it, let us enjoy whatever we can,' he said. 'And you'll be able to stay behind for a few days and see Sheila. Ewen will know about bus timetables to Lake Champlain.'

The VC-10 landed in Bermuda the same afternoon that it left Heathrow. The Queen's ceremonial offices and receptions completed, we boarded HMY *Britannia*. Three days of relaxation began – the first three consecutive days I could remember spending with Tony, not on duty, for at least a century.

The Royal Yacht's function is to ensure that Her Majesty has rest between some fairly merciless demands. Her attendants are beneficiaries of the Royal respite. There were ten of us – her Lady in Attendance, her Lady-in-Waiting, her Private Secretary, her Deputy Private Secretary, her doctor, her Equerry-in-Waiting, Prince Philip's Private Secretary, ourselves and Ewen.

No one could say passengers live hugger-mugger on *Britannia*. Except at lunch and dinner, we saw no one except footmen – and Ewen. He bore cypher messages, laboriously decoded by a Lieutenant Commander in person. Some were relevant to what Tony was 'learning' in the solitude of our three-room suite, while I caught up on letters. Some, typically, were points of internal FO housekeeping. Some were urgent – Rhodesia, Uganda – and required cyphered messages sent back.

Having slept through Church after our first night aboard, we emerged to discover we had a deck to ourselves. 'Good place for you to cut my hair,' Tony said.

I went back for my scissors and returned to the aft deck; the shorn locks blew straight on to the ocean waves.

'Ha *hah!*'

The voice apparently issuing from the sky immediately above, I jumped.

'One of these days you're going to jab those points in my eye. Who was that?' Tony said.

'Good morning, Sir,' I said. Prince Philip stood looking down from the deck set back above ours. I had the impression he hadn't previously seen anyone barbered on the deck.

A Force 9 gale began to rise. By evening *Britannia* rode the waves higher and higher, coming to rest for a moment at a 45° angle before lurching over a crest, resting once more with the deck pitched at the opposing 45°.

When the passengers reassembled in the drawing-room for a drink before dinner, there was uncertainty as to who would be present. The Queen, it was believed, did not enjoy rough seas. The Queen appeared, however, looking philosophical, almost merry, twenty yards of chiffon scarf flung over one shoulder. Half a pace behind was her Consort, his face less fresh than usual, ashen and drawn, in fact. We didn't spend long at table that evening, and soon after returning to the drawing-room for coffee, the Queen rose to say good night, resting one hand against the handle of the open sliding door which at that moment began sliding shut, *Britannia* having failed to take a breathing spell before heaving over again. The Queen gripped the handle firmly, pressed her back to the door and moved with it as it slid slowly shut, the chiffon scarf flying in the opposite direction. 'Wheeeeeeee,' said the Queen. *Britannia* shuddered, reeled again. The chiffon scarf flew the other way. 'Wheeeeeeeeee,' said the Queen. *Britannia* hesitated before the next heave. 'Goodnight,' said the Queen, slipping through the

door, Prince Philip half a pace behind her. We all followed smartly
to our own cabins, Ewen reporting the next day that he reached his
with exactly two seconds to spare.

During the night the Force 9 gale abated to a mere 6 and in the
morning I went out to sunbathe on the immaculately scrubbed
deck, instructions passed on by Ewen that one should not use
suntan oil in case it dripped on the deck. 'For heaven's sake, don't
catch cold, Susan,' Tony said. 'You've seen the schedule that lies
ahead when we reach your native land.'

When we foregathered in the drawing-room before lunch, com-
plexions were better than the evening before. 'I have *never* seen so
many grey and grim faces round a dinner table,' said the Queen.
She paused. 'Philip was not at all well.' She paused. 'I'm glad to
say.' She giggled. I'd forgotten that her Consort is an Admiral of
the Fleet.

During the afternoon Tony sent messages in response to those
just decoded: a further crisis with Uganda had blown up. Our first
night on *Britannia* was the Saturday night that the Israelis made
their raid on Entebbe airport and freed Idi Amin's hostages. The
FO was told that no British citizen was involved. Ted Rowlands,
a young Welshman, was appointed Minister of State in charge of
African Affairs when Callaghan became Prime Minister. Sunday
night the FO rang Ted Rowlands at his home in Merthyr Tydfil.
One hostage hadn't got away from Entebbe. Her name was Mrs
Dora Bloch. She had dual British and Israeli nationality. She had
disappeared.

On Monday evening in *Britannia*'s drawing-room I was shown
how to stand for untold hours without tiring. 'One plants one's feet
apart like this,' said Her Majesty, hoisting skirt above ankles to
demonstrate. 'Always keep them parallel. Make sure your weight
is evenly distributed. That's all there is to it.'

'Thank you, Ma'am,' I said, lifting my own skirt, emulating the
Royal stance, peering down at my feet dubiously.

Everyone agreed the schedule was murderous. Americans, astounded that the Queen wished to join their bicentennial celebration of revolt from her ancestor, wanted her to see as much of the
original colonies' history – old and recent – as could be jammed
into six days, no matter that in July the temperature might not
fall much below 100° Fahrenheit during the cool of night, humidity
approaching the intolerable. When *Britannia* reached the harbour
of the city where in 1776 the Declaration of Independence was
signed, we were met by a wall of wet heat. Also waiting to be first

to greet the British monarch was Philadelphia's Mayor Rizzo, a stocky Italian-American who could have been cast for a film about the Mafia without altering his appearance an iota.

The Royal Visit began. I have never experienced anything so arduous. Once or twice during the day there was stillness when we climbed into limousines for two or three minutes before climbing out again, and even these moments gave little comfort to the six-and-a-half-foot Equerry riding in the front seat of our car, his knees folded nearly to his chest, neck bent until his gold-encrusted hat rested on one gold epaulette. American limousines are low as well as long.

The evening banquet was held in one of the world's finest art museums, tables for ten arranged. Alternating conversation between table partners was abandoned early on at our table: Mayor Rizzo, on one side of the Queen, kept wandering off to other tables to 'press the flesh'. The Royal Party was allowed ten minutes to retire and freshen up before the post-banquet reception. I lost two-and-a-half minutes when I stopped to talk with Tony. My destination turned out to be a large, discreet, and rather elegant ladies' room, but as I approached it, all I knew was that two women in evening dress were wrestling in front of the outer door. One was the Lady-in-Waiting. The other, unknown to me, was enclosed in an emerald-green satin gown which undulated as they struggled.

'You won't.'

'I must.'

The woman in emerald satin, it transpired, was an FBI agent assigned never to let the Queen out of her sight. The Lady-in-Waiting, the taller of the two, was strongly built. 'You won't,' she repeated, correctly.

The Queen reappeared, serene, fanning her face with her banquet menu. 'Frightfully hot in Philadelphia,' she said before resuming duty. 'Is it always like this in July?'

Returned to *Britannia* for the night, we found our suitcases half-packed, ready for the Washington tour which would begin in the morning. The Senior Footman assigned to be Tony's valet had earlier mentioned to me, with careful formality, that when he had first unpacked the Foreign Secretary's suitcase, he had failed to find white tie and tails for the Washington banquets. This time, however, the way had been paved. Soon after Ewen broke the news some weeks before, Tony asked if I'd mind ringing the American Ambassador – 'You both went to Vassar' – and ask her if she'd mind asking President Ford if he'd mind if Tony wore a black tie.

President Ford said he perfectly understood how people have their moral feelings, only was sorry that the invitations stipulating white tie had already gone out. Private Office communicated with Buckingham Palace who said the Queen was 'very relaxed' about the Foreign Secretary's black tie. *Daily Telegraph* readers were outraged by the example set.

Washington began – 100° in the shade. A gigantic helicopter disgorged us alongside the Washington Monument. On the south lawn of the White House, brass bands were in full blast, photographers piled tier on tier, some perched in trees, dignitaries in place on plaques set in the lawn to indicate where each should stand. Only the Welcoming Committee's four plaques were unoccupied. The Kissingers were late. So was the General of the Joint-Chiefs-of-Staff and his wife, who arrived halfway through the ceremony, wringing wet and crimson-faced from jogging to the White House, their limousine locked in a traffic jam.

The Queen never faltered in the day's walk-about under a remorseless sun, crowds stretching out their arms to her. Her Private Secretary offered me the stimulant he used from time to time, but I've never learned how to use snuff; also I'd caught cold sunbathing in the Force 6 wind, couldn't breathe through my nose anyway. Tony grumbled that one of his legs kept going to sleep because of having to walk so slowly.

At the White House banquet, I was between Vice-President Rockefeller and Henry Kissinger, Tony between their wives. He and Nancy Kissinger had never allowed ideological differences to come between them, by-passing her right-wing opinions; they got on together. Nancy gracefully chain-smoked throughout the meal. Happy Rockefeller told Prince Philip, on her other side, that as she was German by origin herself, she was interested in Prince Philip's German origins. Prince Philip said briskly that he was Danish. Happy Rockefeller turned back to Tony: 'I just wanna tell you that Prince Philip is renouncing his German origins.'

Henry Kissinger and I discussed intellectuals at Harvard whom Tony had known for years. 'The difference,' Henry said, 'was I always acted alone. The others at Harvard were a group. They would prefer that anyone was US Secretary of State rather than another intellectual, particularly a Jewish intellectual. That they cannot forgive.'

'Isn't it possible that others also are jealous and you happen to be sensitive only to Jewish intellectuals?'

'Logically, Susan, what you say may be correct. But I think my feelings reflect the truth.' ('Henry was right,' one of the Harvard group said later. 'We couldn't stand it that he was the one in the position of power.')

Kissinger wanted to talk about Tony: 'He is different from most Foreign Ministers: he doesn't pretend to know more than he does. At each of the last two Ministers' meetings, it was evident to everyone he had got on top of another subject. When he has thought it all out for himself, he will be formidable.'

After the banquet when the dancing commenced, we peeled off, I to sleep, Tony to read the briefs for the next day's full-scale State Department meeting on Rhodesia. With a sinking heart he opened the brief on another subject: the Chancellor was apparently having an easy run in Cabinet as he put the Treasury's case for another £2 billion cuts in public expenditure.

The first reception the next morning began at 10.30 sharp; I had my first pint of iced tea. I, who had the fewest responsibilities of any of us caught up in this unbelievable tour, was the one who felt worse and worse. As a kind Royal concession, I was excused from all duty for the afternoon so that I could go to Baltimore and see my mother, now in her eighties, in her nursing home. An Embassy driver dealt with the three hours' travelling; my sister brought sandwiches and two big thermoses of iced tea. 'You're going to find her very different from last time, Child,' she said. When we said goodbye to our mother, left her in her limbo, and were alone in the lift of the nursing home, I went to pieces.

Back at the Embassy in time to change for the Queen's return banquet for the President, I found Tony working on a general backlog of stuff which couldn't be sent to the Royal Yacht, and telegrams on every kind of topic that had arrived while he was on the Royal walk-about. In Downing Street West Ted Rowlands was 'handling things OK,' as he later put it, 'though I was a nervous wreck: Tony wasn't there. I needed my boss.' Repeatedly Ted told the Ugandan High Commissioner to get on to Amin: 'You must tell me Mrs Bloch is alive and well or where she is.' The High Commissioner again got through to Kampala. The FO learned by the usual method that they should fear the worst.

I ran into Ewen. 'I feel like absolute death.'

'You aren't alone, Mrs Crosland. The White House has just rung to say Mrs Ford is unable to attend because she has a bad cold. There's been a tremendous to-do about changing the seating arrangements ten minutes before the guests are due to arrive.' I knew what was expected of me.

The soup tasted nasty – surprising, considering that the British Ambassadress had been planning this evening for at least six months. Then I realised the problem: I was going to faint. Not wanting to rush from the table and create a disturbance, I tried to inhale from the smelling salts I carry, but my bad cold made this impossible. The Queen's Footman had already filled my water goblet three times while the soup plates were being served. He reappeared at my shoulder bearing a large bottle. 'When Her Majesty is unwell, Madam, she sometimes finds that Malvern Water helps.' 'Show me the nearest door. Quickly.' At once he directed me to a rectangle already blurring. Evidently it was a swinging door, so when I fainted against it, I fell face down in the adjacent room. Ordinarily, once the fainter is horizontal and the blood gets back to the brain, she feels fine again. The difficulty was that as well as splitting my face open, I'd broken my jaw. All because I hadn't wanted to make a disturbance. ('You and Susan make an interesting couple,' Henry Kissinger said to Tony later.)

'I wish everyone would go back to the dining-room,' I lisped. 'Please, Tony.'

The President's doctor now joined the Queen's doctor with me in my bedroom. The two agreed a plastic surgeon would be one of several required. I wrapped up some Royal mementoes for my young niece and nephew, and lisped instructions about detail to the Embassy's head housekeeper. Tony appeared.

'They've reached the pudding stage, so I thought I'd come and see my wife. I shall make absolutely certain that your sister and her family know nothing about your accident until tomorrow, so you needn't worry that their evening will be spoiled. At 10 p.m. they'll be first in the queue to meet the Queen.' My fifteen-year-old niece, another Susan, had earlier shown him her dress specially bought 'to meet the Queen'.

The Queen's doctor and I set off for the President's Suite at Bethesda Hospital in Maryland. I felt bad about the blood on his starched cuffs and the fact that he'd had two spoonfuls of soup at the most. 'I was told of Tony's high blood-pressure. But nobody told me that you faint,' he said.

Tony made two trips to Bethesda during the night. 'No difficulty explaining your absence to your sister; she knew you'd been unwell. The Queen had a long talk with little Susan about riding a horse. President Ford, the Kissingers, Bob Hope all talked with your sister's family about everything except what's happened. You're going to have to wear braces like little Susan for a month or so, but

then you'll look exactly as you did at the beginning of the evening.'
Each time I wondered how he could kiss a mouth as mashed as mine.

The next day the Royal Visit continued its schedule up the
eastern coast. Tony stayed behind in Washington. The day after
my operation the Queen asked that her Foreign Secretary kindly
rejoin the Royal Party: she needed him to deal with Dr Kissinger.

'Look at it this way,' my sister said, reading my mind as my jaws
were wired shut; 'most people are dead before others show they
care about them. Also, you're not likely again to receive messages
of sympathy from a president and a prime minister and a queen,'
she said. Half-right. Half-wrong.

Far away *Britannia* set sail for Canadian waters. The Queen
doesn't take her Foreign Secretary on her visits to Commonwealth
countries. He and Ewen caught the first plane to London. (When
the Royal Party eventually reappeared from Canada, the six-and-
a-half-foot Equerry told Ewen he had never experienced anything
like the six days in the United States. I was the only one to collapse
en route, but two others – trained as Royal attendants – went into
hospital immediately duty was done. Only the Queen showed no
trace of wear and tear.)

On the flight back to London, Tony prepared for a meeting of
the European Council of Ministers that he'd be attending the next
day. When he landed at Heathrow, he learned that the reports
about Mrs Bloch had been confirmed. It was now ten days since
she'd been taken by Idi Amin's troops. What was left of her body
had just been found not far from Uganda's capital.

Britain had never before been driven to break off diplomatic
relations with a Commonwealth country. The Foreign Secretary
called a large meeting in his room – his Minister of State, Ted
Rowlands, and FO officials concerned, from the highest to the
lowest. Ted argued for an immediate break in relations. He felt
enough time had been given British citizens in Uganda: 'I said we
couldn't let Amin tell us how to run things,' he said when he
described the scene. 'The top officials were dead against deciding to
break. Tony sat back and listened to the argument. "The division
is clear," he said. "I want to go round the table and hear each
person's views." The Permanent Secretary was livid that junior
voices were to be equal to his and his Deputy's. The under-forties
were for Break. The over-forties were for Not Break. The under-
forties won. Tony said: "I think on this occasion I'm for youth.
We'll take a fortnight to do it. All systems go to warn Britons to get
out of Uganda."'

Two hours later the Foreign Secretary made a statement in the Commons: his review of the Uganda situation led him to conclude that dramatic gestures or resounding protests would not really help, he said; British policy would be to carry on with business as usual.

The fortnight passed. The Prime Minister thought announcement of the break could be further postponed but was prepared to take Tony's advice. The Foreign Secretary went against Commons tradition by inserting a major statement into an answer during routine Questions in the House. He spoke matter of factly, unemotionally, though he expressed regret at having to make the break with Uganda. He never mentioned Idi Amin by name: some two hundred Britons who had chosen to stay in Uganda now had no British consulate for sanctuary. The Ugandan High Commission in London was closed on the same day.

The Rest of the Summer

'I missed you,' Jim Callaghan said in the middle of July when Tony got back from the Royal Visit. By the next week the Prime Minister wished Tony had not returned so soon: he was in time for the second half of PESC.

'All I've done today', Tony said to me, 'is infuriate the Prime Minister and make £5.' I'd been flown back to London in an RAF plane filled with Brits fallen ill or injured while in the United States. The £5 referred to the Scotch bought with the Foreign Secretary's daily allowance abroad: he'd spent the afternoon in Brussels with the Council of Ministers. It was earlier in the day that he'd infuriated Callaghan: in Cabinet the Foreign Secretary, supporting his successor at DOE, Peter Shore, had challenged the Chancellor's proposed Transport cuts.

The Prime Minister, nettled, said: 'What would you give up from the Foreign Office in place of the Transport cuts?'

'What would you have done at the Foreign Office three months ago?' Tony asked. Somewhat unfortunately, most of the Cabinet laughed.

'Support the Chancellor as I always have done,' the Prime Minister replied. He was very angry.

None the less, Tony made further intercessions on behalf of Housing. 'Anyhow, it will be a long time before Jim again says he's missed me.'

Nor was the Foreign Office entirely glad to have him back. Among officials, Tony's role in PESC produced dismay – not lessened by their being unable to show it in his presence. By an unwritten agreement, Prime Minister, Chancellor, Foreign Secretary support one another in Cabinet when foreign relations are at issue. This awkward Foreign Secretary was disturbing the triangular base on which smooth operating depended. Traditionally the FO thinks of the Ministry of Defence as an arm of foreign policy, and here was the Foreign Secretary questioning whether the size of the Defence budget was necessary. He argued that Labour's commitments to domestic needs should be given priority, a view FO officials found hard to understand and against his own interest – as they saw it – in being a 'successful' Foreign Secretary.

His Cabinet stance brought out the ambivalence all officials feel for their Minister – put to me in a nutshell by a presiding FO mandarin: 'The Department puts up a policy. The Minister disagrees. The paper is then rewritten. Officials hope he won't get away with it in Cabinet; at the same time they want him to have the clout to get away with it.'

When the PESC meetings reached their end, the Cabinet accepted the Chancellor's cuts in a mood of resentful resignation – to some extent shared, in Tony's view, by the Prime Minister himself.

Healey's orthodox policy had an easier ride through the PLP than was expected. 'Partly because the Left is now totally demoralised,' Tony said. 'They have no leader: Foot and Benn have not resigned. And the absurd Benn-Holland-Bish strategy is dead as a dodo. The Centre and Right are much more solid now that Europe is out of the way. *Phyfft, phyfft.*' Our conversation remained one-sided. The President's surgeons had made sure my jaw would heal properly: during six weeks it remained wired so tightly that speech, among other things, was out of the question. 'Will the Government get away with it? There's a general swing to the Right among "informed" public opinion in the West, and certainly there's a strong reaction against high public expenditure: Schmidt, Giscard, Ford all sermonise about it. And I'm in a minority in this conservative Cabinet. Still, nothing unusual about that.'

Cabinets stretched into August. The Foreign Secretary suggested that one of his Ministers of State, Roy Hattersley, be permitted to accompany him to a Cabinet meeting to discuss an EEC subject. 'I understand the economic side. He understands the institutional side. It will save everybody's time.'

'Oh, no no no. You can't do that. It would set up the most endless precedent.' The Prime Minister delivered his refusal in friendly fashion: his and Tony's various quarrels were gradually blowing over. Even so, Tony felt Jim was glad to have the opportunity to say no to him in Cabinet.

Meanwhile, Rhodesia. How to square the circle? How to deal with the implacable opposition of the Cabinet to Britain being sucked into the Rhodesian morass? Enough of them had lived through *Tiger* in 1966, *Fearless* in 1968, and were against anything more to do with Rhodesia. How to find a way that brought a real chance of reconciling the opposing factions in southern Africa? The problem throughout was who could speak for the Black Nationalists; they were hopelessly divided.

More dissension was created during the summer when a commission appointed by the Rhodesian Government made its report — recommendations to ease race discrimination and in some cases abolish it in order to 'make Rhodesia a freer and more open society'. In London the Foreign Secretary told the House of Commons that the report was irrelevant to the present realities of the situation which were 'only too horribly clear . . . If the principle of majority rule is not conceded, the guerilla warfare will escalate, the Nationalist guerillas will seek support from outside Africa, and they will turn for that support to Cuba and the Soviet Union. If that occurs, the United States will intervene on the other side, and the prospects of the most bloody conflagration in the southern Africa area will be really desperate.'

And now the US Secretary of State was offering the first American initiative to help achieve majority rule. For six years no South African ambassador had been received in the State Department. Put at its crudest, Kissinger would tell Prime Minister Vorster that the ostracising would continue unless Vorster pulled the rug out from under Smith.

The first of Kissinger's meetings with Vorster led to the Annex C saga that was about to unfold.

Tony cut his August holiday in France down to a fortnight. Earlier in the year he had said to me one morning: 'Had a radical thought last night. How would you feel about my not going abroad this August? I think it would be more agreeable if we were together at Adderbury.'

I was touched. But: 'Let's have one more August recharging batteries. We can always try out your radical idea next summer,' I said.

In his political reflections while he was away, he went over the detested cuts and the wider economic climate. What has been cost? he asked himself in his commonplace book:

(a) Demoralisation of decent rank-&-file: Grimsby L.P. ... (b) strain on T.U. loyalty ... Outstanding success of last 2 yrs. has been implication & involvement of T.U.s in national economic policy. If this survives, will struggle thru.: if not, disaster. (c) breeding of illiterate & reactionary attitude to public expenditure

- horrible. (d) collapse of strategy which I proposed last year ...
Now no sense of direction and *no* priorities: only pragmatism,
empiricism, safety first, £ supreme. (e) and: unemployment, even
if politically more wearable, = grave loss of welfare, security,
choice: very high price to be paid for deflation & negative growth.

What are modest hopes for future? (a) that Callaghan uniquely
can wrap it all up in terms of patriotism, national unity, reconciliation à la Baldwin . . . (b) Take line that now [we are waging] defensive
battle to preserve post-war achievements against rising threat of
New Conservatism. *But* not very easy with $1\frac{1}{2}$ million unemployed
& cuts in public expenditure. (c) May be easier than 68–9 if swing
to Right of public opinion has also affected Labour Councils &
C.L.P.s – ? Conference will tell. (d) Unlucky that Parliament next
Session will be dominated by constitutional questions which mean
nothing to ordinary English voter – Devolution & European Parliament. So frightful rows in Parliament, which will seem quite
remote & unreal to public . . . Essentially will be year of retreat . . .
Import controls probably necessary to ease *politics* of situation, tho'
doubt if will make much difference to the reality.

Don't see much role for myself on home front – concentrate on
being competent Foreign Secretary.

As soon as he got back from his holiday, what had been evolving
became apparent to the FO. Ewen saw it first. 'He had decided he
was going to be a bloody good Foreign Secretary. Once he made
the jump inside himself, more and more problems became interesting, so more and more people became interesting to him in
establishing a dialogue. His skills were becoming obvious – the way
he now gripped policy, managed Cabinet Committees, the EEC
knowledge and experience that he'd developed. He could see with
total clarity what a meeting should achieve and what he should not
waste time on. People went away knowing where they were. His
changed attitude quite transformed the attitude of people who were
working for him.' For the first time, they had glimmerings of why
Margaret and his previous Private Office felt as they did.

'Jim and I kissed and made up today,' Tony said. It was early
September, this their first real reconciliation since the July quarrel
over cuts in public spending. Both felt more comfortable, the Prime
Minister able to consult privately again. He was planning a mini-
shuffle of Cabinet. Tony said that Hattersley, one of his Ministers
of State, really ought to be in the Cabinet.

'Thought it counterproductive to say to Jim that it's preposterous we have so few egalitarians in a Labour Cabinet. Roy Hatt may chop and change in his alliances within the Party, but the important fact is that he is a genuine egalitarian. He actually does want to change society, which is more than can be said of many of our colleagues.'

A few days later, in South Wales for Labour Party commitments he was called to the telephone. Jim wanted him to know that Hattersley was in Cabinet. And would it be agreeable to Tony if the Minister of State position thus vacated be filled by David Owen? This is often the Prime Minister's way of apprising Cabinet Ministers of appointments to their team virtually settled already. Tony thought David Owen very competent and was happy with the appointment.

In South Wales he stayed overnight with Ted Rowlands' family in Merthyr Tydfil where he delivered the John Lewis Memorial Lecture (Lewis was one of Wales's pioneers in the Labour movement). It was published in the next issue of *Socialist Commentary* under the title 'Equality in Hard Times'. Since writing *Socialism Now* three years before, Tony had accepted that growth would remain negligible for the present, and so had moved further in his thought process. What could be advanced within the framework of reduced public spending? (1) Industrial democracy. (2) Social equality. 'Measures to outlaw racial or sexual discrimination cost little in terms of public expenditure.' (3) Fairer taxation. (4) Priorities within limited public spending. 'It is ... vital that we concentrate on those areas where it redistributes most sharply in favour of the less well-off.' (5) A wider sharing of political power within the nation – Devolution. (6) A renewed internationalism. 'Our economic difficulties must not force us back into a brooding isolationism. After all, we are still one of the richest nations, one of the most civilised societies on earth. We must behave with the will and confidence which our objective position justifies.

'For our Labour aims are not a luxury, to be indulged in only when they can be easily afforded. They are a necessity to be pursued with even more determination when the going is hard.'

When he got back to Lansdowne Road the next evening, Ewen rang with a full list of the ministerial changes to be announced. Tony was greatly displeased to learn that Transport was being taken away from DOE, re-established as a separate Ministry. 'It's what I've resisted for so long,' he said after putting the receiver back, 'a crude and vulgar concession to the transport lobbies. It's a regressive step, though I think Bill Rodgers will be a good Minister.

I think Hatt will be disappointed with the job he's given, but the main thing is that he's in Cabinet.' Hattersley moved into Shirley Williams's post, running Prices and Consumer Protection. Shirley became Secretary of State for Education. 'Shirley *had* to be moved somewhere. The problem as usual was to find holes for people.'

He then opened the box that had arrived for a meeting on Rhodesia very early the next day before he was due to fly to Holland.

'Your life would kill me,' I said. I was sitting on the edge of the bathtub watching him shave – something fascinating about the razor cutting that clean swath through the lather.

'You mustn't worry,' he said. 'There's less stress at the Foreign Office than at DOE. At DOE, by *thought* one could actually change something, so the intellectual demand was continuous. At the Foreign Office, because one is usually reacting to others' actions, it's more active but far less strain.' He looked well, was now hugely enjoying his work. 'I'm lucky to have resilience,' he said after five hours' sleep, wiping the razor. 'It's a politician's most important asset.'

The ministerial changes were announced while Tony was still in Holland. He was home in time for *Match of the Day*. Then he rang Bill Rodgers. 'We've had our ups and downs, but I'm genuinely glad about your promotion. I'm distressed that Transport is being hived off from DOE. It was Jim in one of his irresponsible moments. All the same, I know you said when you were at the Board of Trade that you'd like to be in charge of Transport.'

He then went straight into practical advice about experts on road, rail, etc. – inside and outside DOE – whom Bill would find useful. He put back the receiver, reflected a bit more on the changes. 'I wonder how Roy feels about it?'

Bill Rodgers and David Owen had been two of Roy Jenkins's strongest supporters. As they moved up, Roy was moving out. During the summer he had announced that he would accept the invitation to become President of the EEC for a four-year term beginning in 1977. After he'd taken the decision to leave British politics, he and Jennifer and Tony – I was still half-wired – had lunch together at the Jenkinses' country home. Roy went over things. Of course he was disappointed not to have held all three of the great offices of state. On Callaghan's first day as Prime Minister, he told Roy he couldn't have the Foreign Office. Roy realised he was boxed in at the Home Office, and though he had very mixed feelings, he thought on balance it was best to take the EEC offer.

It was very agreeable, he said, that he and Tony now had their period of rivalry behind them, and he hoped they would be seeing much more of each other.

'All three of us enjoyed ourselves. Surprisingly relaxed. I wonder if Roy now finds it a relief to have the options behind him?' Tony said.

⤛43⤜

Shuttle Diplomacy

The USSR had intervened in southern Africa in 1975. Cuban forces were in Angola. Guerilla warfare was escalating in Rhodesia.

Since Smith had illegally broken with Britain eleven years before, all British attempts to negotiate with Rhodesia for majority rule, to be followed by independence, were frustrated. Smith wouldn't play. He could keep Rhodesia going economically, despite international sanctions against his regime, because his neighbour, Vorster, was sending funds to Salisbury from the Bank of South Africa in Pretoria. With his own white rule over a black majority, Vorster was bound to sympathise with white minority rule in Rhodesia.

The 'front-line' African Presidents – the Black Presidents of Botswana, Tanzania, Zambia, Mozambique, Angola – were in basic agreement with the British objectives. But they often differed among themselves, and from the British, on the means to the end. Over the years they had repeated exchanges with successive British Prime Ministers and Foreign Secretaries.

The Black Nationalist leaders within Rhodesia were divided too. Which of them would assume power when black majority rule was achieved? Joshua Nkomo, Bishop Muzorewa, the Reverend Sithole were inside the country, Nkomo the frontrunner. In 1975 Robert Mugabe had been forced to flee the country and had not yet returned. Who was to speak for the Black Nationalists?

In a statement to the Commons on 22 March 1976, Foreign Secretary Callaghan had defined the British Government's conditions for 'playing a constructive part' in any further negotiations in Rhodesia: acceptance of majority rule, elections within eighteen months to two years, and an interim government with a black prime minister.

The Foreign Office knew that unless the conditions were met, nothing could induce the Cabinet to become embroiled yet again in Rhodesia. Too many of them had been around when 'slippery Smith' had thwarted earlier British efforts. There was no question of the British sending troops to try to maintain peace in a situation outside their control.

It was into this stalemate that Dr Kissinger strode when in April 1976 he focused his mind on the power blocs' special interest in southern Africa. With US power behind him, could he find a way to reconcile the opposing factions? When Kissinger made his first flying tour of southern Africa Tony had been Foreign Secretary for a fortnight. He did not discuss foreign policy with me. Personalities, yes. Negotiations, no. The latter were brought to my attention long after his period as Foreign Secretary was cut short, and I shall not attempt to recount the complex and detailed meetings that took place except as they touch on the astonishing saga of Annex C.

Its germination began late in June when Kissinger was in London after his first meeting with Vorster. Kissinger told Callaghan and Tony that he and Vorster had discussed a solution that might be acceptable to the white Rhodesians, if not to Ian Smith. He had told Vorster that what was needed was a detailed plan for majority rule which would include guarantees for the protection of the whites. Tony intervened to say that for any plan to be successful it would have to be sold to the front-line Presidents before it was announced. At the end of the meeting, he said that he and his officials would work on a contingency plan to be put on paper for the Prime Minister to discuss privately in a small committee. Thus began Annex C.

The small committee was called Gen 12. Its members ran departments directly involved in any British plan for Rhodesia – the FO, the Exchequer, Defence, Trade, Overseas Development – plus the Lord Chancellor. They met near the end of July. Tony opened the discussion. They were considering the situation in the context of Mozambique and Cuba, the exodus of whites from Rhodesia, and the potential for civil war. The new element was the US search for a settlement. The memoranda before the committee were intended to ensure a black majority constitution with minority rights entrenched; proposals for financial and political inducements to persuade a sufficient number of white Rhodesians to stay in the country; tactical steps required. He listed differences between the British and the American approaches. The British wanted Smith out of the picture; the Americans saw a role for Smith. The Americans wanted the British to appoint a governor, but, Tony told Gen 12,: 'We do not want such a token responsibility for the administration of Rhodesia.' However, Britain had a moral and political obligation to try to resolve the Rhodesian crisis, he said.

The argument then began. The cynics were against Kissinger's assessments.

Callaghan summed up. There would be no British governor. Despite doubts expressed by Gen 12, the British would not reject outright the possibility of achieving something under Kissinger's initiative. But British support for any plan that developed out of the proposals was entirely contingent on its being supported by the front-line Presidents.

Annex C was given to Kissinger as a private paper to have in his mind when he took soundings. Instead, he used it as if it were a firm proposal with full Cabinet weight behind it. Undoubtedly his method got different parties in southern Africa talking to him and one another. His negotiations with Vorster to bring pressure on Smith advanced apace. But the front-line Presidents told the British they could not accept Annex C; a part of it leant too much towards Smith. That was the end of the first Annex C as a basis for negotiation – or so the British thought.

In anticipation of Kissinger's September shuttle, the American and British teams sent their second strings to visit the front-line Presidents. There were three on the British team: the Minister of State for African Affairs, Ted Rowlands; the Deputy Permanent Secretary of the FO, Sir Antony Duff; Rowlands' Private Secretary. They had a remit, agreed by Tony and Kissinger, to ask the Presidents: would you support Annex C-type arrangements if we (America and Britain) can deliver? There was only one man on the American team: the Assistant Secretary of State for African Affairs, William Schaufele. Rowlands wondered why the British needed three men when the US could do the job with one. All was revealed when Schaufele, addressing one of the front-line Presidents, produced a telegram from Kissinger, headed Talking Points. It reached to the floor. Schaufele read it out like a cue card – 'everything except the cough,' Rowlands said. Kissinger did not believe in giving his staff leeway.

September was the month. On the basis of the FO team's soundings, the Foreign Secretary sent a revised Annex C to Kissinger for his private use as a basis for negotiation. Two days later, Kissinger flew to London for further discussions. Tony's love affair with Henry continued – banter, intellectual analysis, indiscretion mixed with awareness that the US Secretary of State said different things to different people. After the initial badinage, the Foreign Secretary opened their formal meeting by reminding Kissinger: 'We have got to get Smith out of the picture.'

After several more days' shuttling Kissinger was back in London. In the formal discussions at No. 10 it emerged that the original Annex C – intended for Kissinger alone – had been left behind with Vorster, who was in contact with Smith.

That evening the Kissingers had dinner at Lansdowne Road. The four of us talked about other matters. The following morning Kissinger resumed his shuttle. Ted Rowlands thought he should have gone along as well. Tony was adamant: there was no point while Kissinger was carrying this ball.

The Foreign Secretary was getting daily feedback from the relevant FO diplomats about how each front-line President felt about the proposals. Sometimes Kissinger used one set of proposals, sometimes another. He didn't stay in one place long enough to be trapped into supplementary questions. He was in the next capital by then.

Neither form of Annex C had been put to Cabinet: both were exploratory. Why take hypothetical tactics to Cabinet? Nothing to do with Rhodesia could be got through Cabinet if the front-line Presidents were unable to accept it. FO officials were clear that this had been explained to Kissinger time and time again, and that he deliberately chose to misunderstand: this was his great negotiating technique. He never divulged to the British what precisely he was saying to whom.

A very few senior FO officials were aware that privately the Foreign Secretary had come to feel his own judgment in this area might now be better than Kissinger's. Africa was a different world from the power blocs. Did Kissinger understand the fragmented nature of politics in Rhodesia?

'What worries me about Henry,' Tony said over gossip, 'is his tendency to do things impressionistically without keeping in mind what one party has in fact agreed to. Repeatedly I have to send him messages to keep him from bouncing me, even though he might be doing so unintentionally.'

'I gave them different arguments to achieve a common purpose,' Kissinger said to me later. 'That's what diplomacy is about. My outstanding characteristic is that I am a great persuader.'

Alongside the joint struggle to find a basis for negotiations, the two men kept up their habit of badinage. Halfway through September they devised a points system. On ringing the FO at 9.30 a.m. and being put through to Tony on the scrambler in the study at Lansdowne Road, Henry began: 'You score two points for being home at 9.30.' That night when Henry rang again, Tony said into the scrambler: 'You get one point for your originality in phoning London from Zürich via Washington, thus ensuring secrecy through total inaudibility . . . Henry, your voice has disappeared again.'

A highly confidential letter from Kissinger was typed, he explained, because Tony couldn't read his handwriting and would penalise him two points for illegibility.

A vital coded telegram from Downing Street West to Pretoria ended: 'One point for delaying my departure to Grimsby.'

A week after the Foreign Secretary had said to Kissinger, 'We must get Smith out of the picture,' Kissinger sent a message: Vorster preferred the original Annex C, which included the proposal more favourable to Smith. The Foreign Secretary then sent a message saying they could not go back to that concept. He received a further message: Kissinger had handed the revised Annex C to Vorster and left it with him. The next day, Vorster was with Smith. This meant Smith now had both documents.

Kissinger began to report on his second round of talks with Smith. The pattern was changing all the time, but Kissinger was making something happen. He complained indirectly to Tony that UK cavilling over Annex C was jeopardising his, Kissinger's, strategy. On 20 September the Foreign Secretary instructed the FO to prepare a chronology of events concerning the two documents, then flew to Brussels for a meeting of the Council of Ministers. On the 21st, having read the chronology, he instructed that a message be delivered orally to Kissinger making it *absolutely clear* that Britain has a Cabinet system of government. The Cabinet had not endorsed the details, as the Prime Minister had made clear to Dr Kissinger on 6 September. Annex C – in both its forms – had been put forward purely as a discussion document.

That afternoon Tony and I went together to Grimsby for a special reception in honour of a notable retired skipper. We caught the 7.15 a.m. train back to London on the 22nd. When he went into his office, he found that an FO diplomat in southern Africa had put the oral message for Kissinger in writing, making it seem unpleasant and unhelpful. Meanwhile some other officials had let the press know of their deep scepticism of Kissinger's tactics. Palliser was away. The Foreign Secretary called into his office everyone concerned. Curt angry words followed. Immediately afterwards he went to a diplomatic correspondents' lunch and said that he supported Kissinger and deplored the cynics – including those in his own office. (FO cavilling to the press stopped.) 'The trouble with being out of the country so much is that I can't control what happens in London,' Tony said when he came home that night. 'Apart from what it would mean in terms of human welfare, I shall be very happy for Henry if he pulls this off. It will give me great pleasure to see the cynics confounded.'

The next morning, the 23rd, the Foreign Secretary told the Cabinet that the Kissinger tour had produced a basis for an offer which Smith would make publicly. It was the first time anything to do with the American-British initiative had been discussed in Cabinet. He stated which front-line Presidents were in favour, which against. Care had been taken not to endorse the proposals. Kissinger had been irritated, but the British had made clear that the support of the front-line Presidents was essential. Kissinger had gone beyond what had been agreed. The British saw the five points to be announced by Smith as a basis for negotiation only. Kissinger saw it as a commitment.

Most of the Cabinet who took part in the argument were against the whole show. Furthermore, there was no evidence that Kissinger could get his proposals through the US Congress. In any case, Britain must not again get dragged into 'the Rhodesian morass'. But Britain had a debt of honour and a legal responsibility, the Foreign Secretary reminded them.

After Cabinet he had a working lunch with the French Socialist Party leader, Mitterrand, chaired the Cabinet Committee on economics, chaired a meeting with Euro-MPs, came home for supper. 'Gosh, it's nice to be home. Incredible. Absolutely incredible,' he said. After supper we were lying on the sofa opposite the drawing-room coal fire. Twenty minutes later he lifted his left arm, looked at his watch. 'We must be getting on,' he said. Ten minutes after that he left for Heathrow to meet Kissinger.

It was essential that on their drive to No. 10, he and Kissinger be alone in the back of the car. Callaghan had decided to include Denis Healey and Michael Foot and the Lord Chancellor, Elwyn-Jones, at the meeting. It would be useful to show Kissinger that it wasn't only the FO who had been cynical. But if anything was to advance, Kissinger had to be made to understand how British government works, how different Cabinet Ministers' minds work.

Tony was home again before midnight. 'Jim was right to have the others,' he said. 'All three responded amiably when Kissinger quietly but succinctly answered their various questions – for which he was now prepared. The meeting went beautifully. Elwyn told a long anecdote. Michael smiled from time to time with pleasure at dealing with this intellectual. Unlike in Cabinet this morning, Denis was subdued.' In the car, Kissinger had told Tony that no one before had adequately explained to him about Cabinet consensus. Tony felt Kissinger should already have understood.

What he didn't tell me was the substance of the meeting at No. 10. Among other things Kissinger said that his success in delivering Smith had been a combination of arrogance and ignorance. He had told Smith that what Smith could *not* do was put the five points forward and then haggle. The Prime Minister had spoken of the reluctance of Cabinet colleagues to get involved. There was a debt of honour, but there were great difficulties in rushing at the thing.

It was the next morning, 24 September. In Salisbury Ian Smith announced that he had accepted the five points of Dr Kissinger's 'package deal'. Commenting on the conditions of acceptance Mr Smith said: 'In the light of previous experience there will be some understandable scepticism regarding the undertaking that terrorism will cease, but on this occasion the assurance is given, not only on the authority of the United States Government, but of the British Government as well.'

In London, Smith's broadcast was heard with some consternation. The five points in the package deal, which had been sold as 'the British Plan', had never been authorised by the British Government.

That same morning in Downing Street West the US Secretary of State and the Foreign Secretary began their meeting at 9 a.m. Very sharp words were exchanged. The Foreign Secretary re-iterated forcibly that the Cabinet had not endorsed any detailed proposals. The US Secretary of State retorted that everything had to be subordinate to his getting Smith's agreement to majority rule. The Foreign Secretary remarked that history would no doubt judge whether Dr Kissinger was correct.

Then they gave a joint press conference before coming to Lansdowne Road with Nancy Kissinger and the American Ambassador, Anne Armstrong. Eileen had stayed beyond her three hours in order to cope with the world while I washed my hair. The doorbell rang. 'Three American gentlemen are in the hall, Mrs Crosland. They would like to speak to you.' With towel wrapped round my hair I met the forerunners of a squadron of Secret Servicemen. They asked politely to search the house and back garden. They appeared disturbed by the fact that all Val Arnold-Forster had to do was mount the stairs in her own house across the square at the back and aim a gun straight into our drawing-room, and Kissinger's bodyguards would have served in vain. His arrival always provided a spectacle for our neighbours, some of whom leant from their windows, cameras at the ready, when Lansdowne Road was summarily blocked by a seven-car cavalcade, a police van completing the procession.

24 September was the last Friday of the month. In the late afternoon Tony caught the train from King's Cross. It was his Grimsby weekend. The Town was playing at home. Marvellous. He was staying in Grimsby until Sunday when he and I would meet at Blackpool for the Labour Party Conference.

Before Tony reached Blackpool on Sunday 26 September, in Salisbury Smith had started to wriggle out of the five points.

44

Blackpool

I always looked forward to the Labour Party conference – five days at the seaside with Tony. Meals with friends without my cooking. Riding on the trams along the promenade. Walking on the sandy beach watching the waves roll in.

Transport House determines the hierarchical sleeping arrangements at conference, and Tony was not a member of the NEC. 'Do you realise if I was ever elected to the NEC we wouldn't have to pay for this extraordinary room?' he said, as he surveyed the arches and arabesque columns that adorned our sitting-room at the Imperial Hotel. He leant out a window to watch an illuminated tram approach, a cartwheel of winking stars revolving on its roof. We both loved Blackpool's illuminations.

We were joined in our exotic setting by Derek Gladwin, chairman of the Standing Orders Committee, the McCarthys and the two DLs who as usual were arguing with one another about which debate Tony should speak in for the five minutes allowed those lucky enough to be called to the rostrum by that year's Party chairman. At the same time Tony was muttering that he didn't want to enter any of the debates. 'I can't make a decent speech in five minutes,' he said.

'If you want to get on the NEC, you'll damn well have to,' Derek replied.

Had Tony been elected, he could have made his case at greater length from the platform. He first tried for one of the seven seats in the constituency section after Labour went into Opposition in 1970. He was runner-up, in eighth place. During 1971 as he made speeches all round the country, I felt there was an unseen map pinned to the study door, a couple of new flags planted in it each weekend. To his surprise and chagrin, at that year's conference he came ninth. By 1975 he was in twelfth place. He kept on trying.

Despite his shortcomings as an NEC candidate, his standing in the Party permitted us always to have a room facing the sea. In 1976, as a great favour to the Foreign Secretary, he was allowed a sitting-room as well, enabling private meetings to be held other than in the bedroom he shared with his wife. But the urgency of official business could not move Transport House to make any arrangements for a Principal Private Secretary: Ewen was lodged in what he termed a fleapit, blocks away from the Imperial Hotel. When he had sprinted to the Imperial, there was still only one telephone with a scrambler attached to it. That was in the No. 10 suite and surrounded by KEEP OFF signs – not always heeded by the FO.

On Sunday 26 September as we met at Blackpool, Kissinger's initiative in Rhodesia was falling apart. While Ian Smith haggled over the 'package deal', the front-line Presidents publicly dissociated themselves from it. They said they had never agreed to it. They wanted a conference.

Kissinger was in Washington, telephoning frantically to Blackpool. The momentum had got to be kept up. Britain must convene a conference and make an immediate announcement.

Sunday evening Tony was on the scrambler with the KEEP OFF signs surrounding it. This time he was ringing his Minister of State for African Affairs. Ted Rowlands was at home in Merthyr Tydfil, peacefully preparing to go off the next day to Botswana for the celebrations of its tenth birthday. Tony said: 'Get on a plane, Ted, and get out. I'm making an announcement in five minutes that you are going to call on the front-line Presidents to find out whether there is a basis for calling a constitutional conference. I am not going to be bounced. Keep away from the press. I'll do the rest from here.'

Five minutes later the Foreign Secretary issued a carefully-worded statement. The British Government was prepared to help organise a meeting or conference to consider the structure and functions of a transitional government to carry Rhodesia through to majority rule. The African Presidents had not accepted the proposals in their entirety as announced by Mr Smith, but they were willing to look at them as a basis for negotiation.

Smith, as always, had proved a superb tactician. He had never intended to accept majority rule: but he had to make the statement to get out of the corner into which Kissinger had backed him. Once out, Smith unscrambled the whole thing. Nevertheless, the value of Kissinger's September initiative was that Smith had actually used the words 'majority rule'. Even though he went back on the statement two days later, it had undermined white morale. 24 September was the beginning of the end for Smith.

In Blackpool on Monday, 27 September, the Foreign Secretary gave a small lunch for the Socialist International leaders who were visiting conference. Messages flew between southern Africa and Lancashire. After the General and Municipal Workers' dinner that evening – the GMWU was Tony's union – we went back to our suite where another meeting with FO officials began amid the arches and columns. As it was 11.30 p.m., I went to bed next door with a book, laying it aside as one o'clock approached and the murmur of voices in the sitting-room continued. It was their cessation, I imagine, that woke me at 1.30. I found Tony alone, having a nightcap, benign.

'Afraid Kissinger has left us in the shit,' he said equably.

'Intentionally or unintentionally?'

'Intentionally. But for a good cause. It was the only way to break the logjam.'

On Tuesday the 28th, shortly after the NEC election results were announced (Tony went back up to eleventh that year), in southern Africa the Minister of State received another message: he was to stop trying to get agreed terms of reference – just get the lot to meet anywhere for a constitutional conference. When the front-line Presidents were on board, as Ted Rowlands put it, he went to see Smith. They didn't shake hands. Ted sat at the other end of the room from Smith.

'I suppose you've come to tell me I've got to talk to those bloody blacks,' Smith said. That was the most liberal thing he said for the next forty-five minutes.

Ted was seething. But Tony had told him he had to get Smith to the conference. Smith said he'd attend if it was in Rhodesia. Ted told him that wasn't on. When the interview ended, Ted said:

'I take it you will attend a constitutional conference?'

'Yes.'

'What about Geneva?'

'Yes.'

'Thank you.' Ted walked out of Smith's room.

It had been early in September that Tony judged he should hold himself apart as long as Kissinger was running the show. Now Tony was not optimistic about the outcome of the Geneva conference. But it had to be convened.

Meanwhile in Blackpool he made further notes for the speech on Europe that he was making that afternoon at *Socialist Commentary*'s meeting: although he expressed genuine hopes for the EEC, he dissected what he saw as its inflated aspirations.

On Wednesday, between conference debates he wanted to attend, messages on the scrambler and FO consultations alternated with further discussions with members of the Socialist International. Rhodesia was urgent, but East-West relations were not to be ignored. During September Tony had begun forging a tougher line on the USSR. By December he would have the bones of an important speech to deliver next year. (The ideas would form the basis of the FO's general approach into the 1980s.)

Denis Healey thought he would have to miss conference's economic debate: it fell on 30 September, the day he'd be en route to the Commonwealth Finance Ministers' meeting in Hongkong. He'd actually reached Heathrow, been photographed in jaunty summer clothes in anticipation of warmer climes, when he was informed that the pound had staggered alarmingly. He went straight back to No. 11, decided he'd better make a quick trip to Blackpool to speak in that afternoon's economic debate. The Labour Government had entered its most traumatic phase since the energy crisis began.

When the Chancellor mounted the rostrum, he was in bullish form. 'I do not come with a Treasury view. I come from the battlefront ... I left this morning and I have not had anything to eat since I left.'

'Aawww.' The low drawn-out syllable of mock sympathy spread through the hall, delegates then bursting into a great gust of laughter at their own joke. Denis's natural flush deepened. For a moment he was stopped in his tracks. Nothing can throw a speaker more fatally than being laughed at when he's serious. In seconds Denis recovered, plunged on, his command of this difficult audience reasserted.

'That was a considerable feat,' Tony said afterwards.

In his own five-minute speech from the rostrum later that day, the Foreign Secretary told delegates why he had convened the conference in Geneva in a few weeks' time, what was at stake. Mr Smith had not had a change of heart: he had seen the writing on the wall. Delegates cheered. 'The Government, the NEC, and I hope conference this afternoon will show themselves united in our determination to play our part in bringing to Zimbabwe a peace which is firmly rooted, at long, long last, in black majority rule and so in justice and equality.' More applause.

Part of our Blackpool ritual was to lunch with Peter Jenkins and Alan Watkins at Yates' Wine Lodge and discuss the reason why Tony had failed to be elected to the NEC. Britain's two renowned political journalists wanted to know how he thought Labour should solve the economic crisis.

'There isn't a solution.'

Alan rephrased the question. 'The Treasury's policy is collapsing. You must have some idea of your own how to shore it up.'

'No one else has. Why should I?' He was in one of his perverse moods. 'You and Peter are both so clever: you tell us how the economy should be run.'

We reached coffee. Peter's deadline was approaching. 'You're meant to be Labour's great economist, Tony, yet apparently you have no idea how to make the crisis easier for people you profess to want to help.' Peter had been teased long enough.

'Actually, I'd like to know what you think,' I said.

'O.K.' He drawled the letters, sighed, put out his cheroot. A gloomy prognosis followed, his points made even more disheartening by being enumerated. 'Has everyone now got enough to write a column so that I can resume my duty to Queen and Country and bend my mind to foreign affairs?'

'I must go,' Peter said, rising from his chair, angry.

On his way back to conference, Tony strolled with me along the promenade, watching the waves roll over the broad beach. 'Not one of my more successful lunches with those two young men. They expect one to give them a tutorial. Why should I not be allowed a respite like most decent Englishmen?'

'You might have relented sooner. I rather felt for them.'

'So one gathered. You needn't waste your sympathy. I'll bet you five shillings that Peter Jenkins slips a needle in me in his column tomorrow.'

The *Guardian*'s political writer was more subtle. He waited until a Government announcement the following week made plain that the Treasury was in a state of emergency. In Peter's next column he called for a new Chancellor, reminding his readers that the Prime Minister had always intended at some point to swop Mr Crosland and Mr Healey in their jobs. But now, Peter wrote, there was some doubt that Mr Crosland would go to the Treasury because he had so irritated the Prime Minister by 'his intellectual squeamishness and inverted snobbism'.

I'd taken our breakfast back to bed at Lansdowne Road. Tony handed over the *Guardian*, indicating the relevant passage. 'Can you remember how much I bet you?' he said.

The annual Diplomatic Reception is the most onerous single evening sustained by the Royal Family, there being a hundred and fifty accredited countries, all their representatives and spouses to be presented. While the sovereign and her relations dealt with their duties, Tony and I looked at her collection of paintings, sat for a time on a sofa, talked with Rab Butler and one or two other congenial spirits. Just before the Royal Family completed their two-hour test of charm and endurance, the Foreign Secretary and I were shown to the supper room. (Supper turned out to be what I call hors-d'œuvres.) A footman came forward with a salver to offer me some 'supper'. The last time I'd seen him he'd been offering me the bottle of Malvern water. 'I shall never forget the sight of you lying unconscious on that floor, Madam. I have taxed myself ever since.'

'It was absolutely no one's fault but my own.'

The Royal Party entered the room. Angus Ogilvy, who had a bad back anyhow, was ashen. All the men looked pretty done in. The Queen Mother, fresh as a daisy, came up to ask if I was fully recovered. A side effect of my sister's and my fainting, I said, was that our mother stopped taking us to church when we were adolescents: three Sundays running one of us had fainted in the pews.

'Naughty mother,' the Queen Mother replied. 'She should have given you a little sprig of heather. I shall send you one. When my children were young, sometimes they said they couldn't sit through church: "I feel sick. I'm going to faint." I gave them each a little sprig of heather, and they were all right. These things are largely in the mind,' said the Queen Mother.

45

IMF

It was the first week of October. Tony was giving the British Foreign Secretary's annual address to the UN General Assembly. He devoted most of his speech to Rhodesia: none of the parties attending the Geneva conference would be able to claim pre-arranged points; none of the five points made by Mr Smith in his acceptance broadcast of 24 September had been negotiated.

The following day Tony and Henry Kissinger met in New York for formal talks. The discussion was acrimonious. Kissinger said he was amazed at the apparent duplicity of the British in not standing behind their own document. The Foreign Secretary said that Dr Kissinger's knowledge of the principles of the British constitution and government was incomplete.

Yet that evening the two men had a late supper with Nancy at the Kissingers' New York apartment and watched a television debate between President Ford and Jimmy Carter. The American election was drawing near.

In looking back on his southern Africa shuttle, certainly Henry Kissinger felt hard done by. 'Tony behaved with enormous honour throughout,' he said to me later. 'It was the British Government which sort of double-crossed me.' That the British had produced Annex C as a discussion paper only, that it could not have been got through Cabinet even on that basis, that it was never intended to be put to Smith directly – these were beside the point. It was a document. It was given to Kissinger by the Foreign Secretary and the Prime Minister: 'Whether it had gone through Cabinet was their problem,' he said.

Tony flew to Washington for half a day to give a foreign policy speech to the National Press Club. He declined to go into details of British and American discussions about Rhodesia, though he made clear that 'whatever anybody may have said', the coming conference at Geneva could have been called only if the points were open to negotiation. Of the proposed trust fund, he emphasised that its main object was to help independent Zimbabwe, not 'to do A, B, or C for the whites'. The Press Club gave him a navy-blue plastic windbreaker with their insignia on it. 'Just right for Adderbury,' he said over drinks with my sister and her family before he flew back to London that night.

'My dear Henry. I may be falling out of love with him.' Tony had just put the scrambler telephone back on its hook. He had a bad cold and was working at home. 'The extent to which Henry says different things to different people is very striking.'

Ewen, monitoring the call at the Foreign Office, rang back on the scrambler. 'Between the effect of your heavy cold and your general tone, Dr Kissinger can have been in no doubt of your view of American diplomacy,' he said.

How far Kissinger was prepared to be less than straightforward with *him* took Tony aback. Having noted the fact, however, and got over his cold, he adjusted his love affair. His feelings about a very remarkable man were no longer unmixed, but intellectual admiration and affection still predominated.

Tony deliberately did not go to the Geneva talks where Rhodesia's white and African leaders, assisted by five front-line Presidents, assisted by the British and Americans, were supposed to thrash out the details for an interim government to lead Rhodesia to black rule in two years. He felt he would be a more valuable influence at a later, decisive stage if he hadn't personally committed himself to an operation he thought would be a fair shambles. Instead he sent Britain's UN Ambassador and former Labour minister, Ivor Richard, and Ted Rowlands. The Geneva talks opened on 28 October 1976 and were adjourned seven weeks later (and never in fact reconvened).

When Tony would go to Rhodesia was affected by who won the American election on 2 November. When Carter won, it meant Kissinger continued to be US Secretary of State for only the remaining two months of Ford's 'lame-duck' Government. At Lansdowne Road, Tony told Henry of his mixed feelings. With Henry out of office, Tony could assume the role of ideas-generator which he now felt competent to undertake in foreign affairs. At the same time, he would miss Henry.

At Downing Street West, feelings were unmixed. As Kissinger faded out, they saw clearly the vacuum to be filled. They realised that the man they had despaired of a few months before was the obvious man to fill it.

No sooner did they rejoice than the Foreign Secretary behaved in the way the FO deplores: he put his ideals as a Labour Minister and a democratic socialist before what they saw as a Foreign Secretary's role. The IMF crisis of November 1976 had begun.

By the beginning of November the pound was near ruin, so battered that a gigantic loan from the International Monetary Fund had to be negotiated. For three weeks a small team of IMF men made London their home, laying down the terms on which they'd lend to the British Treasury. At the heart of the discussion lay the problem of the Public Sector Borrowing Requirement (PSBR), i.e. the budget deficit – the amount by which public spending exceeded the Government's revenue from taxation. The terms began to leak out before Monday 22 November when Ministers learned the harrowing extent that the PSBR must be reduced – the economy deflated – if the IMF was to lend money to the British Government. Monday saw the start of a very infrequent instance of Ministers getting together outside the Cabinet Room to work on general Government policy, not something specifically related to their own departments.

There were two groups opposing the IMF's terms. On Monday night one group met in Peter Shore's room at the House; Peter, Michael Foot, Tony Benn, John Silkin, Stan Orme, Albert Booth all agreed to oppose the cuts. They planned to put the case for the Cambridge School's alternative. In another room Tony Crosland's group was meeting, but their leader was absent. He was dining at Buckingham Palace.

Monday had been another of those days. In the morning Tony told Ivor Richard his decision to involve the British Government in the actual running of Rhodesia under the interim government being proposed at the Geneva conference. He would ask the Cabinet's approval the next day: they mightn't give it. Early in the afternoon he was told details of the IMF's terms. Then the talks with the President of Venezuela began at No. 10. It was because of President Perez that while Tony's group was meeting at the Commons, he and I were dining at Buckingham Palace. When we got back to Lansdowne Road he said to me: 'For the first time I wonder if the Government can survive. Jim intends to say to our backbenchers: "You can accept the cuts or you can have Mrs Thatcher." Even if the Government survives, does it make such a difference if Labour measures can't be implemented? What the press cannot understand is that this is the most right-wing Labour Government we've had for years.'

He answered the telephone. It was Roy Hattersley, reporting back on the meeting in Tony's room. Harold Lever, Shirley

Williams, David Ennals had been there, and Bill Rodgers had come in halfway through. All opposed cuts. But their opposition was based on different arguments. Ennals and Shirley wanted to protect their departments' budgets. Lever, like Hattersley – and Tony – thought the whole exercise unnecessarily deflationary.

When he put the receiver back Tony was acutely, uncharacteristically, depressed. The cuts would make pointless everything he'd done at Housing and Transport, everything that Barbara and others had done for the social services: these would be dished. 'There must be a better alternative.'

I went to bed. He walked up and down the study floor for another hour and a half, made notes.

On Tuesday Cabinet approved the step forward he proposed for Rhodesia. Then the Chancellor put the IMF's terms to Cabinet. November had brought Denis, tough as he was, close to exhaustion. The Prime Minister's cough – his sign of tension – got worse. All except the most right-wing Ministers felt on a rack. The Chancellor said that Britain must accept the IMF terms or not get the loan.

The Foreign Secretary had passed a message to the Prime Minister, asking to speak next. Tony put the counter-argument he'd thought through the night before.

There was no economic case for the cuts, he said. He dealt with the arguments one by one. With $1\frac{1}{4}$ million unemployed, nobody could say that there was not enough spare capacity to increase exports. Far from reducing the PSBR, the spending cuts would mean higher unemployment, which would in turn mean higher social security payments and lower tax revenue, thus actually increasing the PSBR. In any case, the Treasury forecasts of the PSBR were unreliable; other experts' forecasts were much lower than the Treasury's.

The cuts would massacre the industrial strategy. So far as trade unions were concerned, Jack Jones might agree, but the public sector would not. Without the public sector unions the Social Contract, already deeply damaged by the effects of the cuts on rents and so on, would collapse.

The only serious argument for cuts was one in terms of international confidence. But what would happen to confidence if the Government bowed down and accepted the package, and as a result the Social Contract broke, and the smouldering resentment of the PLP meant that the Government could not deliver the cuts in the House of Commons?

The Government had made its negotiations too public to do

nothing now. He was prepared to see cuts – mainly cosmetic – of one billion pounds, half a billion coming from the sale of shares in Burmah Oil, the other half to be found in the least deflationary way possible. The Government should then say to the IMF, the Americans and the Germans: if you demand any more of us we shall put up the shutters, wind down our defence commitments, introduce a siege economy. As the IMF was even more passionately opposed to protectionism than it was attached to monetarism, this threat would be sufficient to persuade the Fund to lend the money without unacceptable conditions.

Politically the IMF could not refuse the loan. If the Government kept its nerve, it could insist on its own terms – could limit the cuts to 'window-dressing' to appease the irritating and ignorant currency dealers. 'We have to stop paying "danegeld".'

That was the Crosland counter-argument. It was fully noted and ascribed to him in the subsequent Cabinet minutes – an unusual acknowledgment. It was so convincing that some colleagues wondered why he had offered cuts at all. He offered them as a gesture to the Chancellor's international bargaining position. ('We can't give Denis a hopeless negotiating hand,' he told D. Lip.)

The Prime Minister went round the table, then cut the discussion short. Of the thirteen people who spoke, ten took the view that the loan could be obtained on the terms set out by the Foreign Secretary – cuts largely done by mirrors. Only two supported the Chancellor: 'Reg Prentice, who is mad, and Edmund Dell who is in a very very reactionary state of mind. Both thought Denis hadn't gone far enough!' Our gossip that evening was even later than usual. 'It was a dramatic Cabinet – and a very interesting discussion. Jim didn't – as he said last night he would – support Denis. When Jim summed up, he was *excellent*.'

As reports of this Cabinet rocketed round Whitehall, the Treasury knew it had suffered a defeat; it still expected to win in the end. The Cabinet had agreed that before it met again on Thursday, the Prime Minister would communicate with the American President and the German Chancellor and tell them that Britain would not accept the IMF's terms. At that very moment, a Treasury representative was in Bonn putting the case to Chancellor Schmidt before the counter-argument could be heard.

Wednesday was another of those days, begun at 7.40 with Tony going to Heathrow to see off President Perez. He had barely got into his office when the Italian Foreign Minister, Forlani, arrived for talks, lunch, dinner. The Falkland Islands issue was coming to the boil. Rhodesia was never far away. In between, Tony and Roy Hattersley were preparing a paper on an import deposit scheme and wondering if it were possible to move into an alliance with the group gathered round the Cambridge School's alternative of severe restrictions on international trade. Hattersley suggested that his own political adviser, David Hill, make the approach to Tony Benn's political adviser, Frances Morrell. Hill and Morrell were leading figures in Islington politics and knew one another well.

As both groups were fighting the Treasury's deflationary package, Hill said, could they not join forces in a united front?

Morrell replied that the Bennites were not willing to play that game with the Crosland group. Hill was left with the strong impression that Morrell was speaking for Foot, Shore, Silkin, Orme and Booth, as well as for Benn. It seemed strange: Foot was the titular leader of the group, and Shore – as a former President of the Board of Trade – would ordinarily be the member to put forward an economic paper for the group.

At Thursday's Cabinet, the Chancellor was very subdued as he put the Treasury's case. The Foreign Secretary was called upon next as leader of the opposition: he set out the import deposit scheme with which Healey could go back to the IMF and beat them down. The Cabinet would not meet again until the next Wednesday, because the Prime Minister – and his Foreign Secretary – would be attending a European Council in The Hague earlier in the coming week.

Later on that same Thursday, when Tony and Denis Healey were together at a meeting on a different issue, Tony took every opportunity to display support for Denis. Denis was near the end of his tether. (He told Edna he appreciated what Tony was doing.) After a briefing for the Hague discussions, Tony went off to speak at an evening meeting for the Streatham Constituency Labour Party. He was in a good mood: it was still possible that a united front would break the IMF's hold on Healey; and, though Callaghan consistently told Tony that he expected to support his Chancellor in Cabinet, he still had not done so.

It was the last Monday of November when the Prime Minister and Foreign Secretary flew to The Hague. After the European Council's Tuesday meeting, they returned to England. Tony called in at Lansdowne Road and we gossiped for a bit before he had a nap. He was sad about his conversation with Jim on the flight back. Jim, very self-confident and relaxed, said that he would now support Denis. Schmidt had taken a hard line.

'The irony', Tony said, 'is that Ford/Carter will within a month almost certainly take a soft line. Although Jim repeated that all the arguments haven't yet been heard, he expects to accept the IMF's terms. He said it courteously and without animosity. Not in a spirit of confrontation – which is counter-productive with Jim – I inserted arguments to remind him of the growing general opinion against the IMF's terms.'

After supper Tuesday night Tony went off to the House of Commons for divisions. Hattersley had arranged for Tony's group to meet again in his room. It was a disappointing meeting. Bill Rodgers had gone over to the Prentice-Dell hard line. Shirley and David Ennals were undecided what was best to do since they now seemed likely to save some of their departmental budgets. Shirley was talking of putting together a 'compromise' paper to satisfy Healey and the Crosland group and perhaps even Benn. Tony and Harold Lever and Roy Hattersley alone were unchanged in their opposition to the IMF's terms.

At Wednesday's Cabinet the ten Ministers who hadn't spoken before said they would support the Prime Minister in whatever he judged to be best. Callaghan, as he'd said he would, gave Tony Benn the opportunity to set out his case for a siege economy. Benn got carried away by rhetoric, thus further diminishing the possibility of a united front against the Treasury: he was pulverised by Denis. Shirley was attacked in turn by all the prospective parties to the compromise she proposed. Peter Shore made a strong lucid case for import controls of a less wild order than those that Benn had wanted.

Shore's argument was reinforced by the Crosland paper on his import deposit scheme which he'd put to Cabinet the previous Thursday. This still lay on the table, to be brought into play if the IMF did not relent. It was this paper on which the final struggle turned. It did two things: it presented the Treasury with a viable alternative, and it kept open the way to an alliance between those opposing the Treasury.

And during Wednesday's Cabinet it emerged that Healey had moved away from his original demands: the cuts required by the IMF were now almost halved. 'Jim is a foxy character,' Tony said during our gossip when he rang me that night from his room at the House; divisions were going on indefinitely and he wanted me to get some sleep. He was none the less depressed. 'Some things went well this morning but not enough to make Jim change his mind. He'll come out tomorrow in support of the Treasury. I'll tell you more about it over the weekend when the whole thing will have become more coherent. Meanwhile, I must think what I shall say in tomorrow's Cabinet.'

'I'm very sorry it's coming out like this, Tony. Do you mind just because of the cuts or also because of your part in the affair?'

'Inevitably a mixture of the two, but mostly I care about the first. And it's true that when the Prime Minister joins with the Chancellor, usually they are unbeatable and in this case shouldn't be beaten. If it became known – which it would with this leaking Cabinet – that Jim had been defeated by Cabinet, it would be murder. He is our strongest card. I may well switch my argument halfway tomorrow and say this: that in these circumstances we cannot afford not to support the Prime Minister. He is crucial.'

Meanwhile, as I went to sleep on Wednesday night, in his room at the House Tony learned disheartening news about his supporters. Harold Lever said that as a free-trader he could not go along with the import deposit scheme, and anyhow he thought it deflationary. Shirley said the import deposit scheme was protectionist and would damage the Third World. Hattersley alone stood fast. This meant that in a Cabinet of twenty-three, only eight were now opposing the cuts.

When the others had left, Tony told Hattersley of the conversation with Jim on the plane coming back from The Hague. Callaghan had asked him not to repeat the conversation. Tony thought it necessary now to do so. He told his remaining supporter of Jim's intention at the next day's Cabinet, adding that Jim had asked him to keep it to himself.

'He doesn't trust us,' Roy said.

'Of course not. No one would at a time like this,' Tony replied. 'Since I now propose to give my reluctant support to Jim, you must do the same. No time for heroics – or for you to think that your judgment is better than mine.'

Tony then went down the corridor to the Prime Minister's room. 'In Cabinet tomorrow,' he said to Jim, 'I shall say I think you're wrong, but I also think that Cabinet must support you.' In that case, Jim said, he would speak after Denis and before Tony.

Thus, when Cabinet met on 2 December to take its collective decision, as soon as the Chancellor had completed his presentation, the Prime Minister told his colleagues that he supported the Chancellor. The Foreign Secretary spoke next. He said that the Prime Minister's statement had significantly changed the situation. The Treasury's critics could no longer win. Tony remained absolutely unconvinced by the economic arguments which had been used. But his clear political judgment was that, given the position which the

Prime Minister had taken, it would not be right to press the issue. If it became known that the anti-deflationists constituted a large minority in Cabinet, this would ruin confidence not only in currency markets. It could smash up the Party.

Though the outcome was a draw between the Foreign Secretary and the Treasury, Tony was depressed that the Government had been so manoeuvred in advance that it had to make even half the cuts originally demanded.

In December the Cabinet had to decide where to make the cuts. It was at this time that the Foreign Secretary most hurt his top officials, played it quite rough. One of them later told me how they felt about it: 'The Department was fairly relaxed when he took the line that the IMF was a capitalist body with narrow criteria for judging whether a country was doing well or badly, intolerable that a socialist Government should have this philosophy imposed on it.' The FO tended to side with the IMF in the interest of 'international confidence'. 'What irritated officials was his putting domestic needs first. It wasn't just this single December budget when he questioned whether the size of our defence commitment was necessary: it was a running argument. He argued that if the choice had to be made, the cuts should be in defence rather than, say, housing. Iconoclasm and scepticism are not unhealthy, but we felt he was too subjective.'

The FO has always cherished the illusion that foreign policy transcends Party politics. Two Foreign Secretaries widely recognised as remarkable were Labour: Ernest Bevin and George Brown. Ernie was loved throughout the diplomatic service. George was not, because he behaved so abominably at times. But both shared a quality that endeared them to officials: both saw their job in terms solely of advancing British interests abroad. Tony did not. This was maddening for officials – constantly having to take into account things they thought were irrelevant.

His recalcitrance on the Defence budget was bad enough. But he was also unorthodox – lesser FO officials might have said 'unsound' – on free trade. In a sense, free trade is what the Foreign Office is all about. 'He made no bones about the fact that he felt things had changed and we needed to protect our economy more,' this top official continued. 'He was moving towards agreed regulations of trade, whatever our allies abroad might feel. What was so irritating was that he was a very good economist, so he could argue unorthodox economic views cogently.'

'It is ludicrous', Tony said more than once, 'that I have not a single professional economist, committed to the Labour Party, to advise me.' The FO has adequately competent bureaucrats on general international economic matters, but he wanted an alternative voice. He asked Michael Stewart, an economist and former Labour candidate with a lot of Whitehall experience, to come into the FO as his personal economic adviser. Stewart would take leave from his job at London University and start work on 11 February 1977.

The Treasury felt Tony didn't understand their argument against high public expenditure: some officials hoped he would become Chancellor soon so that they could get at him directly. Denis Healey talked openly to the TUC: 'This is the last time you and I will have to argue this point. The next time you will have to argue it with Tony Crosland.'

'Do you want to be Chancellor at a time when apparently nothing can be achieved to further Labour aims?' I asked him during gossip at Lansdowne Road.

'I've mixed feelings. It would be a challenge: I would still like to see if it isn't possible to do better, however frightful the economic situation will be for the next couple of years. I'd also like to stay on at the Foreign Office for another eight months – which is what Jim originally intended. I'm now getting on top of it at an increasing rate. At last Monday's meeting at The Hague, Jim could look to me to make the case in confidence that I knew the subject, unlike the Puerto Rico summit where this patently wasn't so. I'd like it either way, which is a nice feeling.'

'You used to say you weren't interested in foreign affairs.'

'You sure I said that?'

'Frequently to Shirley.'

'It was a silly, childish remark for me to make.' He looked slightly sheepish.

A few days later the Kissingers were in London making their official goodbye. While Nancy did her Christmas shopping, Henry came to Lansdowne Road on Saturday and was introduced to English football: we took him to Stamford Bridge to see Chelsea play Wolves. He'd called in at No. 11 on the previous evening to see the Healeys. Edna told them that in the years at Oxford, when it was obvious that Denis and Tony and Roy Jenkins would be political rivals, she'd always believed it was Tony who would go to the top.

'All this speculation is entertaining,' Tony said, 'but it's footling. Funny if it turns out that the leadership jumps over our generation.'

⇢ 46 ⇠

In His Stride

It was our first Christmas at Adderbury. Instead of three generations of Tony's family gathering at Lansdowne Road on Boxing
Day, we'd held a summer party for them in his Foreign Office
room overlooking Horse Guards Parade, everyone taking turns for
the best view of the Trooping of the Colour below. With Pete at
the University of Hawaii, he and Sheila and the baby were in
Honolulu for Christmas. Ellen-Craig returned to south London to
start the New Year.

'Do you think there's something odd about us?' Tony said. We
were reading either side of the wood fire, which was his responsibility at Adderbury. 'Most people haven't had *one* of the things
we've had together. Must be extremely rare to manage the transi-
tions to each new phase which – while different – have all been so
happy. Extraordinary when one thinks about it. If we're not careful,
we'll end up like Darby and Joan.'

'I've never known who this Darby and Joan were.'

'You expect me to teach you what every English schoolgirl
knows. I'm meant to be thinking about the nation's affairs. They
lived only for each other until they were ninety years old. Something like that.'

From the sitting-room we could see the brook, brown and
swollen, rushing self-importantly past the bottom of the garden,
spilling over into the garden. 'Think I like Adderbury best of all in
winter,' he said. 'Gives an even greater sense of our being alone
together.'

On the floor in neat piles almost encircling his chair was his
holiday work – FO stuff and a big chunk of the Gaitskell biography
that Philip Williams had been working on for ten years. Philip had
asked Tony to read a draft. On his side table was Kingsley Amis's
Alteration. In the so-called study, on a table from The Boltons,
waited the other books brought to read for fun, lying alongside the
scrambler and a tape recorder lent by the FO. On the reels were
the French lessons he gave himself twenty minutes a day when at
Adderbury. He spoke good French but not effortlessly, thought his

six months as President of the EEC Foreign Ministers would be less taxing if he were more fluent. 'Bilingual at the age of four, and one let it go: I shall never forgive myself.'

The McCarthys drove over from Oxford for an extended family lunch – the Leonards and D. Lip were there. After animated dissection of the Labour Party, someone raised a television programme, the first of its kind, being prepared by Granada: it would reconstruct a critical moment in British politics. The moment was the IMF crisis of November 1976. Cabinet Ministers would be acted by journalists, Peter Jenkins to play Tony. Each Minister would need to brief his surrogate if the journalist-actors were to get it right.

'Well, I'm not going to,' Tony said. 'Very uneasy about this kind of candour about Cabinet.'

Margaret McCarthy was furious. 'All the others involved are going to be putting themselves forward in the best light they can. I'm sick of having you lead on these occasions and then be left blushing modestly in a corner while others take the credit.' She laid about Tony as only Margaret could. He began to laugh. In the end, he agreed to discuss the thing generally with Peter Jenkins over lunch at Adderbury. (Peter still didn't get all he wanted.)

Clea had a cushion in front of the fire. She slept more than when he'd given her to the children before we married. 'That cat can't live for ever, Susan. I can see it all: tears streaming down your face. You've got to accept the fact that she's going to die one of these days.' They played a game. Each time he got out of his chair to battle with the fire, shift a log shaped like a rhinoceros, he turned back to find Clea in his chair, pretending to be asleep. He lifted her, still curled up, flat on his hands, replacing her on her proper cushion. 'You *know* that's my chair.' It took two to play the game.

He induced me to join him on a short walk – not one of the hour-long things when he strode up hill and down dale, stopping to examine the seventeenth-century architecture that prevails in Adderbury. We examined our estate, the fairyland half-acre of wild garden, stepped through the door in the hedge, crossed the surging brook and walked the sodden path along the other side. 'Have we really had Adderbury for eighteen months? Incredible,' he said. 'When I realise how fast time is going, I feel a cold hand at my heart.'

He got up from his chair to pour a second cup of tea, giving a tug at the ancient army fatigues dyed bottle green. 'That's that. I finally understand about all these bloody countries. Actually look forward to the next seven months. God it would be marvellous to get Rhodesia settled before I go to the Treasury.'

'When are you going to Rhodesia?'

'Probably in March. Soon after we return from Washington. Jim's taking Audrey, so you'll be expected to come. You'll like that part of my job – be able to see your sister. Interesting to discover what Carter is like. I daresay I'll find six months' to-ing and fro-ing to Brussels a bore, but it's worth it for the challenge: if it's the last thing I do, I'm going to change their ludicrous procedure.' He lit a cheroot. '*Phyffi, phyffi*. Hope Jim doesn't change his mind and swop Denis and me before August. Now that I'm in my stride I've rather taken to this job.'

Despite their differences, some in the Foreign Office had taken to him. With Kissinger gone, a new initiative in Rhodesia was being prepared. In January 1977 Britain assumed the EEC presidency for the first time. FO officials looked forward to a productive six months: the Foreign Secretary's skill as a chairman meant that agreements in the Council of Ministers could be reached economically instead of dragging on for ever. A few top-level civil servants had reservations about the detente speech he was thinking through – more hostile ideologically than they advised – but it was gratifying to have a Foreign Secretary ready to work at this level.

At Adderbury it was late when Tony came to bed. 'Amis's book is so exciting I couldn't wait to see what would happen,' he explained.

On Sunday Chris drove us to the RAF airfield at Northolt to meet the German Chancellor and his Foreign Minister for an overnight summit meeting at Chequers, Schmidt impressive and charming in his seaman's cap. Tony's own white cap, intended for milkers – given him by Frankie Donaldson fifteen years before to keep his hair out of his eyes when playing tennis – must have got caught up in *Britannia*'s laundry: we never set eyes on it again. He so admired the German Chancellor's cap that Schmidt said he'd send him a similar one. Evidently Tony had told the others it was my birthday: when I joined them for drinks before their working dinner, an Anglo-German rendering of 'Happy Birthday' boomed forth.

Over supper for two, Audrey Callaghan said: 'You've never been to Dorneywood.' Dorneywood was the country house a philanthropist had presented to the nation for the Foreign Secretary's use.

'There's been so little time alone, Audrey, and we wanted to be at Adderbury.'

'Why don't you give Dorneywood a try? It's very beautiful and not too large. You have to pay for the food and drink, of course, but the staff buys and cooks and washes up. It would be nice for you, Susan.' Another factor was new to me: Dorneywood's staff had to be in constant attendance whether the Foreign Secretary was there or not: if he had no interest in the place, the trustees intended transferring it to some other body. Later that night while the Germans took a swim in Chequers' indoor pool, Tony joined me in a four-poster bed. We decided to have a look at Dorneywood.

The next free weekend, however, was spent at Adderbury. Walking at the bottom of the garden where the brook swirled past, Tony said again: 'I feel a cold hand at my heart. Haven't thought about death for a long time. Gives one an odd feeling.'

'Do you want to talk about it?'

'Over our pre-dinner drink?'

We were sitting either side of the fire. 'It's not that I'm afraid of death. What I mind about it is there's so much I still want to do.' He wasn't talking just about political objectives. 'I haven't even seen all of my own country. Still, not a lot one can do about it. Just wanted to tell you.'

Because we knew each other's thoughts so well, we sometimes spoke elliptically. I was thinking about people when they're very old – someone like my mother – who often would rather be dead than like that. I said: 'Now that human beings have adapted to the trauma of the birth pill, don't you think they'll soon accept the idea of a death pill?'

He was out of his chair and standing over me. He was seldom angry with me – had never been like this. 'How can you talk like that? Suicide is the most cowardly thing I can think of.'

'You've never said that before. You know how much I mind when people say that.'

'I say it now because I want you to know I think it. You have two daughters. You have an infant granddaughter. To commit suicide would be the most cowardly thing you could do.'

'I wasn't talking about now. I was talking about thirty, forty years from now.'

'I don't think you were.'

He was so – what? – intense that I no longer felt sure what I had been talking about. I certainly thought it was a long time ahead. Perhaps it wasn't. He'd shaken me.

'We won't go on about it. You know how I feel.' He returned to his chair. 'Let's have our second drink and read and recover our evening. Over sups we can move on to a more agreeable subject.'

Dorneywood was as Audrey described, except that Tony was irritated by the ground-floor windows being sealed. All doors had to be propped open, including the front door of the house, to get a breath of air into the drawing-room where he worked in an armchair. This meant the detective suffered over the loss of security, the Foreign Secretary suffered over the loss of privacy. The windows would be in use by our next visit, we were told.

Over dinner prepared and served by someone else I said: 'As there's no country house that goes with the Treasury, perhaps we ought to exploit Dorneywood while you're still at the Foreign Office, alternating with Adderbury when a weekend away is possible. I love Adderbury more and more, but we'll have it to enjoy for the rest of our lives. Dorneywood is available only for the next six months: we could use it to entertain people we've not been able to see for years.'

'Marvellous place to hold seminars,' he said. 'Michael Stewart starts working for me on Friday. I could get people together here and actually thrash something out. Then everyone could walk round the park and enjoy the place. We'd give them lunch without your having to cook it.'

In its serene park, the house was of human proportions, light and airy – not some vast impersonal heap. Only the master bedroom was furnished in the magisterial, massive style admired at the turn of the century. The Callaghans used it when Jim was Foreign Secretary, and we were put there for our first weekend because I'd said we would like a double bed. At the other end of the corridor was a far prettier room with two outlooks, flawed only by its twin beds. Dorneywood's trustees took a poor view of rearranging the benefactor's furniture. The housekeeper and I devised a way to make the twin beds suitable for conjugal life. The Croslands would try out that room on their next visit. 'Come look at it, Tony,' I said before lunch.

We returned in the afternoon to the master bedroom with its dark mahogany – looming outsize double-bed, tall mirror on castors, expressions of the Victorians' heightened sense of virtue and vice. Round the walls, closely arrayed, stood Victorian statesmen, each engraved eminence in his window, so to speak. 'Do you find it makes you feel slightly wicked having all those dignitaries gazing down upon us?'

'You are childish,' he said. When he woke, he looked at his watch. 'We must be getting on,' he said. 'Want to get in two-and-a-half hours on detente before dinner. What are you going to do?'

'That will be your epitaph – carved on your tombstone in huge block letters: WE MUST BE GETTING ON.'

' "Never a dull moment" will be carved on yours,' he said. 'Wish I could remember when you first said that. Something catastrophic had just happened.'

'Was it when we were driving back from Sandwich and that thing the English call the Big End fell out of your car? Some garage coped while you took me on a long walk to a village with half-timbered houses and a church that had a chequered tower. Chilham? It was a very hot day.'

'Wasn't that. Something else. Wish my memory was better.' He looked at his watch. 'Chattering as if we hadn't a care in the world. We really must be getting on.'

He was giving the detente speech to the Diplomatic and Commonwealth Writers' Association in the first week of March. The central section was intended to be published complete in itself. Tony felt that some British diplomats were too soft with the USSR, unwilling to interfere in Russia's internal affairs – namely, human rights – lest trade be adversely affected. He felt the risk should be taken if any effective outside influence was to be wielded on behalf of the dissidents. In the speech he was ventilating the whole philosophy of Communist Russia. He had fired his first ideological shot over the Soviet bows at a NATO meeting in December.

In the early 1970s there had been a kind of euphoria about an alteration in the Soviet attitude. He was asserting that the USSR is intrinsically aggressive. Unless this was acknowledged, detente would simply deteriorate into a charade from which only the Soviet Union would benefit. He was shifting from use of the word 'detente' to 'management of East-West relations'. It was possible, he said, to manage these in such a way as to permit a greater range of contacts – trade, cultural, and so on – while also pressing one's own values.

He could get away with this, the FO realised, because he was rock solid in his knowledge of international socialism. All the same they thought the speech too provocative, were concerned that he cited Brezhnev by name. At Dorneywood he made the speech even more abrasive: 'Very well. If this is the challenge of the high priests of Marxism, let ideological battle be done. I am happy to pick up the gauntlet. I can think of no better way of demonstrating the barrenness of Communist state collectivism than engaging on equal terms in the struggle for ideas.'

The Hattersleys came to Sunday lunch at Dorneywood. We went for a long walk afterwards through the crisp frosted parkland, Tony in his red-leather carpet slippers and a long belted overcoat. 'Belonged to my first wife's brother,' he said in explanation of how a coat could be moth-eaten and fashionable at the same time: the passage of twenty-five years had brought it into vogue again.

While we strolled through the greenhouse, he and Roy Hattersley talked about the need for a new book on socialism. 'We have got to keep making the point', Tony said to him, 'that the far Left are not the only people who can claim a socialist theory while the rest of us are thought to be mere pragmatists and administrators.' The distinction he made within the Party was between the radical thinkers and what he called the ameliorators of the Right. 'It's not enough to disagree with the Marxists *et al*. The Centre must remember and keep reminding people that we are ideologists too.'

When Molly and Roy left, Tony returned to detente.

He'd marked in his Labour Party pocket diary which weekends would be free for the next six months. I went through these with the housekeeper, deciding which would be used for seminars and lunches at Dorneywood. 'You mean there's a future for us, Madam?' he said. I felt bad I hadn't appreciated their position before.

◆ 47 ◆

An 'Ultimate' Weekend

On the evening of Tuesday 8 February the No. 2 Private Secretary rang from the Foreign Office: the Brussels meeting on fishery policy was still going on, the Secretary of State mightn't get home that night.

'He threatened before he left to change the other Ministers' desultory habits even if it meant keeping them up all night until they agreed.'

'The Secretary of State is the only one under threat, Mrs Crosland. The other Foreign Ministers can go home to bed and leave someone in their place.'

Later Ewen rang from Brussels, cheerful as usual, though they wouldn't get back until Wednesday. 'It's gone very well indeed, and the Secretary of State is not giving up now. With luck we'll get a couple of hours' sleep before we fly back to London tomorrow. He'll call in at Lansdowne Road on the way to the Foreign Office. He's in top form, getting especial pleasure from teasing Dr Owen.'

David Owen had campaigned long and hard for the EEC, and Tony thought this intense young man – whom he liked but also liked keeping under control – might as well deal with the institutional side, which in any case he knew better than Tony. 'Dr Owen is an expert in these matters and will explain them now,' he would say at the Council, turning without prior warning to his Minister of State. Ewen was amused. David, however competent, began to feel the strain.

Tony stopped by Lansdowne Road on Wednesday, had an hour's sleep. Knotting his tie again he made a face at himself in the mirror. 'Could look more fresh, I suppose. Good thing one's resilient.' That night he gave a small dinner party at Carlton Gardens for the departing American Ambassador, Anne Armstrong. Protocol was largely set aside in seating arrangements, congeniality taken into account. Tony Benn was on my left in the middle of the long table, sitting directly across from his host. Quite a few wives were American, Tony appointing Diane Lever an honorary American for the occasion. His after-dinner speech reflected neither stress nor fatigue. As soon as the guest of honour had departed, a television set was summoned from the nether regions. The Foreign Secretary put a chair two feet in front of it and watched the last ten minutes of a football match: he'd miss it altogether if he waited until we got home.

Thursday after Cabinet, Cabinet Committee, meetings on de-tente, Rhodesia, Fish, he was home for dinner before returning for ten o'clock divisions at the House. 'Let's lie on the sofa for twenty minutes,' he said after supper. 'Gosh, it's nice to be home. Abso-lutely incredible.' Twenty minutes later he looked at his watch. 'We must be getting on.'

We'd fixed to go to south London at lunchtime on Friday for Camberwell School of Art's exhibition of the final-year students' work. I was sitting on the edge of the bath, watching him shave. 'Why don't I ring Ellen-Craig and tell her we'll come see her paintings next week?'

'You haven't seen the Diary for next week. It'll have to be today or never,' he said.

On our way to Camberwell he talked of his pleasure at a meeting he'd just had with his economic adviser, Michael Stewart. 'Having someone inside the Foreign Office who grasps Labour's domestic priorities is going to be invaluable,' he said. Friday was Michael Stewart's first day at the Foreign Office. 'By the way, there's a message from the Consul in Mexico City saying Mark did receive the telegram.' My sister's twenty-year-old son, not given to effu-siveness, had written Tony a letter of unequivocal admiration. Tony was so touched that he was uncertain how to answer: he settled on a telegram. 'Wish I knew if Mark actually received my telegram,' he'd said the week before. 'Would be terrible if he thought I hadn't bothered to answer.' So that was now all right.

At Camberwell the caretaker thoughtfully forgot to tell the Principal when the Foreign Secretary arrived at the gallery, so Tony and Ellen-Craig had time alone together, he totally engrossed in what she had to show him while I wandered through other rooms. 'You both looked really speedy when you stepped out of that car and came up the stairs,' she said when she rang me later, 'you in that big hat and Tony taking three steps at a time.'

He rarely returned to Oxford, but at a Buckingham Palace lunch in November for President Perez, two paths – long diverged – had recrossed. 'Am I seeing things, Susan? The man over there looks just like Raymond Carr. Except he's wearing a moustache.'

The tall figure shambled across the marble floor. Under the

moustache Raymond grinned at this unlikely venue for reunion. 'What the hell are you doing here?' he said.

'Something to do with being Foreign Secretary. For that matter, what are you doing here?'

'Something to do with my tomes on Spanish colonies.'

They had arranged to meet again over dinner at St Antony's College, Oxford, where Raymond was Warden, and the dinner was this particular Friday.

Tony left the Foreign Office in time to go first to the Radcliffe Infirmary where Philip Williams was recovering from an illness, but was slightly delayed by Oxford's one-way traffic system. He and Philip discussed the Gaitskell biography which was nearing completion.

At St Antony's Tony sat between Raymond and a lively young don. 'Why have you put me next to a woman who only wants to talk about the EEC? Don't you realise it's killing me?' he grumbled to Raymond.

After dinner he asked for a small seminar so he could tap the collective wisdom of St Antony's Russian and East European Centre. He would redraft the detente speech on Sunday evening.

Chris dropped us off at Adderbury, took the detective on to the hotel in Banbury. 'Absurd waste of the taxpayer's money,' Tony said. He walked round the garden: the February snowdrops had closed for the night, but the frosted grass and branches stripped for winter were whitened by the stars. He walked through the house, came back to the sitting-room for a nightcap by the fire. 'I'd wondered if Dorneywood might diminish Adderbury,' he said. 'It's the other way round: it's enhanced the sense of privacy at Adderbury. If I pop off tomorrow, you mustn't think Adderbury has been wasted: already we've had so much happiness here.'

Saturday evening we celebrated our thirteenth wedding anniversary. He was excited when he returned from his post-dinner walk. 'You must come outside. I've never seen the stars so bright.' I stepped to the door too late. 'Oh. They've just gone in,' he said, disappointed that I'd missed them. When he came up to bed he said: 'Stayed up later than I'd intended. Was enjoying thinking about how we're going to make the most of Dorneywood for the next six months and give pleasure to friends in so doing.'

We slept late on Sunday. While I made breakfast he went out to buy the newspapers. We glanced through them. 'There's an article by Alex Comfort in the *Sunday Times Magazine*,' he said. 'It should interest us both. Don't let me forget to read it tonight.'

When he returned from his morning walk it was long past noon. I was in the courtyard when he came striding down the lane, swinging his arms, wearing the blue windbreaker with the insignia on it, the red muffler Sheila had made him for Christmas tucked into the collar. 'Adderbury is an absolutely ravishing village. This is an "ultimate" weekend,' he said.

Twenty minutes later we were having belated mid-morning coffee, he working on Rhodesia papers. He had to refill his pen from the bottle in my desk, always grumbled about this task. 'Are you sure pens used to run out so soon?' he said, returning to his chair. I was at the table in the window and had just started a letter to Sheila. 'Something has happened,' he said.

Because he often mimed to entertain me, spoke in a solemn voice about things trivial, as I turned in my chair I imagined ink from the newly-filled pen had leaked on to something quite unimportant. Ewen said later how strange it was to see on the Rhodesian papers where the pen had stopped in mid-letter. 'I can't feel my right side,' Tony said.

I used the telephone in the same room so he'd know what I was saying. The London GP was out on rounds, wouldn't be back for an hour. I told his wife we couldn't wait that long. Tony reached over with his left hand to the side table at his right, unhurriedly picked up the mug, drank some coffee, put the mug back. He reached over with his left hand for a cheroot, planted it between his lips, picked up the box of matches with his left hand and then stopped, looking at it. 'I'll be back in a second,' I said to the GP's wife. 'I have to put down the telephone while I light my husband's cigar.' I moved a small table from my side of the fireplace and set it on his left with an ashtray on it. The GP's wife and I finished our conversation.

The consultant I rang in Oxford asked me the colour of Tony's face. I said it was good; yes, he was speaking clearly. In that case it was almost certainly a twenty-four-hour spasm and by that evening he should be recovering the use of his right side. It would take the consultant half an hour to get to us from Oxford: meanwhile he'd get hold of a local GP.

'Bloody hell,' Tony said, with the quick impatient shake of the head. While we waited, I was sitting on the floor by the side of him that could feel. He was smoking a cheroot, looking out the glass door leading on to the garden. The snowdrops were open in the sunshine. When he started to tell me something and the words poured out as gibberish, he stopped. We were both silent. He tipped the ash from the cheroot into the ashtray. When there was a problem to which he couldn't see the answer, he used to make a tock-tock-tock sound with his tongue. 'Tock-tock-tock,' he said.

We looked through the glass door at the brook flooding brown along the bottom of the garden. 'I'll bet you'd like me to move your papers,' I said. 'You always take a dim view of my stepping on them with my high heels.' I carried the piles one by one and lined them along a wall where he could see they were still in order.

A man walked in. The GP was reassuring, efficient as he made various tests. He too said it was a twenty-four-hour spasm, saw no reason why Tony shouldn't stay at home while it passed. I rang his sister Elsie: someone else was needed in the house while I stayed in the room with Tony. Of course she'd come. I must try not to worry: their father had suffered a similar spasm once when he was at the War Office: he'd completely recovered and gone back to work full-time.

The consultant walked in. Though they'd only once been introduced in Oxford, it sounded right when he said: 'Hullo, Tony. You're not feeling too good I gather.' The picture remained fixed in the consultant's mind: Tony half-turned his head, gave a rather wry smile with the good side of his face, as if to indicate something was wrong with the right side and he knew it was severe damage. The consultant said later: 'He seemed to be indicating a sort of anticipatory attitude of will and acceptance. "Oh damn this thing." It's difficult to analyse, but certainly it wasn't fear. He was concerned, but throughout those hours he never struck me as a man who was frightened of accepting the consequences.'

The consultant told Tony that when you had a muscular spasm on your right side it also affected your speech temporarily and he mustn't worry about the one-sided conversation. The consultant was sitting on a child's bench he'd pulled up. The GP was standing by Tony's chair. I was sitting on the floor by his good side. Clea made one of her graceful leaps from the floor to his shoulder that didn't feel and lay there.

So he'd know I understood, I said that this muscular spasm must be particularly difficult for him as ever since I'd known him he'd had a recurrent war nightmare in which he couldn't move one leg. Both doctors said there wasn't too long to wait: it was a twenty-four-hour spasm. Tony looked at his watch.

The doctors left the room. They came back. They told him they thought he'd be more comfortable if he went into the Radcliffe

Infirmary in Oxford for the night, had everything checked over while they were about it. He'd need a fortnight's convalescence, so one night in hospital didn't really make any difference. It'd be more comfortable to go to Oxford by ambulance. Had we a telephone extension?

The GP stayed with Tony while I went to the kitchen with the consultant. He made telephone calls. I listened to the medical jargon. He finished. I asked him to tell me the exact meaning of the jargon. It wasn't the short-lived spasm they'd hoped. Tony would probably be paralysed for the rest of his life on the right side. Though they didn't know the extent of the brain damage, the haemorrhage had already done so much injury that his mental powers could never be fully restored.

The ambulance men were closing the doors when I pushed them open again and jumped out. 'I must get my card with the Government telephone numbers on it.'

'He's so big,' one of the nurses said in the intensive care unit in the National Health ward, but by placing him diagonally the bed was just about long enough. It was 10 p.m. by now, and we were alone. The bed was wider than our sofa at home: I put my high-heeled shoes under the chair, folded my skirt neatly on it. In medical language he was entering a comatose state, but still conscious. I said: 'What has happened apparently happens all the time. It's not a stroke. By lunchtime tomorrow you'll be able to speak and move just like before. Where shall we go for the fortnight's convalescence? Adderbury or Dorneywood? We can decide tomorrow.' Some of his left side still responded. He lifted his left arm and turned the wrist inwards. 'At least for once you can sleep late on a Monday morning. And by lunchtime tomorrow you'll be exactly as you were at the beginning of this afternoon.'

He was looking at his watch.

PART THREE

►►48◄◄

The End of the Story

When we'd got out of the ambulance at the Radcliffe Infirmary, messages were waiting for me to ring the Prime Minister and Ewen Fergusson. Eventually I did so. I was unforthcoming: I was stalling for time, had not quite closed the door on a miracle. It didn't occur to me that both men already knew what was happening. Nor did I realise that the Prime Minister had to assume the Foreign Secretary's role. I said he'd felt unwell earlier so we'd decided to have a general check-up. Ewen should think in terms of my husband being away for a fortnight. With Jim I edged nearer the truth – Tony had lost the feeling in one foot. Yes, of course I'd ring Jim the next day.

It was the next day in the Radcliffe Infirmary. No miracle was evident. He was deeply unconscious. Somewhere in that hospital is the office of its Governor, younger than I expected a Governor to be, his hair very curly, cut in an Afro-style that suited him. He was wry and helpful, kept sending for more milk each time I emptied my tumbler.

'It's kind of you to let me use your telephone.' I looked at my card with the Government numbers on it, asked for the Prime Minister.

'Hullo, Susan. How are things going there?' Something the matter with Jim's voice.

'Things here are bad. He's not going to get well. The damage is still going on. It can't be reversed. We're not going to put him on one of those life-saving machines.'

'I think you're being very brave.'

'There's no alternative.'

I looked at my card of Government telephone numbers. Ewen came on the line. Something the matter with his voice.

'He's not going to get well. I want David Lipsey to tell the children. Is that clear?'

'Yes.'

'Ellen-Craig will be at her art school. I don't know Sheila's telephone number in Honolulu.'

'We'll have that.'

'The man at the Embassy in Washington – the one who is friends with my sister and her husband. Will you get him to tell my sister? Ask him to tell her not to come now. I'll want her after it's over. But not now. Is that clear?'

'Yes.'

'My husband's elder sister already knows, so she'll look after that end. I want Ellen-Craig and David to come as soon as possible. Is that clear?'

'Yes.'

'I'll say goodbye then, Ewen.'

Someone came into Tony's room. 'Mr Lipsey needs to speak to you on the telephone in the Governor's office. I'll take you a back way.'

'I think you ought to ring Sheila yourself, Susan.' Something terrible had happened to David's voice. 'Pete was crying but capably distressed. He told Sheila and I heard her shouting.' He gave me the Honolulu number.

'Someone will have to sort out this telephone bill,' I said to the Governor. He poured me another glass of milk.

'I wish we could be there,' Sheila said.

'There must be someone at the university to lend you the money. We'll reimburse them. I know it's a lot, but after all, this isn't going to happen again.' The Governor swivelled his chair round so he wasn't looking at me.

Someone came into Tony's room. 'Superintendent Alan Dickinson is in the Governor's office.' Alan was the Foreign Secretary's senior detective.

'We're driving to Adderbury. Isn't there something we can get for you?'

'No, thank you, Alan.'

He looked troubled. 'Don't you want us to bring you a change of clothes?'

'On that table beside my husband's chair in the sitting-room there's a bracelet in some tissue paper. He gave it to me for our wedding anniversary the night before. The paper is so scrumpled that it might be thrown away. Will you make sure it's all right?'

Alan still stood there. He said the detective who'd been at the Banbury hotel was very sorry I hadn't rung him. He would have liked to have been of help.

'Please apologise for me, Alan. I forgot he was there.'

A nurse came into Tony's room. She was carrying a patient's white hospital gown. Like Tony's, but not so big. 'I'll leave this here,' she said. 'You'll be more comfortable in it.' Later she returned with the crumpled tissue paper and the bracelet. 'Superintent Dickinson asked me to give you this.'

Most of the time the room was still, just the two of us. At the same time, the room was full. The twenty years that I was telescoping into one-sided conversation sometimes made me burst out laughing. Every two hours the nurses came in and turned him on to his other side – 'He's so big' – but all I had then to do was rearrange arms. His left hand could still take hold, I was certain.

Upstairs in one of the hospital guestrooms, Ellen-Craig unwrapped fish and chips. Once a day she left the Radcliffe Infirmary to buy supper which we ate together. I got restless quickly, wanted to get back in bed with Tony. There was a back stairway, so I stopped changing out of the hospital gown after the first day or two. 'Funny to think all this is going on in here and for once no one outside knows it's happening.'

'People outside do know something, Mama. The hospital hasn't had anything like this before. That man with the curly hair is under a strain. I've stopped bothering to go a roundabout way to reach Tony's ward. I just walk straight past the photographers. They think I work here. One of Tony's detectives stands just outside the ward. Probably you haven't noticed him.'

David came into Tony's room. 'Granada Television have rung about "The Cabinet in Crisis". It's that film they were preparing about the IMF. It's meant to go out tonight. They advertised it in advance and don't know whether to cancel it. They're not happy about showing a film with someone acting Tony. They think it might offend you.'

'Why should it offend me? It doesn't make the slightest difference to me.'

'I'm sorry, Susan. If they're to show it tonight, they need you to say something more positive.'

'You say, David, whatever they want me to say.'

Ellen-Craig was efficient, composed, throughout the week at the Radcliffe Infirmary. Over our fish and chips she said: 'When you were having a bath this morning and I went into Tony's room, David was sitting there with him. He was reading *The Times*. He's had a lot to deal with. Do you think we should look at the news on that set down the corridor? He's had to handle all that.' David was at a table with microphones on it, talking about the Foreign Secretary's condition. He kept looking down, brushing one hand under his spectacles.

'Where are all those people he's talking to?'

'They're in this building, Mama. It's nice of that curly-haired man to make sure that you and Tony are unaware of anything outside Tony's room.'

'He has a very strong heart, that man of yours,' the consultant said, standing beside Tony. 'There's no way to predict a timetable.'

The Economist goes to the printers on Wednesday nights. On Monday afternoon and evening, evidently, Dick Leonard wrote Tony's obituary, imagining he would be dead before the magazine appeared on Friday. On Wednesday night Tony was still alive. Dick's editor asked him if he thought they could still run the obituary. It was called 'Goodbye, Tony'. David came into Tony's room to ask me.

'Tell Dick it feels right for him to say his goodbye while Tony is still alive.' (Dick had only to change the word 'died' to 'was struck down'. Unknown to me until four years later, a lot of people were taken aback when what was clearly an obituary appeared on Friday before Tony was dead.)

On Thursday the consultant came into Tony's room to say: 'Sheila and Pete and the baby have reached Heathrow. Tony's driver will have them here in an hour.' Sophia was just two. Pete carried her in his arms when he came in the room and stood, looking at Tony. 'Grandpa Toto is sleeping,' he said.

In the corridor of the guestrooms, Sophia raced up and down. If she let her feet go out in front of her, the floor was so highly polished that it was like being on a slide. For the first time I noticed the tension on the Governor's face. 'I'm taking Sophia to Adderbury,' Pete said to the Governor. 'She and I will wait there,' he said to Sheila and Ellen-Craig and me.

Tony's and my luck held: six nights and five days at the Radcliffe Infirmary gave us time for a long farewell.

Late Saturday morning, Bill McCarthy drove Sheila and Ellen-Craig and David and me to Adderbury. David rode in front with Bill. Surrounded by the silence in his car, Bill talked to himself aloud about Oxford's one-way traffic system. 'Terrible. Terrible. Can never find my way without my navigator,' he said, referring to his wife.

Early Monday morning, Pete gathered snowdrops from the garden. Chris drove us back to Oxford. I returned to the Radcliffe Infirmary. We set out for the crematorium.

'That must be it,' Chris said, slowing down as we approached

the gates where police and photographers waited. The police unlocked the gates, locked them behind us. Not long afterwards the
police unlocked the gates again.

At Adderbury I said goodbye to Chris.

That evening, from Ellen-Craig's bedroom, the shouting of
Tony's name began. When it started again the following afternoon,
Sheila rang the GP who had entered our life nine days before. I
recognised the criss-cross pattern of dried blood that scored
Ellen-Craig's face: it matched the pattern of the haircord carpet.
Along with sedation, the GP gave her some salve to help heal her
face before we made the familiar journey from King's Cross to
Grimsby.

A gale was sweeping over the North Sea when *Brenda Fisher* set
out from Grimsby. A photographer from the local paper was
allowed to accompany us. The boat carrying the national media
was instructed to keep at a distance.

The ten passengers on *Brenda Fisher* climbed on to the deck into
the tearing gale.

'I think we should turn back soon, Mrs Crosland.' The skipper's
voice was immediately behind me. 'We're taking in water.'

'I want to go farther out.'

The first handful of grey soot blew back over me: *Brenda Fisher*
was pointed straight into the wind in an effort to reduce her
pitching. Each handful that I threw over the sea was instantly
returned by the gale. I flung the box with the remaining ashes as
far as I could, and it fell into the waves. The skipper's anxiety was
considerable: almost immediately *Brenda Fisher* swung in a complete half-circle and began the return journey to Grimsby.

'Look back, Mama. Look at the sea. Where you threw Tony's
ashes. It's like molten gold.' The winter sun must then have
dropped below the horizon: at once the sea was the colour of lead.

'When you were burying his ashes in the sea,' Ellen-Craig said
some weeks later, 'I felt very mad at him. Especially the way the
light was on the water: he had lived his life the way he wanted and
come into our life and left – and died. With the light it seemed he
had led such a good life, but it was *his* life, not ours. Probably those
feelings – my anger – were caused by so many other people mourn-
ing him – that they had a right to him. It was funny: just as at the
Radcliffe Infirmary when he seemed definitely young, even when
the ashes were being scattered it was Tony Croslandy.'

I noticed the first night at the Radcliffe Infirmary that the
triangle of concentration engraved between his brows – I liked that

triangle – was less deeply incised. In the five days that followed, all
the furrows gradually smoothed out. Before the week ended, he
looked younger than when I first met him.

At the Westminster Abbey Service of Thanksgiving, politicians
and dignitaries, already in their places in the transepts, wondered
who would sit in the section cordoned off on the left of the altar,
opposite where the family would be. A coachload of Grimbarians
was ushered to these seats. The ushers wore khaki, some with the
paratrooper's badge stitched on the right sleeve, others with five
black ribbons spread out like a fan on the back of the tunic. Tony
maintained that he'd only joined up so he could wear the flash of
the Royal Welch Fusiliers. When he'd been doing a Party meeting
not so many weeks before in Cardiff, he took time off to hear the
Caerphilly Male Voice Choir rehearsing. A mass of Welsh voices
pouring forth 'Cwm Rhondda' always made tears come down his
face, and he'd asked if he could have a go at conducting it. 'I waved
the baton like anything,' he said when he returned to Lansdowne
Road. A coach brought the Choir from Caerphilly to Westminster
Abbey. After the service appeared to be concluded, somewhere
above the choir screen, out of sight, these massed voices broke into
'Cwm Rhondda'. The Welsh, fittingly, had the last word.

A few days later I received a letter from a spokesman for the
Transport and General Workers' Union in Grimsby, the first of
the letters asking me to stand for Parliament in Tony's place. I
grasped that I would make a good candidate, but I lacked both the
temperament and the stamina to make a good MP. In any case, I
could hardly bear to go outside our home. Austin Mitchell was
selected as Labour candidate. I told Muriel Barker, then chairman
of the local Party, that I'd come to Grimsby if it was thought
necessary. Halfway through the campaign Muriel rang.

'I don't need to tell you what I'm going to ask,' she said. I went
for one large meeting, a fairly emotional affair, did the interviews
with the local press and radio, caught the next train back to King's
Cross.

At Ashfield another by-election – caused by David Marquand's
leaving British politics to join Roy Jenkins's Commission in Brussels – was held the same day as Grimsby's. Economic problems
facing the Labour Government in 1977 were horrific, the electorate
resentful. Ashfield, with its majority of nearly 23,000, was one of
Labour's safest seats. Grimsby, with its smallish majority, was the
worry.

In the early hours of Friday morning, the television announced the results. Media pundits were bemused: the opposite of their predictions had occurred. Labour was wiped out at Ashfield. Austin Mitchell held Grimsby for Labour with a majority of 520 votes.

The two results made no sense, stated the political editor of *The Times*, nor could its leader writer fathom the matter: Mr Anthony Crosland, for all his qualities, was not likely to have been truly accepted by the mass of Grimsby voters as one of their own: personal regard may have played little part in Labour's holding Grimsby.

'Sod the patronising buggers,' said one of the by-election workers in Grimsby's Labour Party office where they were handing round the national press reports of their 'shock' win. He flung *The Times* to the floor. 'It's people like the fancy-pants boys who wrote that – who think they're so bloody superior – who couldn't understand Tony. My God it was a pleasure to watch him put them down.' He started to cry. That being unmanly, he left the crowded office and went down the narrow steep stairs to the door which leads outside.

Appendix

Who's Who: a guide using Tony's departments as illustration
(and including only characters in the story)

WESTMINSTER
*Politicians**
Key
S of S: Secretary of State
Min: Minister
Min of S: Minister of State
Parly Sec: Parliamentary Under-
  Secretary of State
†PPS: Parliamentary
  Private Secretary

WHITEHALL
Civil servants
Key
Perm Sec: Permanent Secretary
Dep Sec: Deputy Secretary
Asst Sec: Assistant Secretary
Prin Pvt Sec: Principal Private
  Secretary
Pvt Sec: Private Secretary

‡Ec Adv: Economic Adviser

DEPARTMENT OF ECONOMIC AFFAIRS (DEA)
Oct 1964–Jan 1965

George Brown
S OF S (1946–6)

Anthony Crosland
Min of S

William Rodgers
Parly Sec (1964–7)

Sir Eric Roll
Perm Sec

Sir Donald MacDougall
Director-General

Tom Caulcott
Prin Pvt Sec

DEPARTMENT OF EDUCATION AND SCIENCE
Jan 1965–Aug 1967

Anthony Crosland
S OF S

Reginald Prentice
Min of S (1964–6)

Shirley Williams
Min of S (1967–9)

Jennie Lee
Parly Sec (1965–7)
Min of S (1967–70)

Christopher Price
†PPS (1966–7)

Toby Weaver
Dep Sec

Wilma Harte
Asst Sec

Fred Goshawk
Pvt Sec

* capital letters denote a Cabinet Minister
† not a prime ministerial appointment
‡ temporary civil servant

BOARD OF TRADE
Aug 1967–Oct 1969

Anthony Crosland
PRESIDENT

Lord [Wilfred] Brown
Min of S (1965–70)

Edmund Dell
Min of S (1968–9)

William Rodgers
Min of S (1968–9)

Roy Croft
Prin Pvt Sec

Wilfred Beckerman
‡Ec Adv to the PRES (1967–9)

DEPARTMENT OF LOCAL GOVERNMENT AND REGIONAL PLANNING
Oct 1969–June 1970

Anthony Crosland
S OF S

DEPARTMENT OF THE ENVIRONMENT (DOE)
March 1974–April 1976

Anthony Crosland
S OF S

John Silkin
Min for Planning & Local
   Govt (1974)
MIN for Planning & Local
   Govt (1974–6)

Gordon Oakes
Parly Sec (1974–6)

Peter Hardy
†PPS

Sir Ian Bancroft
Perm Sec

Sir Robert Marshall
2nd Perm Sec

Sir Idwal Pugh
2nd Perm Sec

Andrew Semple
Prin Pvt Sec

Terry Heiser
Prin Pvt Sec

David McDonald
Pvt Sec

Noreen Bovill
Pvt Sec

Margaret Turner
Pvt Sec

* capital letters denote a Cabinet Minister
† not a prime ministerial appointment
‡ temporary civil servant

FOREIGN AND COMMONWEALTH OFFICE (FO)
April 1976–Feb 1977

Anthony Crosland
FOREIGN SECRETARY (S OF S)

Edward Rowlands
Min of S (1976–9)

Roy Hattersley
Min of S (1974–Sep 1976)

David Owen
Min of S (Sep 1976–Feb 1977,
then appointed FOREIGN
SECRETARY)

Peter Hardy
†PPS

Sir Michael Palliser
Perm Sec

Sir Antony Duff
Dep Sec

Ewen Fergusson
Prin Pvt Sec

Margaret Turner
Pvt Sec

Michael Stewart
‡Special Ec Adv to FOR SEC
(Feb 1977–8)

LP Leaders since 1935

Clement Attlee 1935–55
PM 1945–51

Hugh Gaitskell 1955–63

Harold Wilson 1963–76
PM 1964–70, 1974–6

James Callaghan 1976–80
PM 1976–9

Michael Foot 1980–

General elections since 1945

July 1945, Feb 1950, Oct 1951,
May 1955, Oct 1959, Oct 1964,
March 1966, June 1970, Feb
1974, Oct 1974, May 1979

Other characters in the story

Sir William Armstrong
Joint Perm Sec of the Treasury
(1962–8), Official Head of
Home Civil Service (1968–74)

Thomas Balogh
‡Ec Adv to the Cabinet (1964–7)
‡PM's own consultant (1968)

Nicholas Kaldor
‡Special Adv to the Ch of the
Exch (1964–8, 1974–6)

Robert Neild
‡Ec Adv to the Treasury
(1964–7)

Index

(Titles are those applicable at the time of this story.)